GUNSLINGERGIRL.

YU AIDA PRESENTS

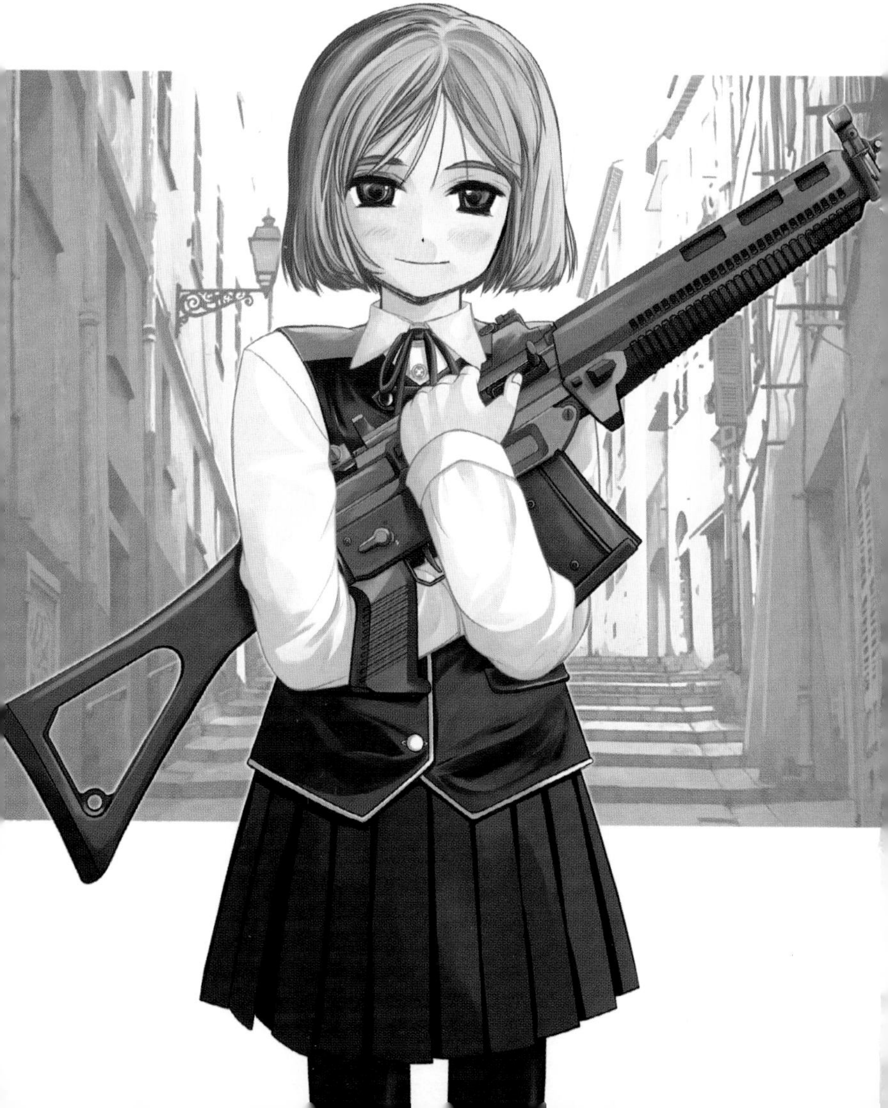

C O N T E N T S

Vol.1

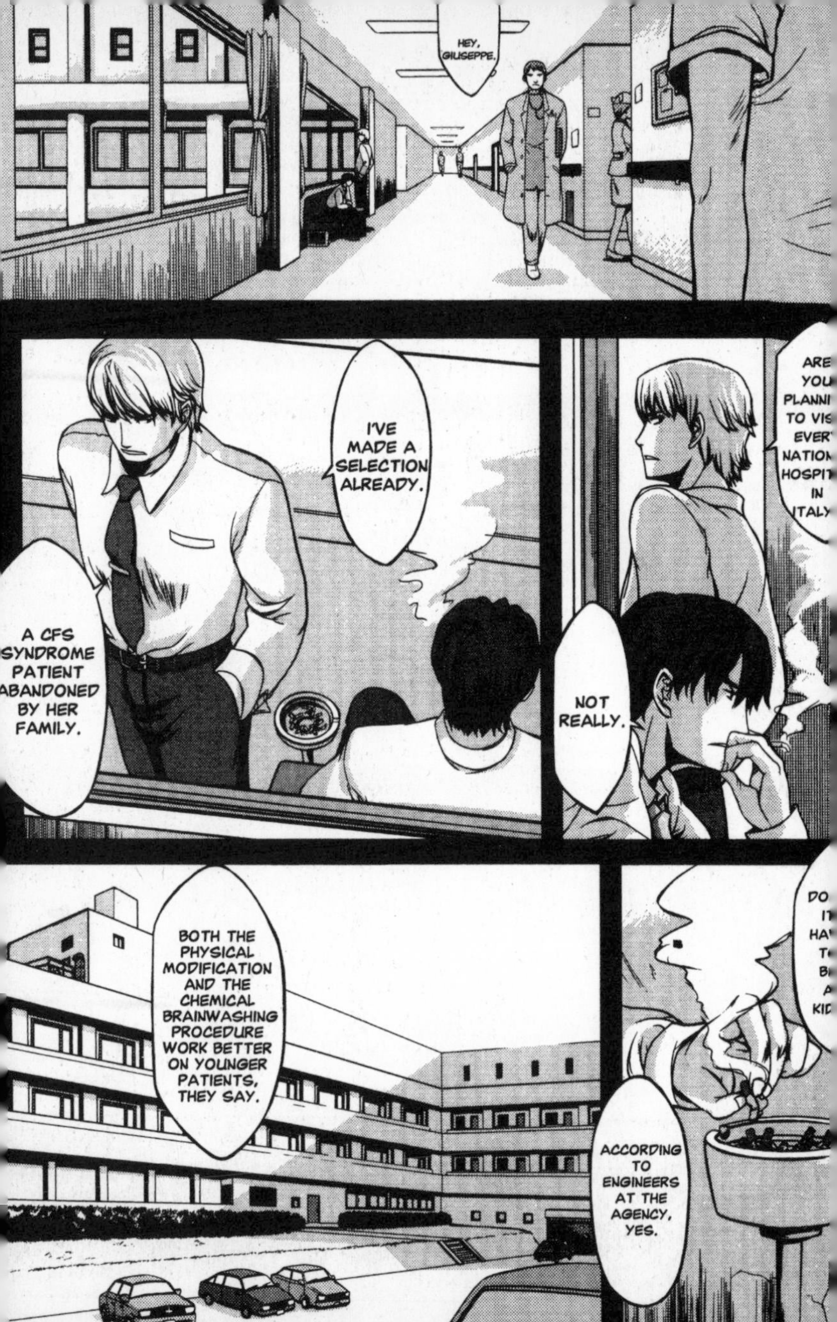
HEY, GIUSEPPE.
ARE YOU PLANNI TO VIS EVERY NATION HOSPIT IN ITALY
NOT REALLY.
I'VE MADE A SELECTION ALREADY.
A CFS SYNDROME PATIENT ABANDONED BY HER FAMILY.
DO IT HA T B A KID
ACCORDING TO ENGINEERS AT THE AGENCY, YES.
BOTH THE PHYSICAL MODIFICATION AND THE CHEMICAL BRAINWASHING PROCEDURE WORK BETTER ON YOUNGER PATIENTS, THEY SAY.

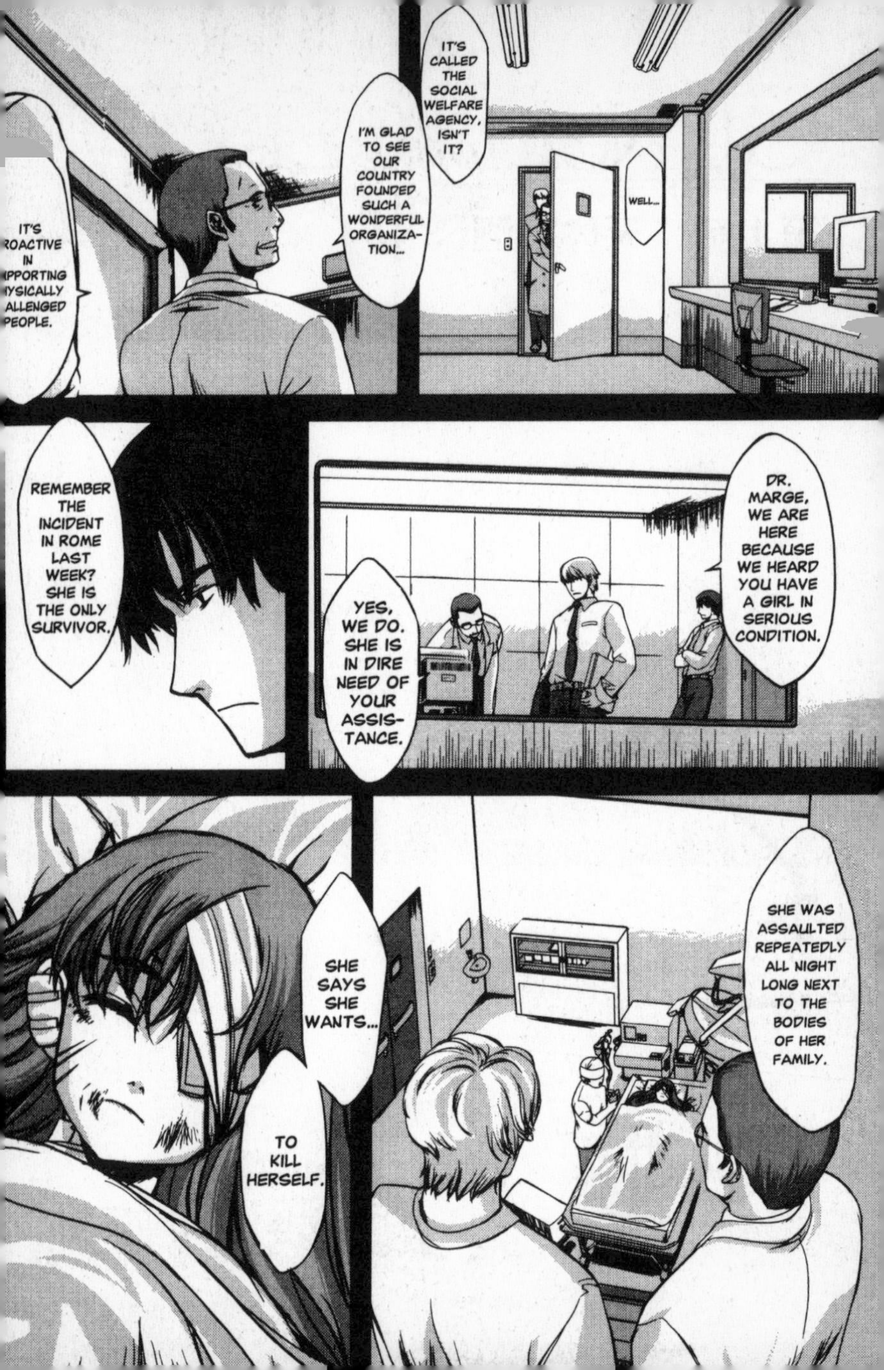
IT'S ROACTIVE IN PPORTING YSICALLY ALLENGED PEOPLE.
I'M GLAD TO SEE OUR COUNTRY FOUNDED SUCH A WONDERFUL ORGANIZA-TION...
IT'S CALLED THE SOCIAL WELFARE AGENCY, ISN'T IT?
WELL...
REMEMBER THE INCIDENT IN ROME LAST WEEK? SHE IS THE ONLY SURVIVOR.
DR. MARGE, WE ARE HERE BECAUSE WE HEARD YOU HAVE A GIRL IN SERIOUS CONDITION.
YES, WE DO. SHE IS IN DIRE NEED OF YOUR ASSIS-TANCE.
SHE SAYS SHE WANTS...
TO KILL HERSELF.
SHE WAS ASSAULTED REPEATEDLY ALL NIGHT LONG NEXT TO THE BODIES OF HER FAMILY.

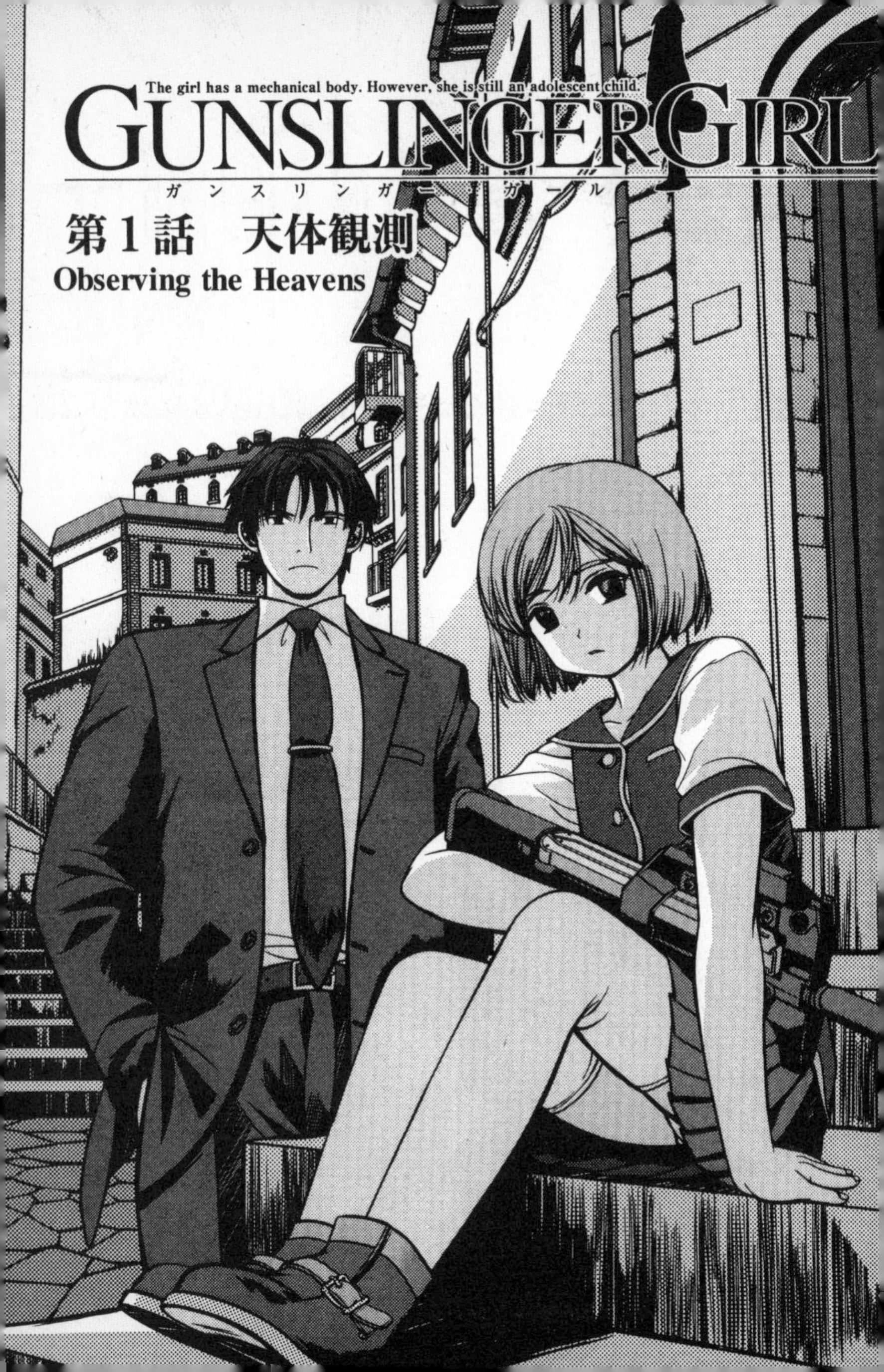

The girl has a mechanical body. However, she is still an adolescent child.
GUNSLINGER GIRL
ガンスリンガー ガール
第1話　天体観測
Observing the Heavens

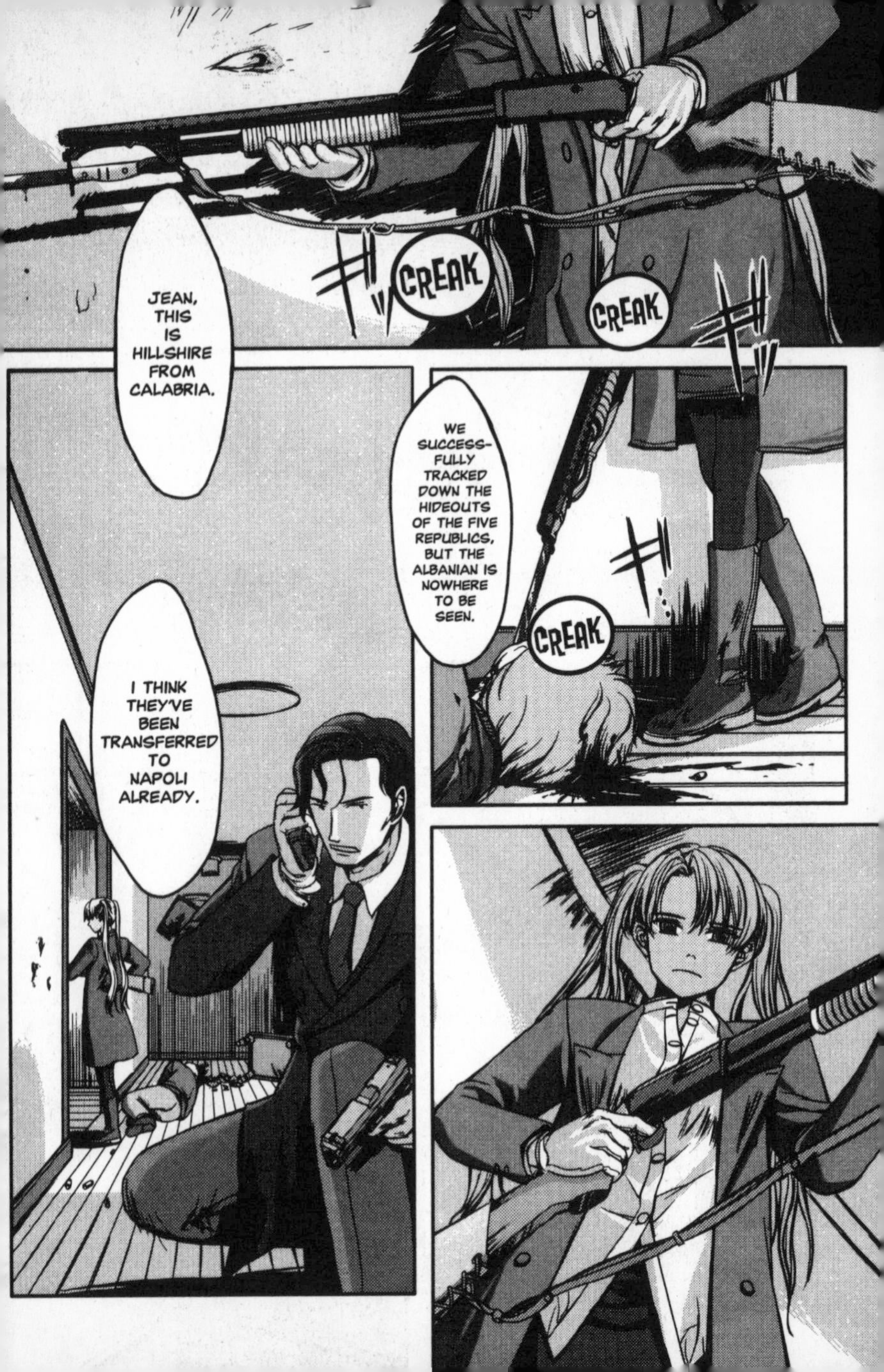
CREAK
CREAK
JEAN, THIS IS HILLSHIRE FROM CALABRIA.
WE SUCCESS-FULLY TRACKED DOWN THE HIDEOUTS OF THE FIVE REPUBLICS, BUT THE ALBANIAN IS NOWHERE TO BE SEEN.
CREAK
I THINK THEY'VE BEEN TRANSFERRED TO NAPOLI ALREADY.

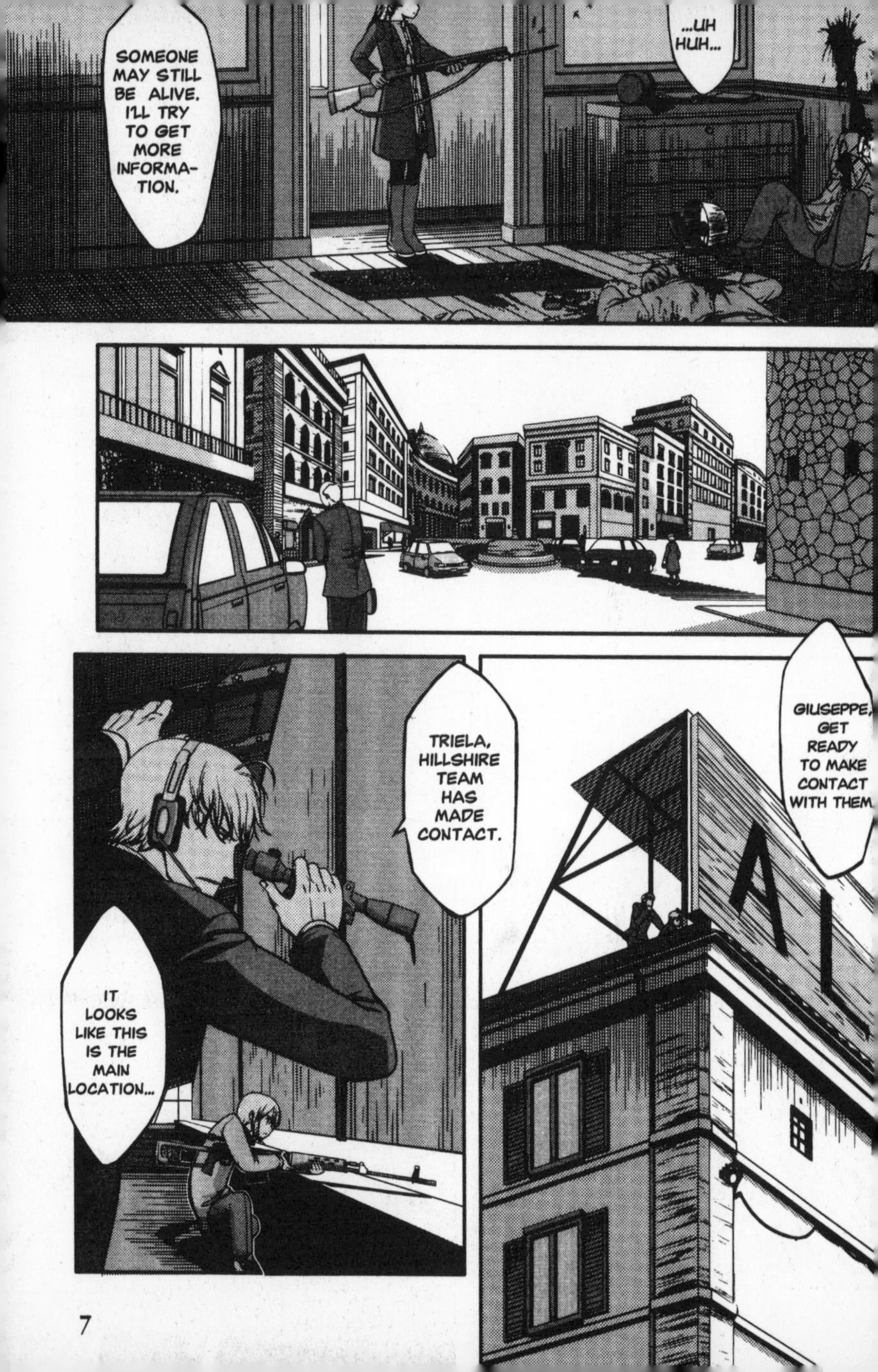
SOMEONE MAY STILL BE ALIVE. I'LL TRY TO GET MORE INFORMA- TION.
...UH HUH...
GIUSEPPE, GET READY TO MAKE CONTACT WITH THEM.
TRIELA, HILLSHIRE TEAM HAS MADE CONTACT.
IT LOOKS LIKE THIS IS THE MAIN LOCATION...

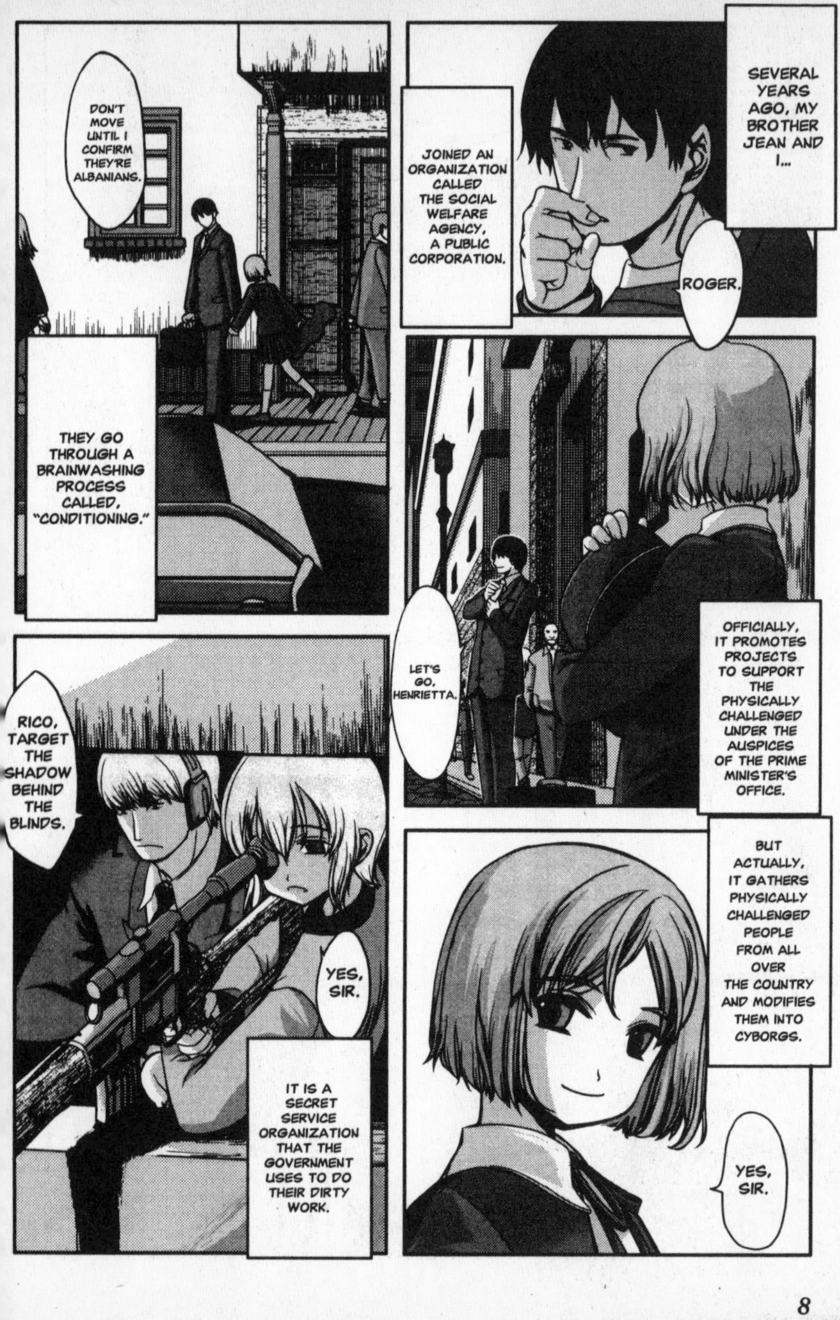
SEVERAL YEARS AGO, MY BROTHER JEAN AND I...
JOINED AN ORGANIZATION CALLED THE SOCIAL WELFARE AGENCY, A PUBLIC CORPORATION.
ROGER.
DON'T MOVE UNTIL I CONFIRM THEY'RE ALBANIANS.
THEY GO THROUGH A BRAINWASHING PROCESS CALLED, "CONDITIONING."
OFFICIALLY, IT PROMOTES PROJECTS TO SUPPORT THE PHYSICALLY CHALLENGED UNDER THE AUSPICES OF THE PRIME MINISTER'S OFFICE.
LET'S GO, HENRIETTA.
BUT ACTUALLY, IT GATHERS PHYSICALLY CHALLENGED PEOPLE FROM ALL OVER THE COUNTRY AND MODIFIES THEM INTO CYBORGS.
YES, SIR.
RICO, TARGET THE SHADOW BEHIND THE BLINDS.
YES, SIR.
IT IS A SECRET SERVICE ORGANIZATION THAT THE GOVERNMENT USES TO DO THEIR DIRTY WORK.

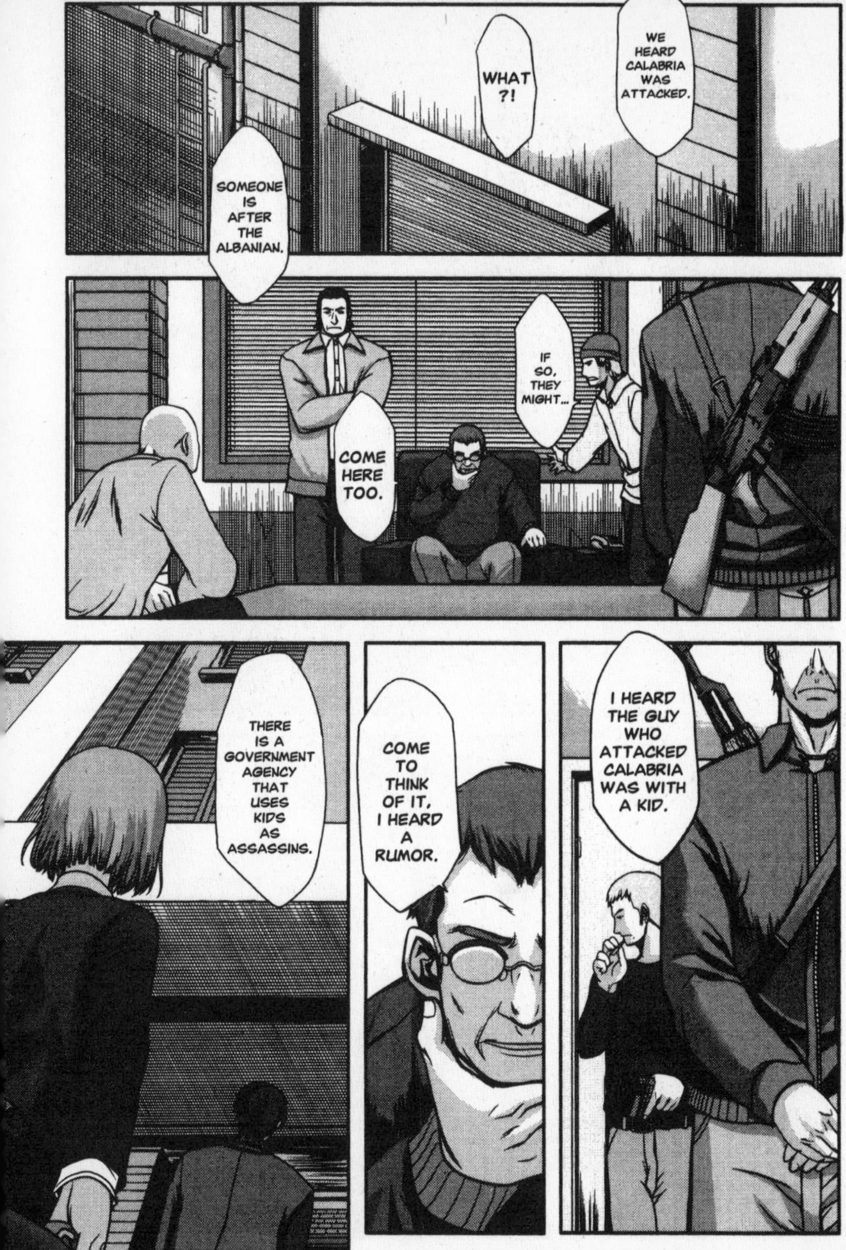
WE HEARD CALABRIA WAS ATTACKED.
WHAT?!
SOMEONE IS AFTER THE ALBANIAN.
IF SO, THEY MIGHT...
COME HERE TOO.
I HEARD THE GUY WHO ATTACKED CALABRIA WAS WITH A KID.
COME TO THINK OF IT, I HEARD A RUMOR.
THERE IS A GOVERNMENT AGENCY THAT USES KIDS AS ASSASSINS.

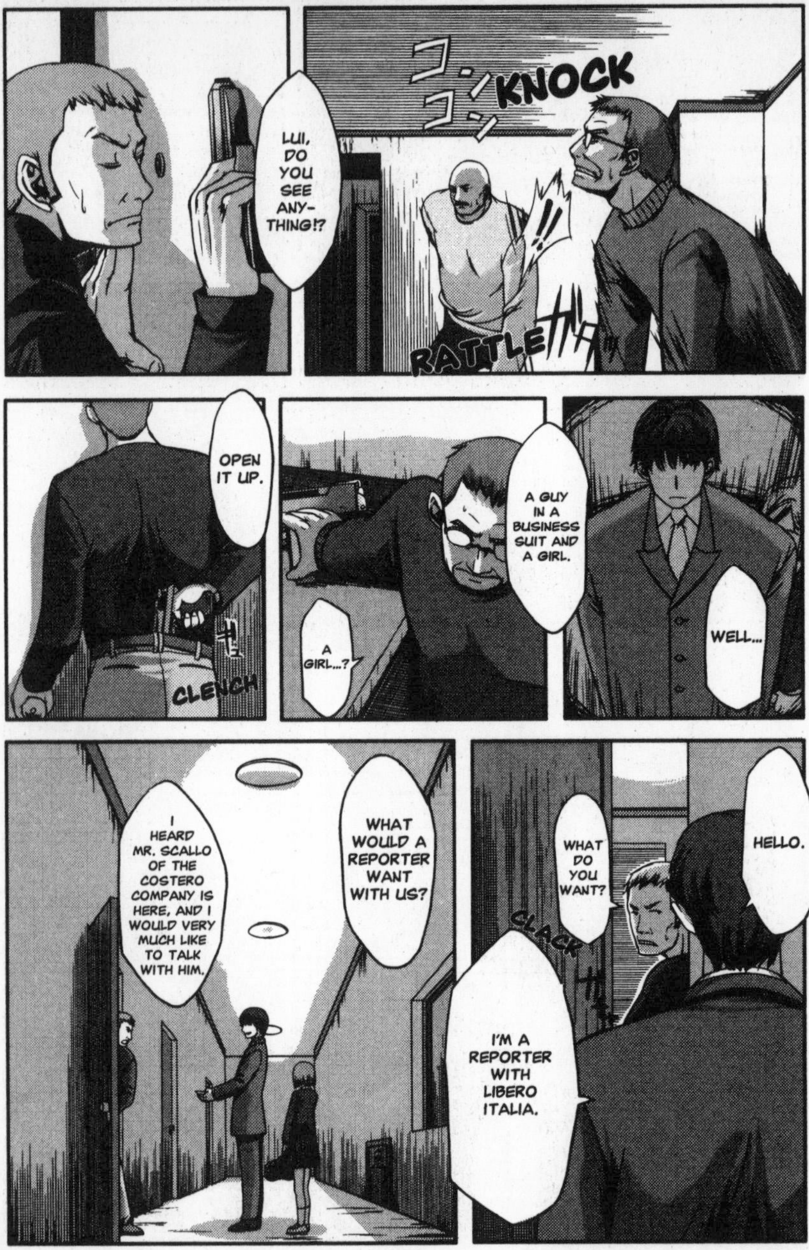
KNOCK
LUI, DO YOU SEE ANYTHING!?
RATTLE
OPEN IT UP.
CLENCH
A GUY IN A BUSINESS SUIT AND A GIRL.
A GIRL...?
WELL...
HELLO.
WHAT DO YOU WANT?
CLACK
I'M A REPORTER WITH LIBERO ITALIA.
WHAT WOULD A REPORTER WANT WITH US?
I HEARD MR. SCALLO OF THE COSTERO COMPANY IS HERE, AND I WOULD VERY MUCH LIKE TO TALK WITH HIM.

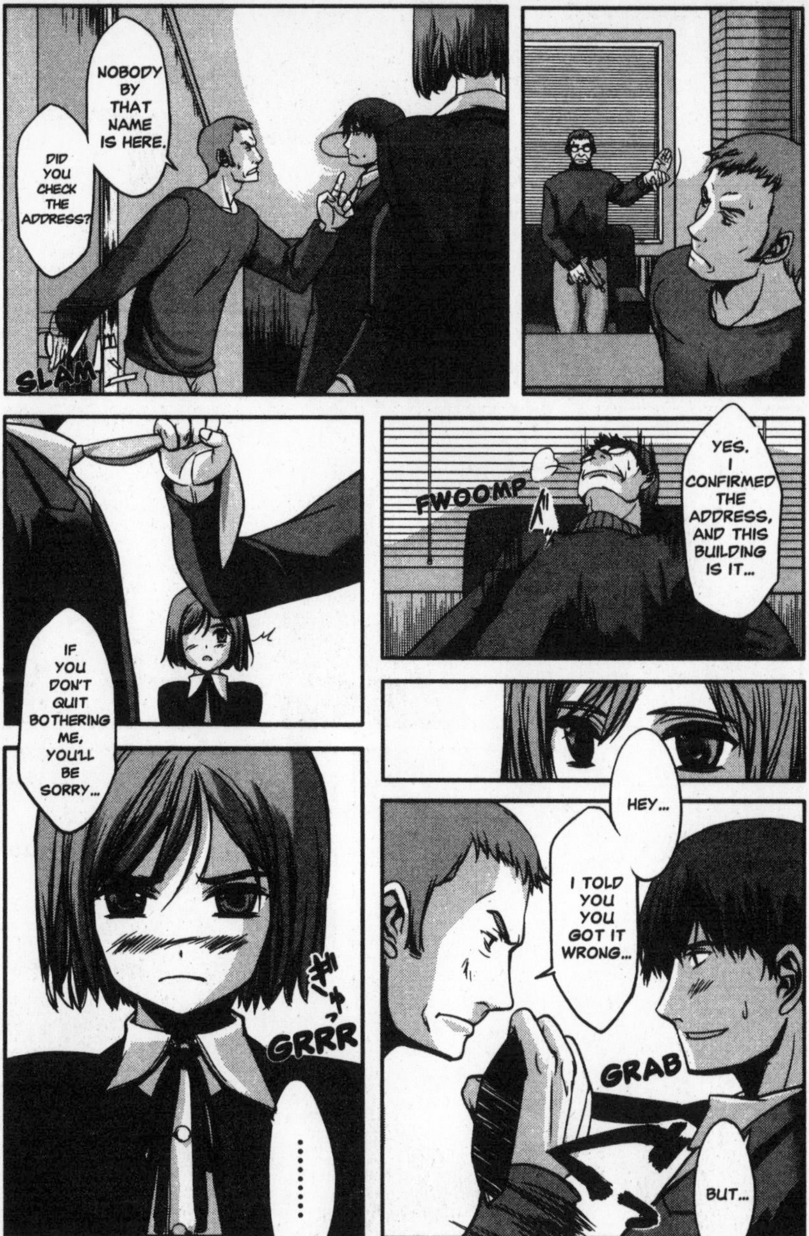
NOBODY BY THAT NAME IS HERE.
DID YOU CHECK THE ADDRESS?
SLAM
YES. I CONFIRMED THE ADDRESS, AND THIS BUILDING IS IT...
FWOOMP
IF YOU DON'T QUIT BOTHERING ME, YOU'LL BE SORRY...
HEY...
I TOLD YOU YOU GOT IT WRONG...
GRAB
BUT...
GRRR
....

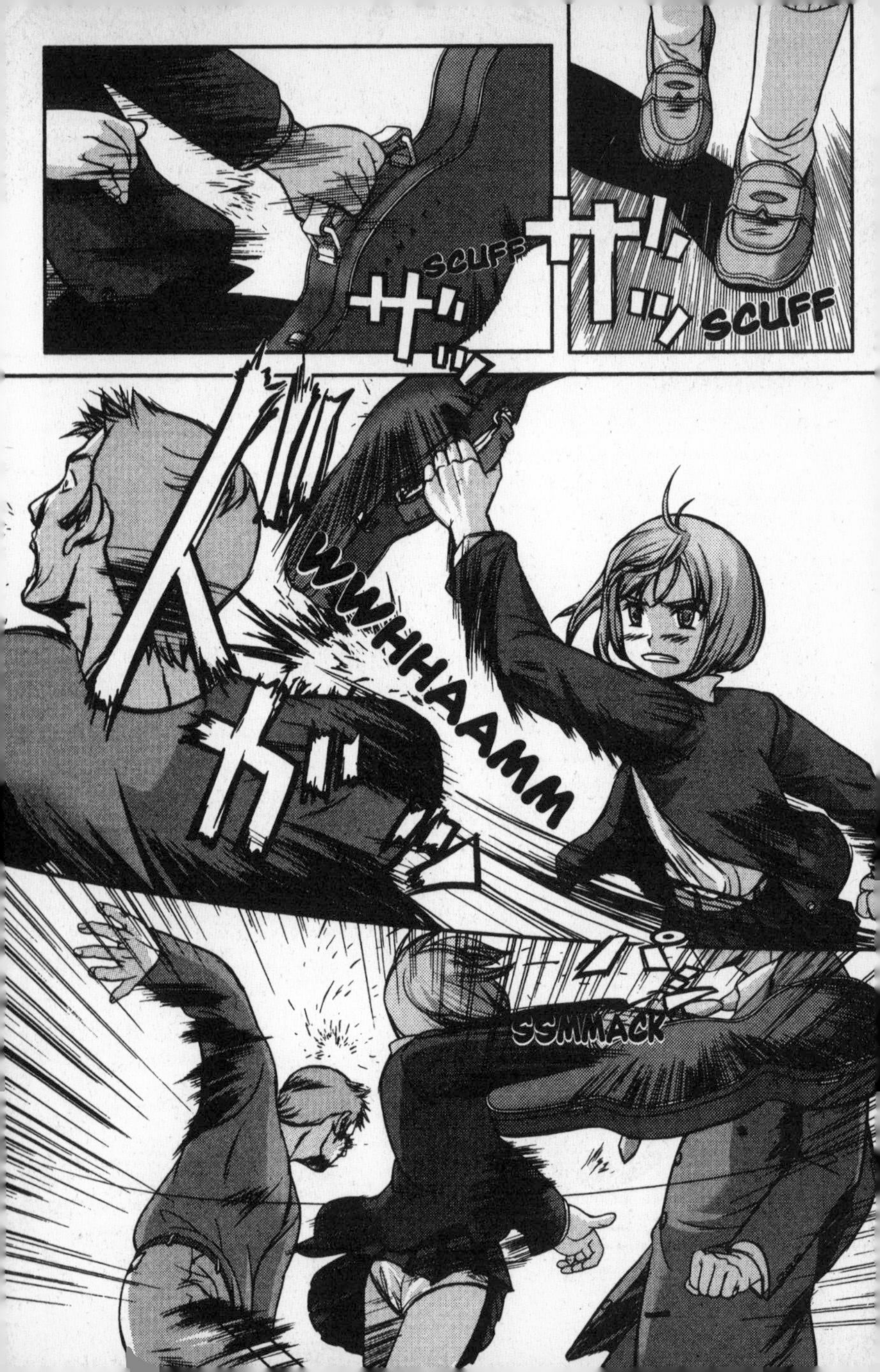

SCUFF
SCUFF
WWHHAAAMM
SSMMACK

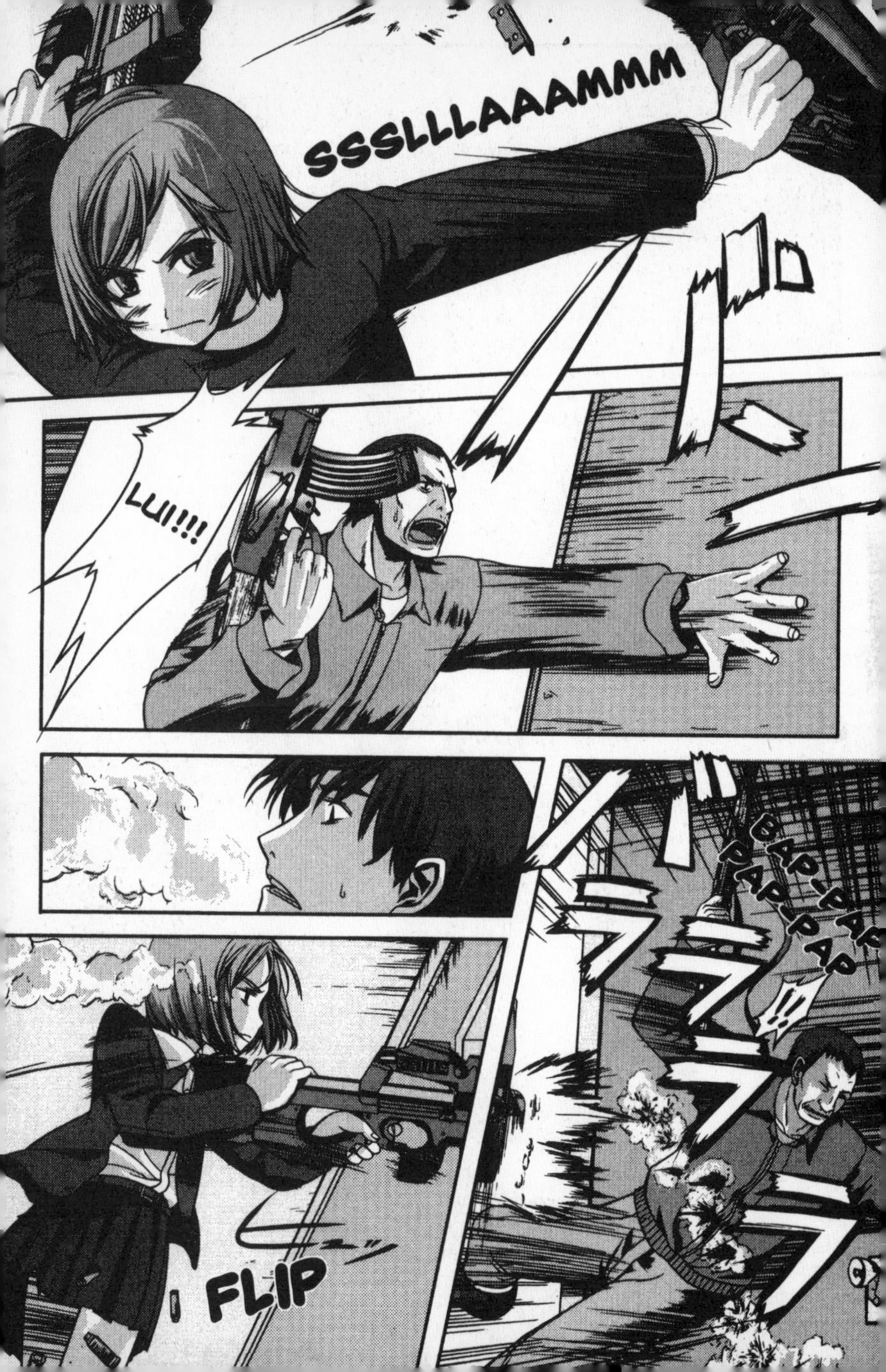
SSSLLLAAAMMM
LUI!!!
BAP-PAP PAP-PAP
FLIP

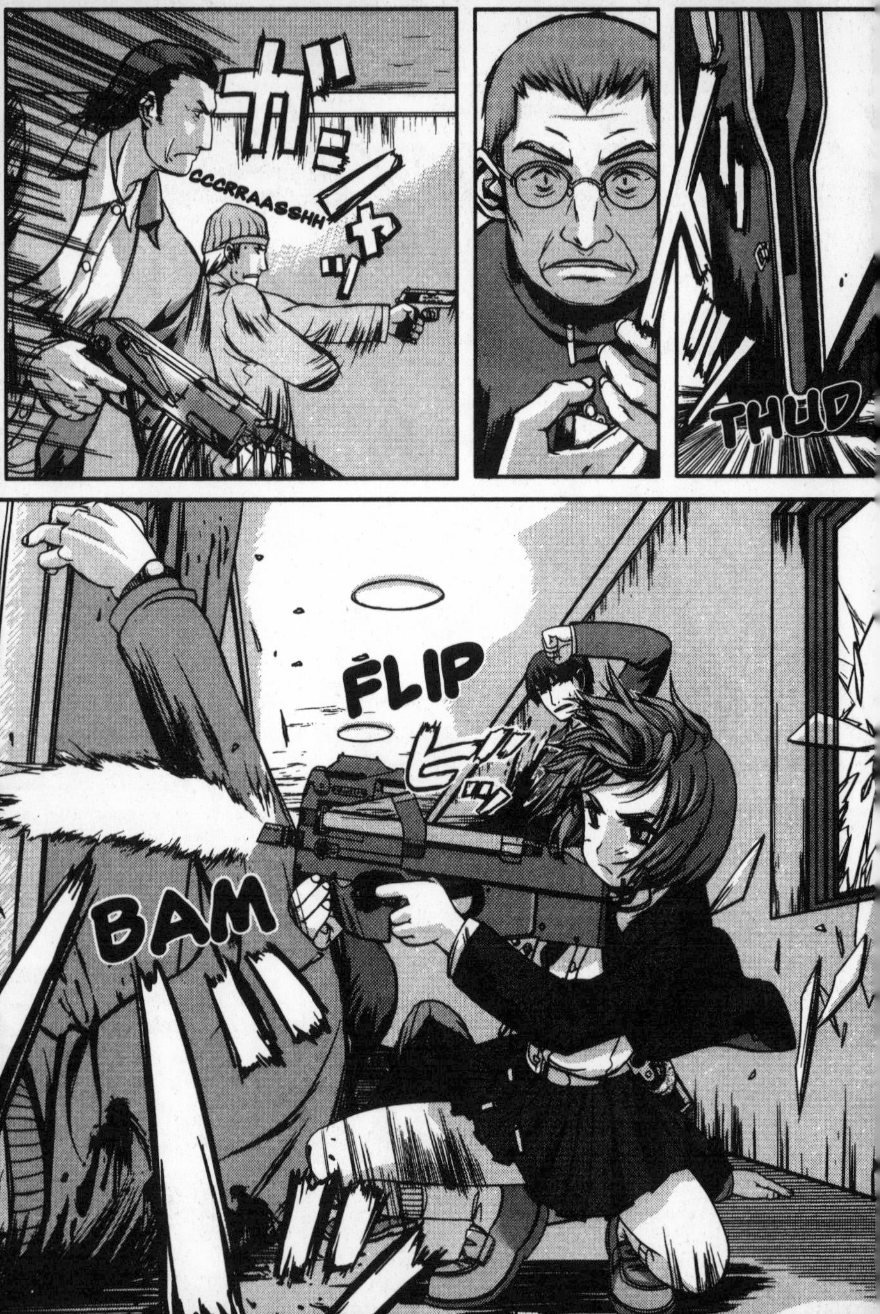
CCCRRAASSHH
THUD
FLIP
BAM

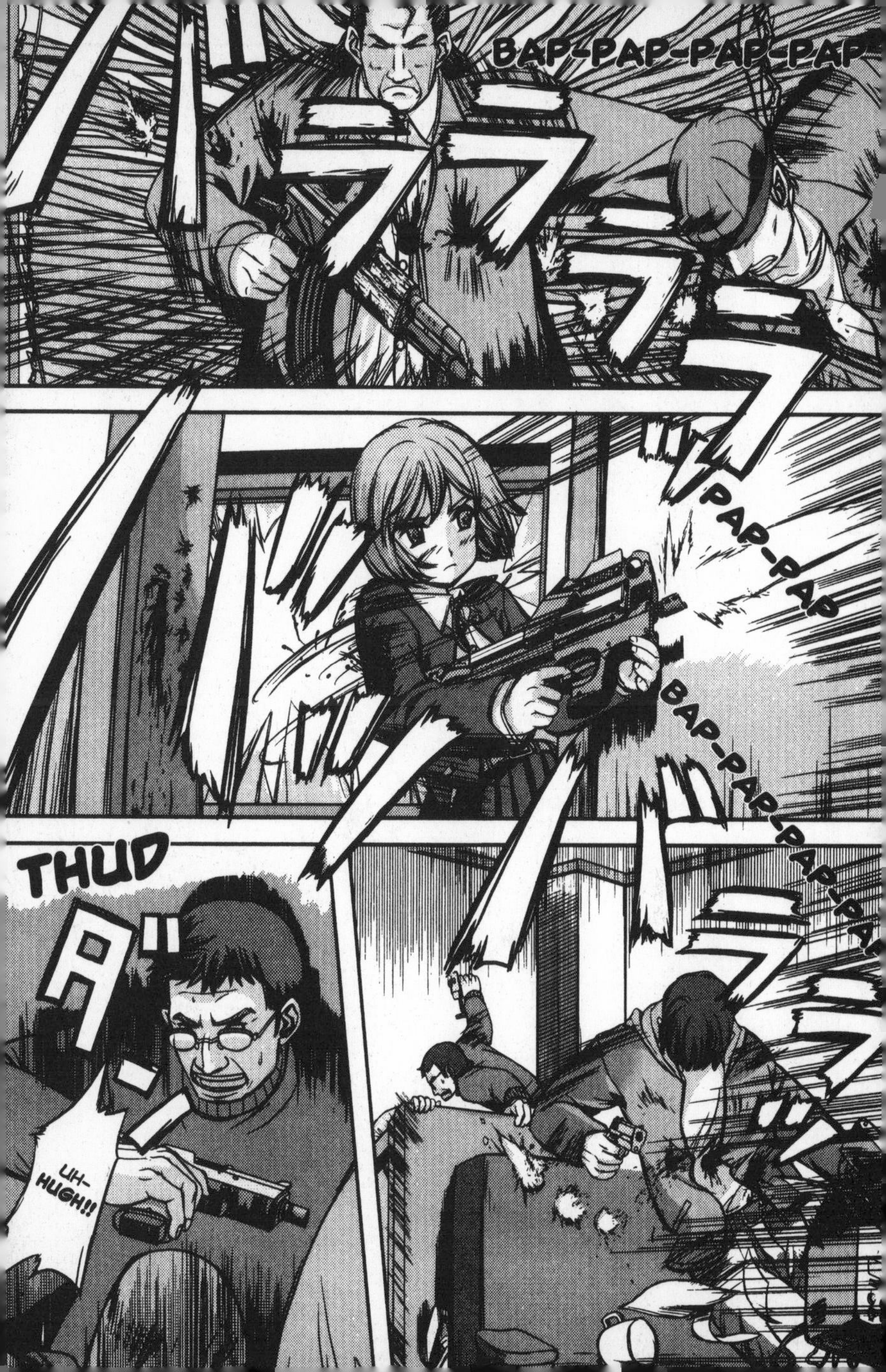
BAP-PAP-PAP-PAP-
PAP-PAP-PAP
BAP-PAP-PAP-PAP-PA
THUD
UH-HUGH!!

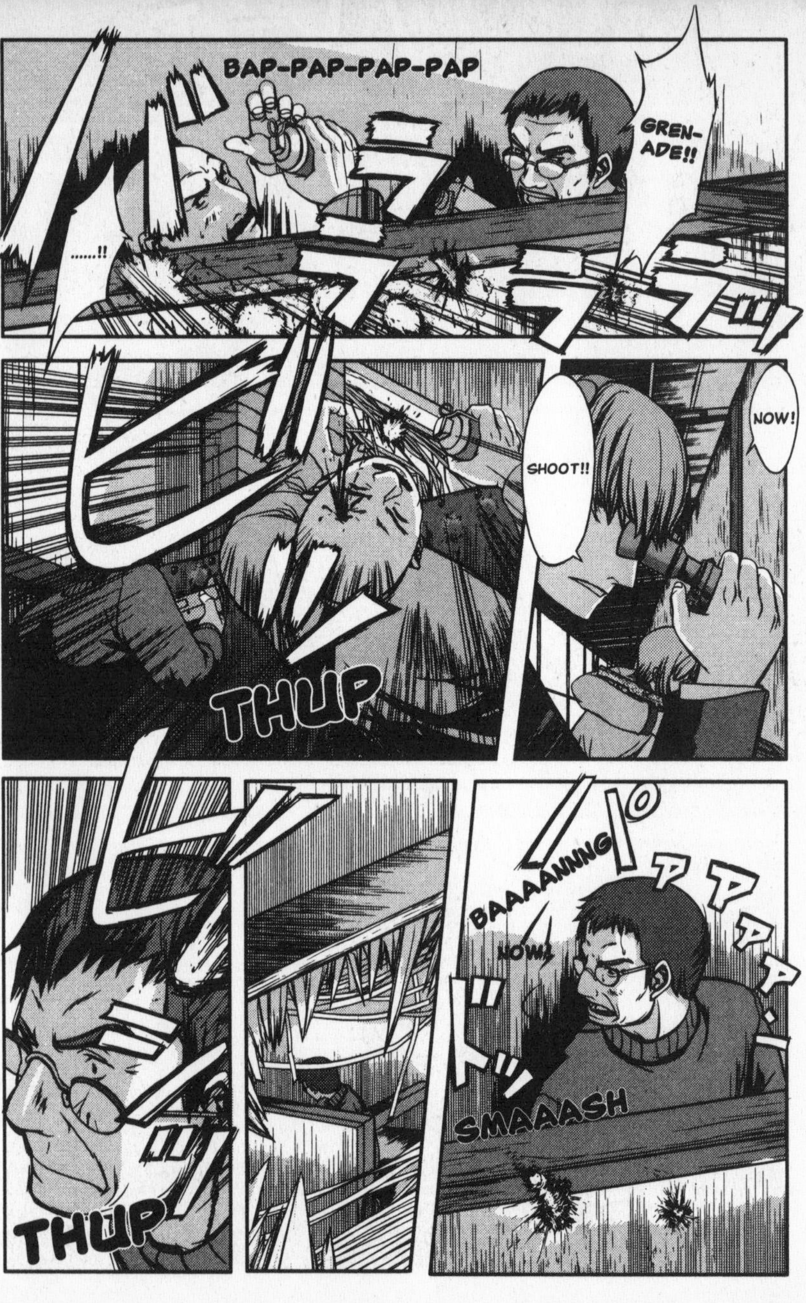
BAP-PAP-PAP-PAP
GREN-
ADE!!
......!!
NOW!
SHOOT!!
THUP
BAAAANNING
NOW!
SMAAASH
THUP

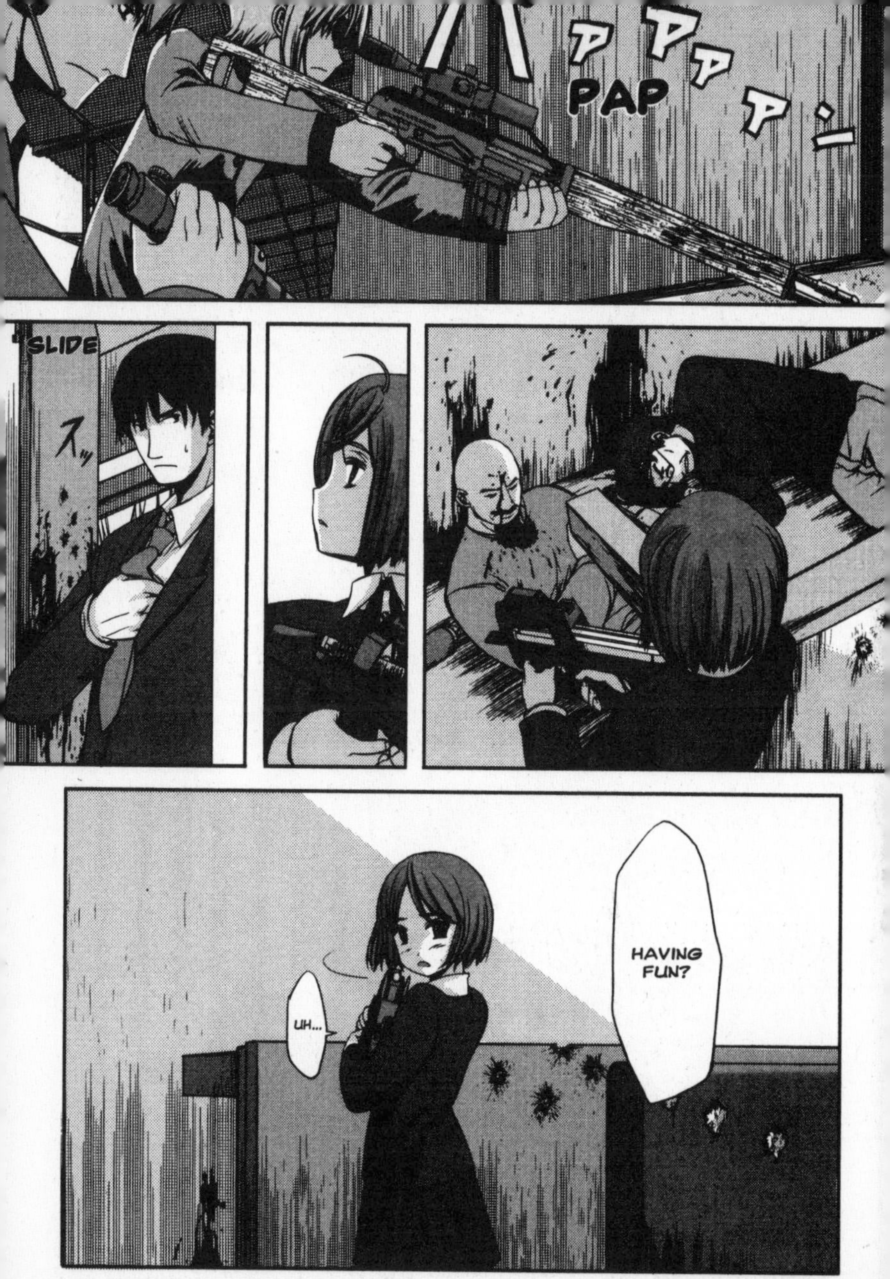
PAP
SLIDE
スッ
HAVING FUN?
UH...

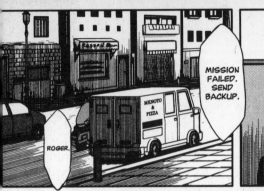
ROGER.

MISSION FAILED. SEND BACKUP.

HEY, FERRO,

EXCUSE ME...

WHY DID YOU GO OUT OF CONTROL?

HENRIETTA,

WELL...

I CAN'T LET ANYONE HURT YOU...

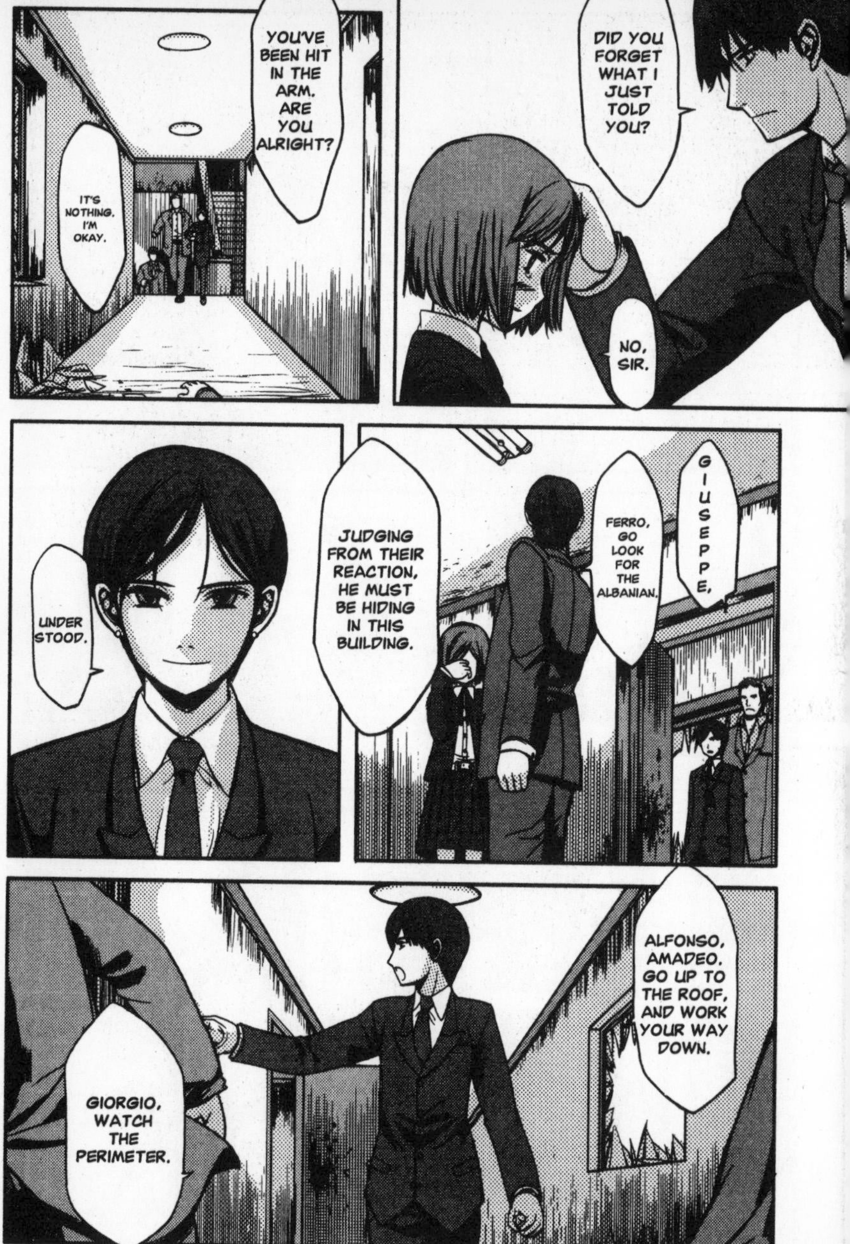
DID YOU FORGET WHAT I JUST TOLD YOU?
NO, SIR.
YOU'VE BEEN HIT IN THE ARM. ARE YOU ALRIGHT?
IT'S NOTHING. I'M OKAY.
GIUSEPPE,
FERRO, GO LOOK FOR THE ALBANIAN.
JUDGING FROM THEIR REACTION, HE MUST BE HIDING IN THIS BUILDING.
UNDER STOOD.
ALFONSO, AMADEO. GO UP TO THE ROOF, AND WORK YOUR WAY DOWN.
GIORGIO, WATCH THE PERIMETER.

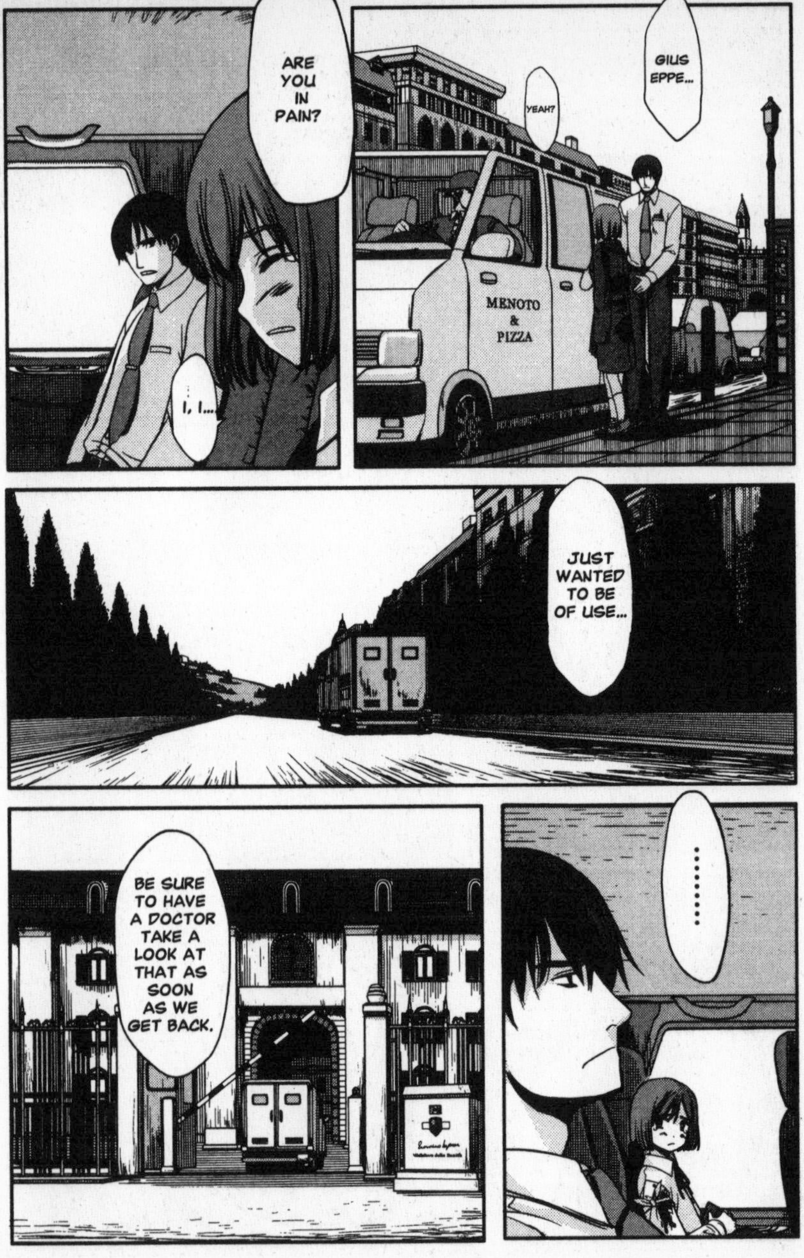
GIUS EPPE...
YEAH?
ARE YOU IN PAIN?
I, I...
JUST WANTED TO BE OF USE...
MENOTO & PIZZA
......
BE SURE TO HAVE A DOCTOR TAKE A LOOK AT THAT AS SOON AS WE GET BACK.

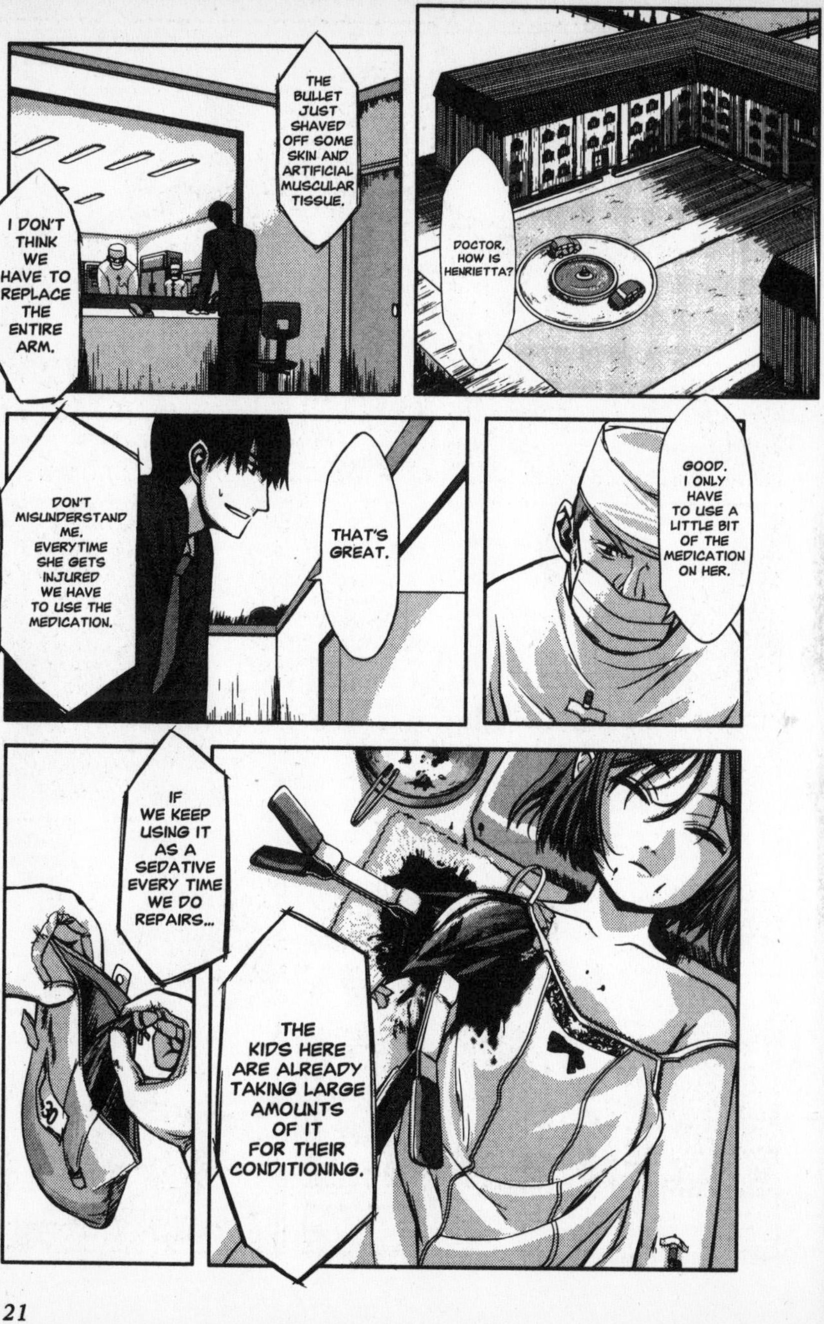
DOCTOR, HOW IS HENRIETTA?
THE BULLET JUST SHAVED OFF SOME SKIN AND ARTIFICIAL MUSCULAR TISSUE.
I DON'T THINK WE HAVE TO REPLACE THE ENTIRE ARM.
GOOD. I ONLY HAVE TO USE A LITTLE BIT OF THE MEDICATION ON HER.
THAT'S GREAT.
DON'T MISUNDERSTAND ME. EVERYTIME SHE GETS INJURED WE HAVE TO USE THE MEDICATION.
IF WE KEEP USING IT AS A SEDATIVE EVERY TIME WE DO REPAIRS...
THE KIDS HERE ARE ALREADY TAKING LARGE AMOUNTS OF IT FOR THEIR CONDITIONING.

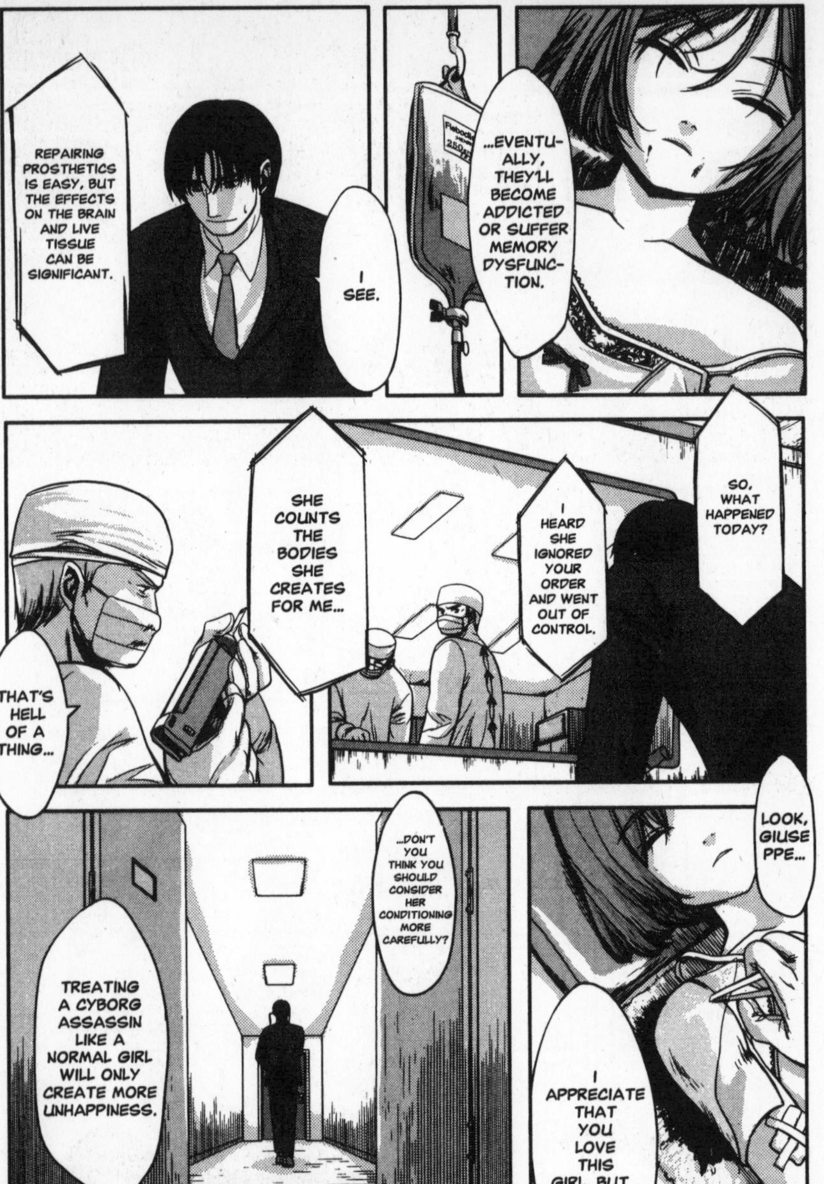
REPAIRING PROSTHETICS IS EASY, BUT THE EFFECTS ON THE BRAIN AND LIVE TISSUE CAN BE SIGNIFICANT.
I SEE.
...EVENTUALLY, THEY'LL BECOME ADDICTED OR SUFFER MEMORY DYSFUNCTION.
SHE COUNTS THE BODIES SHE CREATES FOR ME...
THAT'S HELL OF A THING...
I HEARD SHE IGNORED YOUR ORDER AND WENT OUT OF CONTROL.
SO, WHAT HAPPENED TODAY?
TREATING A CYBORG ASSASSIN LIKE A NORMAL GIRL WILL ONLY CREATE MORE UNHAPPINESS.
...DON'T YOU THINK YOU SHOULD CONSIDER HER CONDITIONING MORE CAREFULLY?
LOOK, GIUSEPPE...
I APPRECIATE THAT YOU LOVE THIS GIRL, BUT...

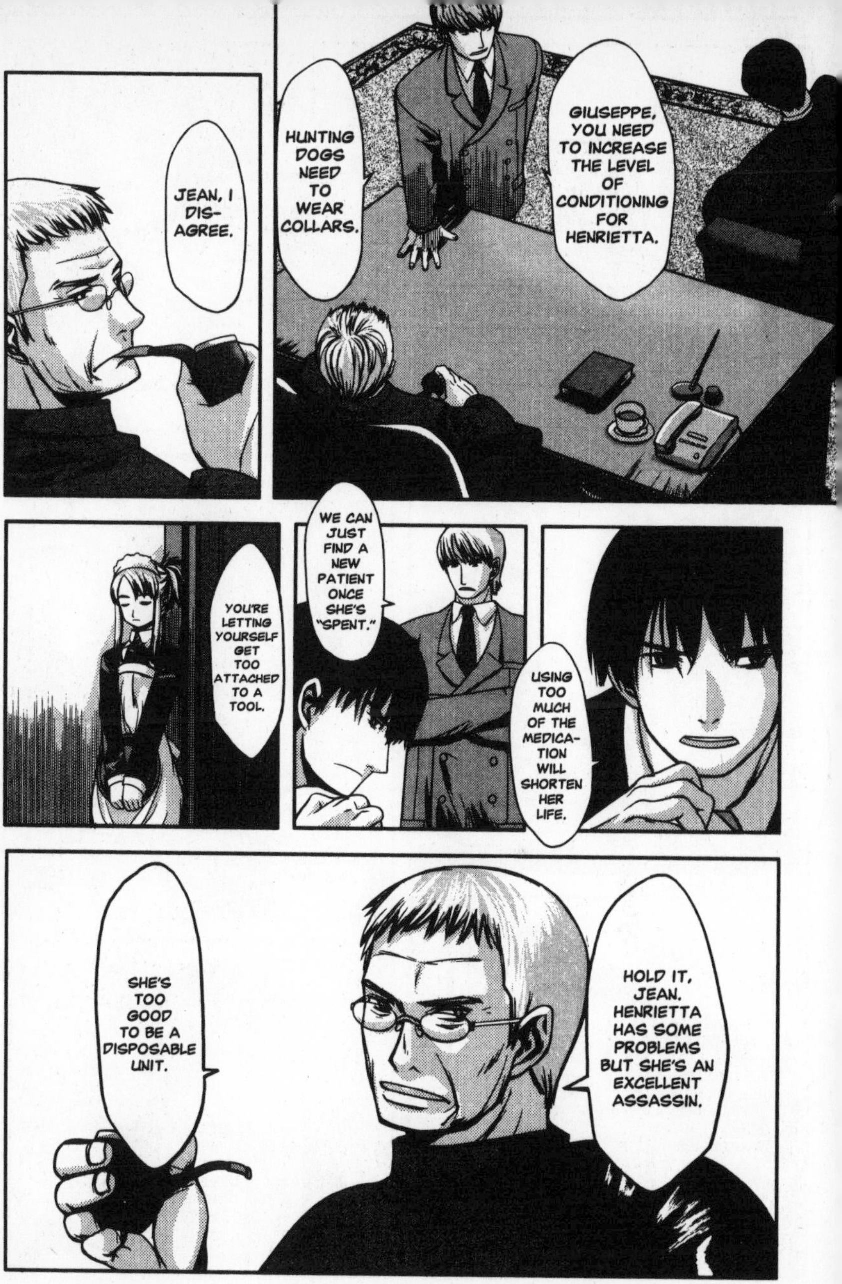
GIUSEPPE, YOU NEED TO INCREASE THE LEVEL OF CONDITIONING FOR HENRIETTA.
HUNTING DOGS NEED TO WEAR COLLARS.
JEAN, I DIS-AGREE.
USING TOO MUCH OF THE MEDICA-TION WILL SHORTEN HER LIFE.
WE CAN JUST FIND A NEW PATIENT ONCE SHE'S "SPENT."
YOU'RE LETTING YOURSELF GET TOO ATTACHED TO A TOOL.
HOLD IT, JEAN. HENRIETTA HAS SOME PROBLEMS BUT SHE'S AN EXCELLENT ASSASSIN.
SHE'S TOO GOOD TO BE A DISPOSABLE UNIT.

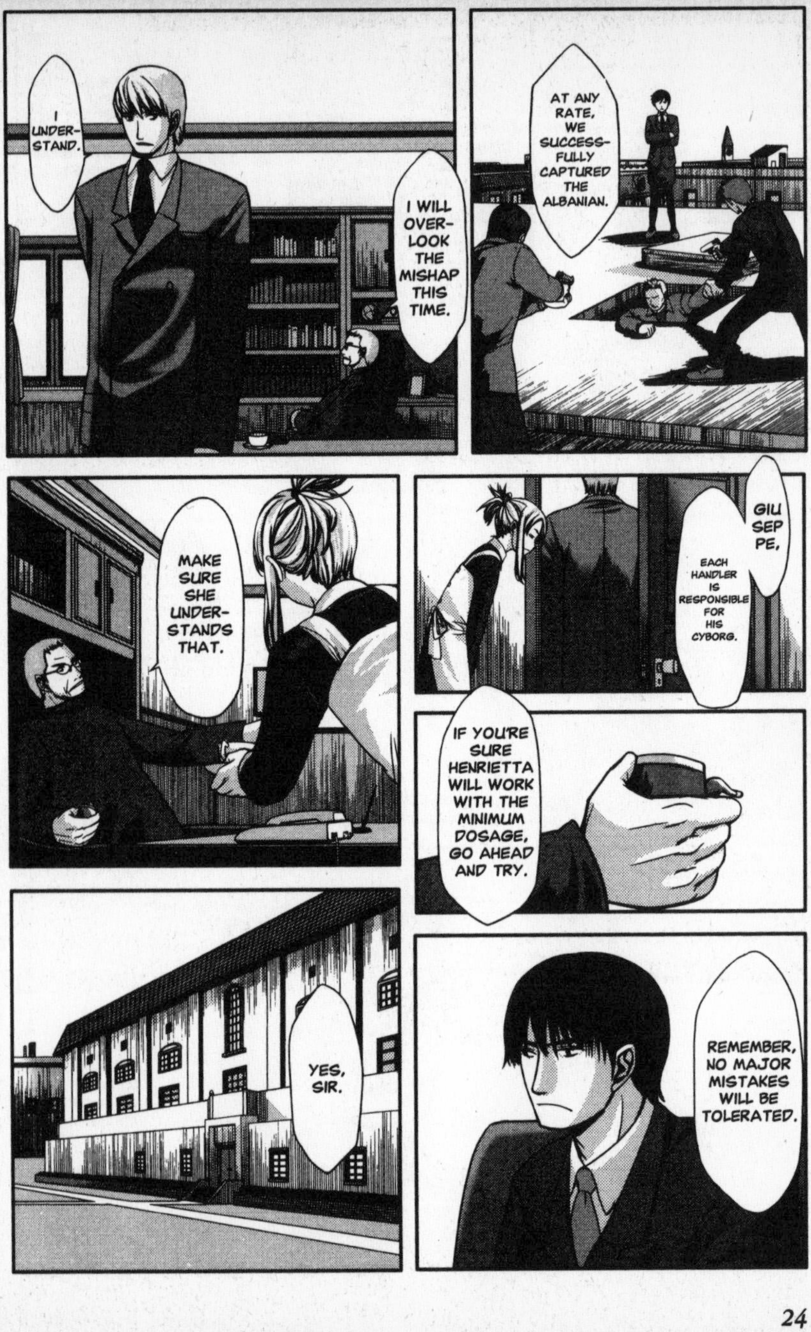
AT ANY RATE, WE SUCCESSFULLY CAPTURED THE ALBANIAN.
I WILL OVER-LOOK THE MISHAP THIS TIME.
I UNDER-STAND.
GIU SEP PE,
EACH HANDLER IS RESPONSIBLE FOR HIS CYBORG.
MAKE SURE SHE UNDER-STANDS THAT.
IF YOU'RE SURE HENRIETTA WILL WORK WITH THE MINIMUM DOSAGE, GO AHEAD AND TRY.
REMEMBER, NO MAJOR MISTAKES WILL BE TOLERATED.
YES, SIR.

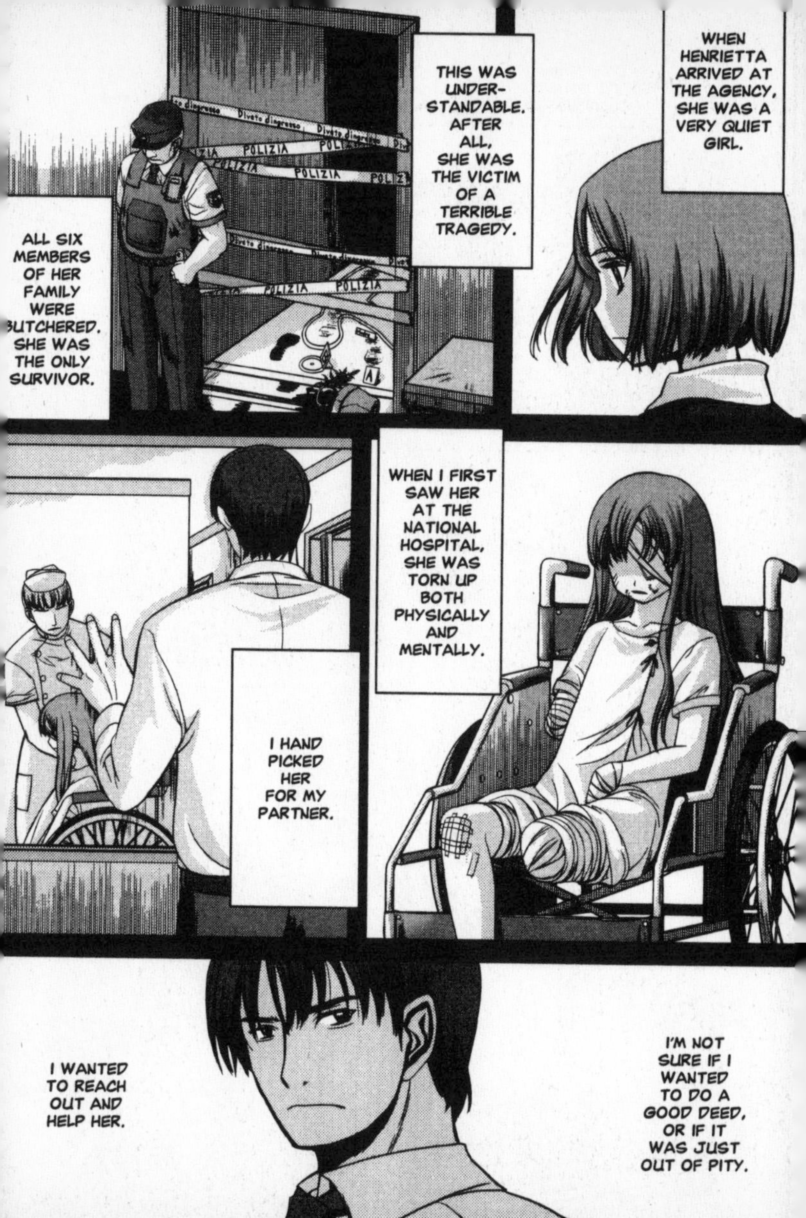
WHEN HENRIETTA ARRIVED AT THE AGENCY, SHE WAS A VERY QUIET GIRL.
THIS WAS UNDER-STANDABLE. AFTER ALL, SHE WAS THE VICTIM OF A TERRIBLE TRAGEDY.
POLIZIA
ALL SIX MEMBERS OF HER FAMILY WERE BUTCHERED. SHE WAS THE ONLY SURVIVOR.
WHEN I FIRST SAW HER AT THE NATIONAL HOSPITAL, SHE WAS TORN UP BOTH PHYSICALLY AND MENTALLY.
I HAND PICKED HER FOR MY PARTNER.
I'M NOT SURE IF I WANTED TO DO A GOOD DEED, OR IF IT WAS JUST OUT OF PITY.
I WANTED TO REACH OUT AND HELP HER.

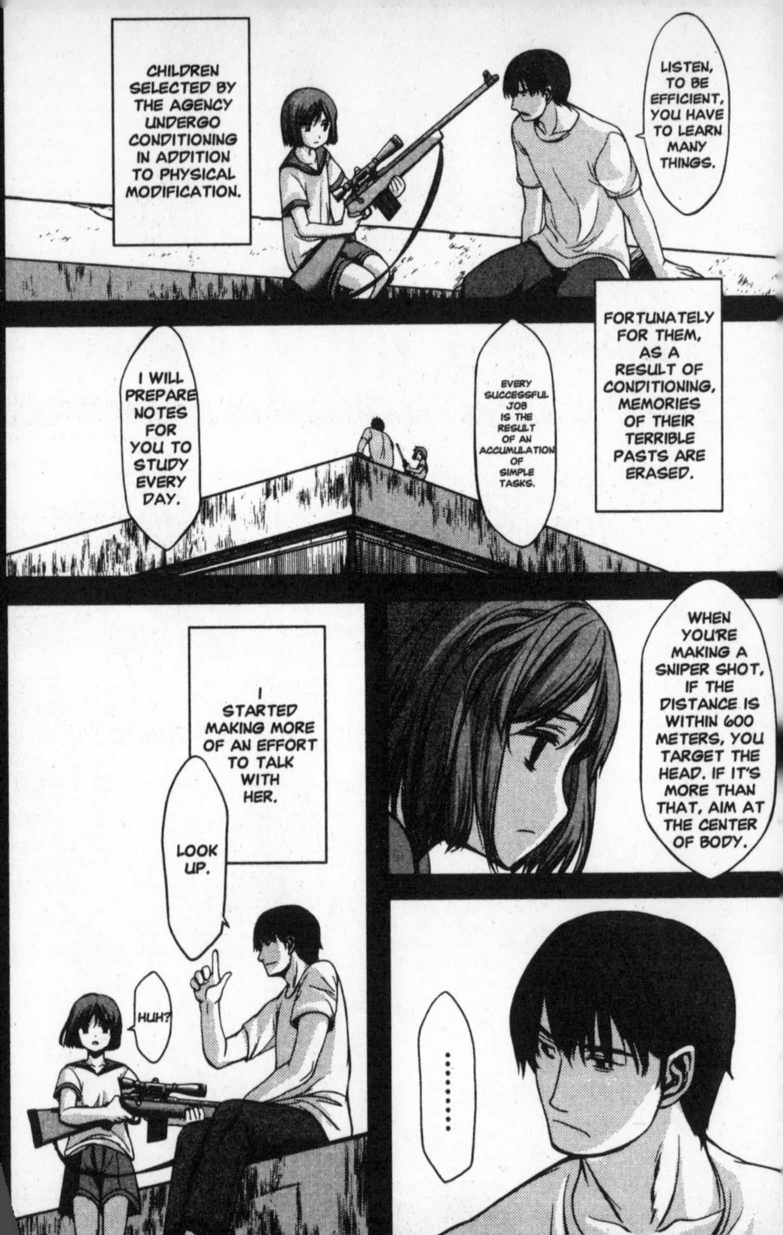
LISTEN, TO BE EFFICIENT, YOU HAVE TO LEARN MANY THINGS.
CHILDREN SELECTED BY THE AGENCY UNDERGO CONDITIONING IN ADDITION TO PHYSICAL MODIFICATION.
FORTUNATELY FOR THEM, AS A RESULT OF CONDITIONING, MEMORIES OF THEIR TERRIBLE PASTS ARE ERASED.
EVERY SUCCESSFUL JOB IS THE RESULT OF AN ACCUMULATION OF SIMPLE TASKS.
I WILL PREPARE NOTES FOR YOU TO STUDY EVERY DAY.
WHEN YOU'RE MAKING A SNIPER SHOT, IF THE DISTANCE IS WITHIN 600 METERS, YOU TARGET THE HEAD. IF IT'S MORE THAN THAT, AIM AT THE CENTER OF BODY.
....
I STARTED MAKING MORE OF AN EFFORT TO TALK WITH HER.
LOOK UP.
HUH?

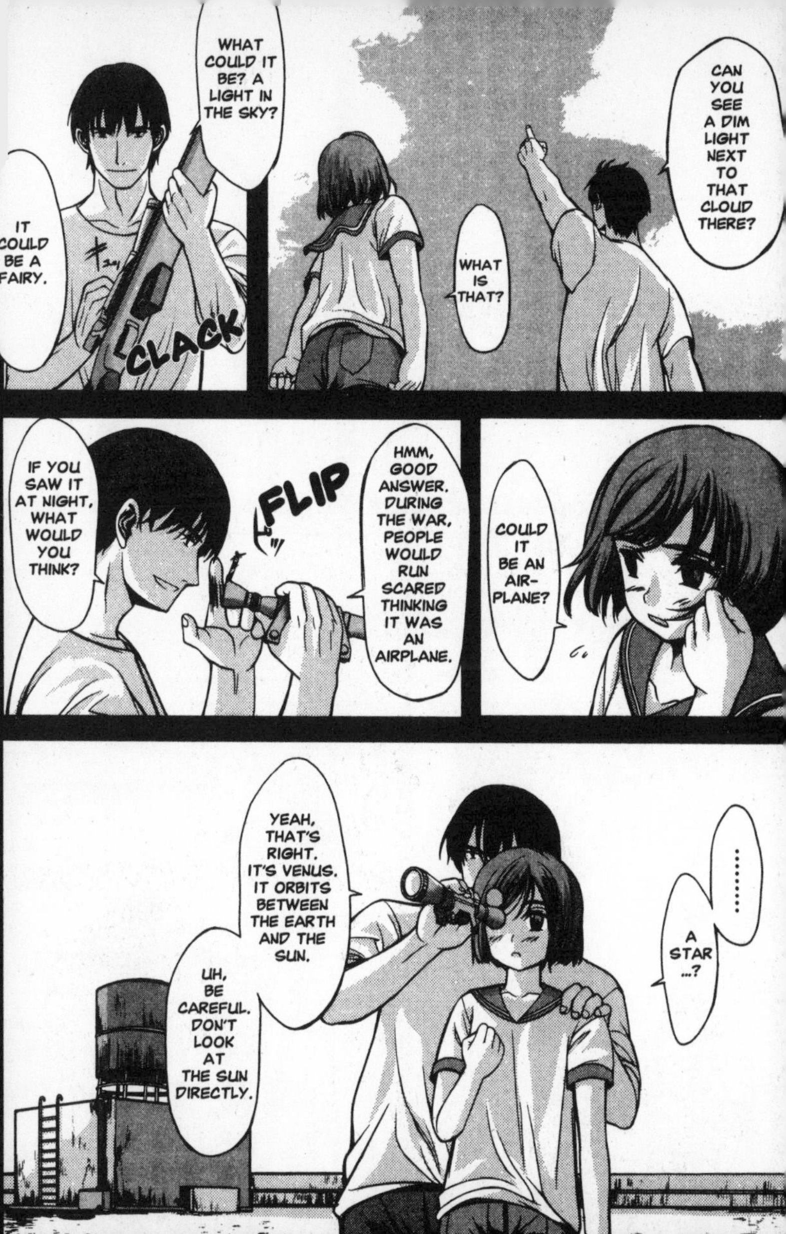
CAN YOU SEE A DIM LIGHT NEXT TO THAT CLOUD THERE?
WHAT IS THAT?
WHAT COULD IT BE? A LIGHT IN THE SKY?
IT COULD BE A FAIRY.
CLACK
COULD IT BE AN AIR-PLANE?
HMM, GOOD ANSWER. DURING THE WAR, PEOPLE WOULD RUN SCARED THINKING IT WAS AN AIRPLANE.
FLIP
IF YOU SAW IT AT NIGHT, WHAT WOULD YOU THINK?
....
A STAR ...?
YEAH, THAT'S RIGHT. IT'S VENUS. IT ORBITS BETWEEN THE EARTH AND THE SUN.
UH, BE CAREFUL. DON'T LOOK AT THE SUN DIRECTLY.

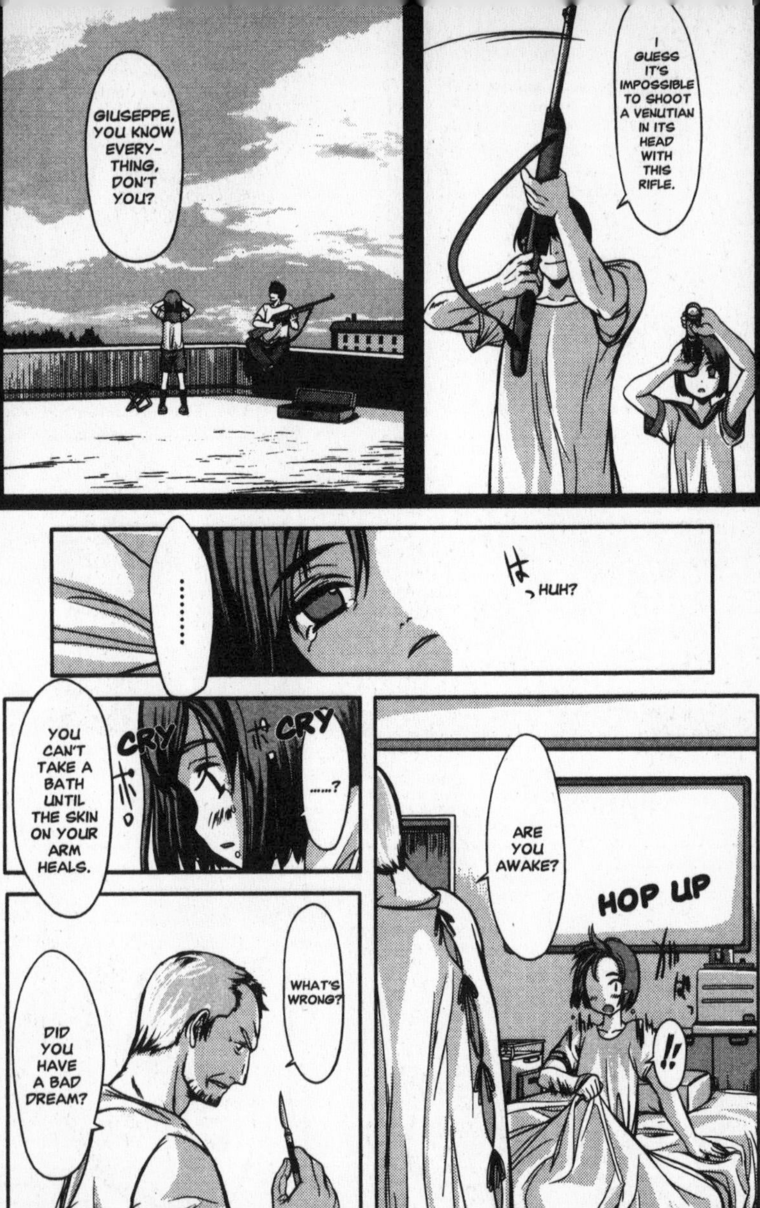
I GUESS IT'S IMPOSSIBLE TO SHOOT A VENUTIAN IN ITS HEAD WITH THIS RIFLE.
GIUSEPPE, YOU KNOW EVERY-THING, DON'T YOU?
は、HUH?
......
CRY CRY
......?
YOU CAN'T TAKE A BATH UNTIL THE SKIN ON YOUR ARM HEALS.
ARE YOU AWAKE?
HOP UP
!!
WHAT'S WRONG?
DID YOU HAVE A BAD DREAM?

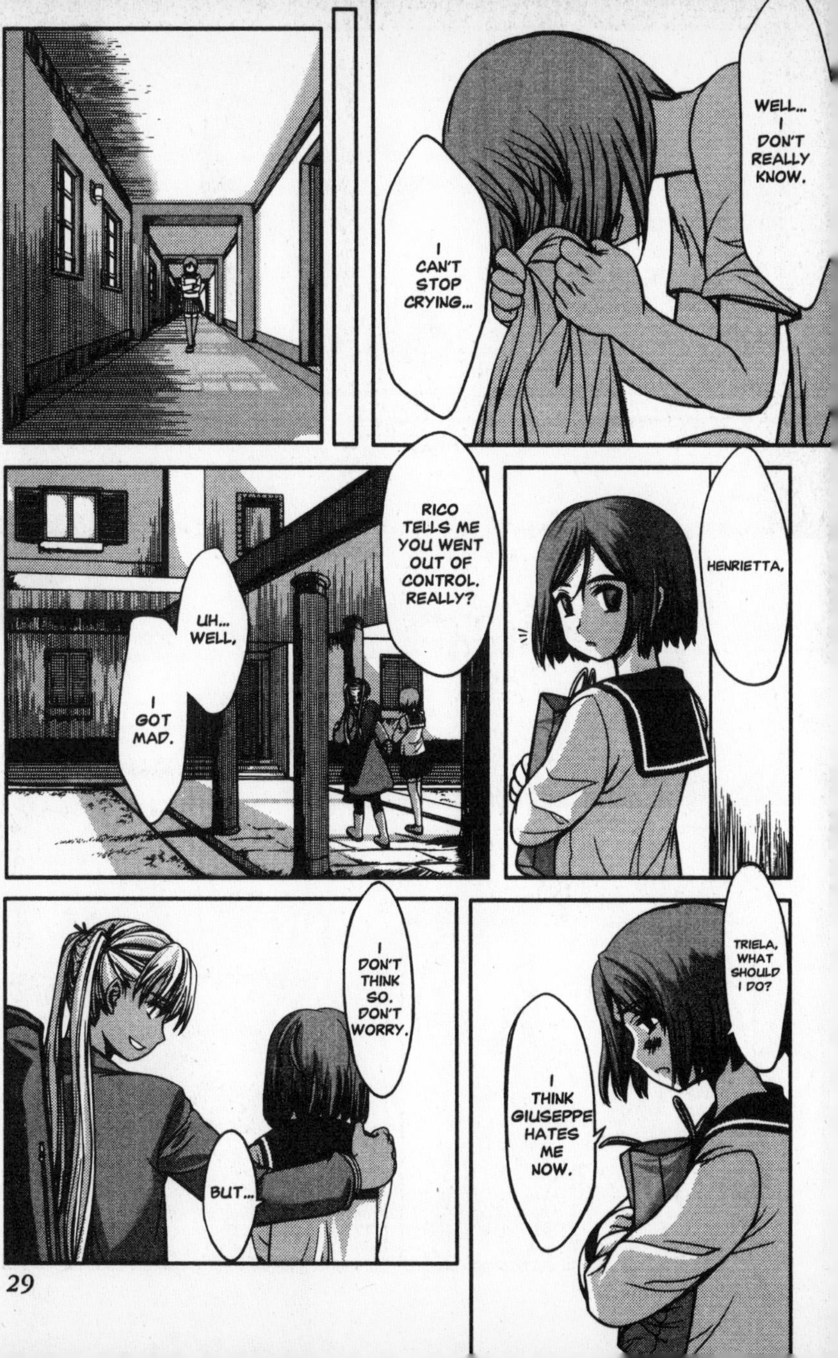
WELL... I DON'T REALLY KNOW.
I CAN'T STOP CRYING...
HENRIETTA,
RICO TELLS ME YOU WENT OUT OF CONTROL. REALLY?
UH... WELL,
I GOT MAD.
TRIELA, WHAT SHOULD I DO?
I THINK GIUSEPPE HATES ME NOW.
I DON'T THINK SO. DON'T WORRY.
BUT...

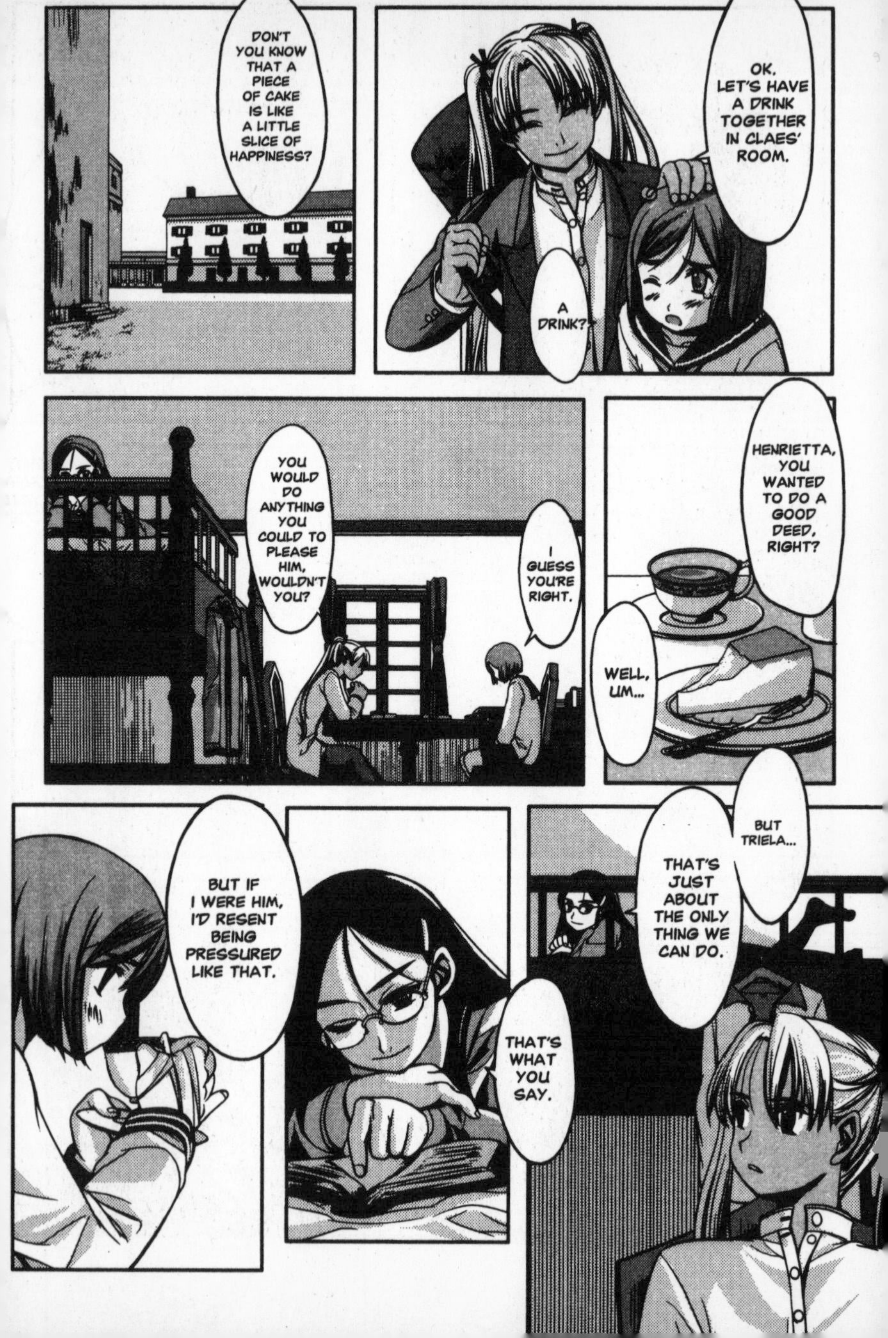
DON'T YOU KNOW THAT A PIECE OF CAKE IS LIKE A LITTLE SLICE OF HAPPINESS?
OK. LET'S HAVE A DRINK TOGETHER IN CLAES' ROOM.
A DRINK?
YOU WOULD DO ANYTHING YOU COULD TO PLEASE HIM, WOULDN'T YOU?
I GUESS YOU'RE RIGHT.
HENRIETTA, YOU WANTED TO DO A GOOD DEED, RIGHT?
WELL, UM...
BUT IF I WERE HIM, I'D RESENT BEING PRESSURED LIKE THAT.
THAT'S WHAT YOU SAY.
BUT TRIELA...
THAT'S JUST ABOUT THE ONLY THING WE CAN DO.

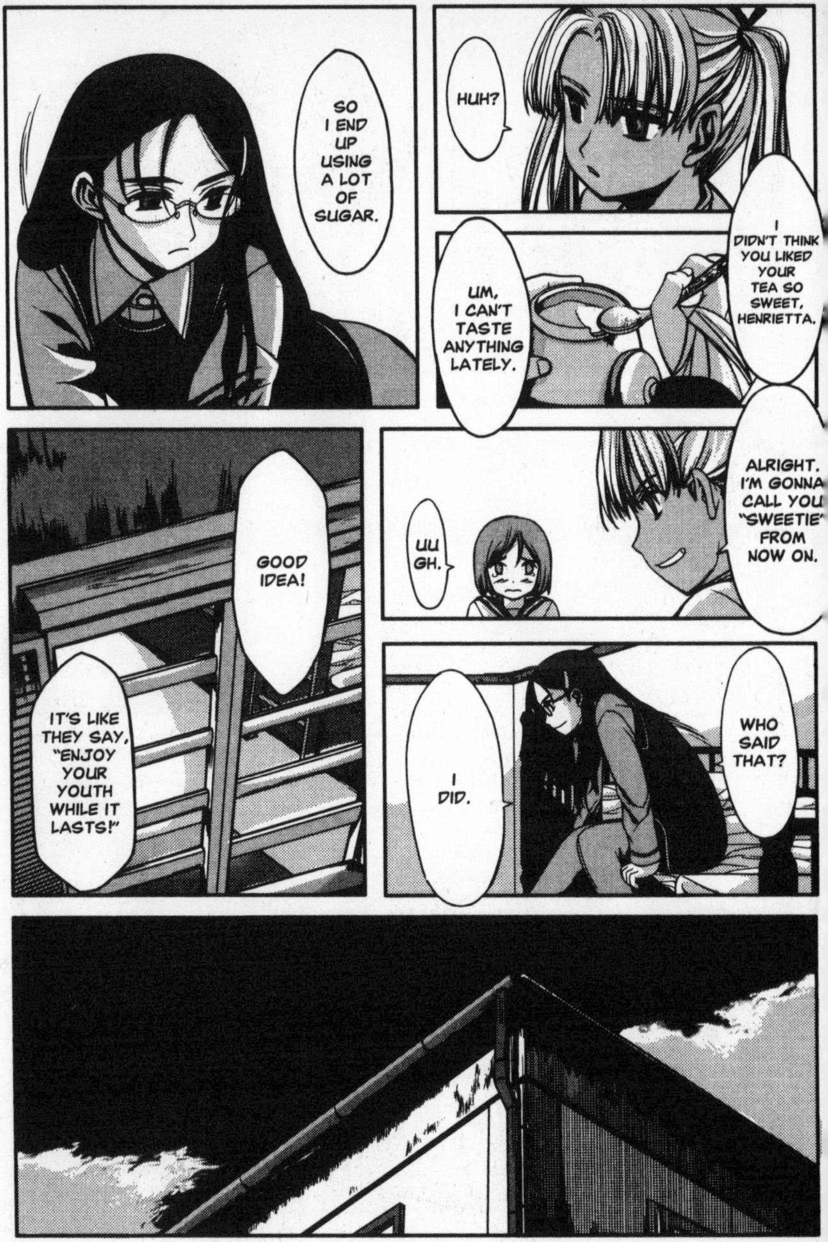
HUH?
I DIDN'T THINK YOU LIKED YOUR TEA SO SWEET, HENRIETTA.
UM, I CAN'T TASTE ANYTHING LATELY.
SO I END UP USING A LOT OF SUGAR.
ALRIGHT. I'M GONNA CALL YOU "SWEETIE" FROM NOW ON.
UU GH.
WHO SAID THAT?
I DID.
GOOD IDEA!
IT'S LIKE THEY SAY, "ENJOY YOUR YOUTH WHILE IT LASTS!"

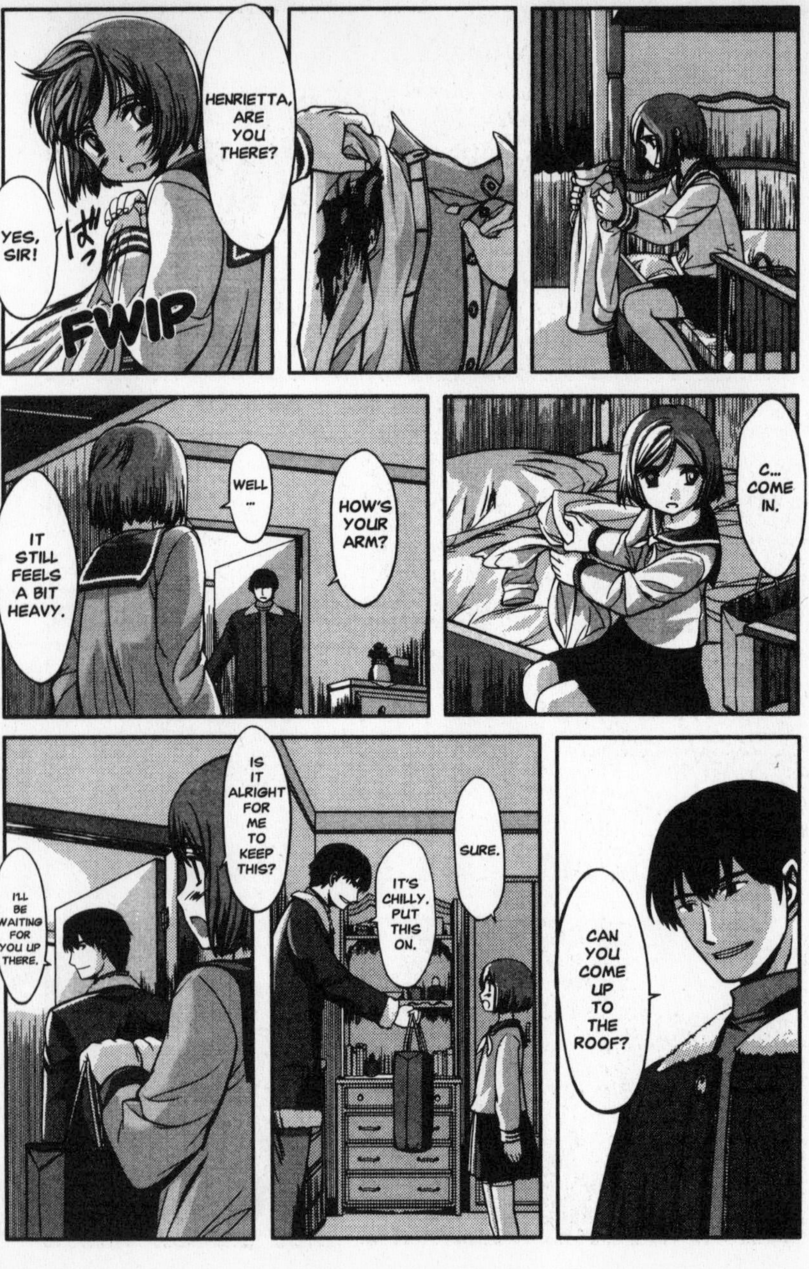
HENRIETTA, ARE YOU THERE?
YES, SIR!
ばっ
FWIP
C... COME IN.
HOW'S YOUR ARM?
WELL ...
IT STILL FEELS A BIT HEAVY.
CAN YOU COME UP TO THE ROOF?
IT'S CHILLY, PUT THIS ON.
IS IT ALRIGHT FOR ME TO KEEP THIS?
SURE.
I'LL BE WAITING FOR YOU UP THERE.

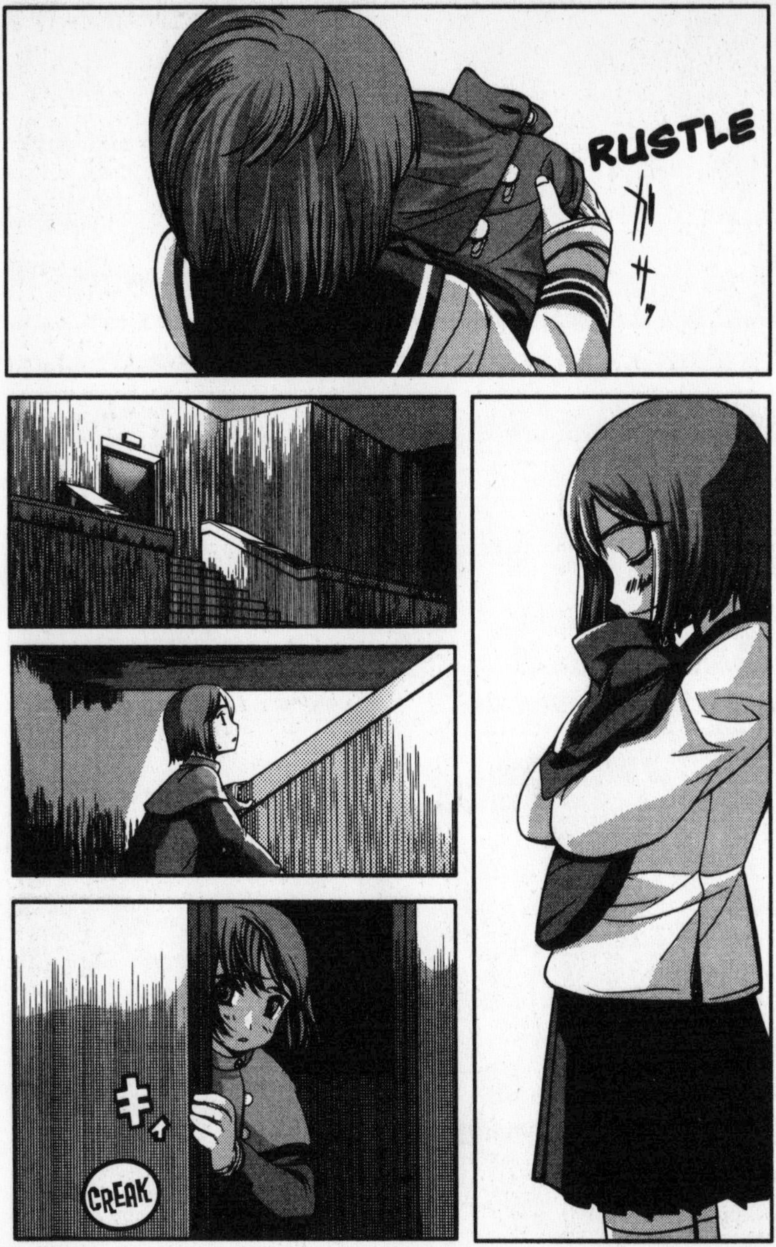
RUSTLE
ガサッ
キィ
CREAK

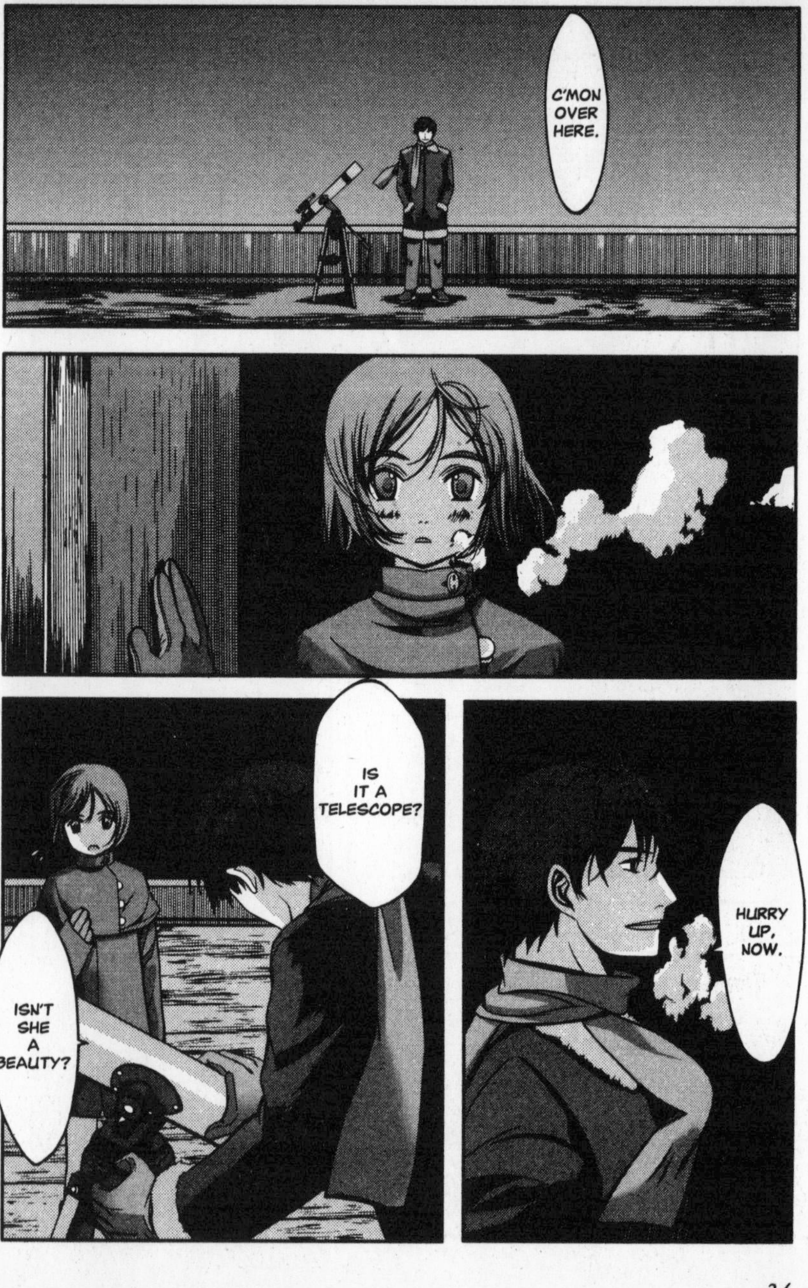
C'MON OVER HERE.
HURRY UP, NOW.
IS IT A TELESCOPE?
ISN'T SHE A BEAUTY?

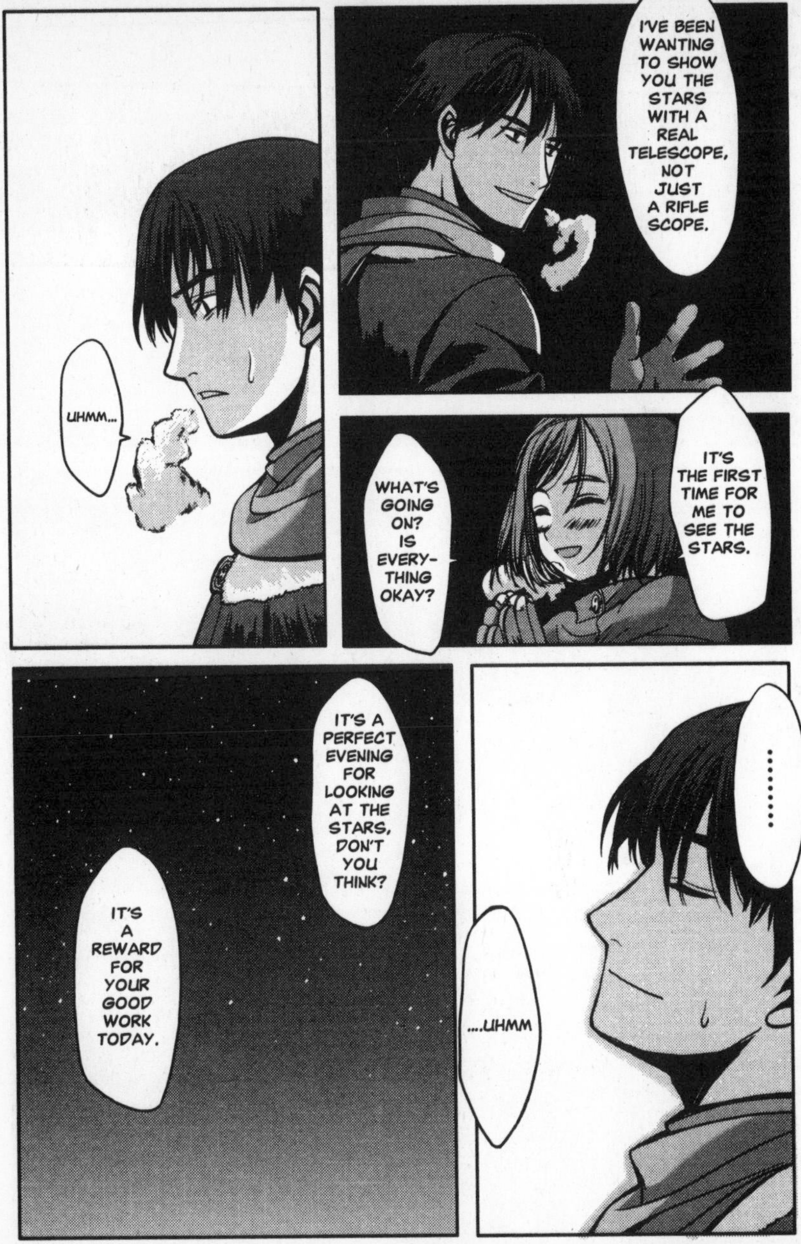
I'VE BEEN WANTING TO SHOW YOU THE STARS WITH A REAL TELESCOPE, NOT JUST A RIFLE SCOPE.
IT'S THE FIRST TIME FOR ME TO SEE THE STARS.
WHAT'S GOING ON? IS EVERY-THING OKAY?
UHMM...
....
....UHMM
IT'S A PERFECT EVENING FOR LOOKING AT THE STARS, DON'T YOU THINK?
IT'S A REWARD FOR YOUR GOOD WORK TODAY.

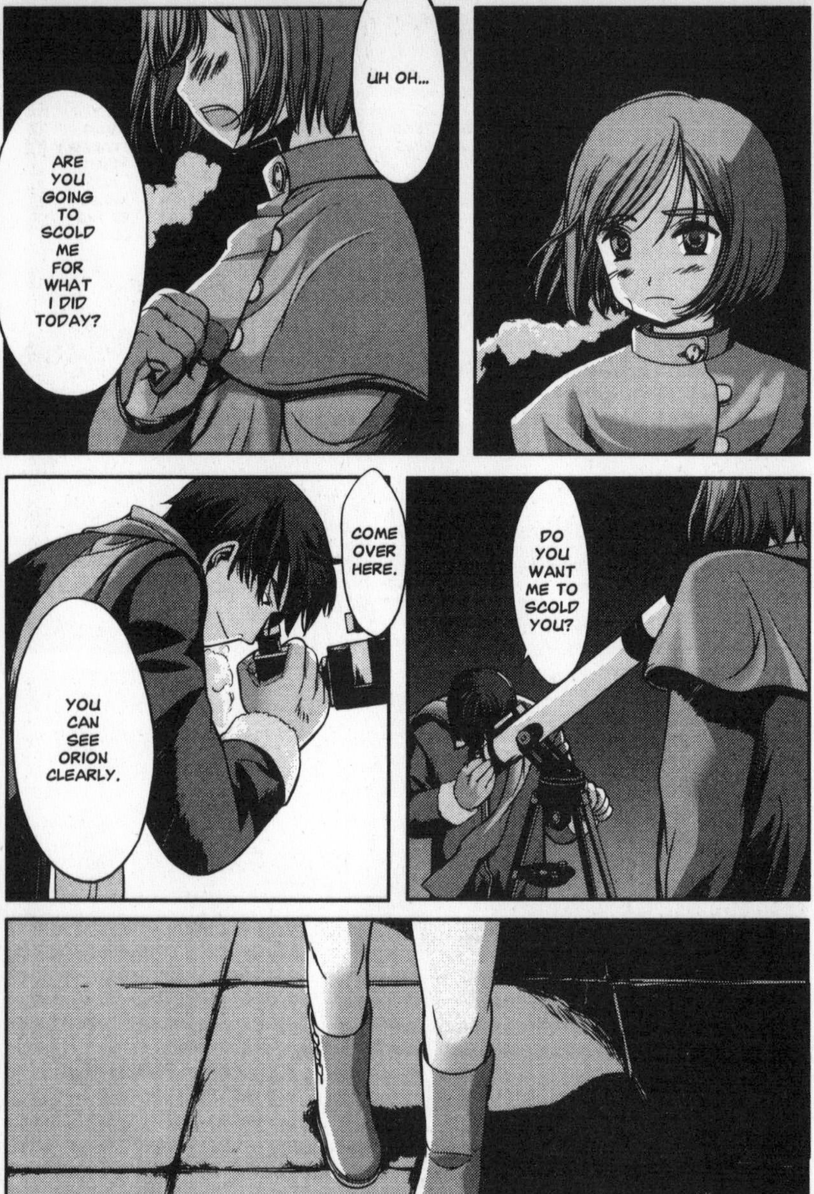
UH OH...
ARE YOU GOING TO SCOLD ME FOR WHAT I DID TODAY?
COME OVER HERE.
YOU CAN SEE ORION CLEARLY.
DO YOU WANT ME TO SCOLD YOU?

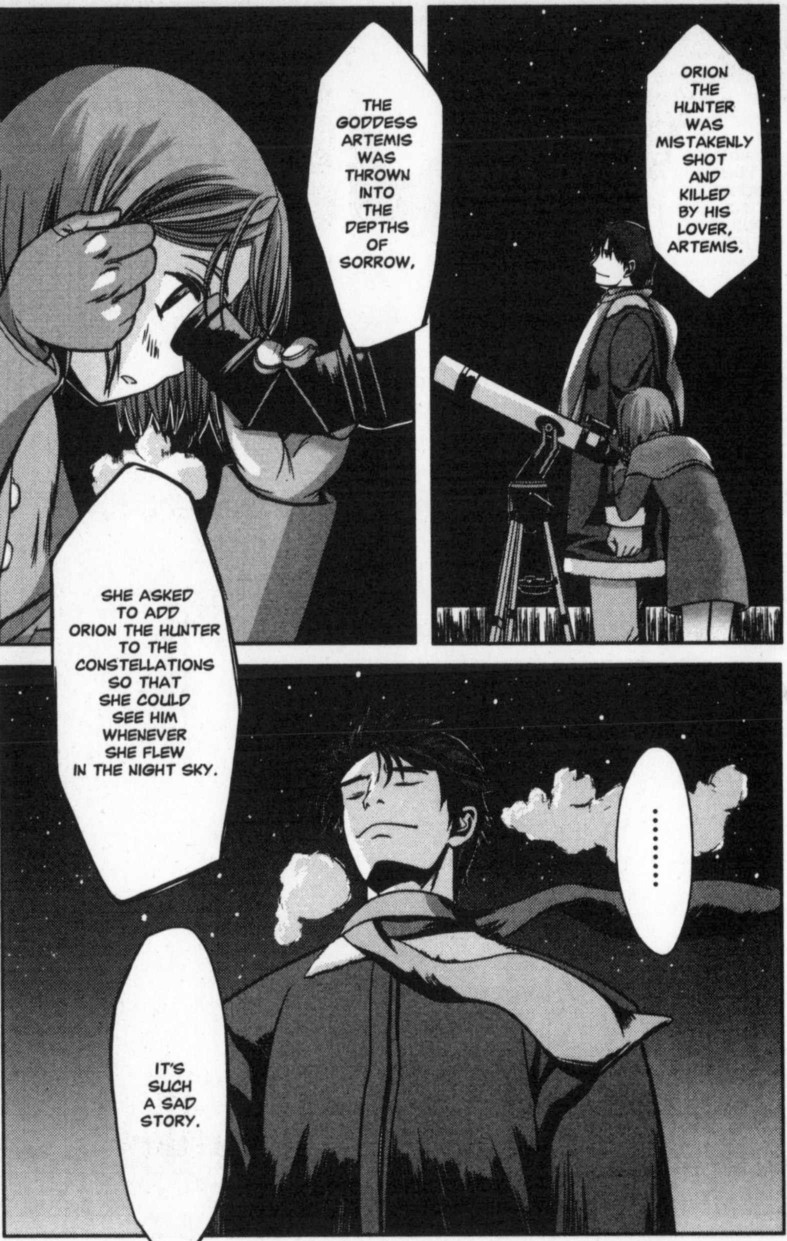
ORION THE HUNTER WAS MISTAKENLY SHOT AND KILLED BY HIS LOVER, ARTEMIS.
THE GODDESS ARTEMIS WAS THROWN INTO THE DEPTHS OF SORROW,
SHE ASKED TO ADD ORION THE HUNTER TO THE CONSTELLATIONS SO THAT SHE COULD SEE HIM WHENEVER SHE FLEW IN THE NIGHT SKY.
......
IT'S SUCH A SAD STORY.

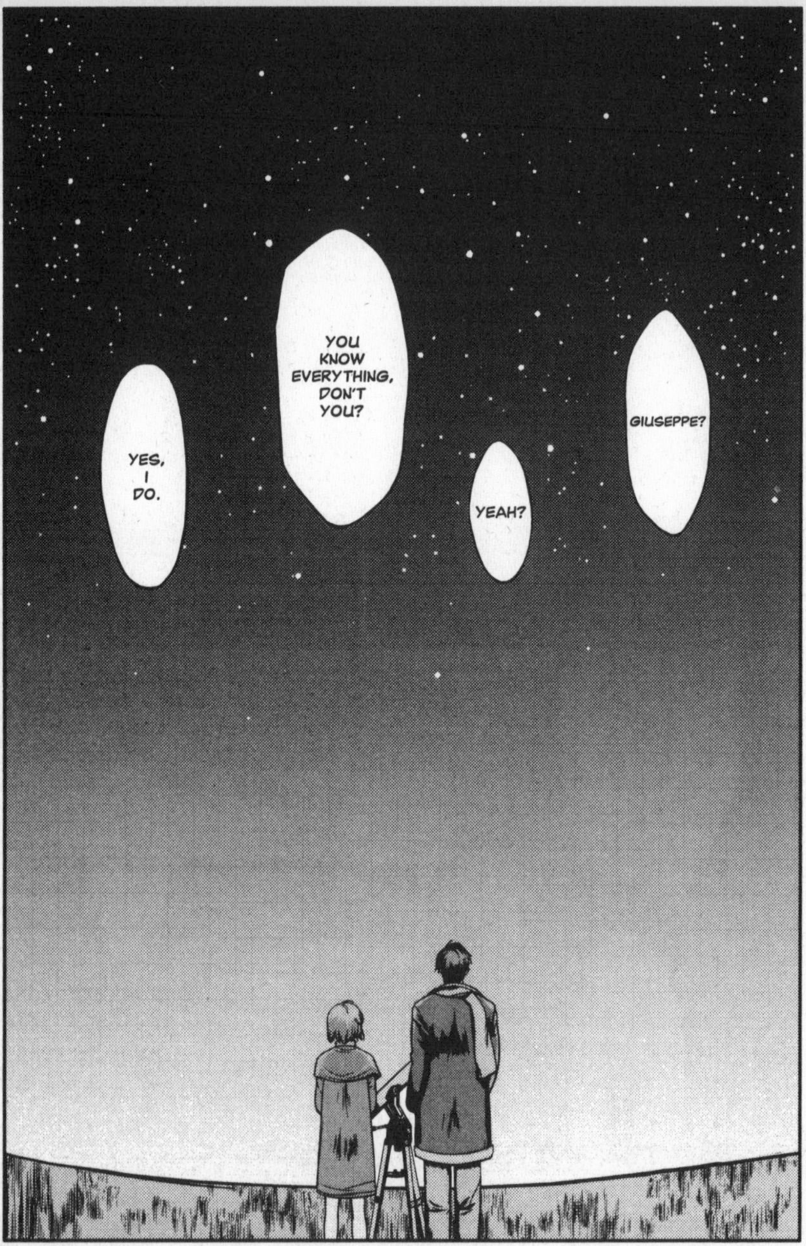
GIUSEPPE?
YEAH?
YOU KNOW EVERYTHING, DON'T YOU?
YES, I DO.

GUNSLINGERGIRL.

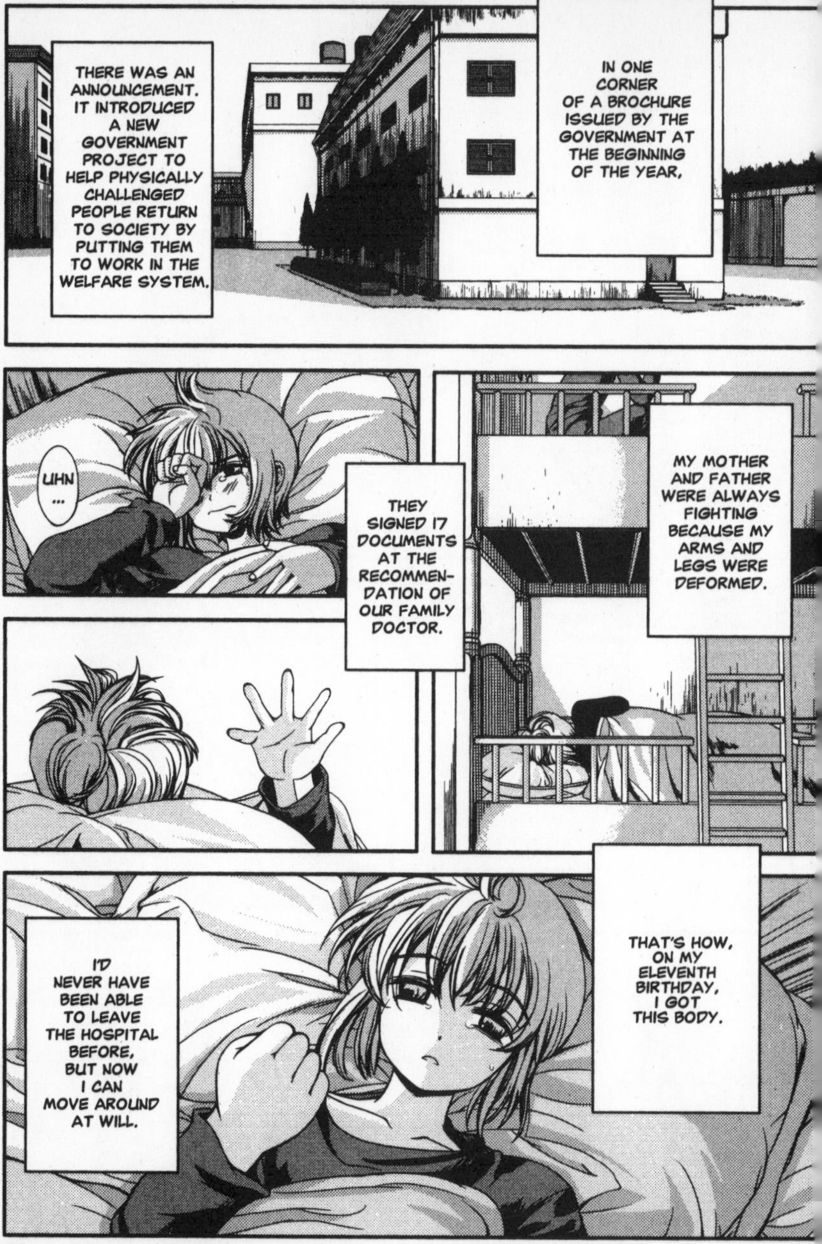
IN ONE CORNER OF A BROCHURE ISSUED BY THE GOVERNMENT AT THE BEGINNING OF THE YEAR,
THERE WAS AN ANNOUNCEMENT. IT INTRODUCED A NEW GOVERNMENT PROJECT TO HELP PHYSICALLY CHALLENGED PEOPLE RETURN TO SOCIETY BY PUTTING THEM TO WORK IN THE WELFARE SYSTEM.
MY MOTHER AND FATHER WERE ALWAYS FIGHTING BECAUSE MY ARMS AND LEGS WERE DEFORMED.
THEY SIGNED 17 DOCUMENTS AT THE RECOMMENDATION OF OUR FAMILY DOCTOR.
UHN ...
THAT'S HOW, ON MY ELEVENTH BIRTHDAY, I GOT THIS BODY.
I'D NEVER HAVE BEEN ABLE TO LEAVE THE HOSPITAL BEFORE, BUT NOW I CAN MOVE AROUND AT WILL.

第 2 話 Love thy neighbor

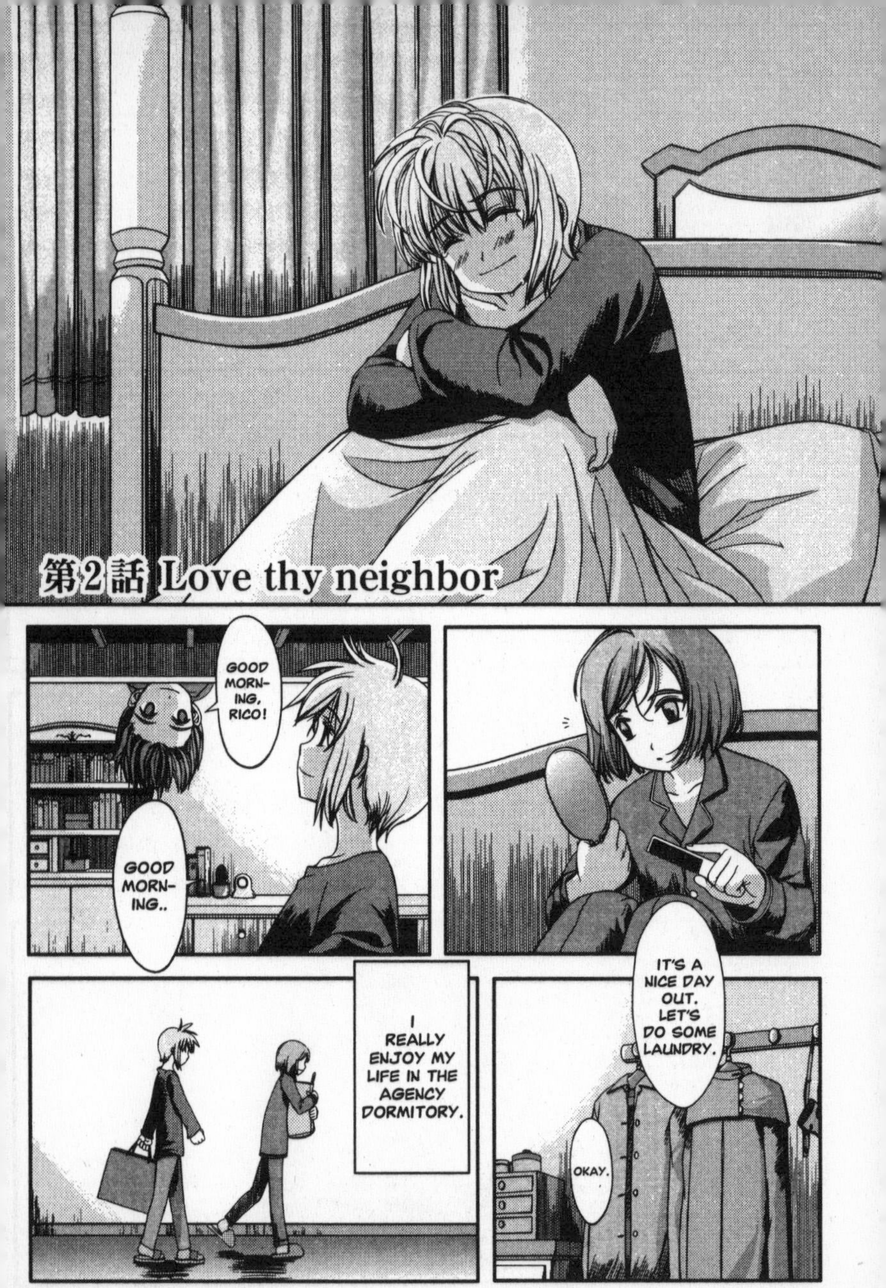
第2話 Love thy neighbor
GOOD MORNING, RICO!
GOOD MORNING..
I REALLY ENJOY MY LIFE IN THE AGENCY DORMITORY.
IT'S A NICE DAY OUT. LET'S DO SOME LAUNDRY.
OKAY.

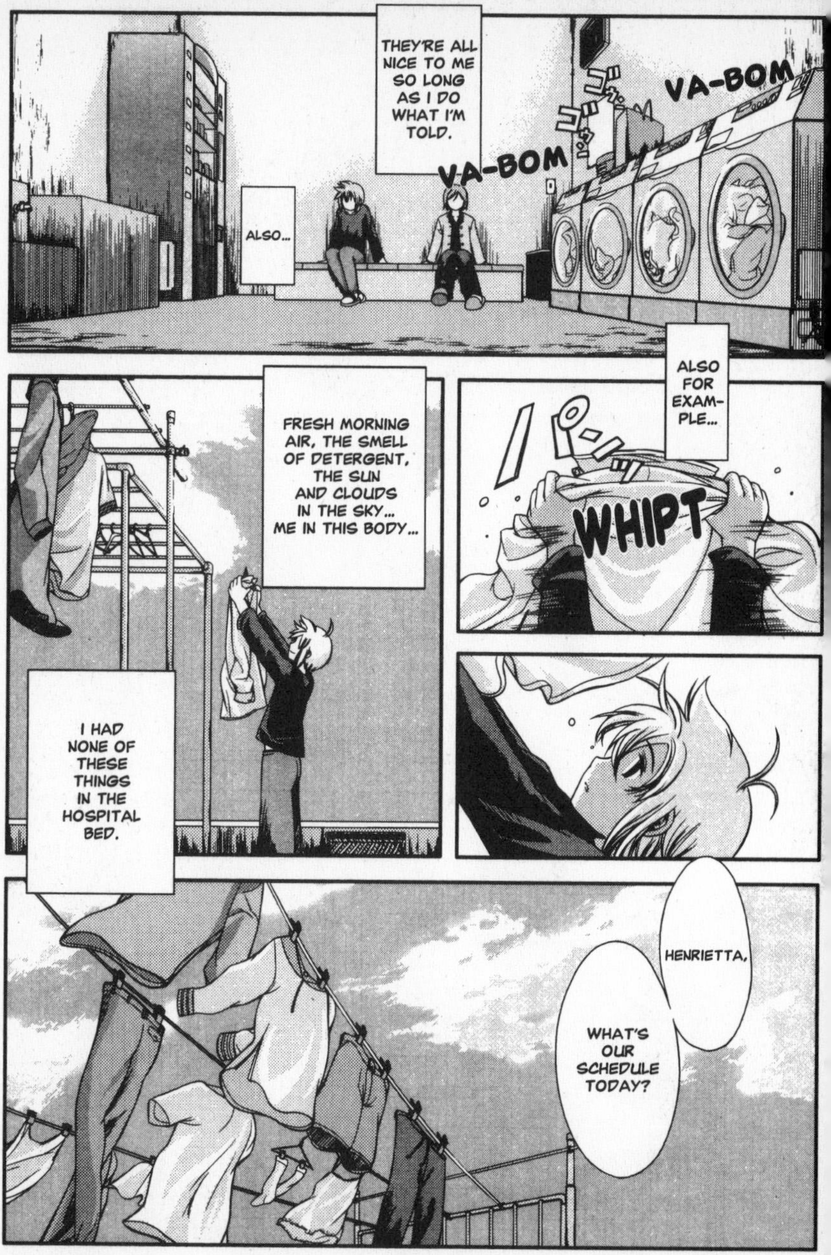

VA-BOM
VA-BOM
THEY'RE ALL NICE TO ME SO LONG AS I DO WHAT I'M TOLD.
ALSO...
ALSO FOR EXAMPLE...
WHIPT
FRESH MORNING AIR, THE SMELL OF DETERGENT, THE SUN AND CLOUDS IN THE SKY... ME IN THIS BODY...
I HAD NONE OF THESE THINGS IN THE HOSPITAL BED.
HENRIETTA,
WHAT'S OUR SCHEDULE TODAY?

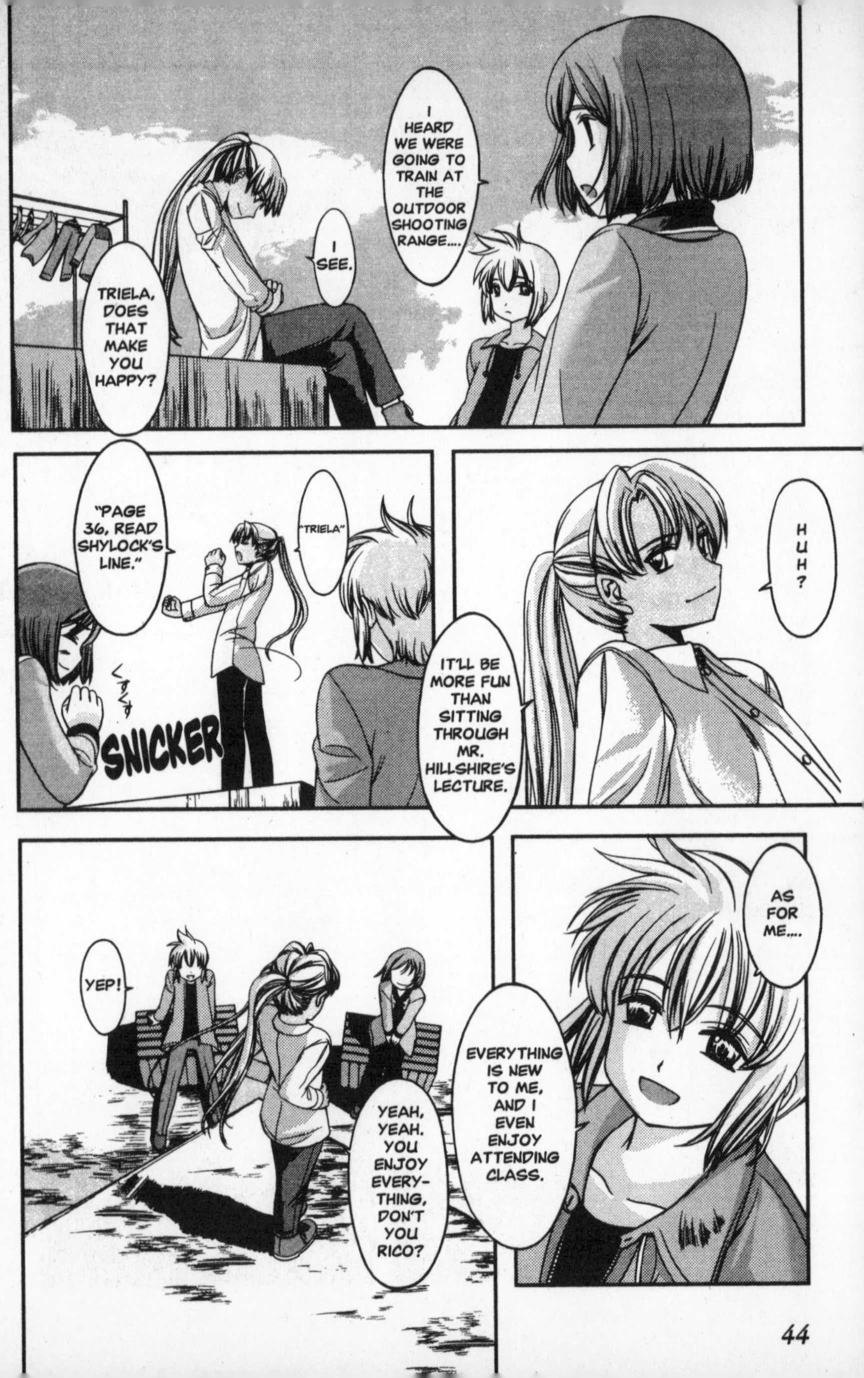
I HEARD WE WERE GOING TO TRAIN AT THE OUTDOOR SHOOTING RANGE....
I SEE.
TRIELA, DOES THAT MAKE YOU HAPPY?
HUH?
IT'LL BE MORE FUN THAN SITTING THROUGH MR. HILLSHIRE'S LECTURE.
"TRIELA"
"PAGE 36, READ SHYLOCK'S LINE."
SNICKER
AS FOR ME....
EVERYTHING IS NEW TO ME, AND I EVEN ENJOY ATTENDING CLASS.
YEAH, YEAH. YOU ENJOY EVERY-THING, DON'T YOU RICO?
YEP!

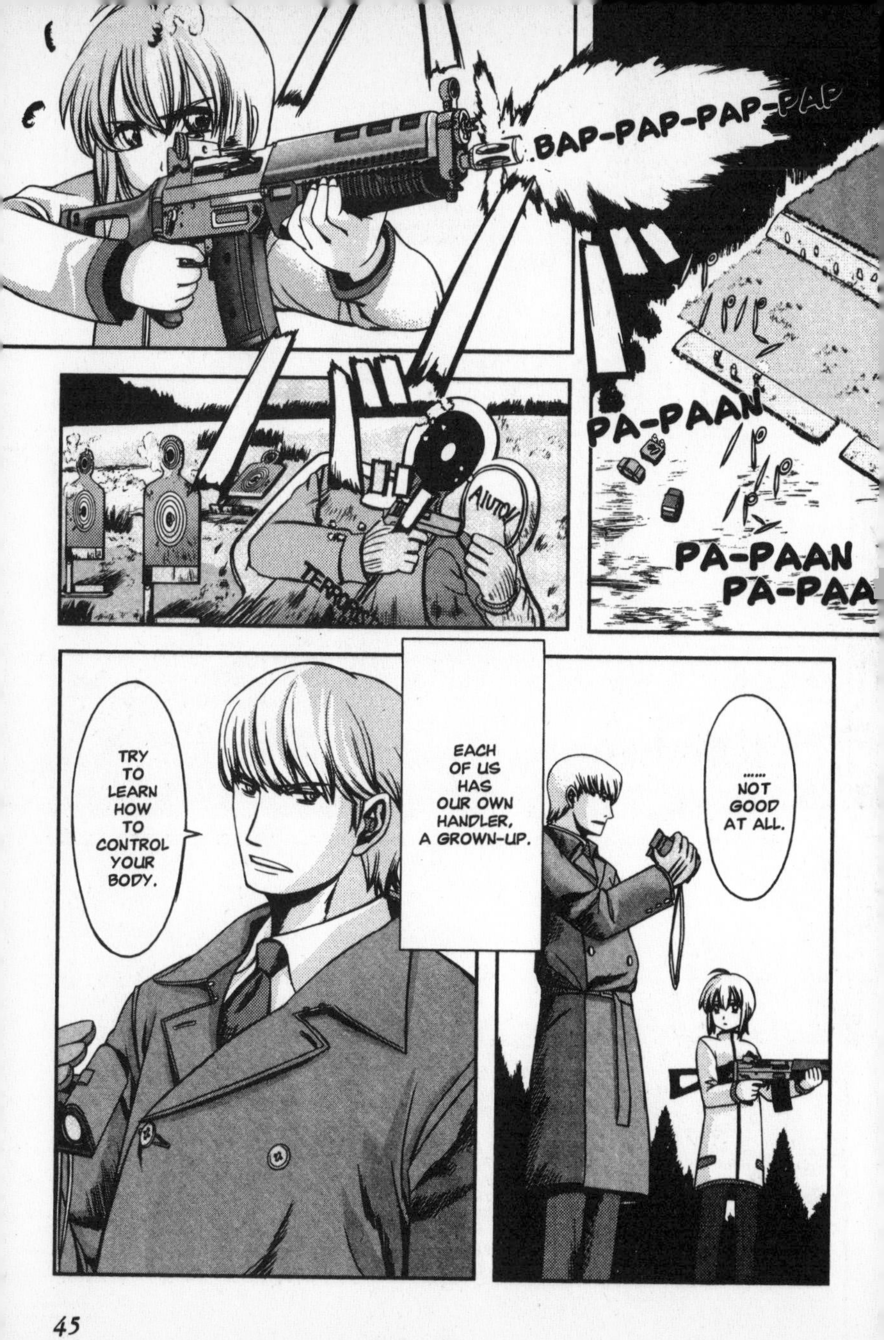
BAP-PAP-PAP-PAP-PAP
PA-PAAN
PA-PAAN
PA-PAA
AIUTO
...... NOT GOOD AT ALL.
EACH OF US HAS OUR OWN HANDLER, A GROWN-UP.
TRY TO LEARN HOW TO CONTROL YOUR BODY.

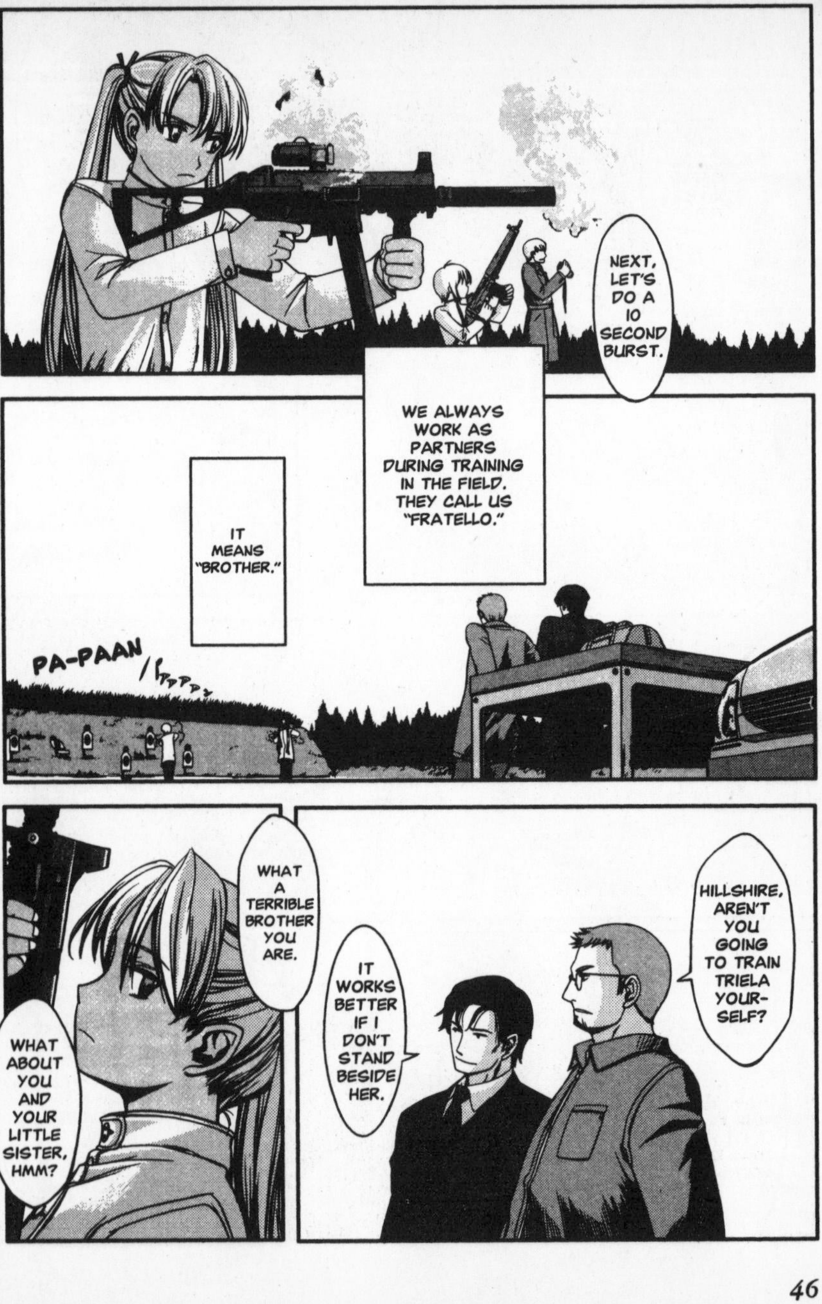
NEXT, LET'S DO A 10 SECOND BURST.
WE ALWAYS WORK AS PARTNERS DURING TRAINING IN THE FIELD. THEY CALL US "FRATELLO."
IT MEANS "BROTHER."
PA-PAAN
HILLSHIRE, AREN'T YOU GOING TO TRAIN TRIELA YOUR-SELF?
IT WORKS BETTER IF I DON'T STAND BESIDE HER.
WHAT A TERRIBLE BROTHER YOU ARE.
WHAT ABOUT YOU AND YOUR LITTLE SISTER, HMM?

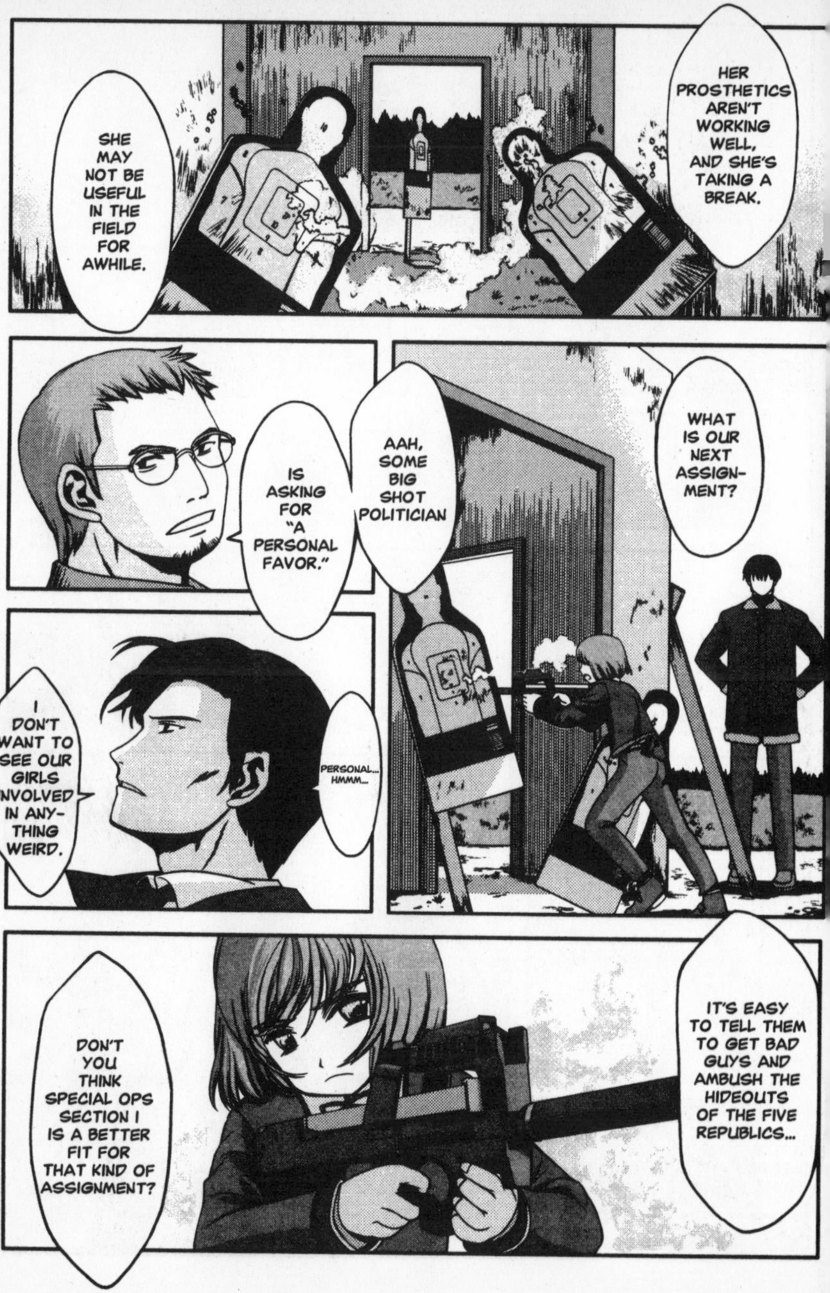

HER PROSTHETICS AREN'T WORKING WELL, AND SHE'S TAKING A BREAK.
SHE MAY NOT BE USEFUL IN THE FIELD FOR AWHILE.
WHAT IS OUR NEXT ASSIGN-MENT?
AAH, SOME BIG SHOT POLITICIAN
IS ASKING FOR "A PERSONAL FAVOR."
PERSONAL... HMMM...
I DON'T WANT TO SEE OUR GIRLS INVOLVED IN ANY-THING WEIRD.
IT'S EASY TO TELL THEM TO GET BAD GUYS AND AMBUSH THE HIDEOUTS OF THE FIVE REPUBLICS...
DON'T YOU THINK SPECIAL OPS SECTION I IS A BETTER FIT FOR THAT KIND OF ASSIGNMENT?

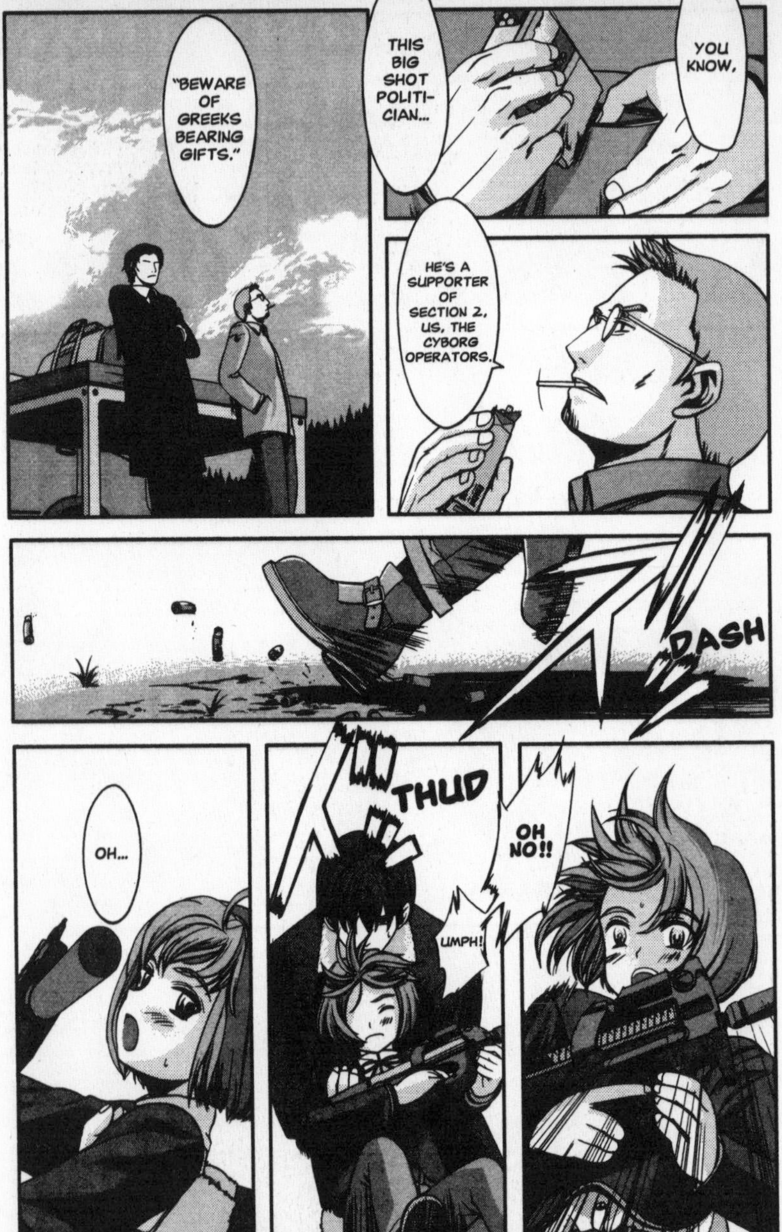
"BEWARE OF GREEKS BEARING GIFTS."
THIS BIG SHOT POLITI-CIAN...
YOU KNOW,
HE'S A SUPPORTER OF SECTION 2, US, THE CYBORG OPERATORS.
DASH
OH...
THUD
UMPH!
OH NO!!

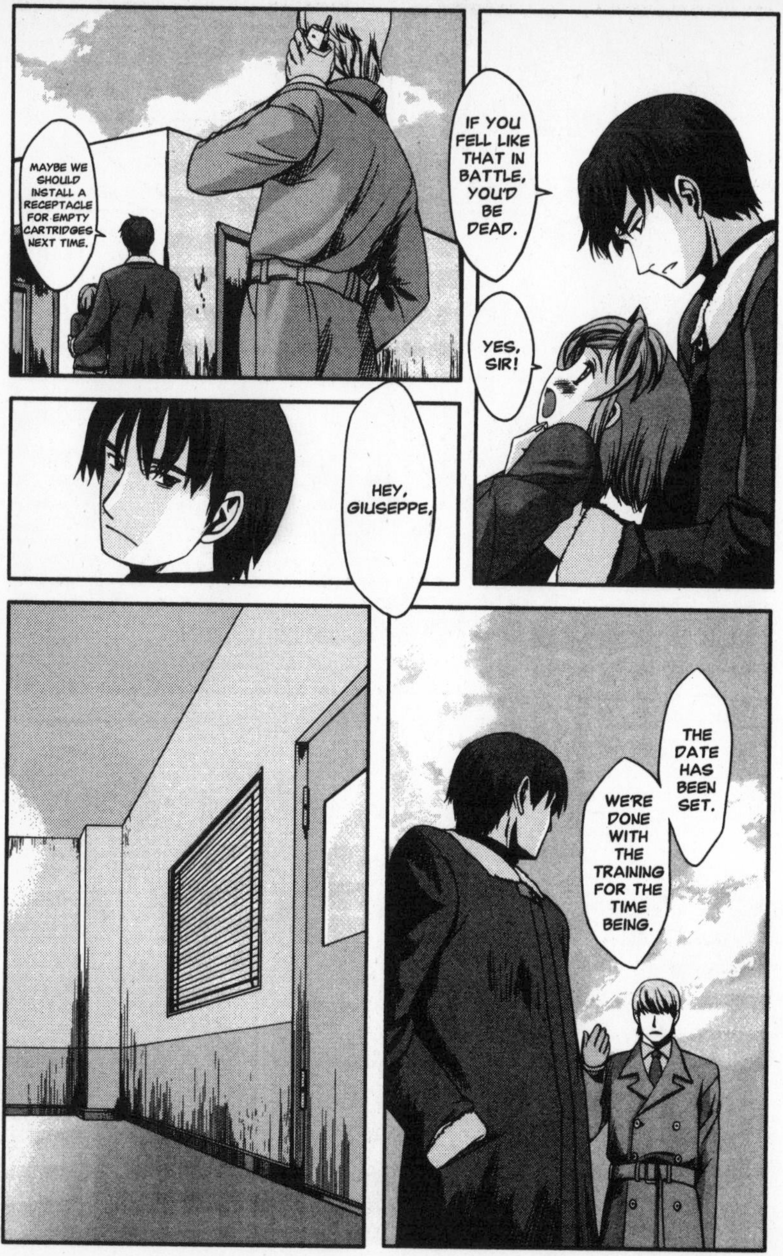
MAYBE WE SHOULD INSTALL A RECEPTACLE FOR EMPTY CARTRIDGES NEXT TIME.
IF YOU FELL LIKE THAT IN BATTLE, YOU'D BE DEAD.
YES, SIR!
HEY, GIUSEPPE,
THE DATE HAS BEEN SET.
WE'RE DONE WITH THE TRAINING FOR THE TIME BEING.

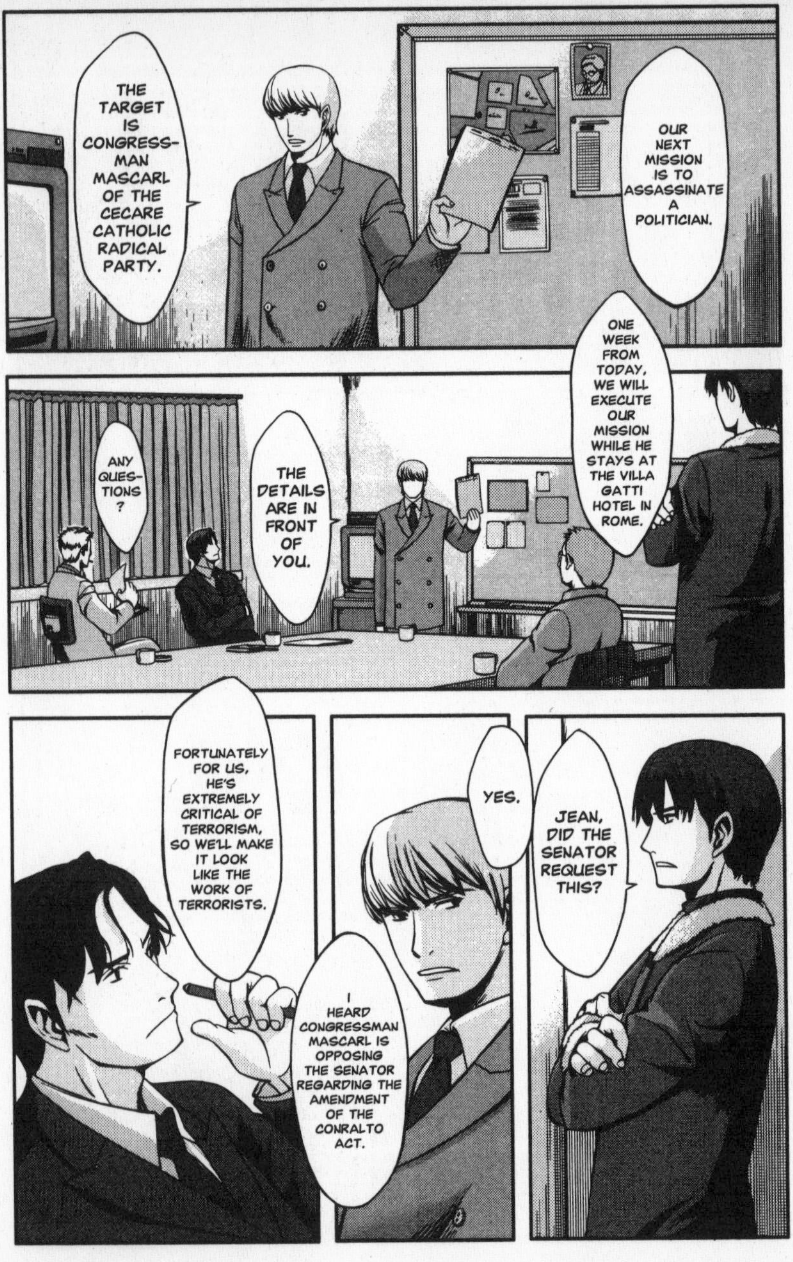

OUR NEXT MISSION IS TO ASSASSINATE A POLITICIAN.
THE TARGET IS CONGRESSMAN MASCARL OF THE CECARE CATHOLIC RADICAL PARTY.
ONE WEEK FROM TODAY, WE WILL EXECUTE OUR MISSION WHILE HE STAYS AT THE VILLA GATTI HOTEL IN ROME.
THE DETAILS ARE IN FRONT OF YOU.
ANY QUESTIONS?
FORTUNATELY FOR US, HE'S EXTREMELY CRITICAL OF TERRORISM, SO WE'LL MAKE IT LOOK LIKE THE WORK OF TERRORISTS.
I HEARD CONGRESSMAN MASCARL IS OPPOSING THE SENATOR REGARDING THE AMENDMENT OF THE CONRALTO ACT.
JEAN, DID THE SENATOR REQUEST THIS?
YES.

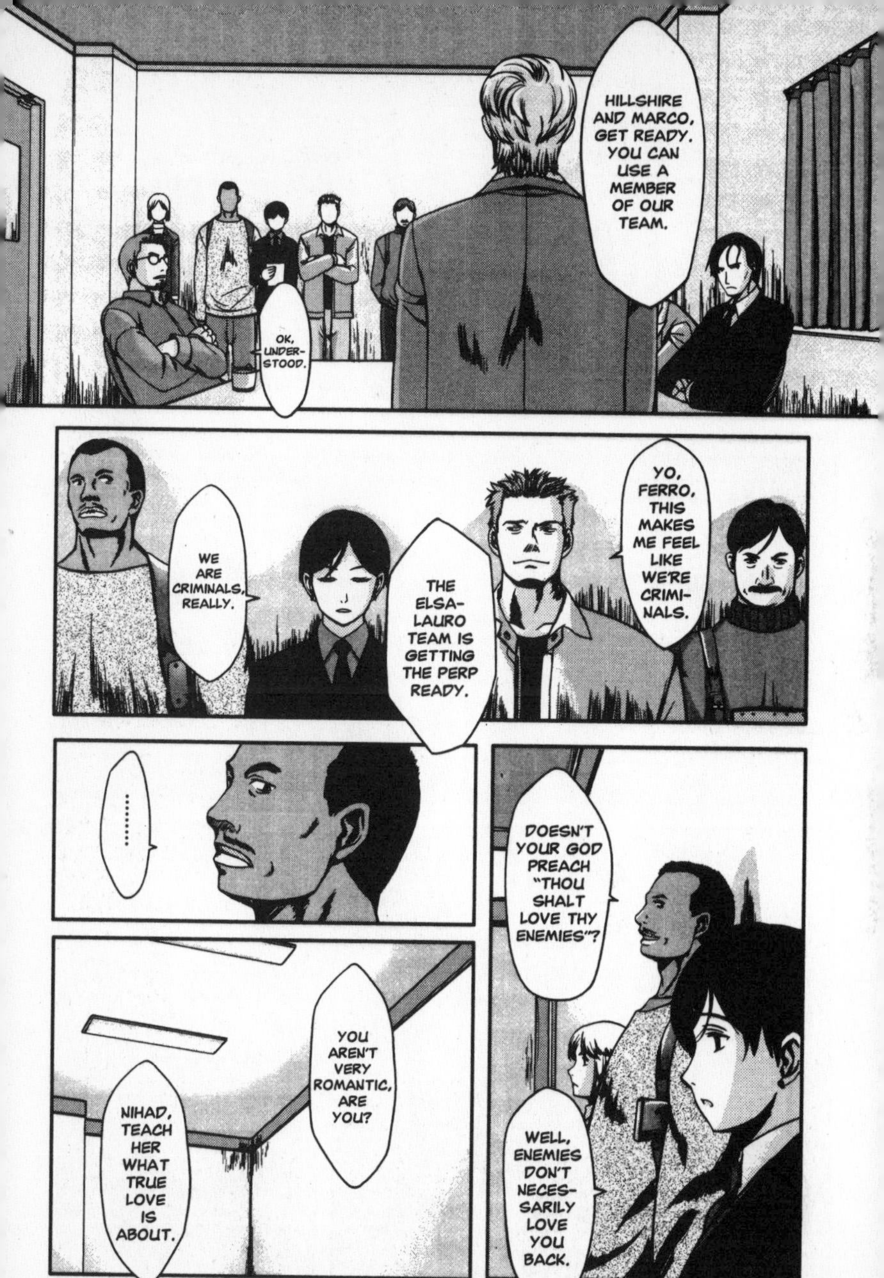
HILLSHIRE AND MARCO, GET READY. YOU CAN USE A MEMBER OF OUR TEAM.
OK, UNDER-STOOD.
YO, FERRO, THIS MAKES ME FEEL LIKE WE'RE CRIMI-NALS.
THE ELSA-LAURO TEAM IS GETTING THE PERP READY.
WE ARE CRIMINALS, REALLY.
DOESN'T YOUR GOD PREACH "THOU SHALT LOVE THY ENEMIES"?
......
WELL, ENEMIES DON'T NECES-SARILY LOVE YOU BACK.
YOU AREN'T VERY ROMANTIC, ARE YOU?
NIHAD, TEACH HER WHAT TRUE LOVE IS ABOUT.

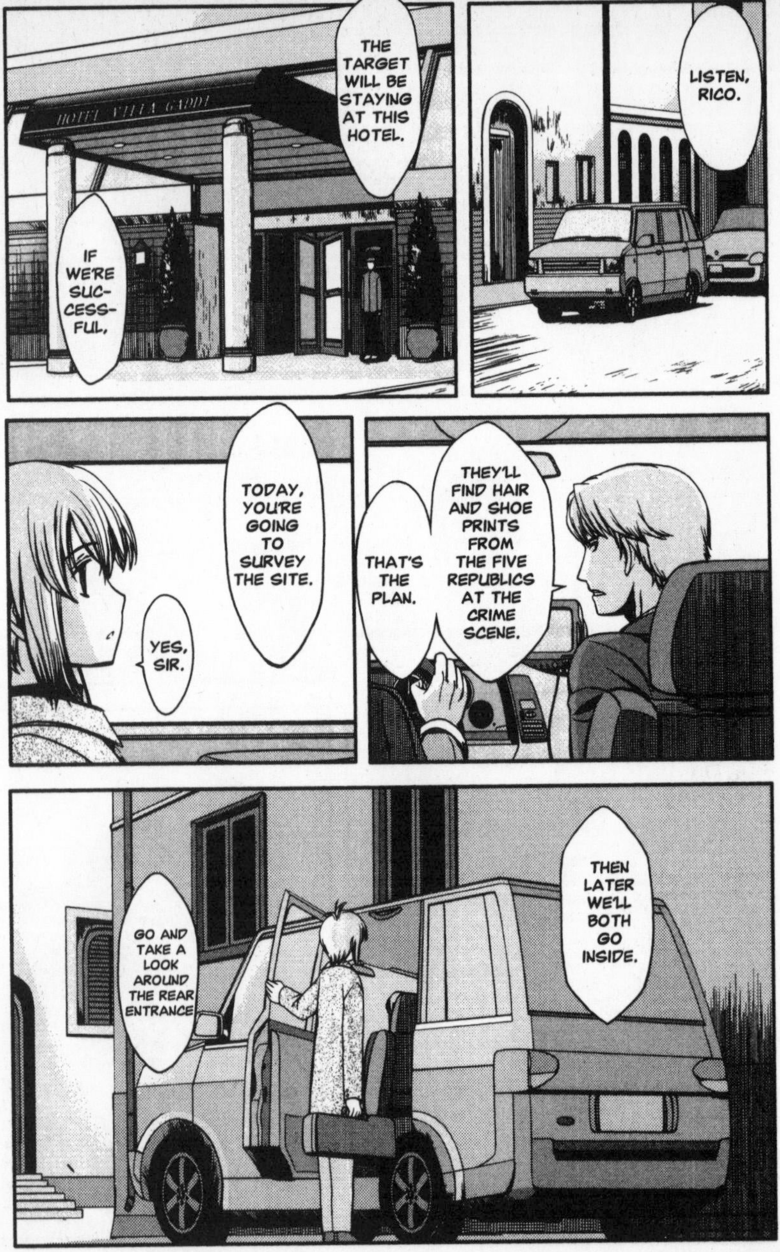
LISTEN, RICO.
THE TARGET WILL BE STAYING AT THIS HOTEL.
IF WE'RE SUC-CESS-FUL,
HOTEL VILLA GARDA
THEY'LL FIND HAIR AND SHOE PRINTS FROM THE FIVE REPUBLICS AT THE CRIME SCENE.
THAT'S THE PLAN.
TODAY, YOU'RE GOING TO SURVEY THE SITE.
YES, SIR.
THEN LATER WE'LL BOTH GO INSIDE.
GO AND TAKE A LOOK AROUND THE REAR ENTRANCE

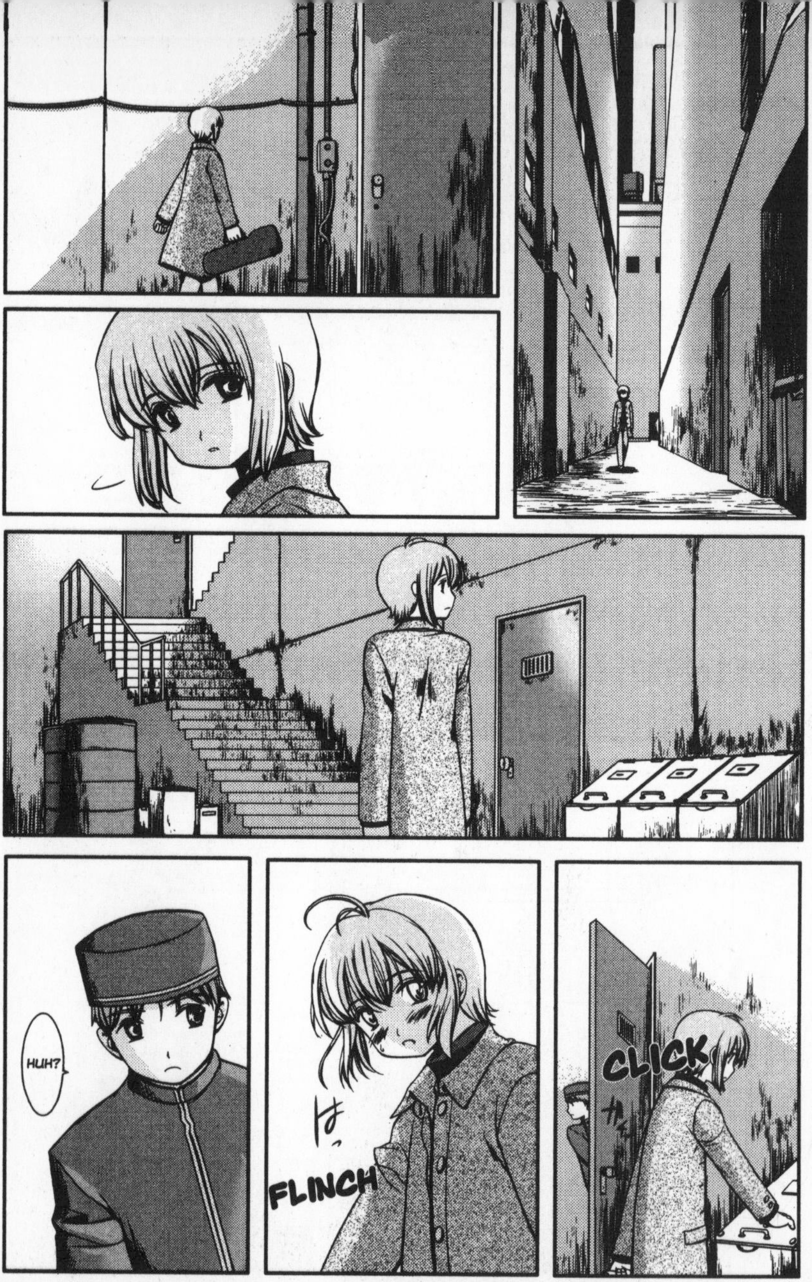
HUH?
は
FLINCH
CLICK

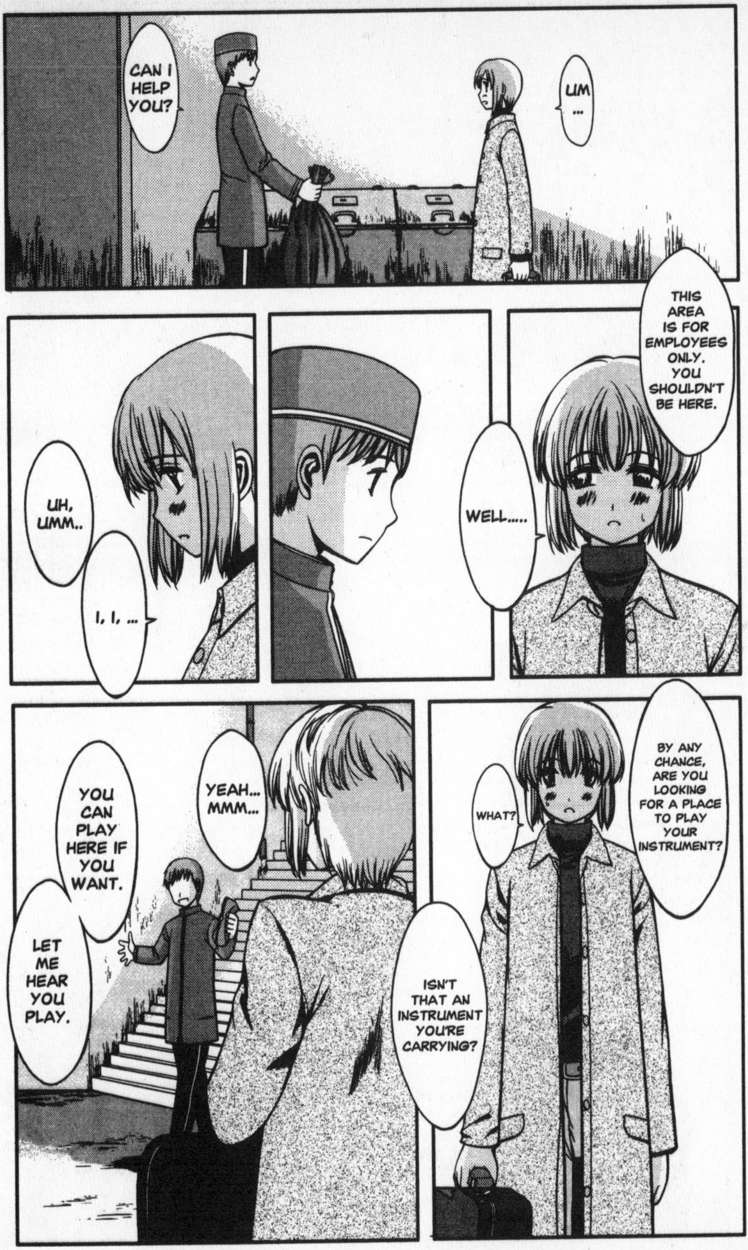
CAN I HELP YOU?
UM ...
THIS AREA IS FOR EMPLOYEES ONLY. YOU SHOULDN'T BE HERE.
WELL.....
UH, UMM..
I, I, ...
BY ANY CHANCE, ARE YOU LOOKING FOR A PLACE TO PLAY YOUR INSTRUMENT?
WHAT?
ISN'T THAT AN INSTRUMENT YOU'RE CARRYING?
YEAH... MMM...
YOU CAN PLAY HERE IF YOU WANT.
LET ME HEAR YOU PLAY.

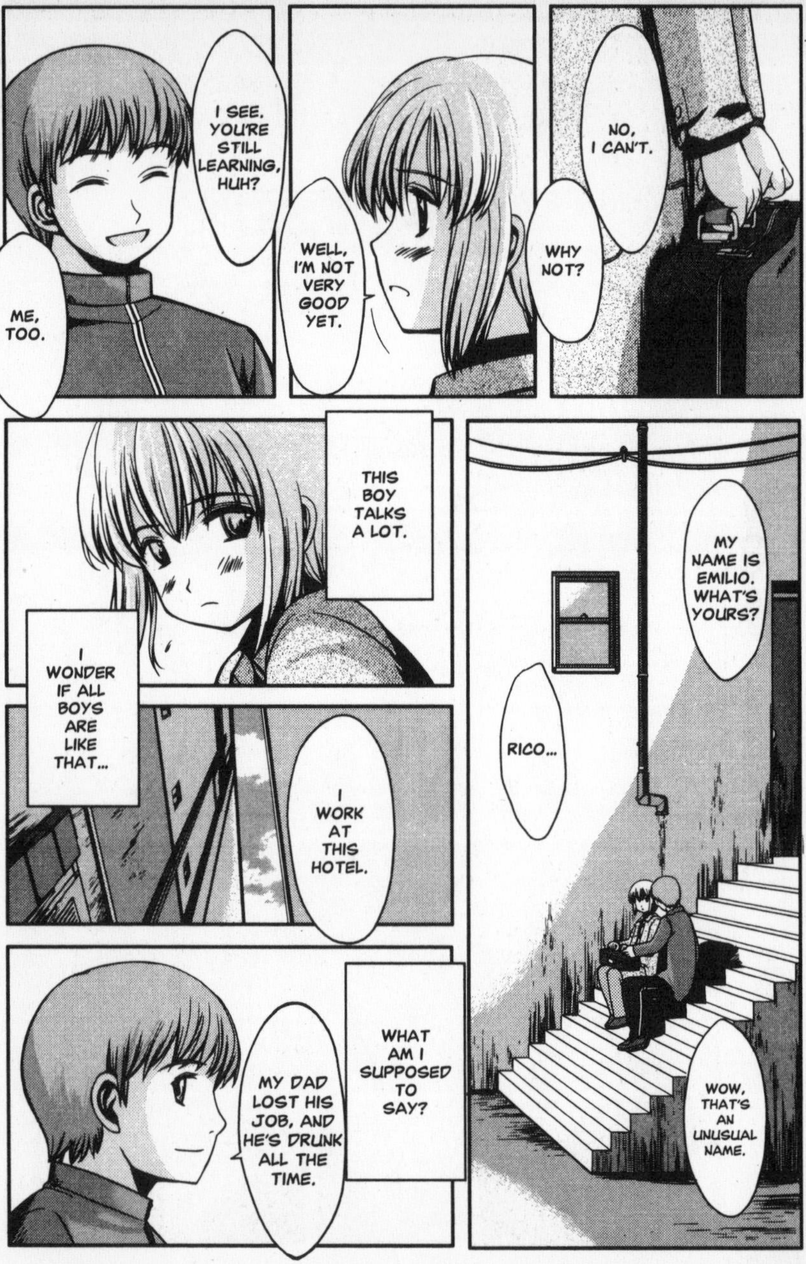
NO, I CAN'T.
WHY NOT?
WELL, I'M NOT VERY GOOD YET.
I SEE. YOU'RE STILL LEARNING, HUH?
ME, TOO.
MY NAME IS EMILIO. WHAT'S YOURS?
RICO...
WOW, THAT'S AN UNUSUAL NAME.
THIS BOY TALKS A LOT.
I WONDER IF ALL BOYS ARE LIKE THAT...
I WORK AT THIS HOTEL.
WHAT AM I SUPPOSED TO SAY?
MY DAD LOST HIS JOB, AND HE'S DRUNK ALL THE TIME.

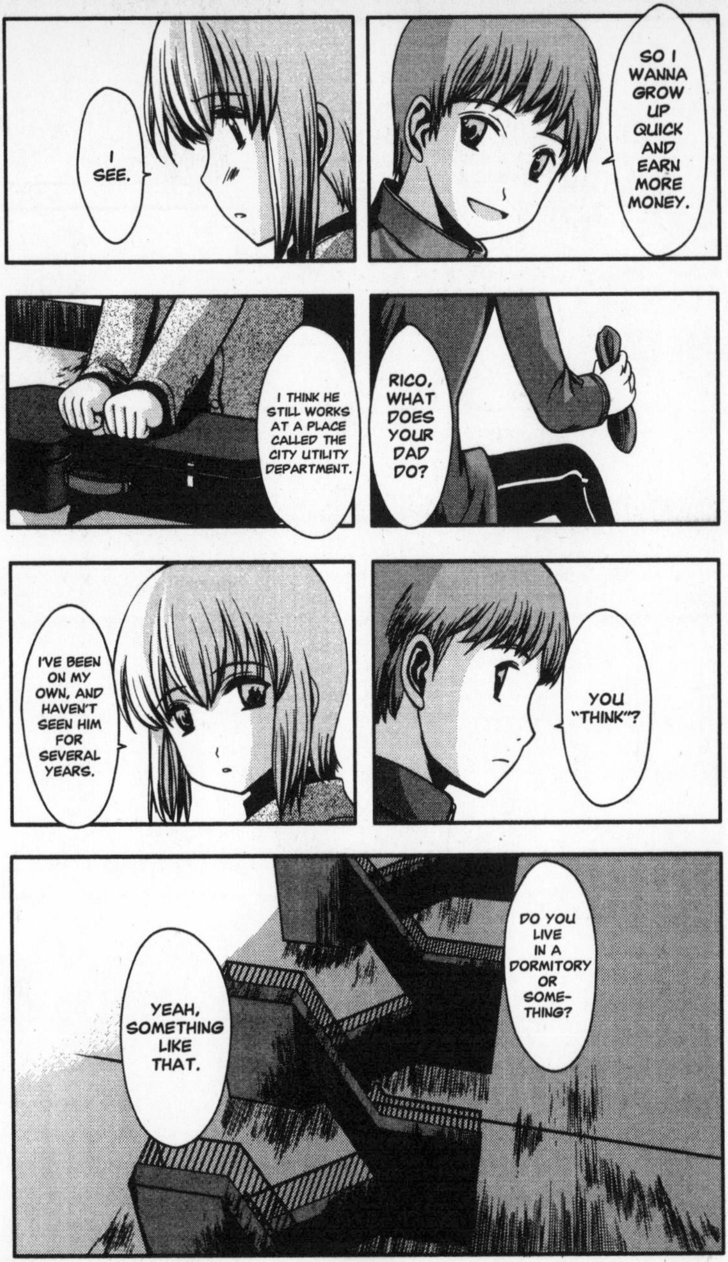
SO I WANNA GROW UP QUICK AND EARN MORE MONEY.
I SEE.
RICO, WHAT DOES YOUR DAD DO?
I THINK HE STILL WORKS AT A PLACE CALLED THE CITY UTILITY DEPARTMENT.
YOU "THINK"?
I'VE BEEN ON MY OWN, AND HAVEN'T SEEN HIM FOR SEVERAL YEARS.
DO YOU LIVE IN A DORMITORY OR SOME-THING?
YEAH, SOMETHING LIKE THAT.

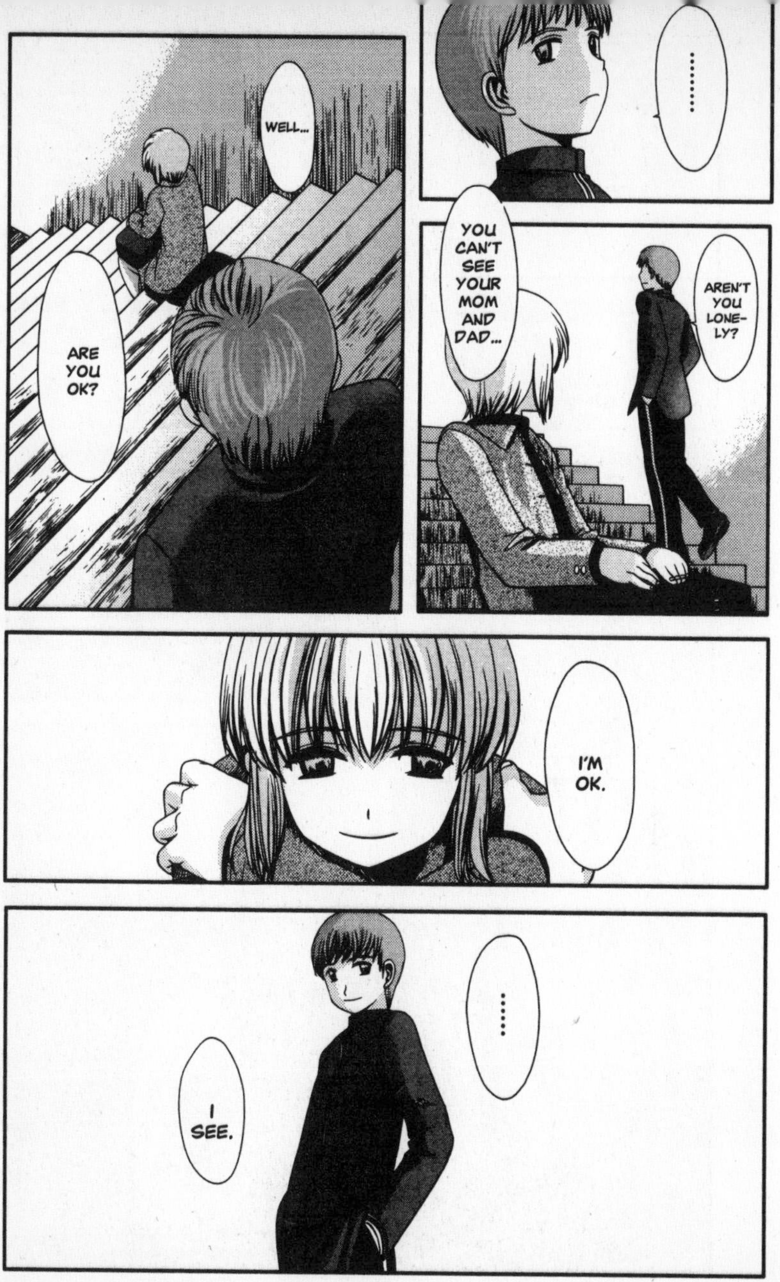
......
YOU CAN'T SEE YOUR MOM AND DAD...
AREN'T YOU LONE-LY?
WELL...
ARE YOU OK?
I'M OK.
......
I SEE.

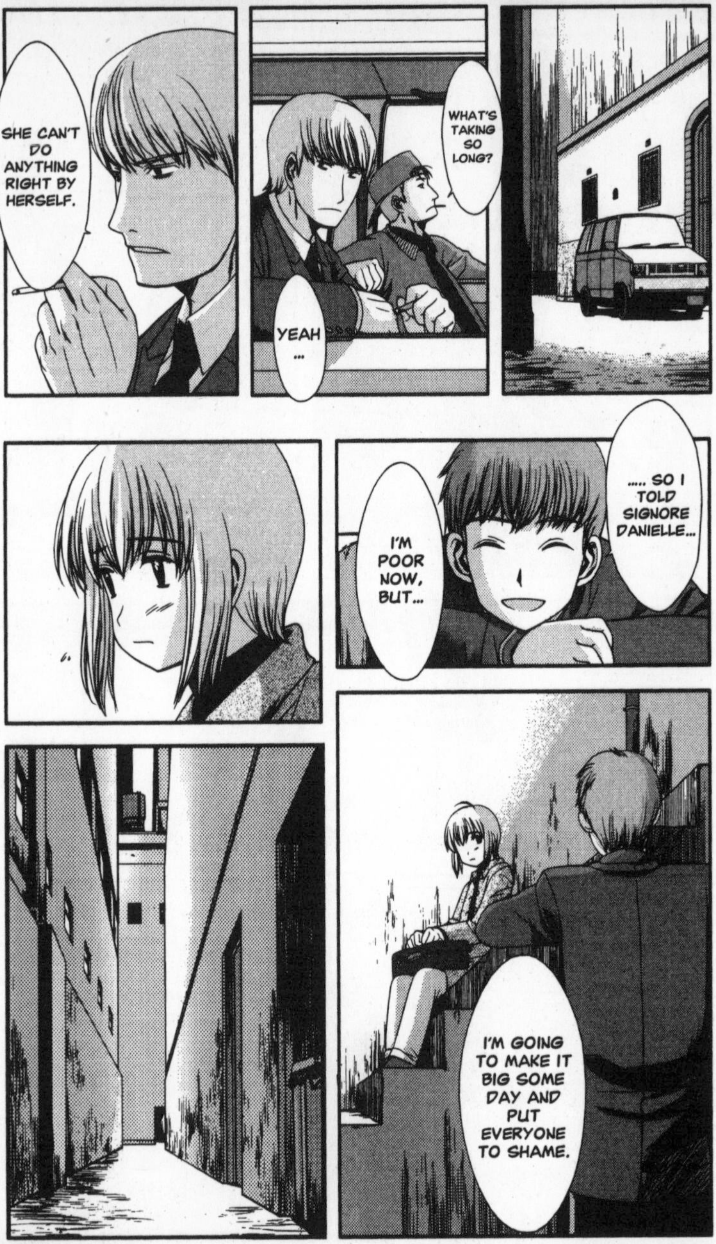
WHAT'S TAKING SO LONG?
YEAH ...
SHE CAN'T DO ANYTHING RIGHT BY HERSELF.
..... SO I TOLD SIGNORE DANIELLE...
I'M POOR NOW, BUT...
I'M GOING TO MAKE IT BIG SOME DAY AND PUT EVERYONE TO SHAME.

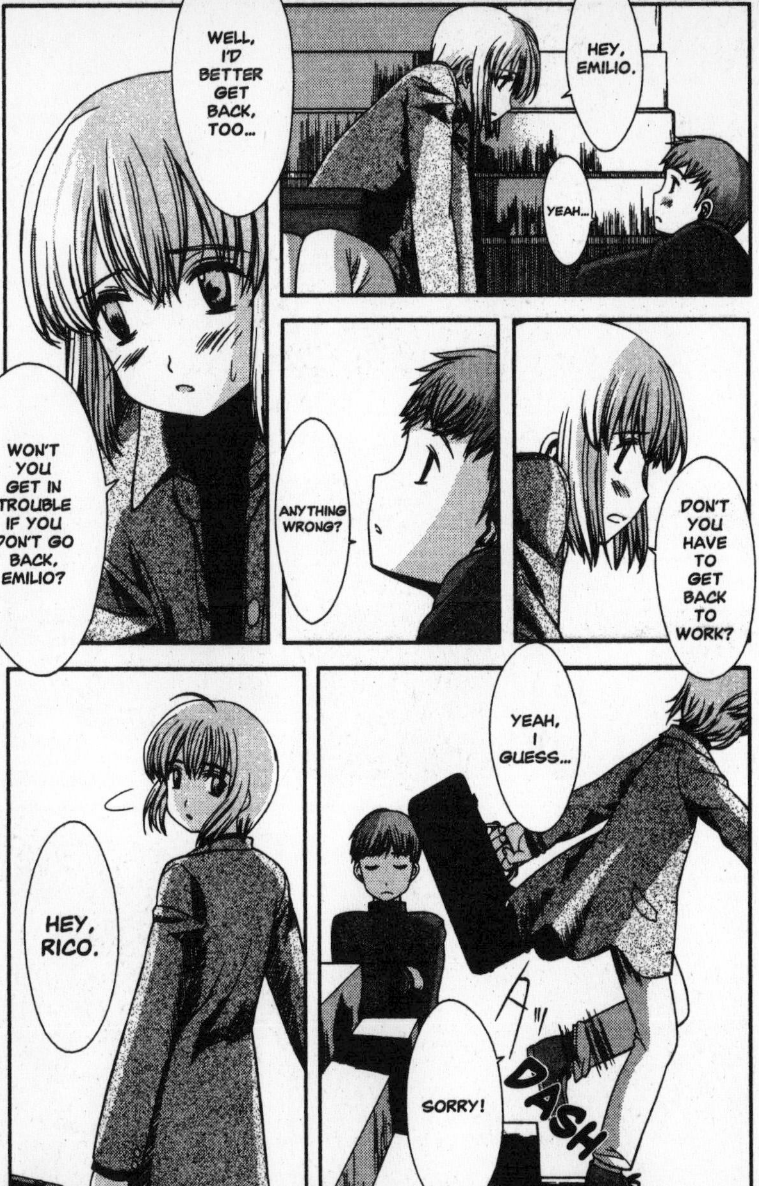
HEY, EMILIO.
YEAH...
WELL, I'D BETTER GET BACK, TOO...
DON'T YOU HAVE TO GET BACK TO WORK?
ANYTHING WRONG?
WON'T YOU GET IN TROUBLE IF YOU DON'T GO BACK, EMILIO?
YEAH, I GUESS...
SORRY!
DASH
HEY, RICO.

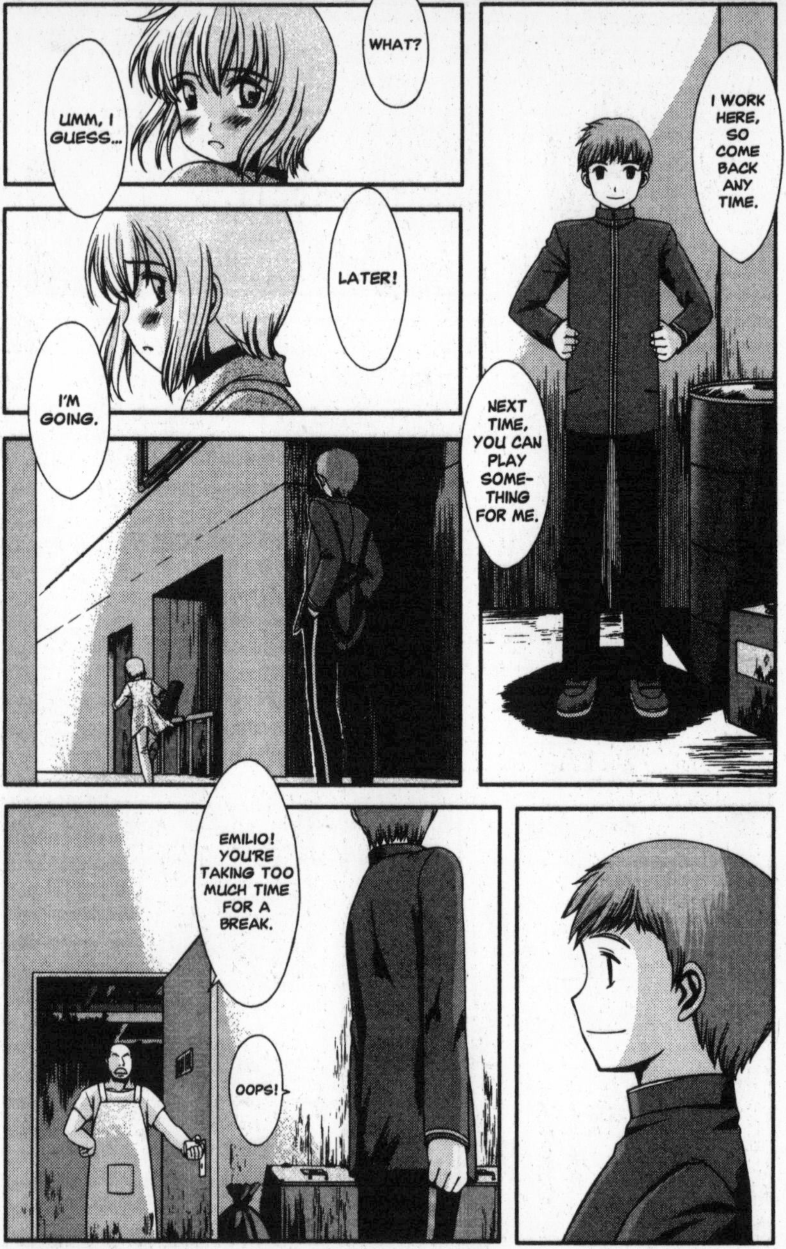
I WORK HERE, SO COME BACK ANY TIME.
NEXT TIME, YOU CAN PLAY SOME-THING FOR ME.
WHAT?
UMM, I GUESS...
LATER!
I'M GOING.
EMILIO! YOU'RE TAKING TOO MUCH TIME FOR A BREAK.
OOPS!

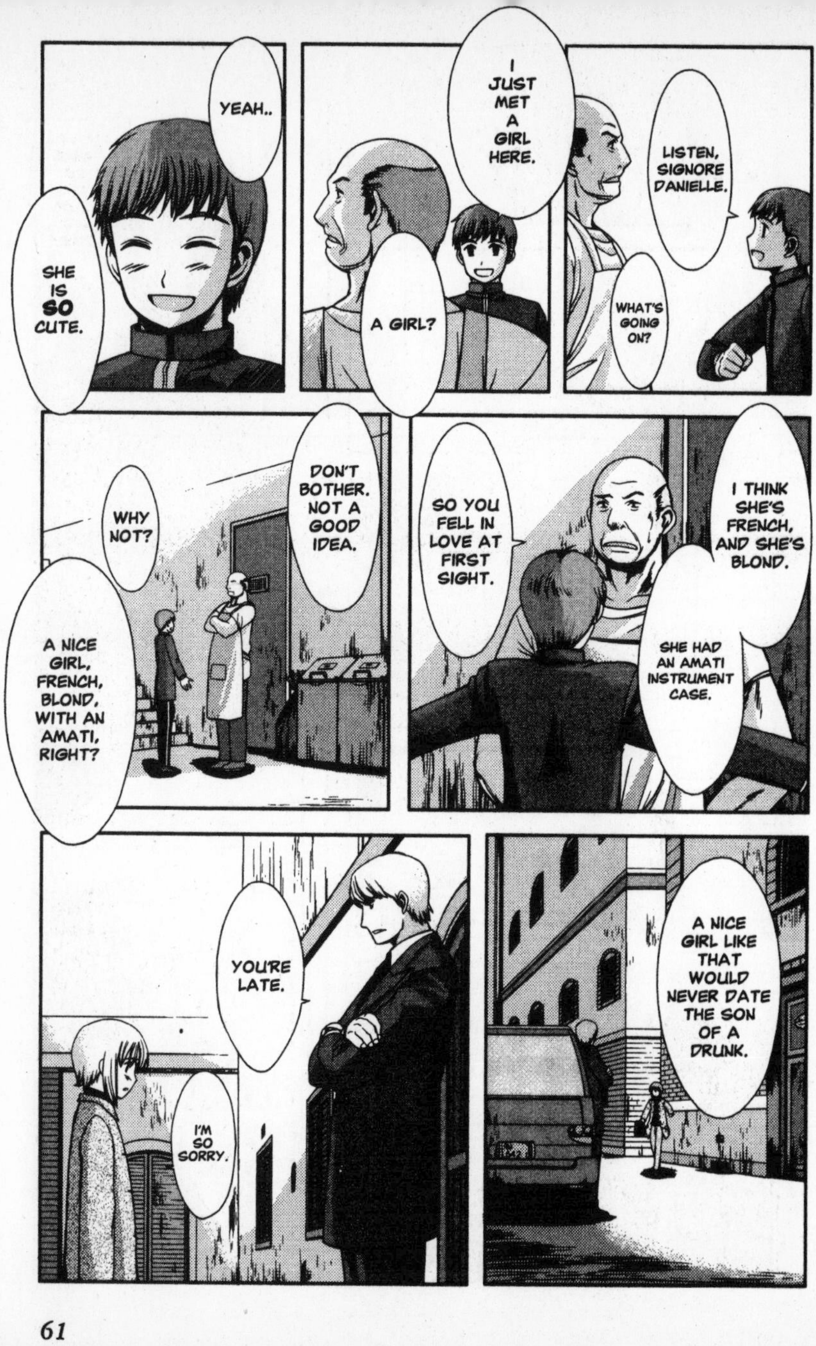
LISTEN, SIGNORE DANIELLE.
WHAT'S GOING ON?
I JUST MET A GIRL HERE.
A GIRL?
YEAH..
SHE IS **SO** CUTE.
I THINK SHE'S FRENCH, AND SHE'S BLOND.
SHE HAD AN AMATI INSTRUMENT CASE.
SO YOU FELL IN LOVE AT FIRST SIGHT.
DON'T BOTHER. NOT A GOOD IDEA.
WHY NOT?
A NICE GIRL, FRENCH, BLOND, WITH AN AMATI, RIGHT?
A NICE GIRL LIKE THAT WOULD NEVER DATE THE SON OF A DRUNK.
YOU'RE LATE.
I'M SO SORRY.

DID YOU RUN INTO SOMEONE THERE?

IF ANYONE SEES YOU WHILE YOU'RE ON DUTY,

NO, SIR.

YOU MUST KILL THEM.

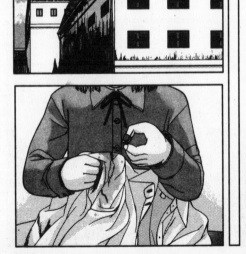

YES, SIR.

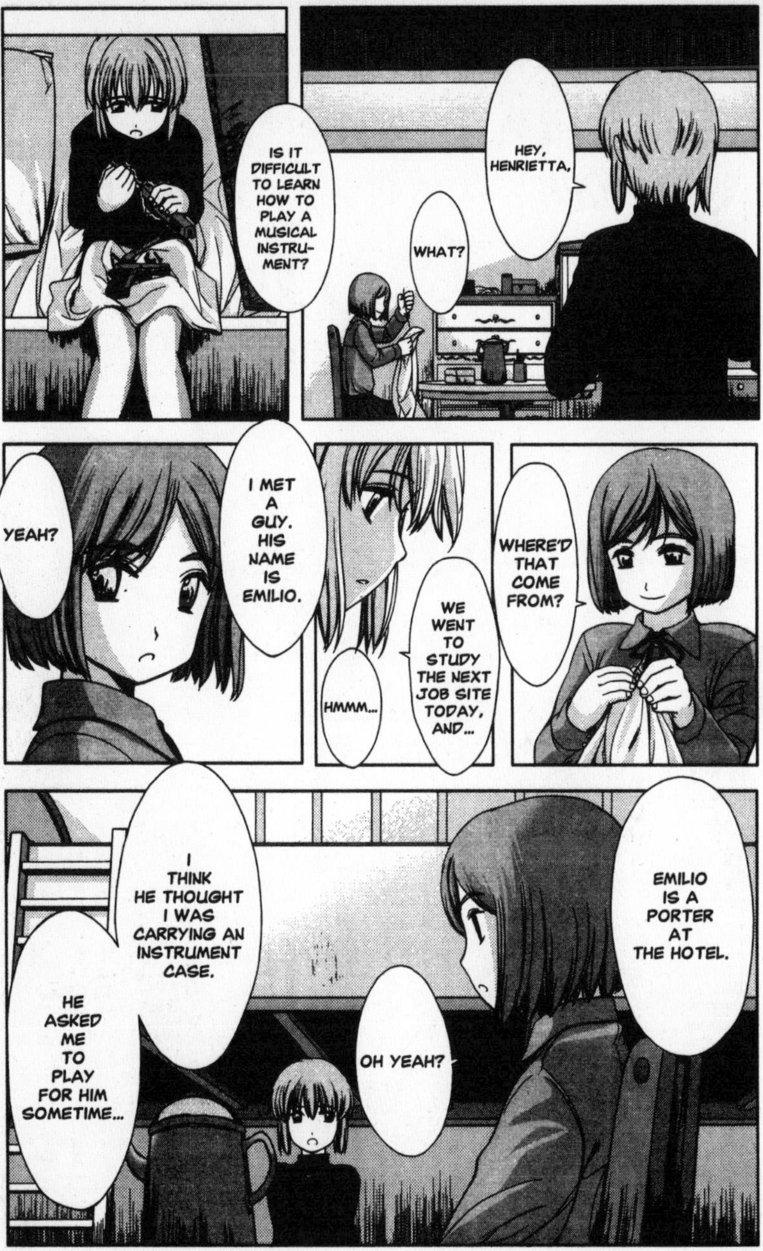
HEY, HENRIETTA,
WHAT?
IS IT DIFFICULT TO LEARN HOW TO PLAY A MUSICAL INSTRU-MENT?
WHERE'D THAT COME FROM?
WE WENT TO STUDY THE NEXT JOB SITE TODAY, AND...
HMMM...
I MET A GUY. HIS NAME IS EMILIO.
YEAH?
EMILIO IS A PORTER AT THE HOTEL.
OH YEAH?
I THINK HE THOUGHT I WAS CARRYING AN INSTRUMENT CASE.
HE ASKED ME TO PLAY FOR HIM SOMETIME...

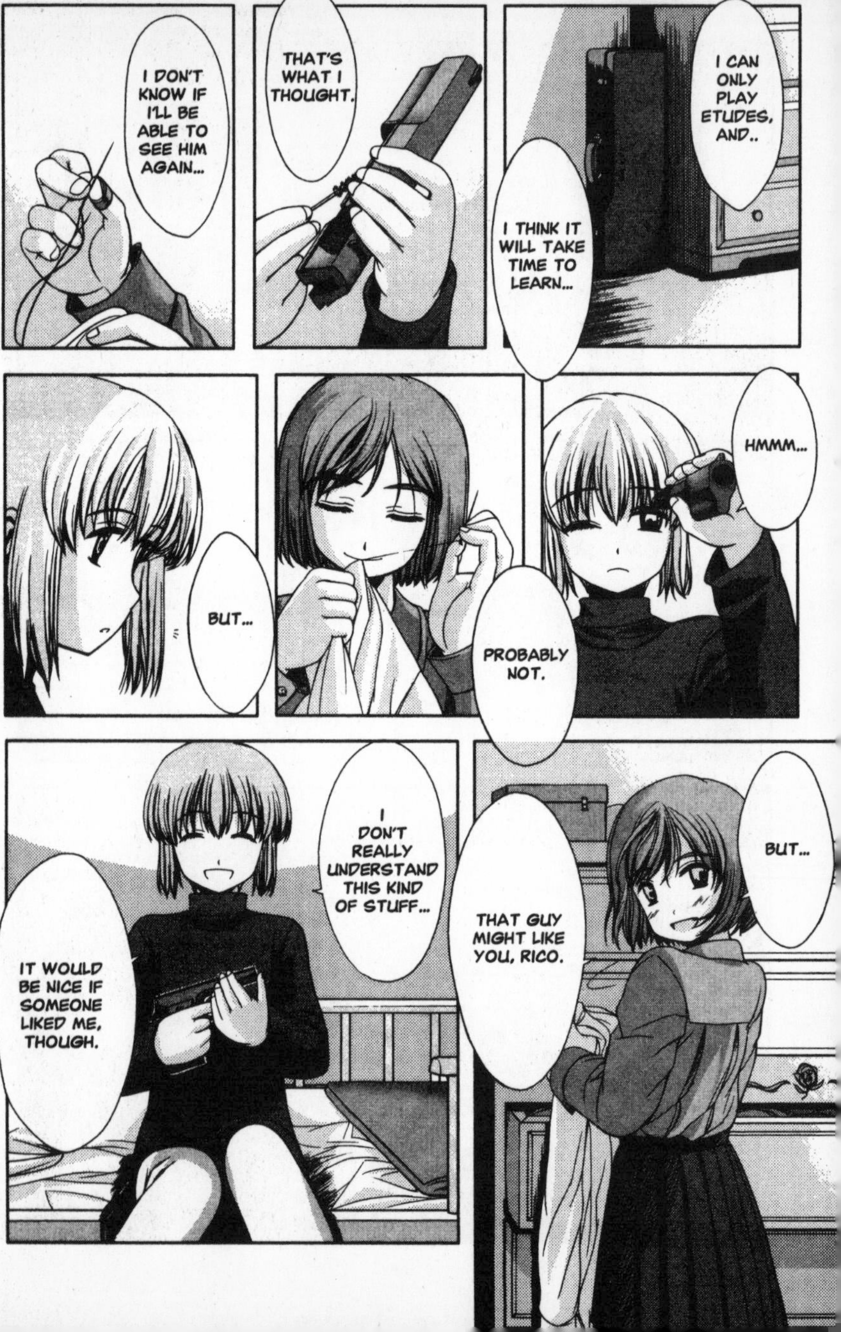
I DON'T KNOW IF I'LL BE ABLE TO SEE HIM AGAIN...
THAT'S WHAT I THOUGHT.
I CAN ONLY PLAY ETUDES, AND..
I THINK IT WILL TAKE TIME TO LEARN...
BUT...
HMMM...
PROBABLY NOT.
I DON'T REALLY UNDERSTAND THIS KIND OF STUFF...
IT WOULD BE NICE IF SOMEONE LIKED ME, THOUGH.
BUT...
THAT GUY MIGHT LIKE YOU, RICO.

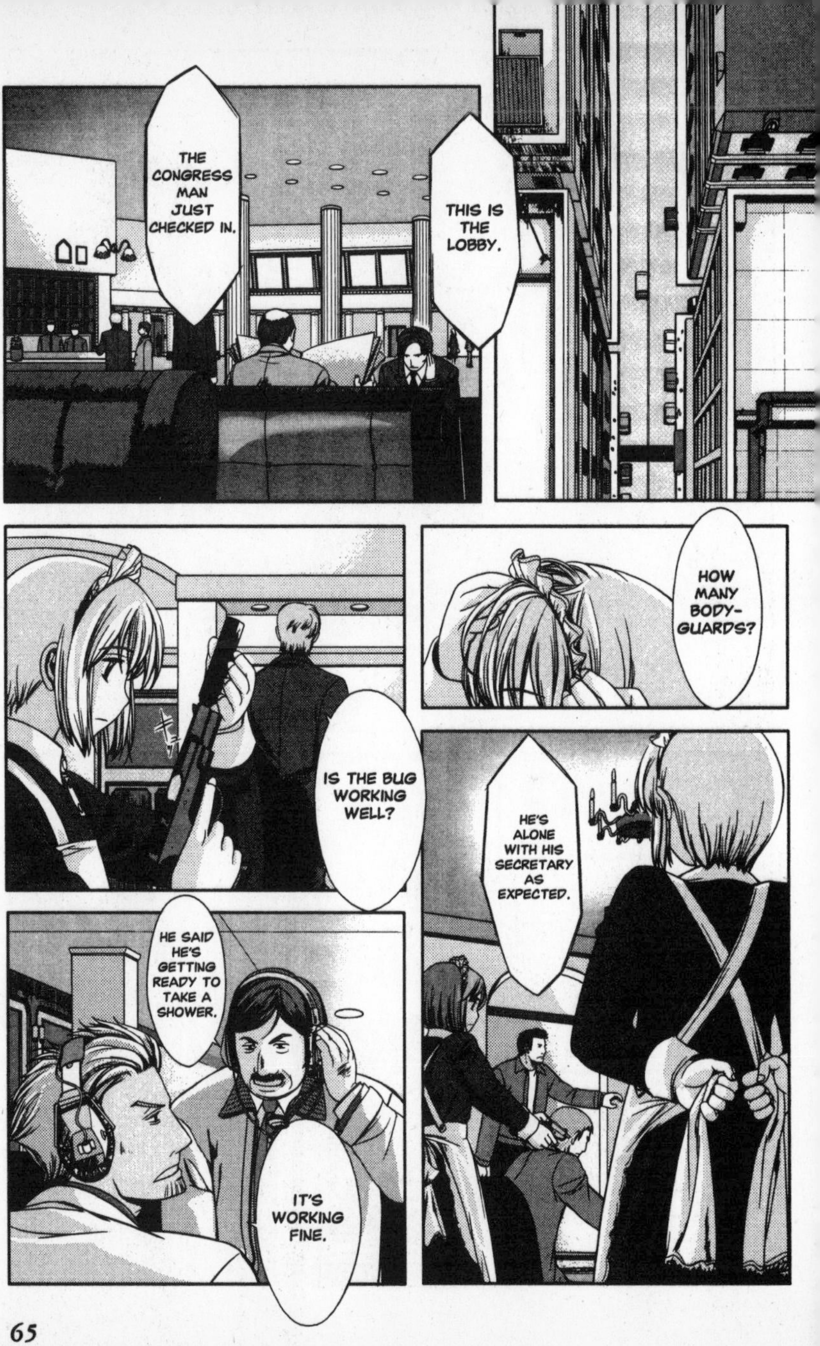
THIS IS THE LOBBY.
THE CONGRESS MAN JUST CHECKED IN.
HOW MANY BODY-GUARDS?
IS THE BUG WORKING WELL?
HE'S ALONE WITH HIS SECRETARY AS EXPECTED.
HE SAID HE'S GETTING READY TO TAKE A SHOWER.
IT'S WORKING FINE.

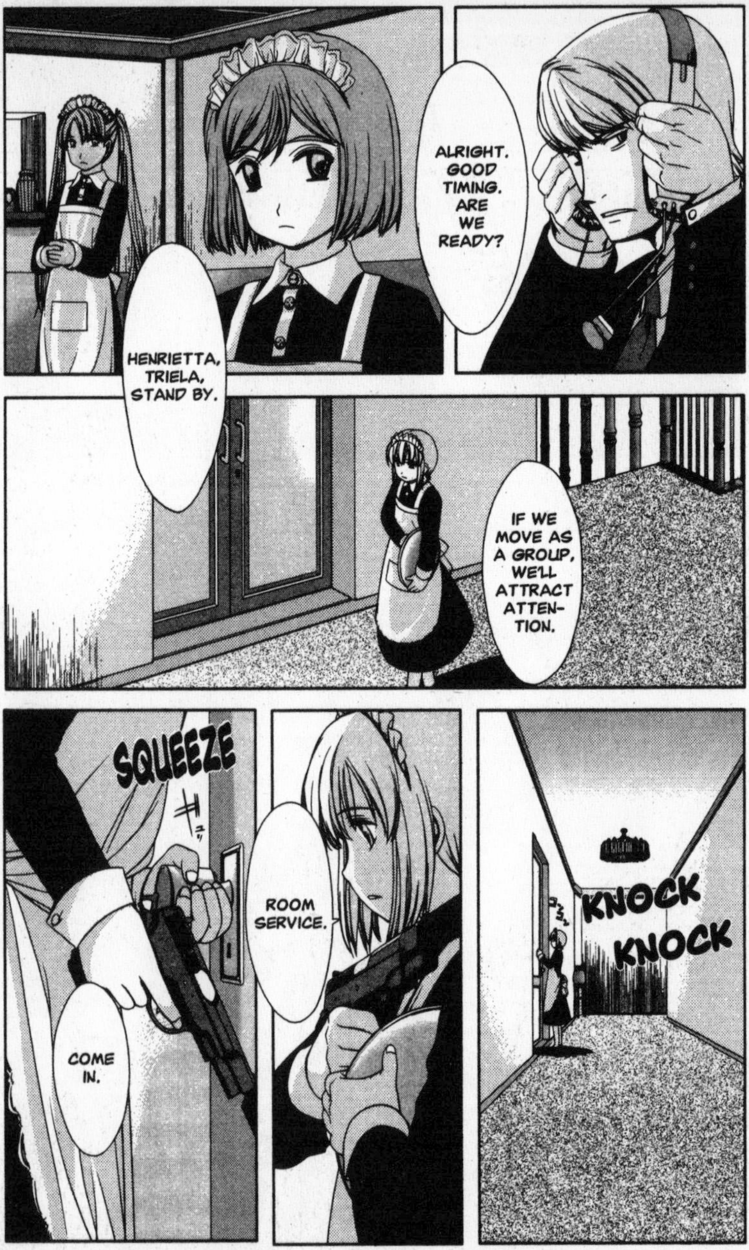
ALRIGHT. GOOD TIMING. ARE WE READY?
HENRIETTA, TRIELA, STAND BY.
IF WE MOVE AS A GROUP, WE'LL ATTRACT ATTENTION.
KNOCK KNOCK
ROOM SERVICE.
SQUEEZE
COME IN.

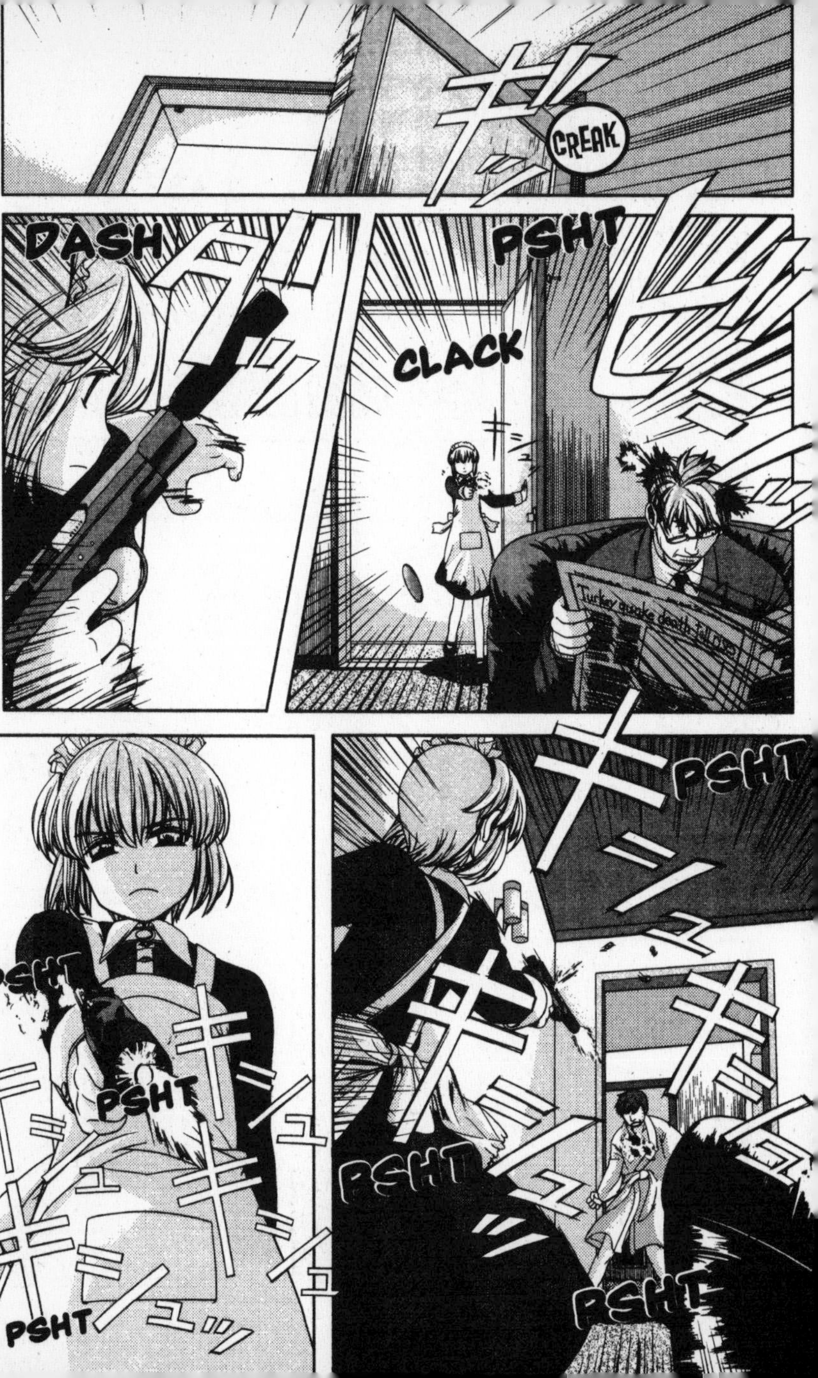
CREAK
PSHT
CLACK
Turkey quake death toll
DASH
PSHT
PSHT
PSHT
PSHT
PSHT
PSHT

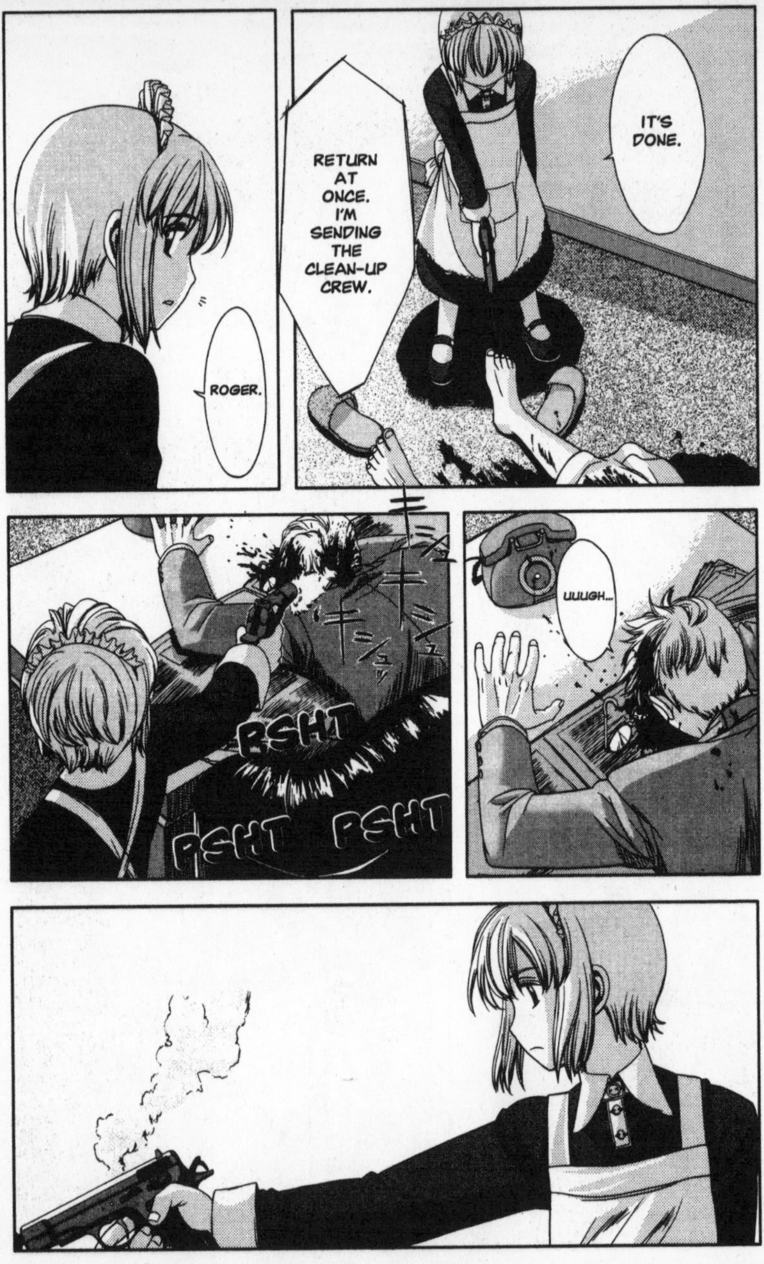
IT'S DONE.
RETURN AT ONCE. I'M SENDING THE CLEAN-UP CREW.
ROGER.
UUUGH...
PSHT
PSHT
PSHT

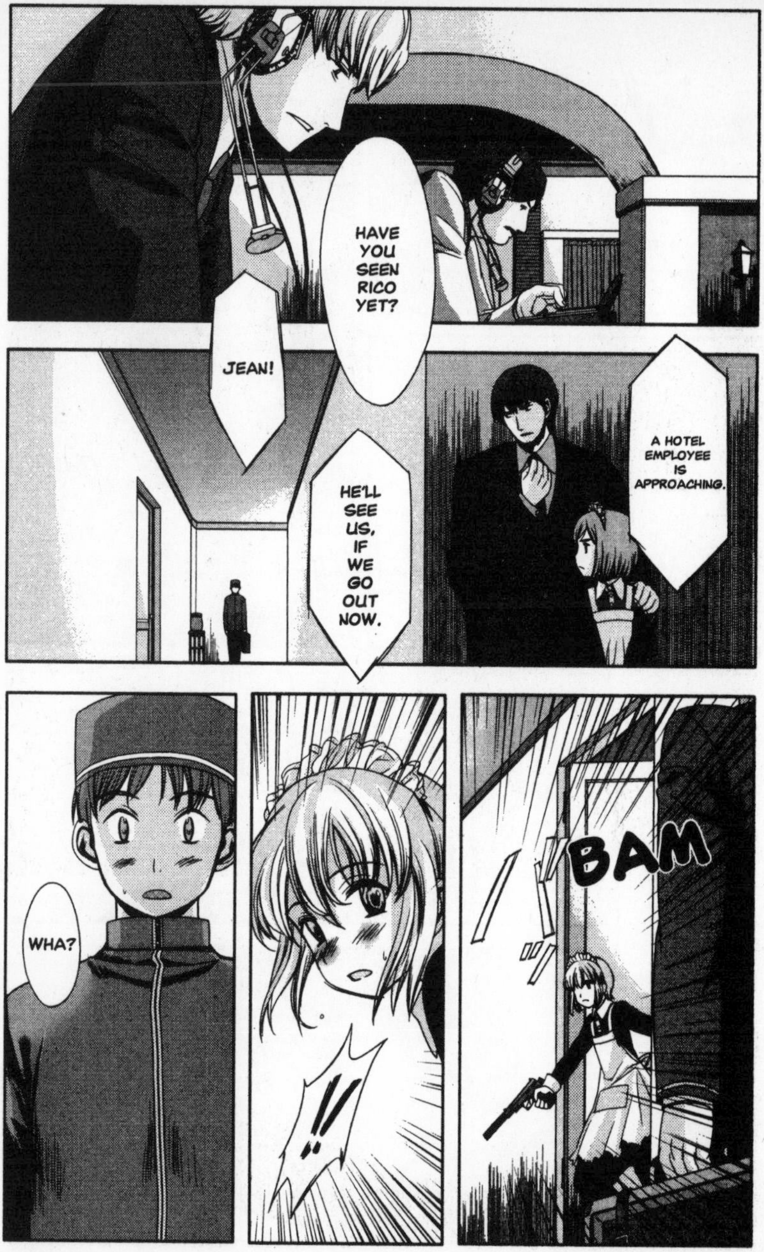
HAVE YOU SEEN RICO YET?
JEAN!
A HOTEL EMPLOYEE IS APPROACHING.
HE'LL SEE US, IF WE GO OUT NOW.
BAM
!!
WHA?

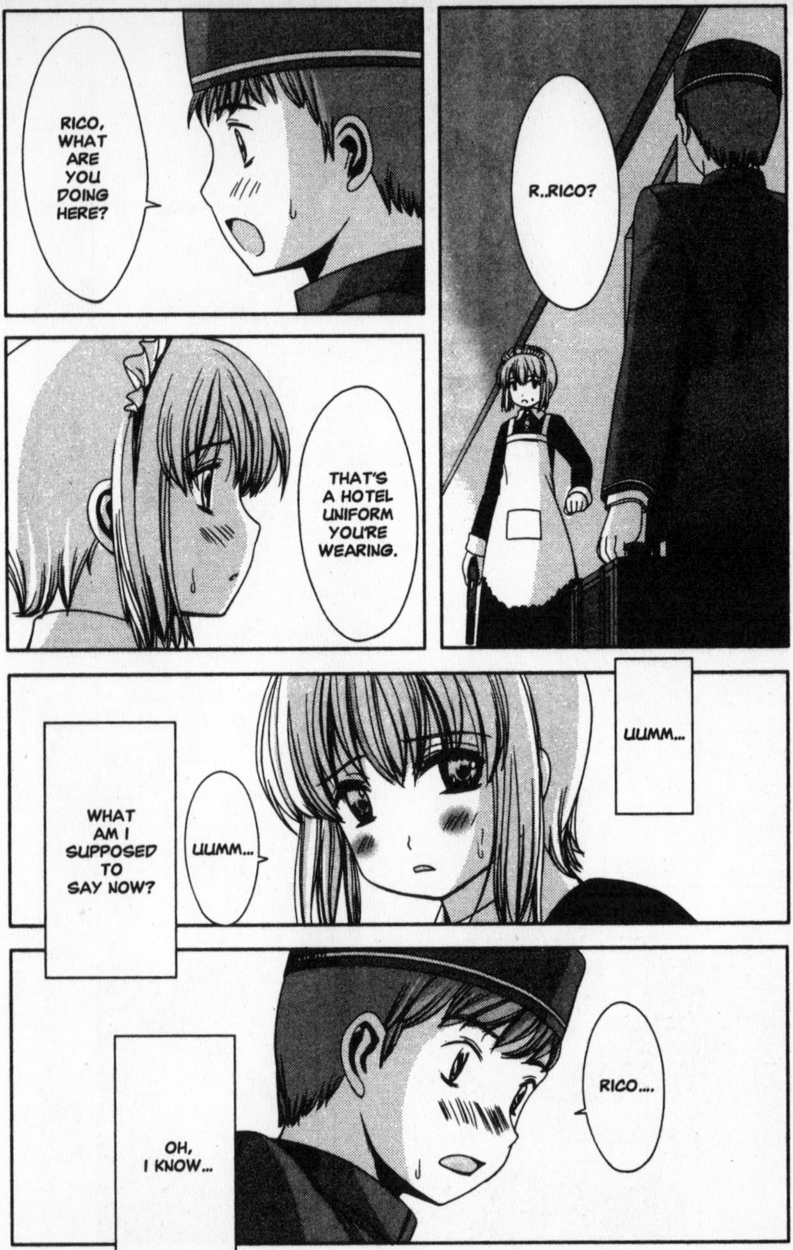
R..RICO?
RICO, WHAT ARE YOU DOING HERE?
THAT'S A HOTEL UNIFORM YOU'RE WEARING.
UUMM...
UUMM...
WHAT AM I SUPPOSED TO SAY NOW?
RICO....
OH, I KNOW...

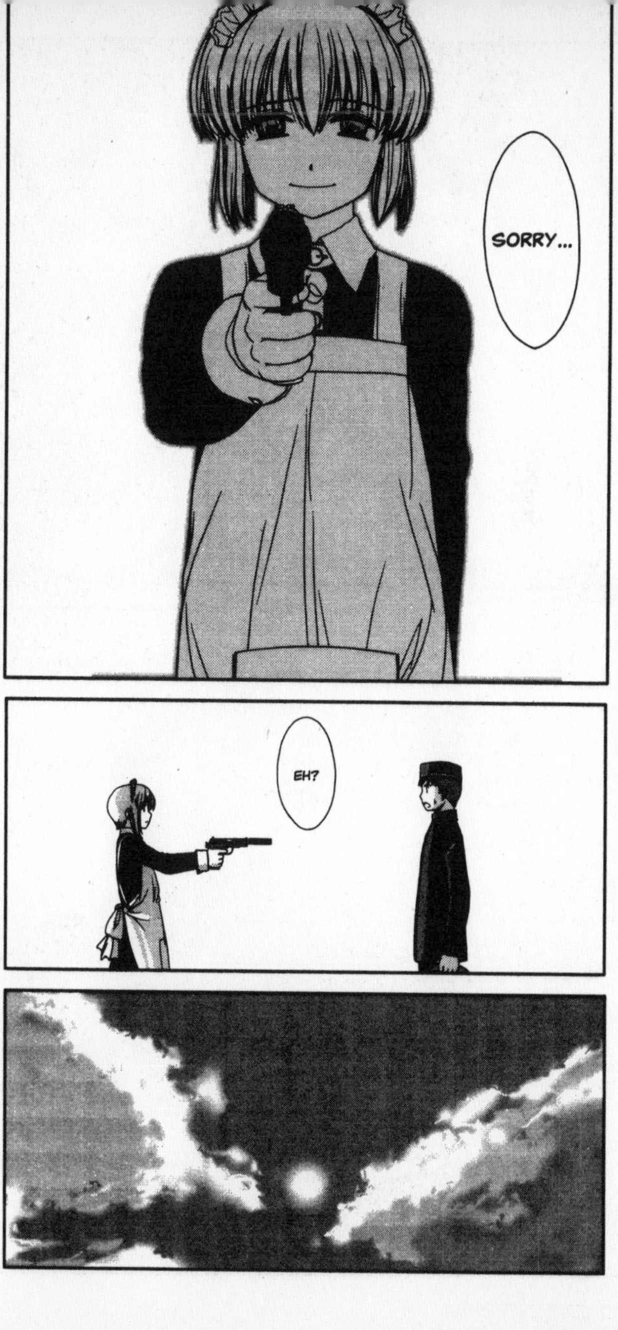
SORRY...
EH?

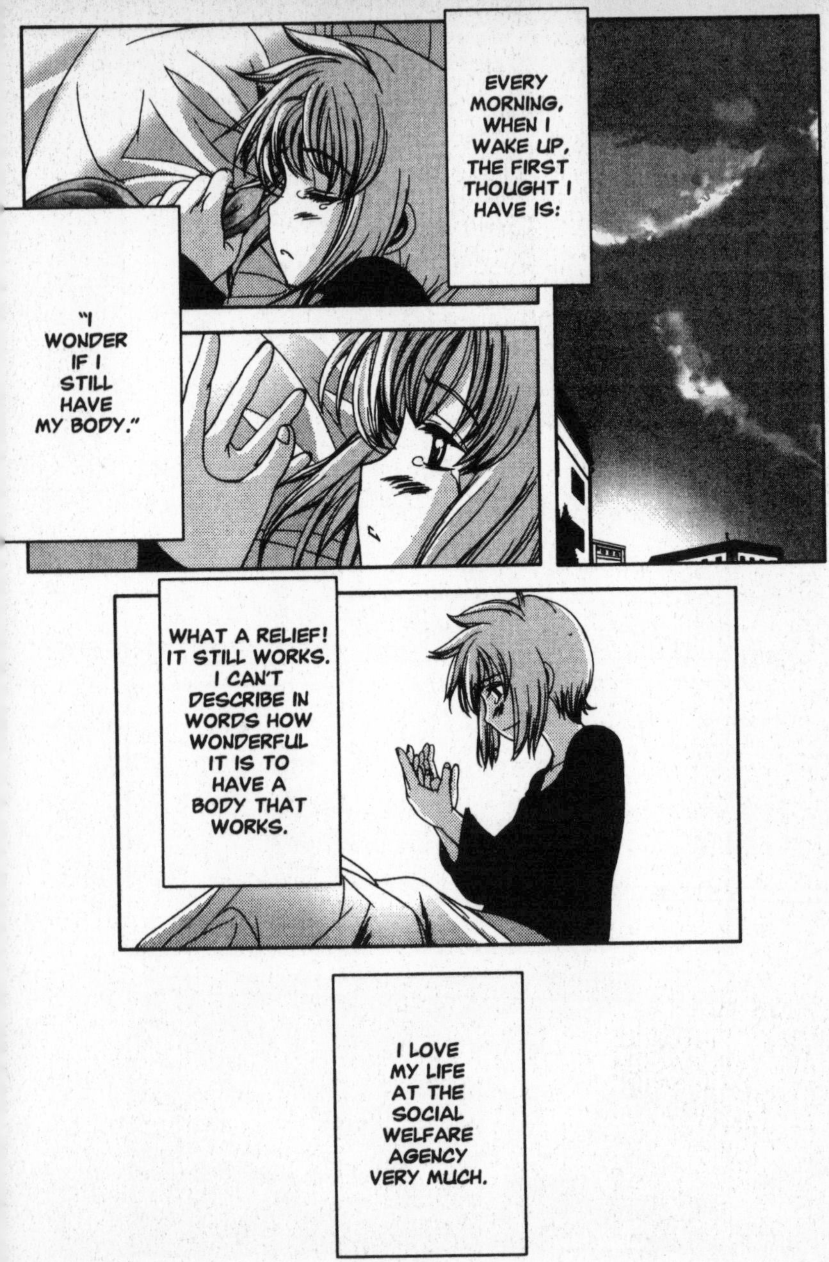
EVERY MORNING, WHEN I WAKE UP, THE FIRST THOUGHT I HAVE IS:
"I WONDER IF I STILL HAVE MY BODY."
WHAT A RELIEF! IT STILL WORKS. I CAN'T DESCRIBE IN WORDS HOW WONDERFUL IT IS TO HAVE A BODY THAT WORKS.
I LOVE MY LIFE AT THE SOCIAL WELFARE AGENCY VERY MUCH.

GunslingerGirl

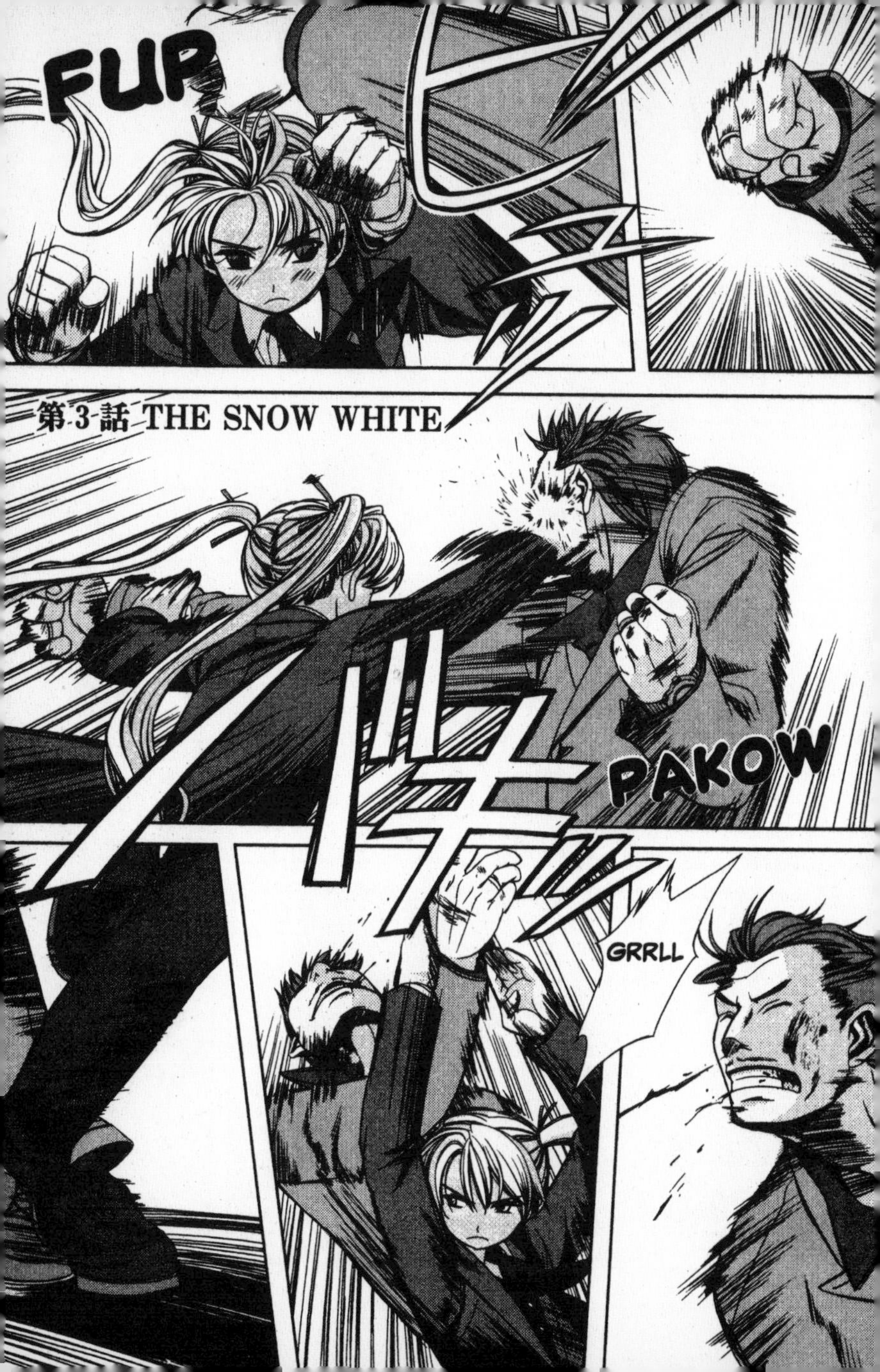
FUP
第3話 THE SNOW WHITE
PAKOW
GRRLL

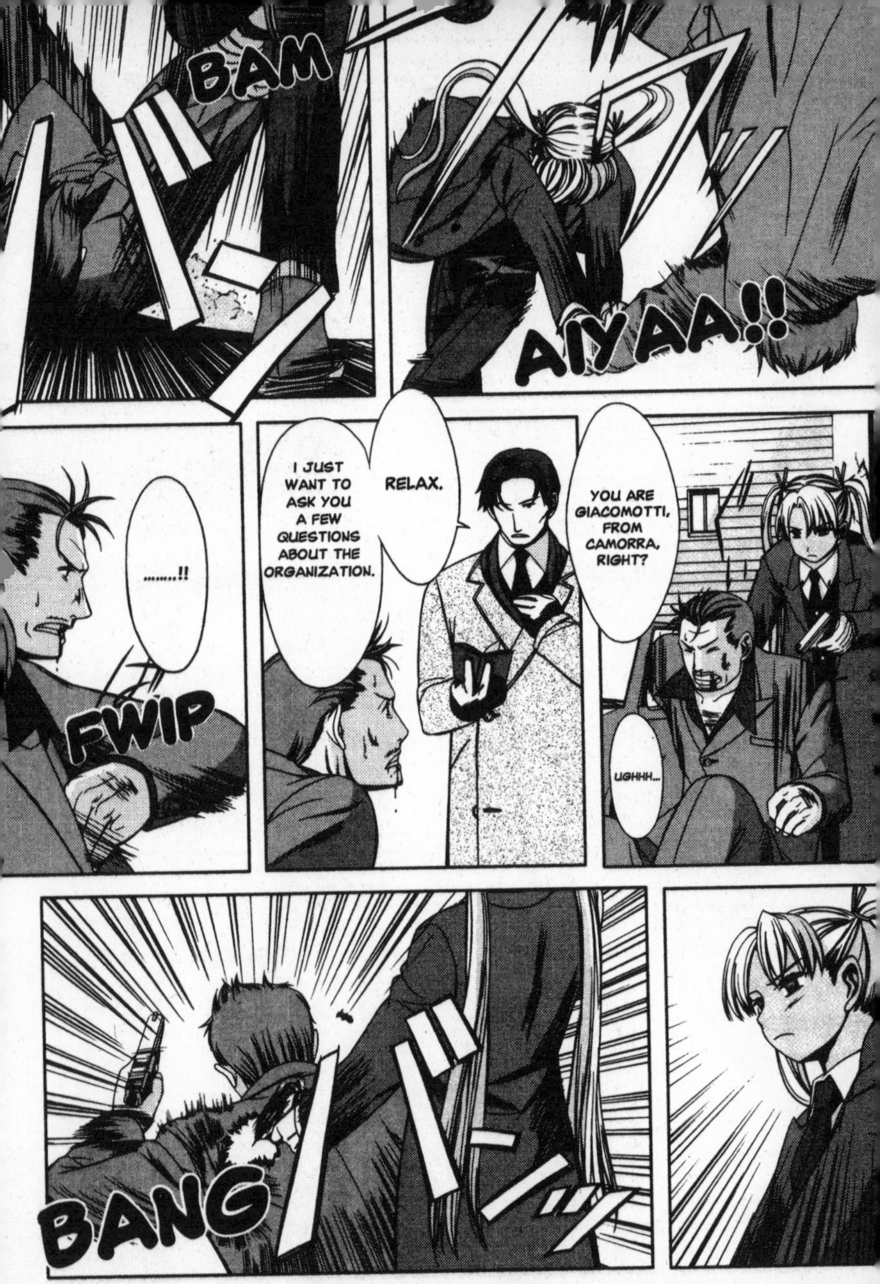
AIYAA!!
BAM
YOU ARE GIACOMOTTI, FROM CAMORRA, RIGHT?
UGHHH...
RELAX.
I JUST WANT TO ASK YOU A FEW QUESTIONS ABOUT THE ORGANIZATION.
........!!
FWIP
BANG

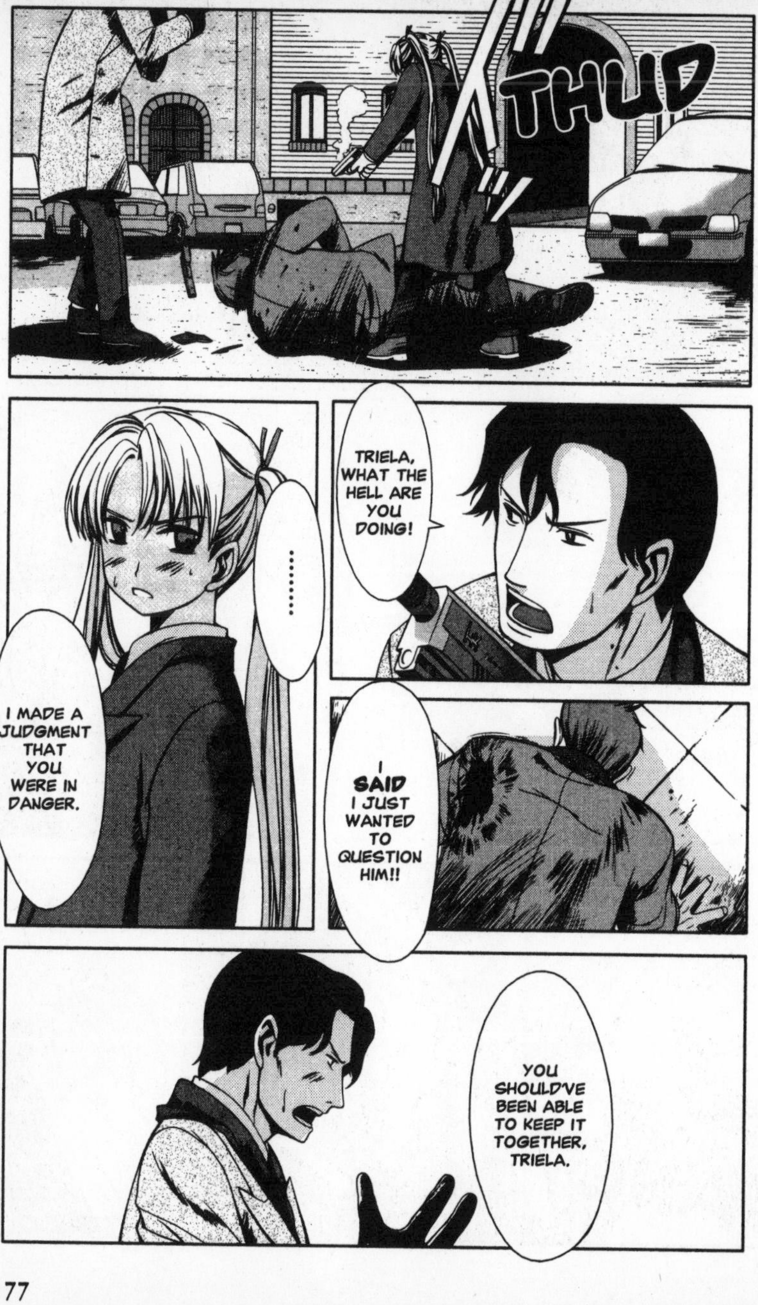
THUD
TRIELA, WHAT THE HELL ARE YOU DOING!
......
I MADE A JUDGMENT THAT YOU WERE IN DANGER.
I SAID I JUST WANTED TO QUESTION HIM!!
YOU SHOULD'VE BEEN ABLE TO KEEP IT TOGETHER, TRIELA.

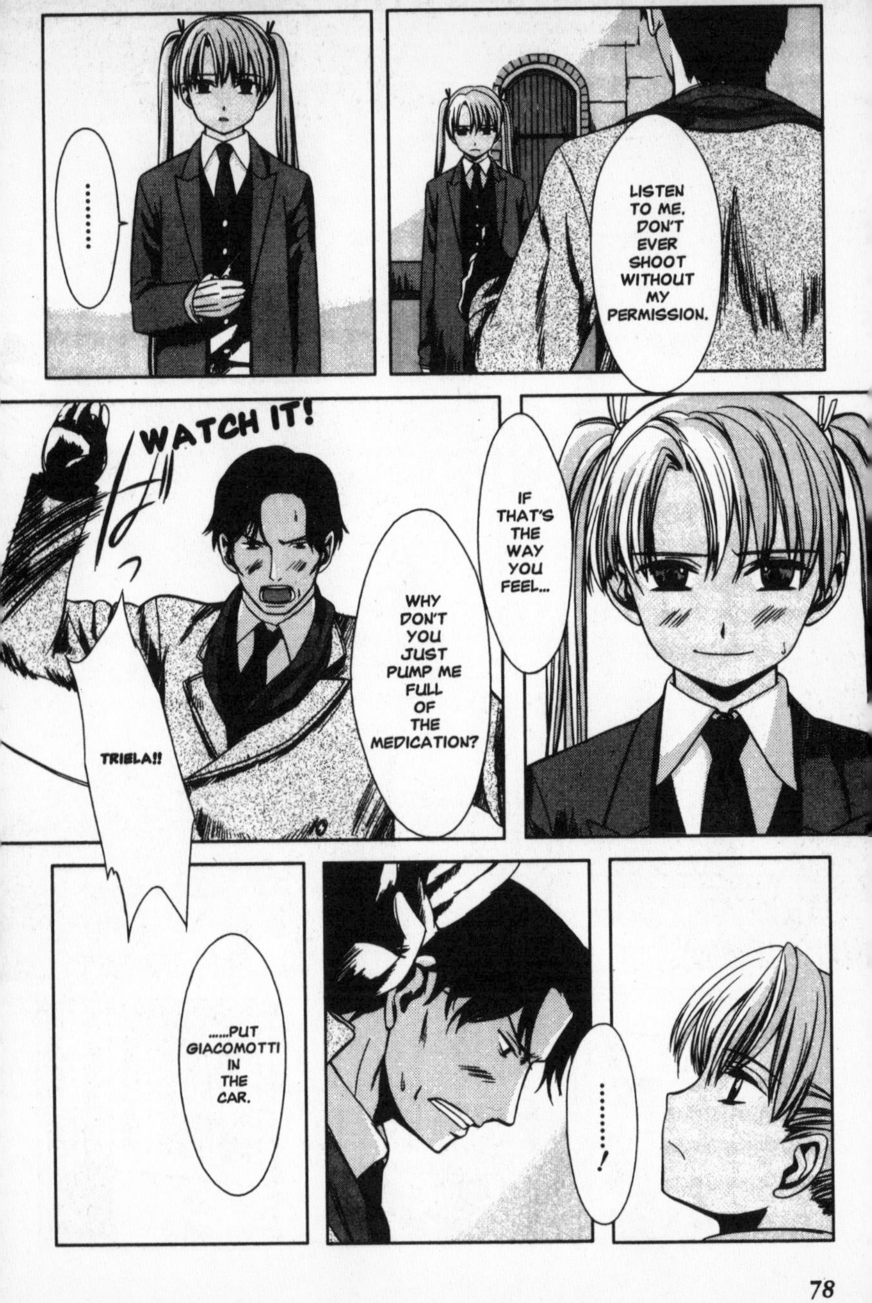
LISTEN TO ME. DON'T EVER SHOOT WITHOUT MY PERMISSION.
....
IF THAT'S THE WAY YOU FEEL...
WHY DON'T YOU JUST PUMP ME FULL OF THE MEDICATION?
WATCH IT!
TRIELA!!
.......!
......PUT GIACOMOTTI IN THE CAR.

第3話 THE SNOW WHITE

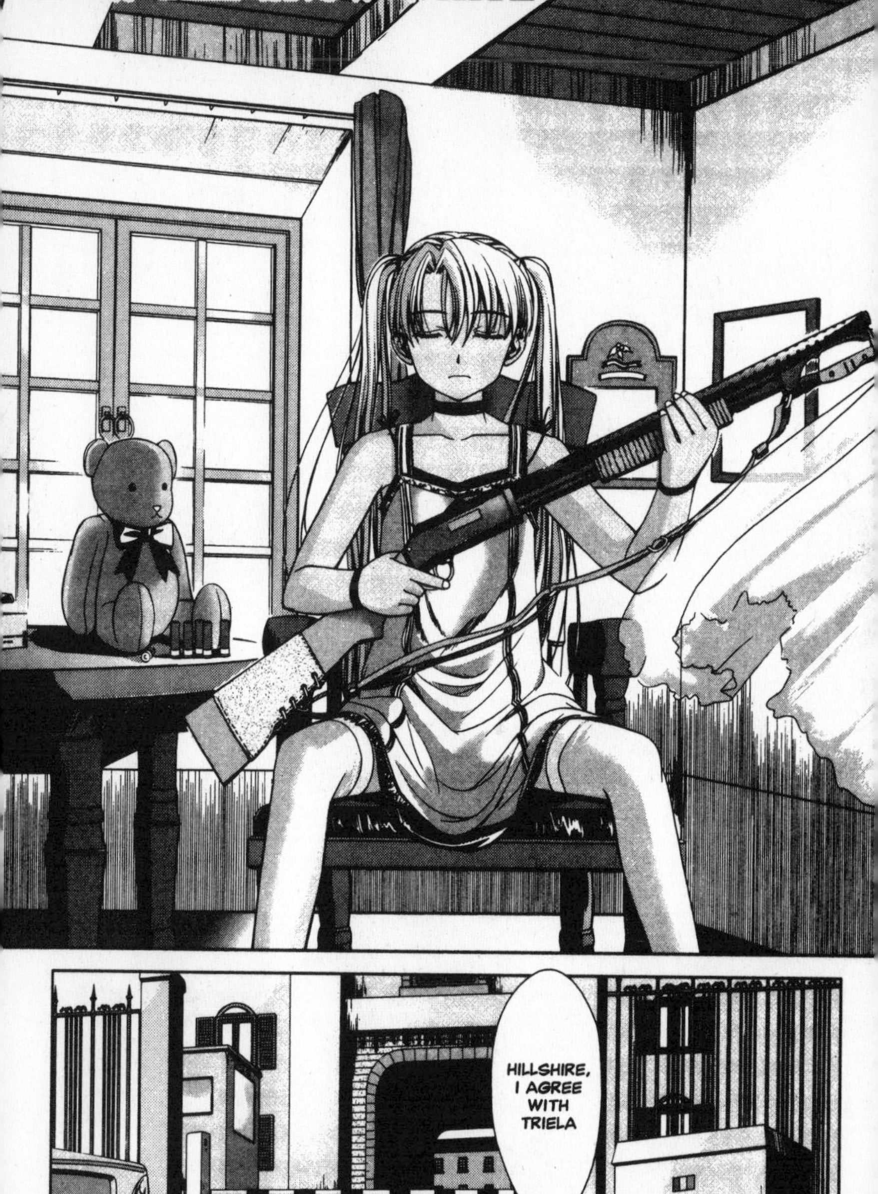
HILLSHIRE, I AGREE WITH TRIELA

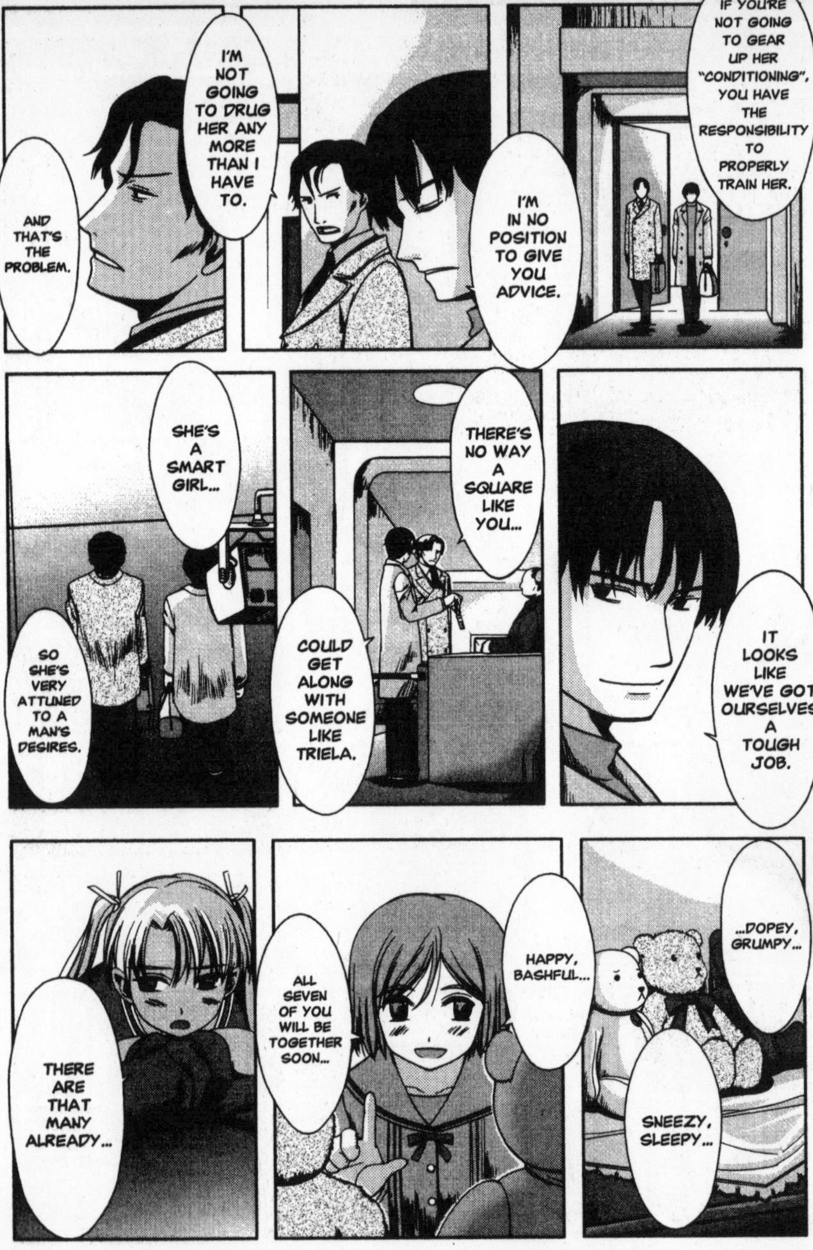
IF YOU'RE NOT GOING TO GEAR UP HER "CONDITIONING", YOU HAVE THE RESPONSIBILITY TO PROPERLY TRAIN HER.
I'M IN NO POSITION TO GIVE YOU ADVICE.
I'M NOT GOING TO DRUG HER ANY MORE THAN I HAVE TO.
AND THAT'S THE PROBLEM.
IT LOOKS LIKE WE'VE GOT OURSELVES A TOUGH JOB.
THERE'S NO WAY A SQUARE LIKE YOU...
COULD GET ALONG WITH SOMEONE LIKE TRIELA.
SHE'S A SMART GIRL...
SO SHE'S VERY ATTUNED TO A MAN'S DESIRES.
...DOPEY, GRUMPY...
SNEEZY, SLEEPY...
HAPPY, BASHFUL...
ALL SEVEN OF YOU WILL BE TOGETHER SOON...
THERE ARE THAT MANY ALREADY...

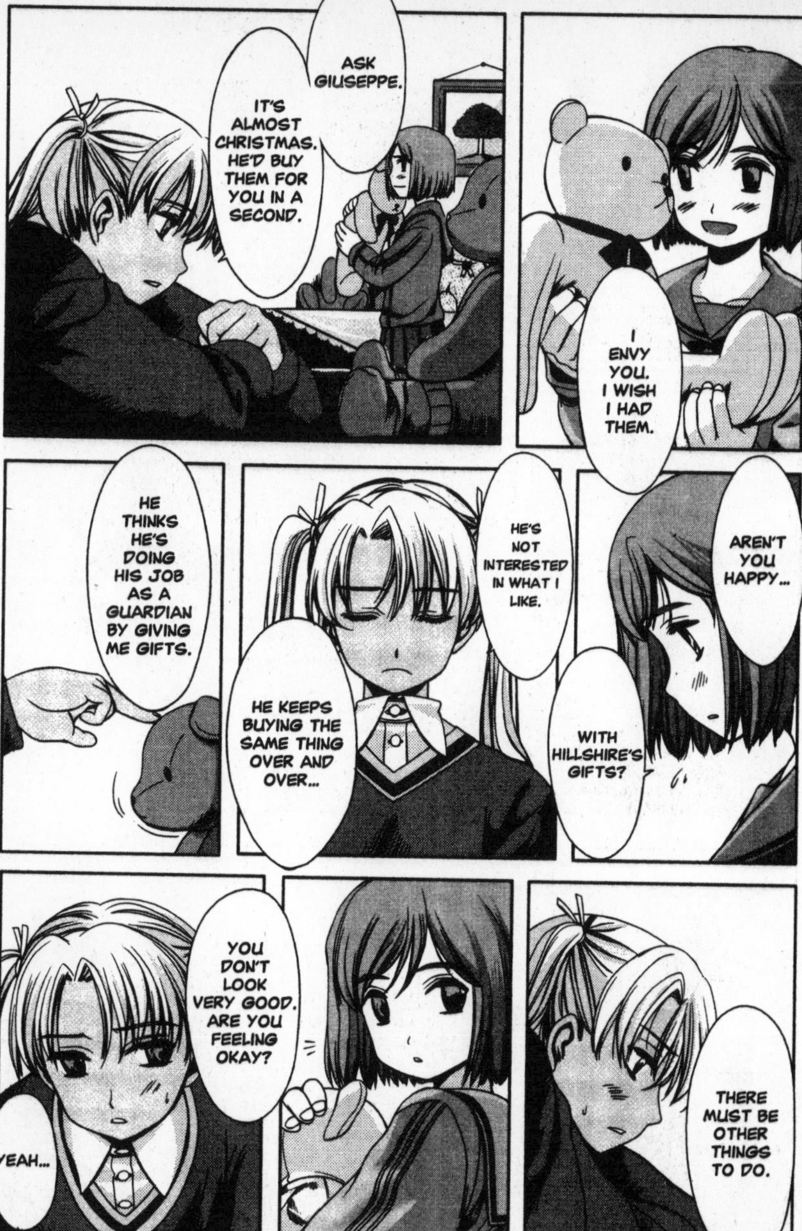
I ENVY YOU. I WISH I HAD THEM.
ASK GIUSEPPE.
IT'S ALMOST CHRISTMAS. HE'D BUY THEM FOR YOU IN A SECOND.
AREN'T YOU HAPPY...
WITH HILLSHIRE'S GIFTS?
HE'S NOT INTERESTED IN WHAT I LIKE.
HE KEEPS BUYING THE SAME THING OVER AND OVER...
HE THINKS HE'S DOING HIS JOB AS A GUARDIAN BY GIVING ME GIFTS.
THERE MUST BE OTHER THINGS TO DO.
YOU DON'T LOOK VERY GOOD. ARE YOU FEELING OKAY?
YEAH...

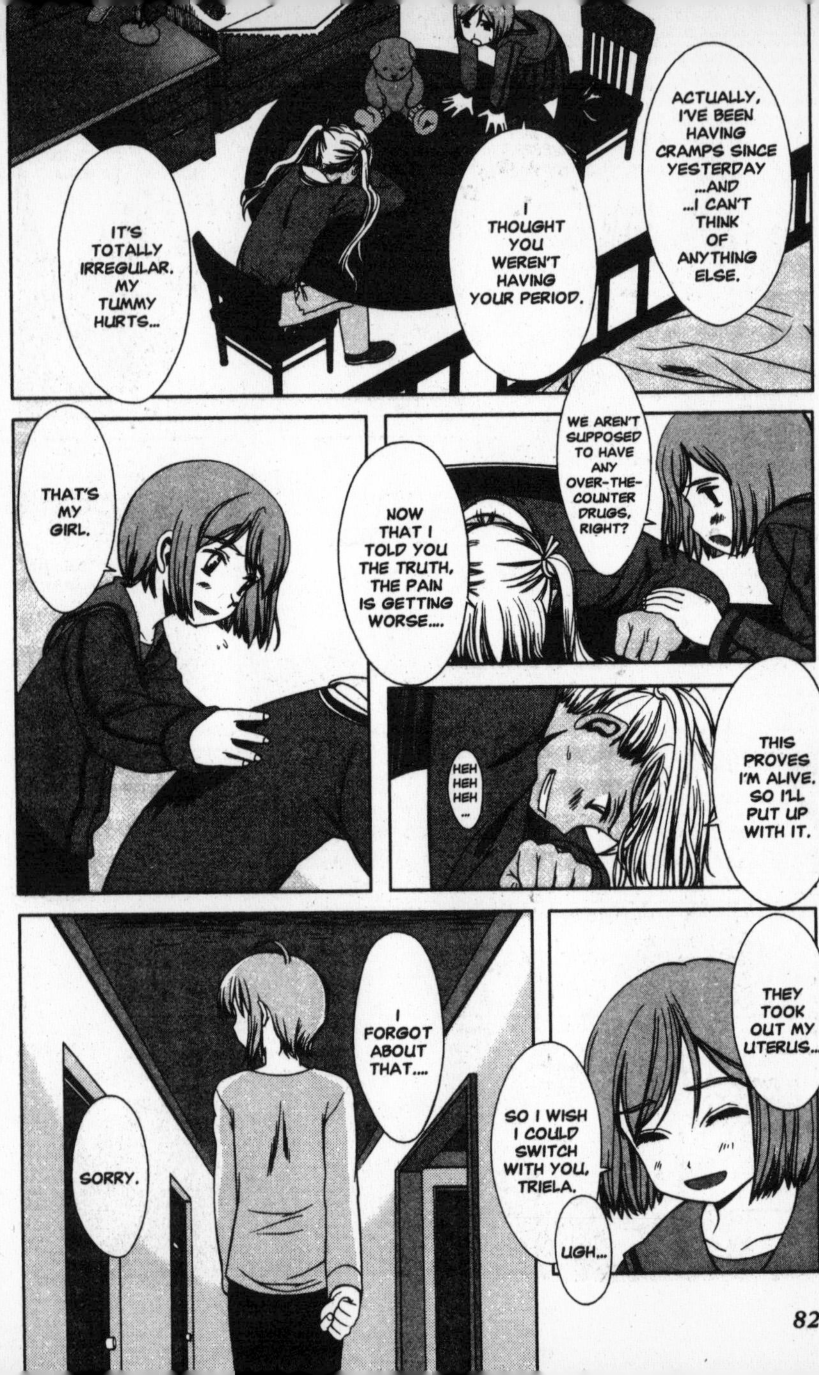
ACTUALLY, I'VE BEEN HAVING CRAMPS SINCE YESTERDAY ...AND ...I CAN'T THINK OF ANYTHING ELSE.
I THOUGHT YOU WEREN'T HAVING YOUR PERIOD.
IT'S TOTALLY IRREGULAR. MY TUMMY HURTS...
WE AREN'T SUPPOSED TO HAVE ANY OVER-THE-COUNTER DRUGS, RIGHT?
NOW THAT I TOLD YOU THE TRUTH, THE PAIN IS GETTING WORSE....
THIS PROVES I'M ALIVE. SO I'LL PUT UP WITH IT.
HEH HEH HEH ...
THAT'S MY GIRL.
THEY TOOK OUT MY UTERUS...
SO I WISH I COULD SWITCH WITH YOU, TRIELA.
UGH...
I FORGOT ABOUT THAT....
SORRY.

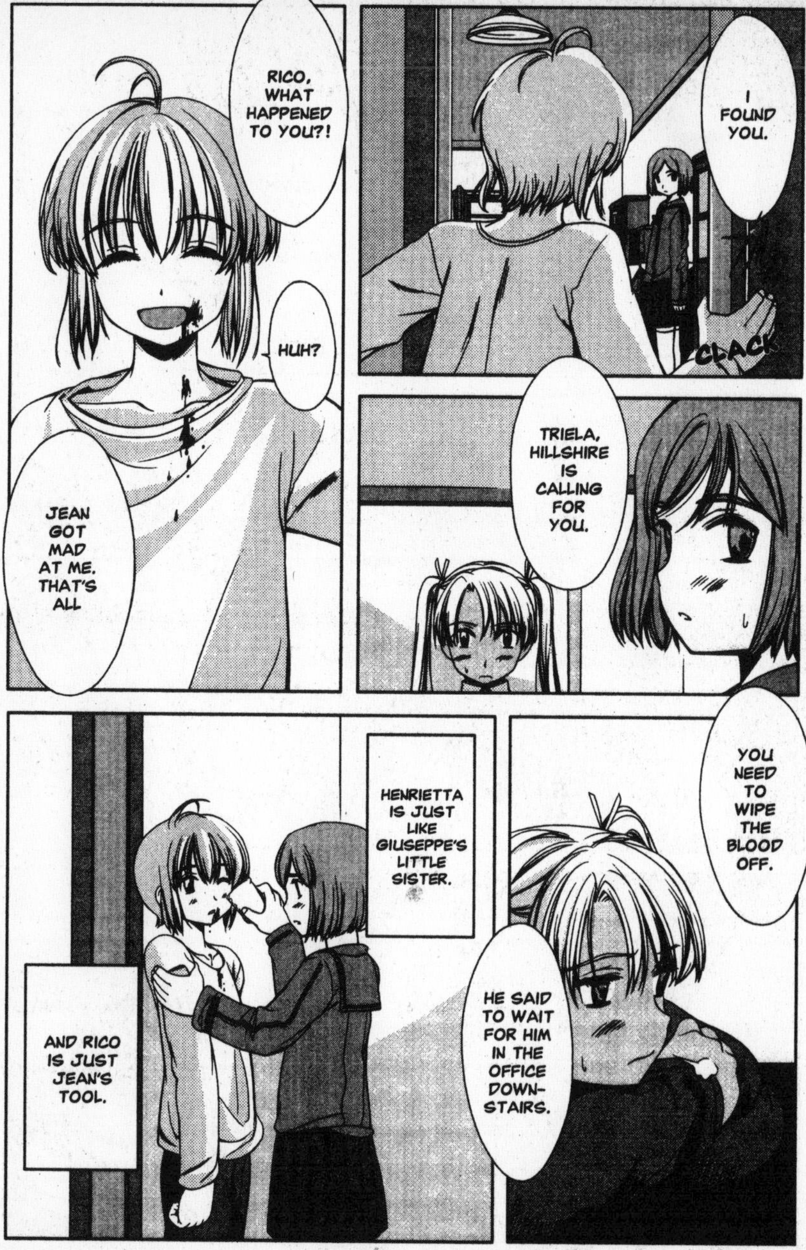
I FOUND YOU.
CLACK
RICO, WHAT HAPPENED TO YOU?!
HUH?
JEAN GOT MAD AT ME. THAT'S ALL
TRIELA, HILLSHIRE IS CALLING FOR YOU.
YOU NEED TO WIPE THE BLOOD OFF.
HE SAID TO WAIT FOR HIM IN THE OFFICE DOWN-STAIRS.
HENRIETTA IS JUST LIKE GIUSEPPE'S LITTLE SISTER.
AND RICO IS JUST JEAN'S TOOL.

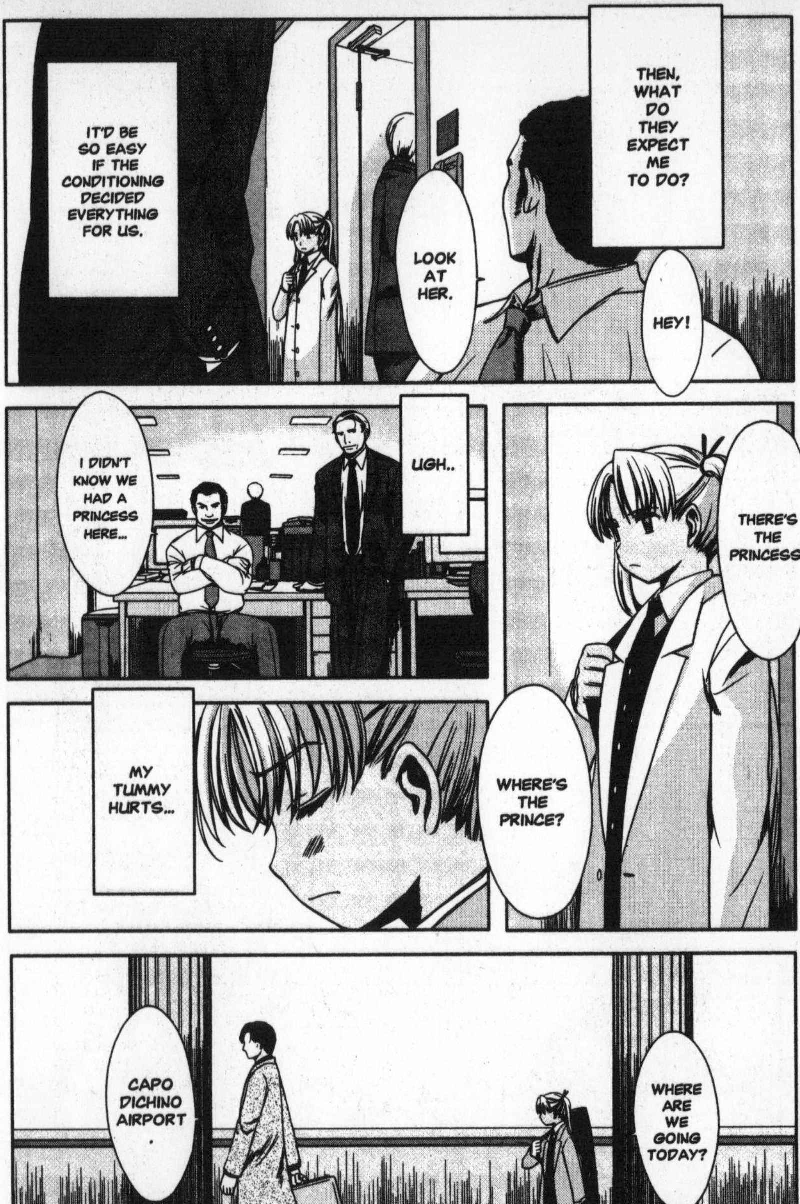
THEN, WHAT DO THEY EXPECT ME TO DO?
HEY!
LOOK AT HER.
IT'D BE SO EASY IF THE CONDITIONING DECIDED EVERYTHING FOR US.
THERE'S THE PRINCESS.
WHERE'S THE PRINCE?
UGH..
I DIDN'T KNOW WE HAD A PRINCESS HERE...
MY TUMMY HURTS...
WHERE ARE WE GOING TODAY?
CAPO DICHINO AIRPORT.

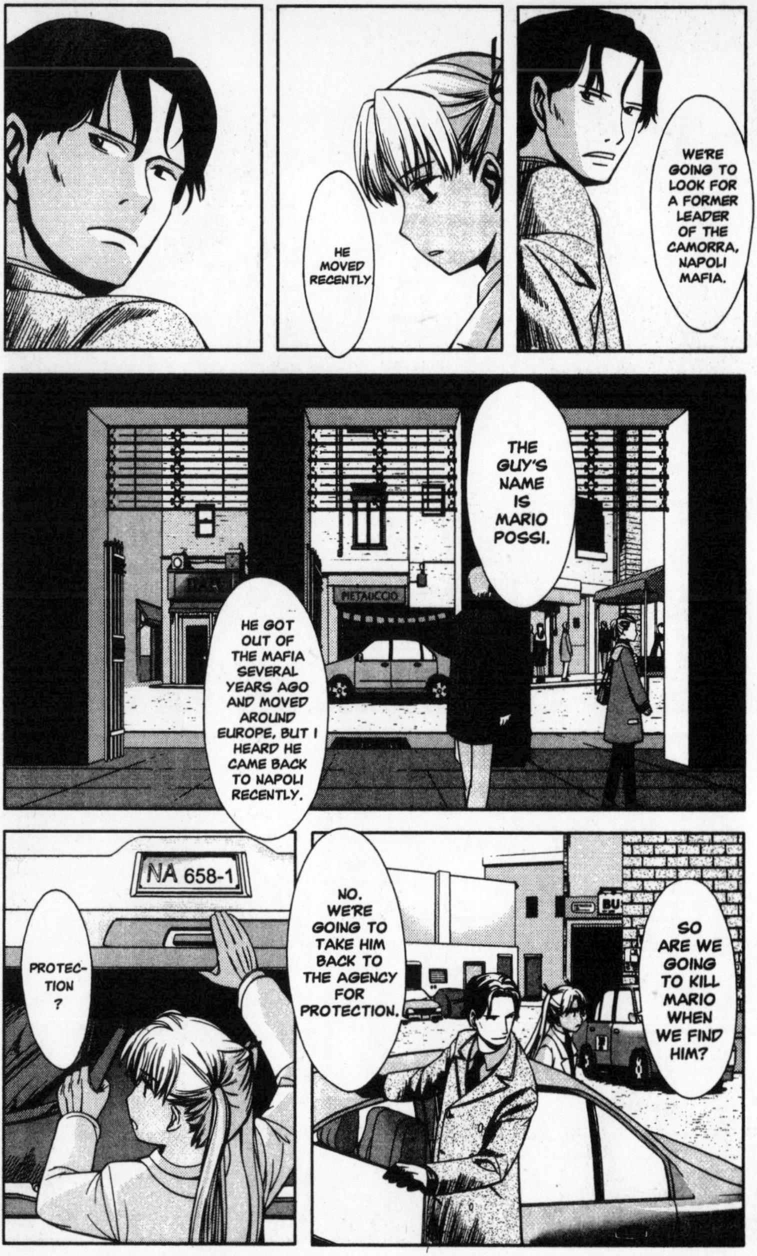

WE'RE GOING TO LOOK FOR A FORMER LEADER OF THE CAMORRA, NAPOLI MAFIA.
HE MOVED RECENTLY.
THE GUY'S NAME IS MARIO POSSI.
HE GOT OUT OF THE MAFIA SEVERAL YEARS AGO AND MOVED AROUND EUROPE, BUT I HEARD HE CAME BACK TO NAPOLI RECENTLY.
SO ARE WE GOING TO KILL MARIO WHEN WE FIND HIM?
NO. WE'RE GOING TO TAKE HIM BACK TO THE AGENCY FOR PROTECTION.
NA 658-1
PROTECTION?

WHEN THE CAMORRA'S BOSS GOES TO COURT, WE'LL NEED A WITNESS WHO KNOWS HIS BUSINESS.
WE'LL OFFER MARIO IMMUNITY IN EXCHANGE FOR HIS TESTIMONY.
THE MAFIA WILL TRY TO STOP HIM, OF COURSE.
THAT MEANS...
MARIO WILL GET KILLED IF WE DON'T DO ANYTHING, RIGHT?
EXACTLY.
WE'LL FIND HIM AND KEEP HIM UNDER PROTECTIVE CUSTODY UNTIL THE COURT DATE.
THEN...
5 EURO
WHY ARE **WE** TAKING THIS ASSIGNMENT, AND NOT SECTION I?
MARIO AND I GO BACK A LONG WAY.
I KNOW A LOT OF PLACES HE MIGHT DROP BY IN THIS TOWN.

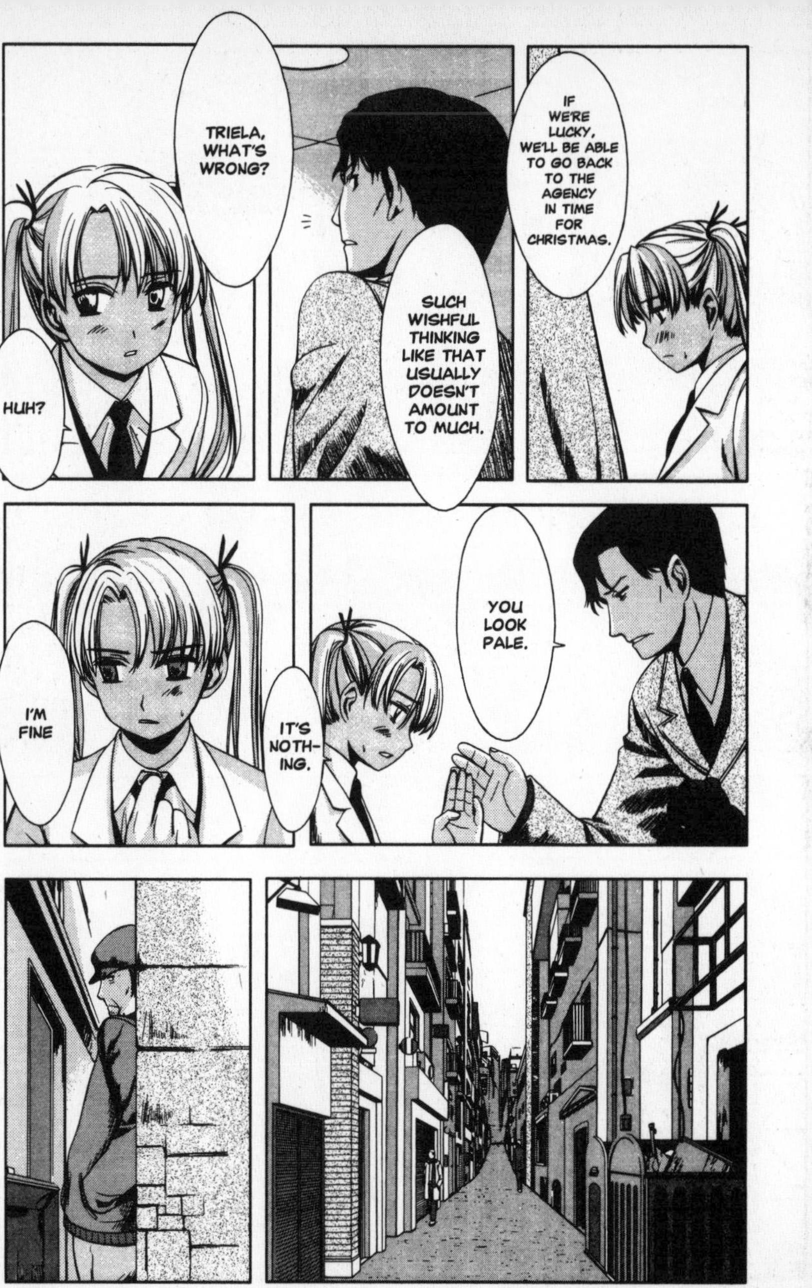
IF WE'RE LUCKY, WE'LL BE ABLE TO GO BACK TO THE AGENCY IN TIME FOR CHRISTMAS.
SUCH WISHFUL THINKING LIKE THAT USUALLY DOESN'T AMOUNT TO MUCH.
TRIELA, WHAT'S WRONG?
HUH?
YOU LOOK PALE.
IT'S NOTH-ING.
I'M FINE

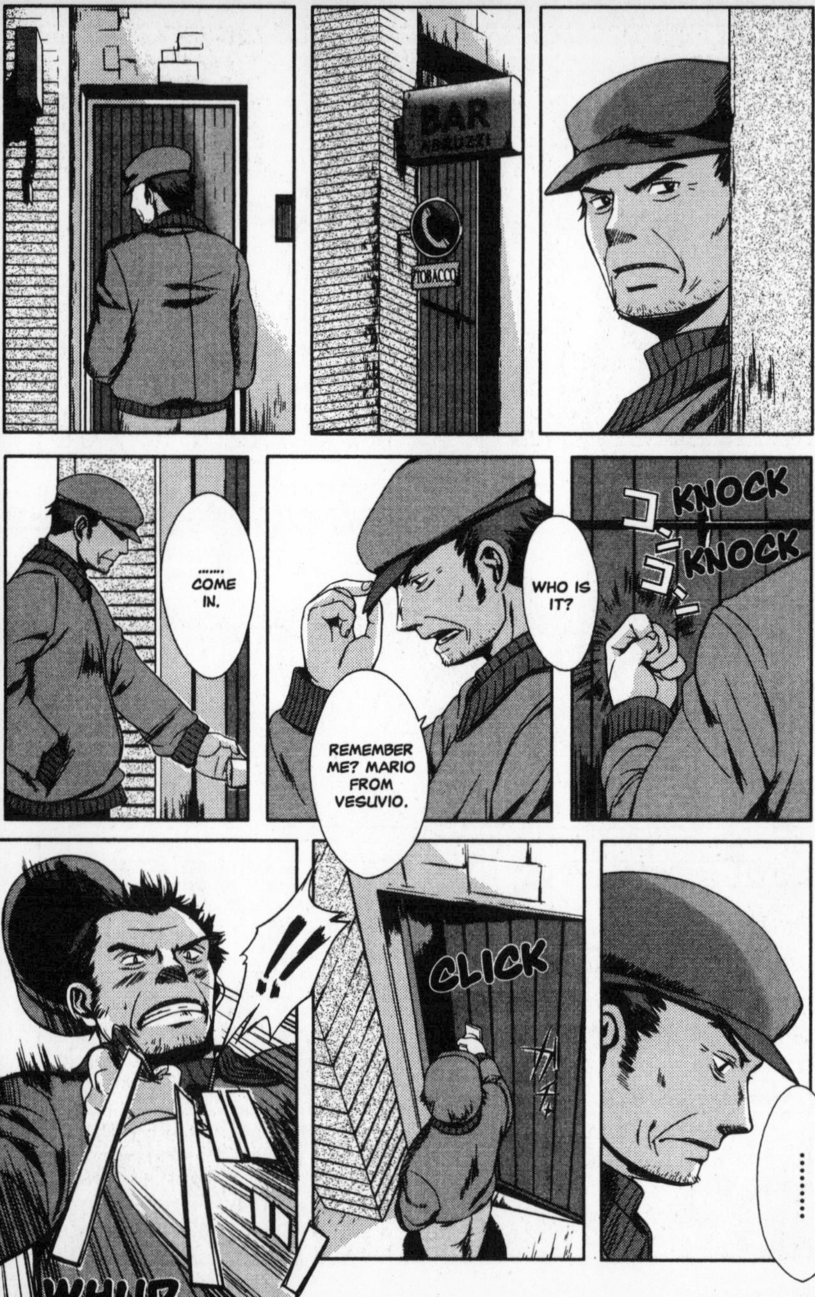
BAR
TOBACCO
KNOCK
KNOCK
WHO IS IT?
REMEMBER ME? MARIO FROM VESUVIO.
.... COME IN.
....
CLICK
!!
WHUD

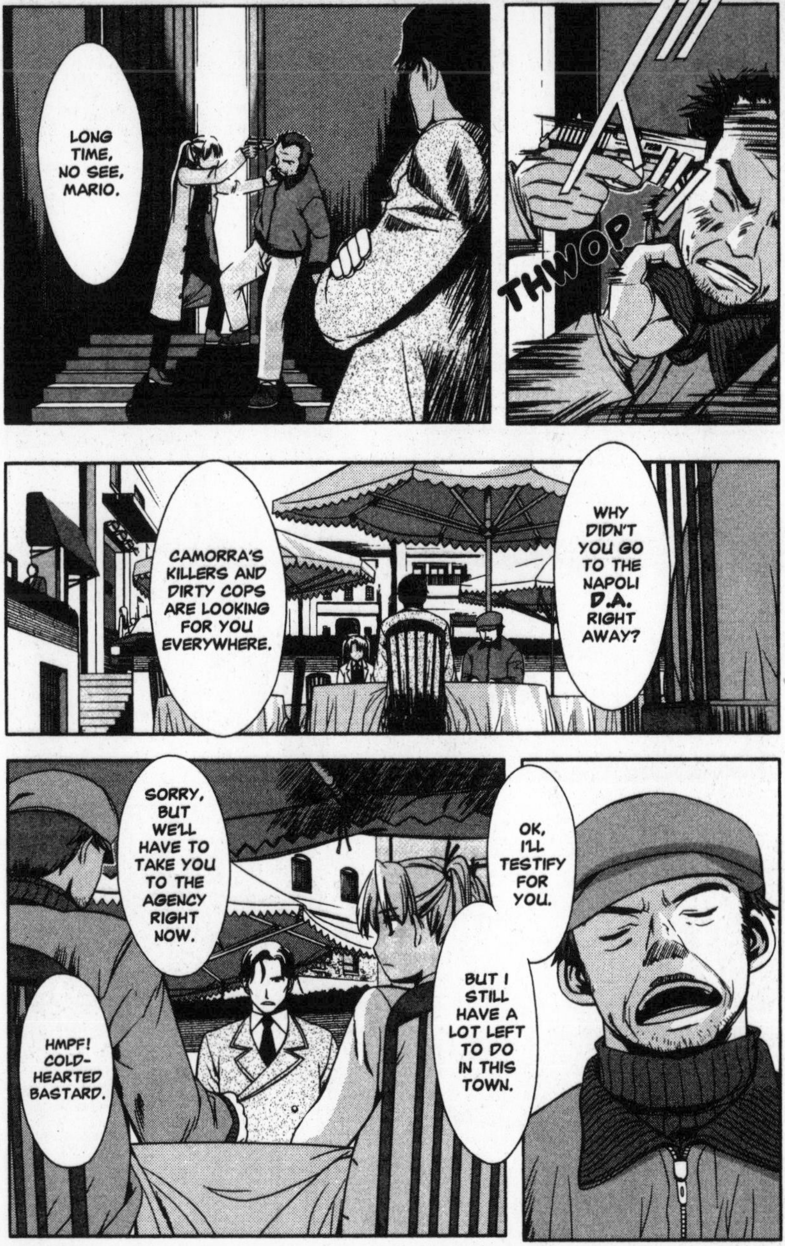
THWOP
LONG TIME, NO SEE, MARIO.
WHY DIDN'T YOU GO TO THE NAPOLI D.A. RIGHT AWAY?
CAMORRA'S KILLERS AND DIRTY COPS ARE LOOKING FOR YOU EVERYWHERE.
OK, I'LL TESTIFY FOR YOU.
BUT I STILL HAVE A LOT LEFT TO DO IN THIS TOWN.
SORRY, BUT WE'LL HAVE TO TAKE YOU TO THE AGENCY RIGHT NOW.
HMPF! COLD-HEARTED BASTARD.

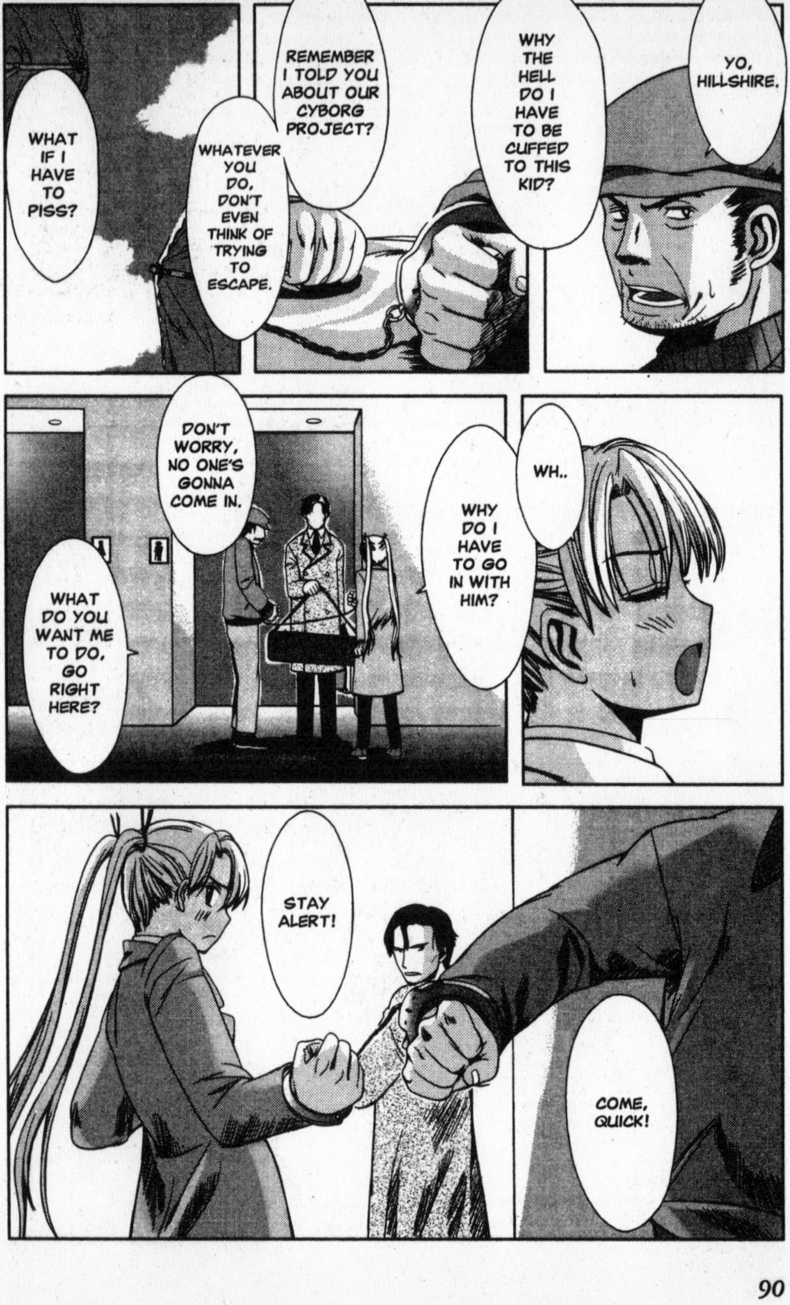
YO, HILLSHIRE.
WHY THE HELL DO I HAVE TO BE CUFFED TO THIS KID?
REMEMBER I TOLD YOU ABOUT OUR CYBORG PROJECT?
WHATEVER YOU DO, DON'T EVEN THINK OF TRYING TO ESCAPE.
WHAT IF I HAVE TO PISS?
WH..
WHY DO I HAVE TO GO IN WITH HIM?
DON'T WORRY, NO ONE'S GONNA COME IN.
WHAT DO YOU WANT ME TO DO, GO RIGHT HERE?
COME, QUICK!
STAY ALERT!

.... HURRY UP!

DON'T RUSH ME.

HE DOESN'T LOOK LIKE THE KIND OF GUY WHO'D HAVE A FRIEND IN THE MAFIA.

WHY ARE ALL YOU AGENCY GUYS SO IMPATIENT?

A LONG TIME AGO, A ROOKIE EUROPOL DETECTIVE CAUGHT A BIG SHOT FROM CAMORRA IN AMSTERDAM.

SORT OF...

DID YOU HEAR ABOUT THE AGENCY FROM HILLSHIRE?

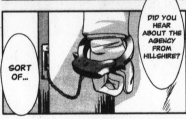

THAT ROOKIE DETECTIVE WAS HILLSHIRE, AND THE BIG SHOT HE LET GO WAS ME.

CAMORRA'S BLACK MARKET TOBACCO BUSINESS WASN'T PAYING,

AND THEY WERE "EXPORTING" BABIES BY WAY OF AMSTERDAM.

EUROPOL?

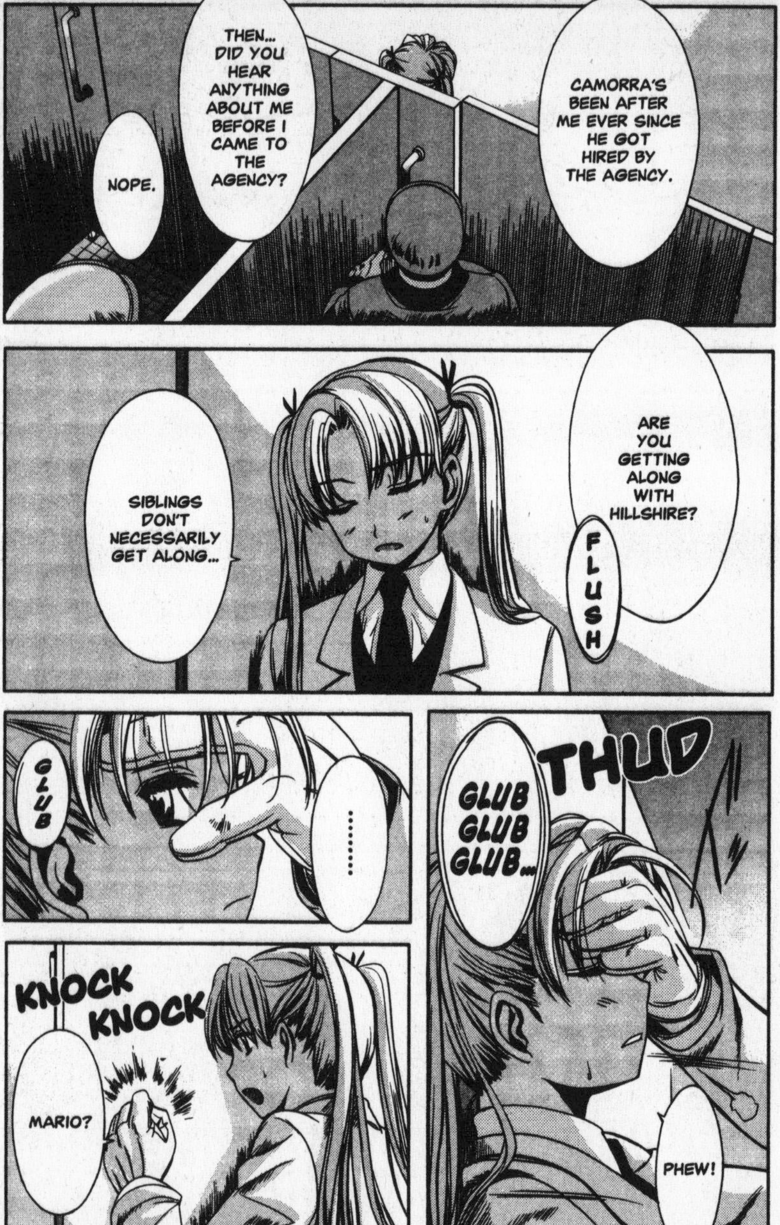
CAMORRA'S BEEN AFTER ME EVER SINCE HE GOT HIRED BY THE AGENCY.
THEN... DID YOU HEAR ANYTHING ABOUT ME BEFORE I CAME TO THE AGENCY?
NOPE.
ARE YOU GETTING ALONG WITH HILLSHIRE?
FLUSH
SIBLINGS DON'T NECESSARILY GET ALONG...
THUD
GLUB GLUB GLUB...
PHEW!
......
GLUB
KNOCK KNOCK
MARIO?

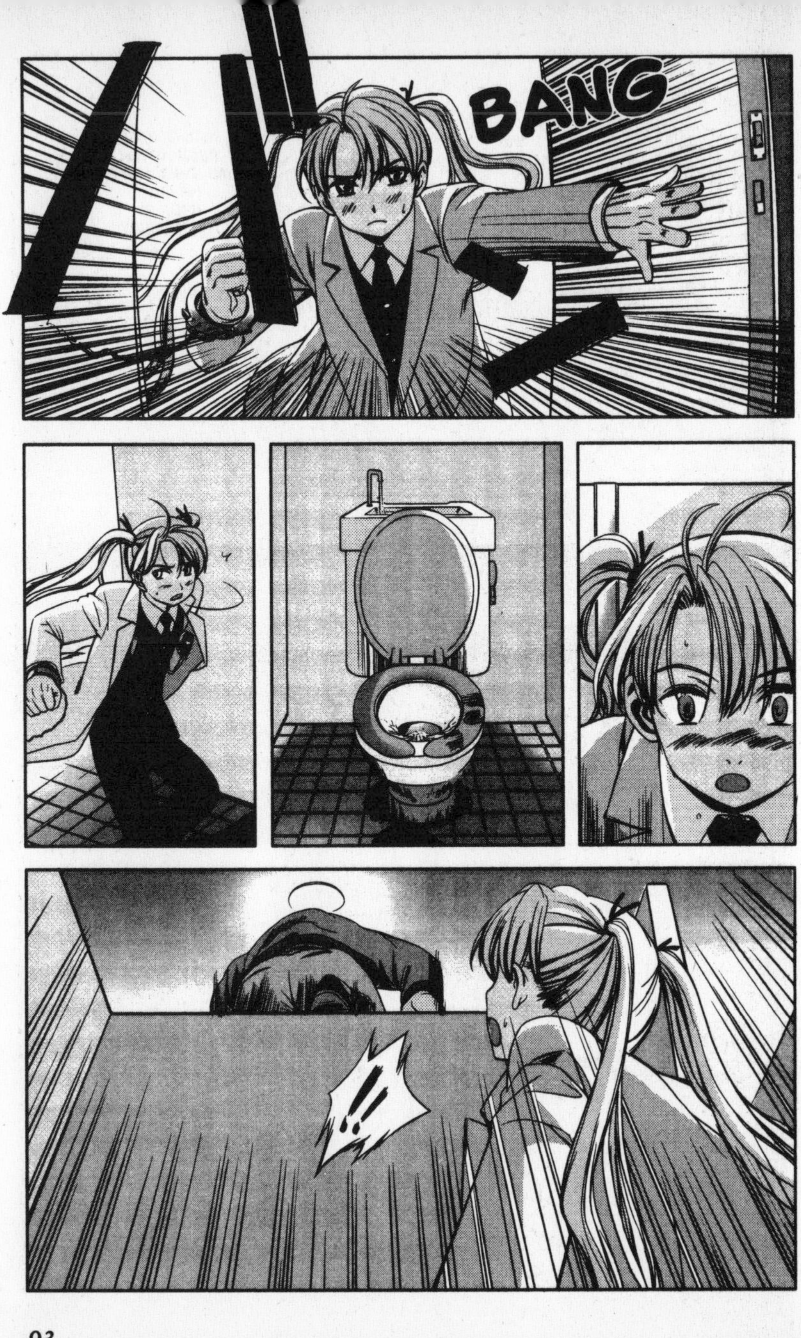
BANG
!!

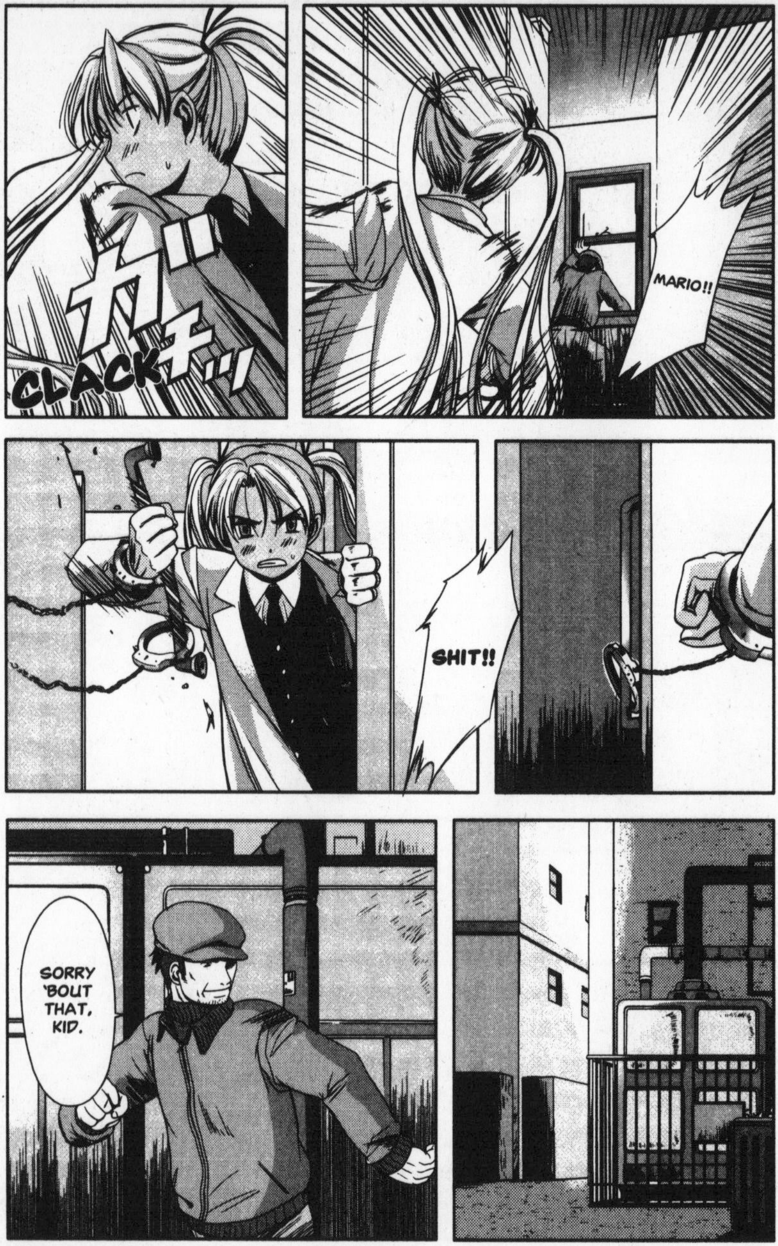
カチッ
CLACK
MARIO!!
SHIT!!
SORRY 'BOUT THAT, KID.

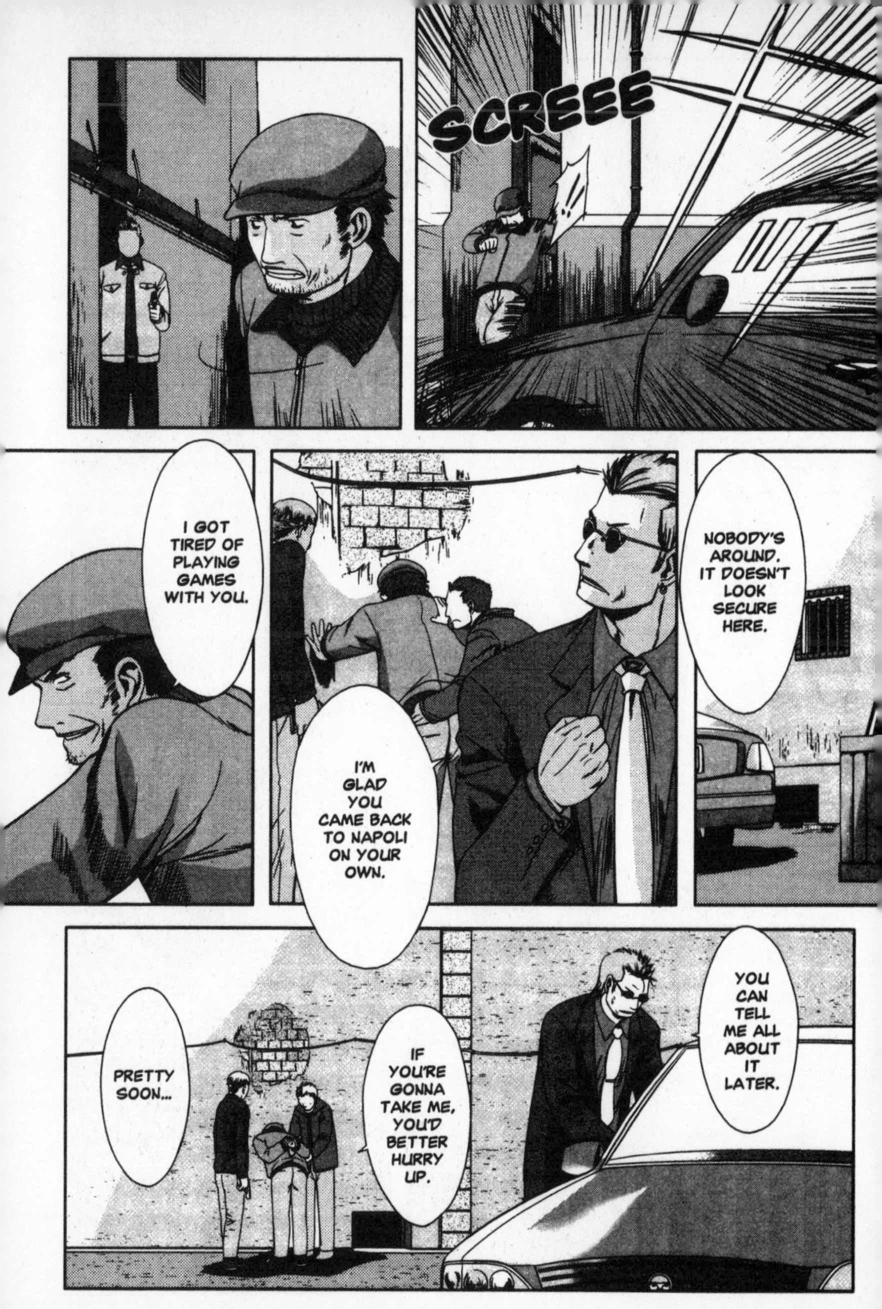
SCREEE
!!
I GOT TIRED OF PLAYING GAMES WITH YOU.
NOBODY'S AROUND. IT DOESN'T LOOK SECURE HERE.
I'M GLAD YOU CAME BACK TO NAPOLI ON YOUR OWN.
YOU CAN TELL ME ALL ABOUT IT LATER.
IF YOU'RE GONNA TAKE ME, YOU'D BETTER HURRY UP.
PRETTY SOON...

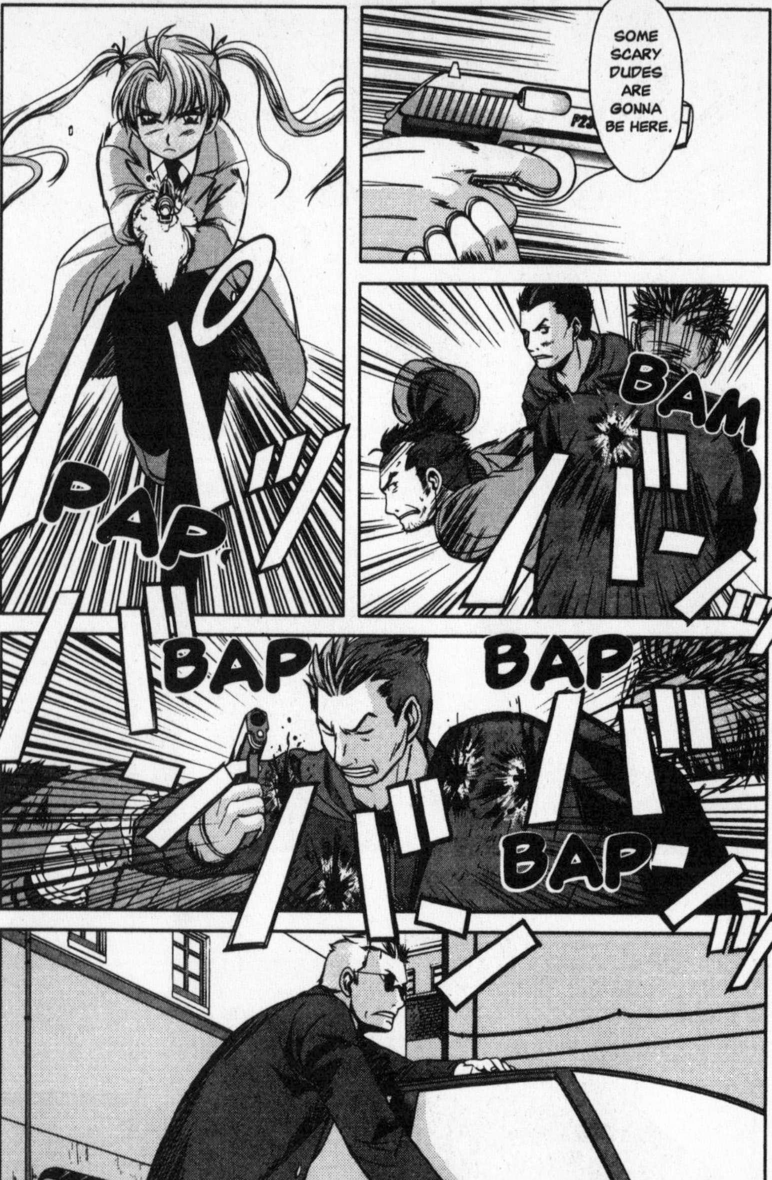

SOME SCARY DUDES ARE GONNA BE HERE.
PAP
BAM
BAP
BAP
BAP-

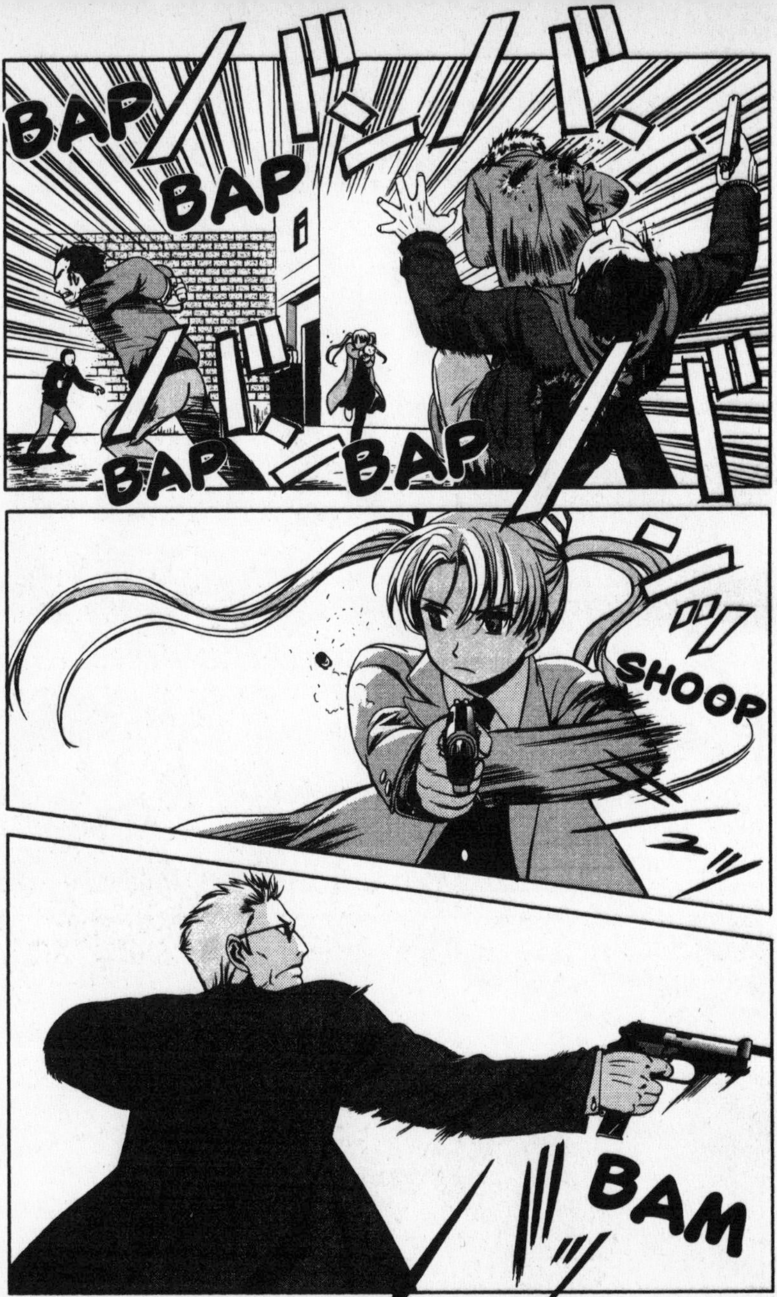
BAP
BAP
BAP
BAP
SHOOP
BAM

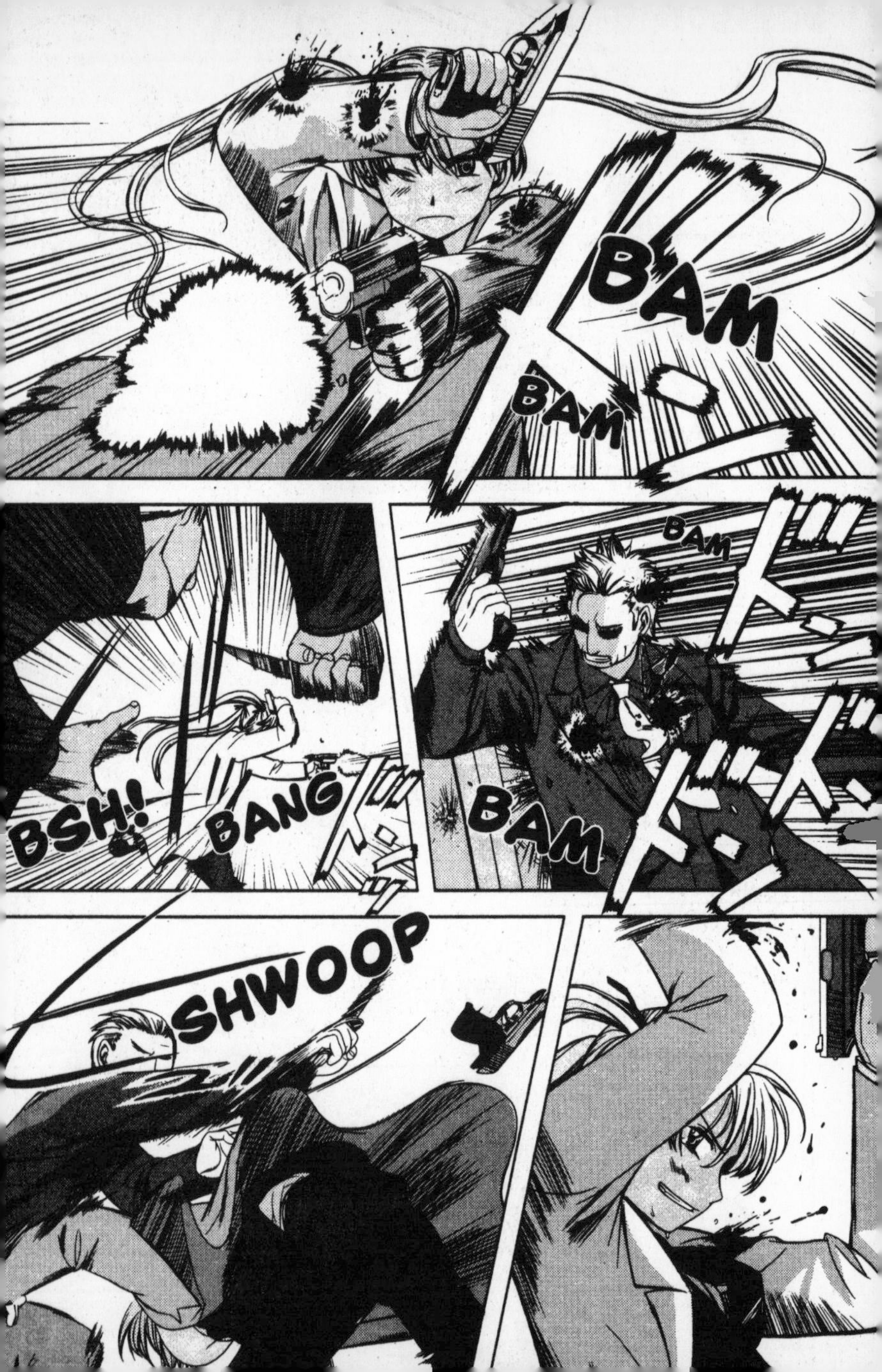

BAM
BAM
BAM
BAM
BANG
BSH!
SHWOOP

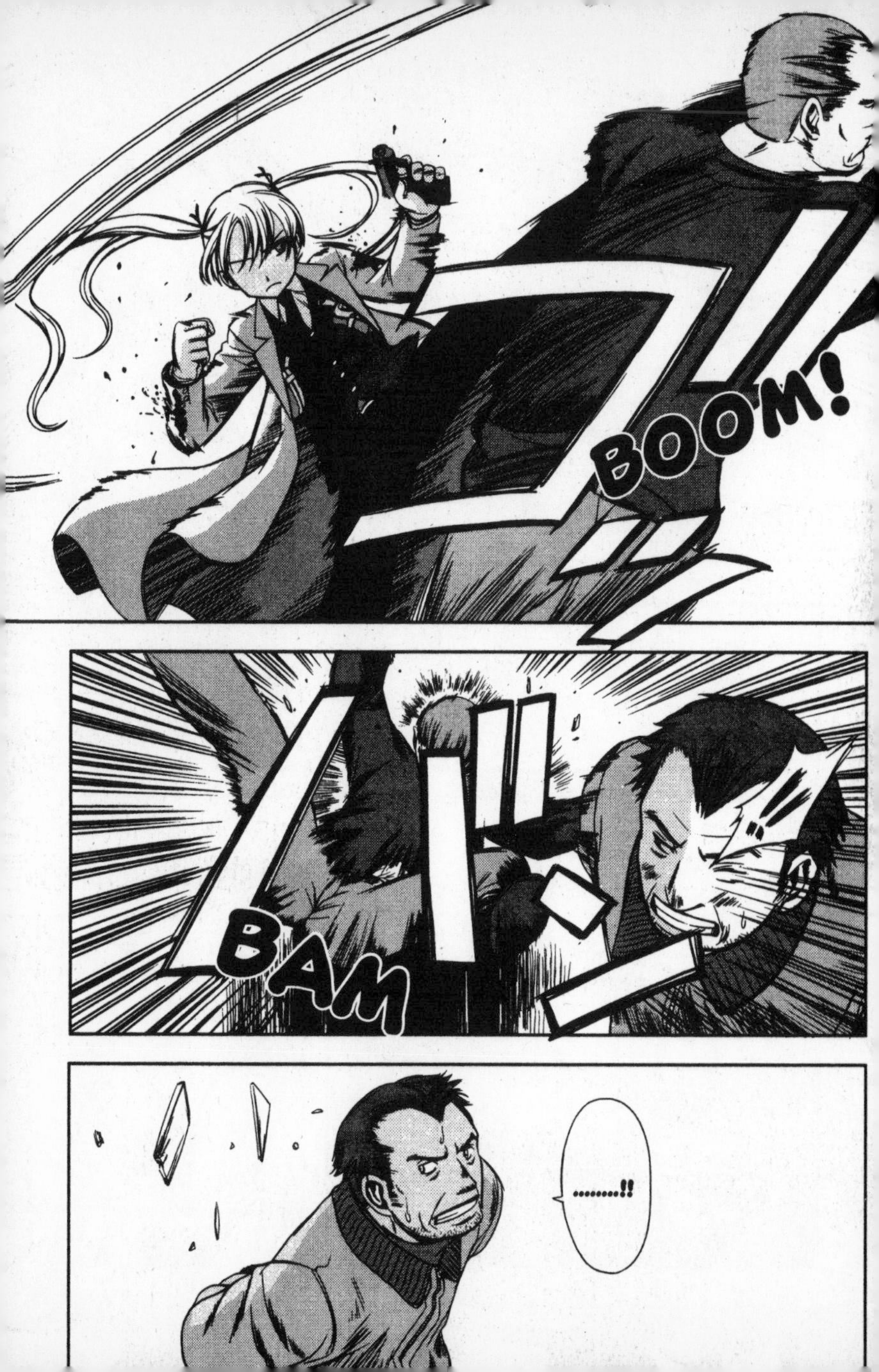
BOOM!
BAM
.........!!

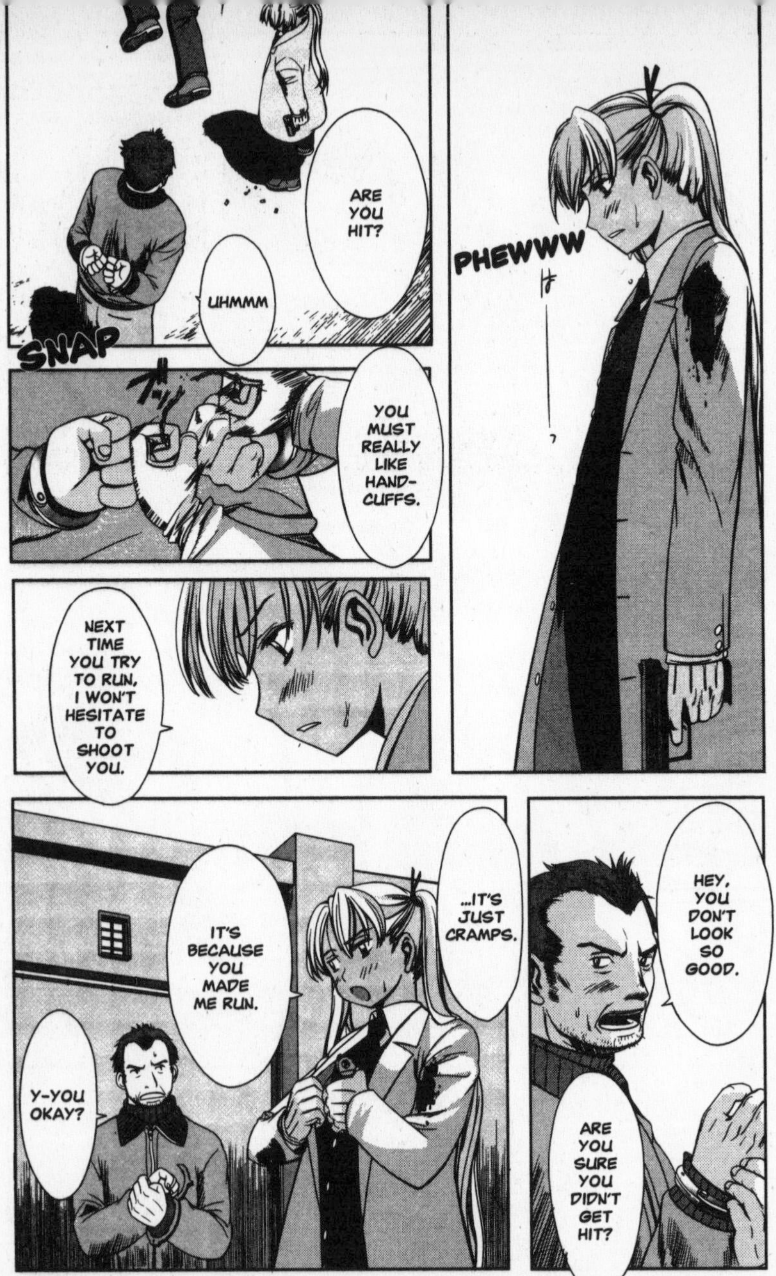
PHEWWW
ARE YOU HIT?
UHMMM
SNAP
YOU MUST REALLY LIKE HAND-CUFFS.
NEXT TIME YOU TRY TO RUN, I WON'T HESITATE TO SHOOT YOU.
HEY, YOU DON'T LOOK SO GOOD.
ARE YOU SURE YOU DIDN'T GET HIT?
...IT'S JUST CRAMPS.
IT'S BECAUSE YOU MADE ME RUN.
Y-YOU OKAY?

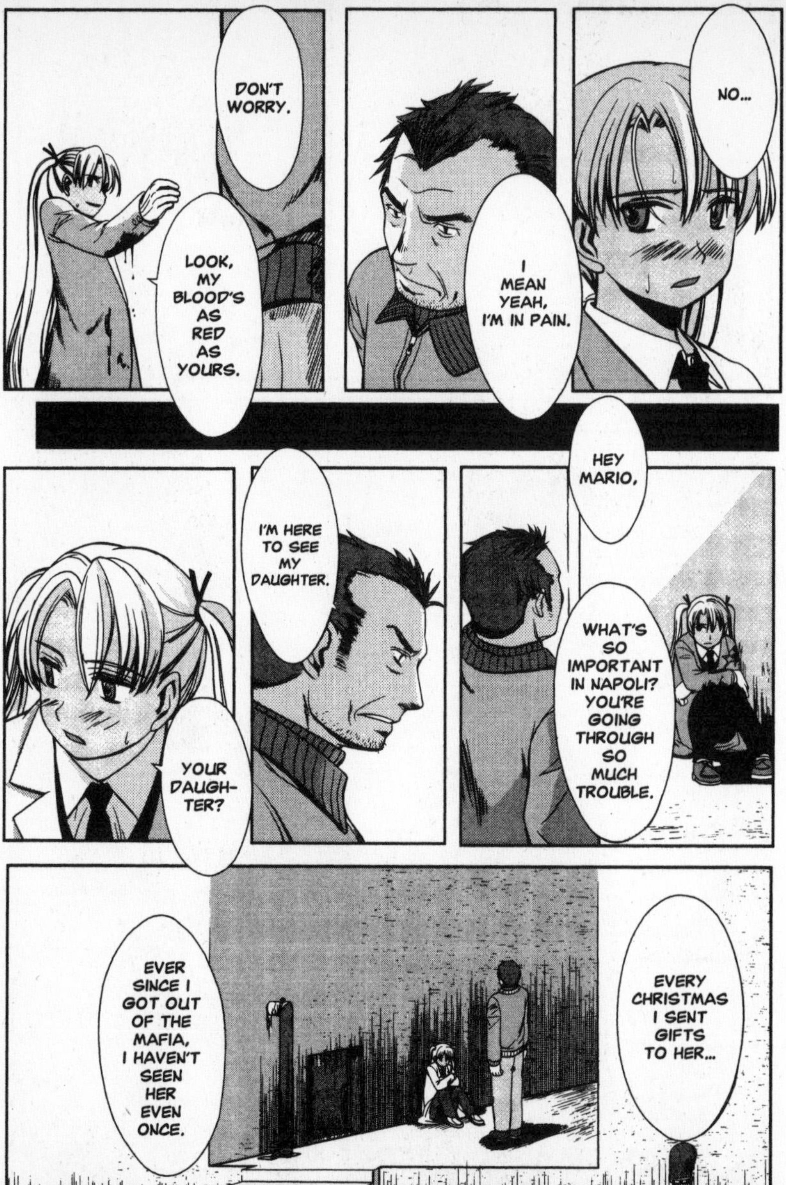
DON'T WORRY.
LOOK, MY BLOOD'S AS RED AS YOURS.
I MEAN YEAH, I'M IN PAIN.
NO...
I'M HERE TO SEE MY DAUGHTER.
YOUR DAUGH-TER?
HEY MARIO,
WHAT'S SO IMPORTANT IN NAPOLI? YOU'RE GOING THROUGH SO MUCH TROUBLE.
EVER SINCE I GOT OUT OF THE MAFIA, I HAVEN'T SEEN HER EVEN ONCE.
EVERY CHRISTMAS I SENT GIFTS TO HER...

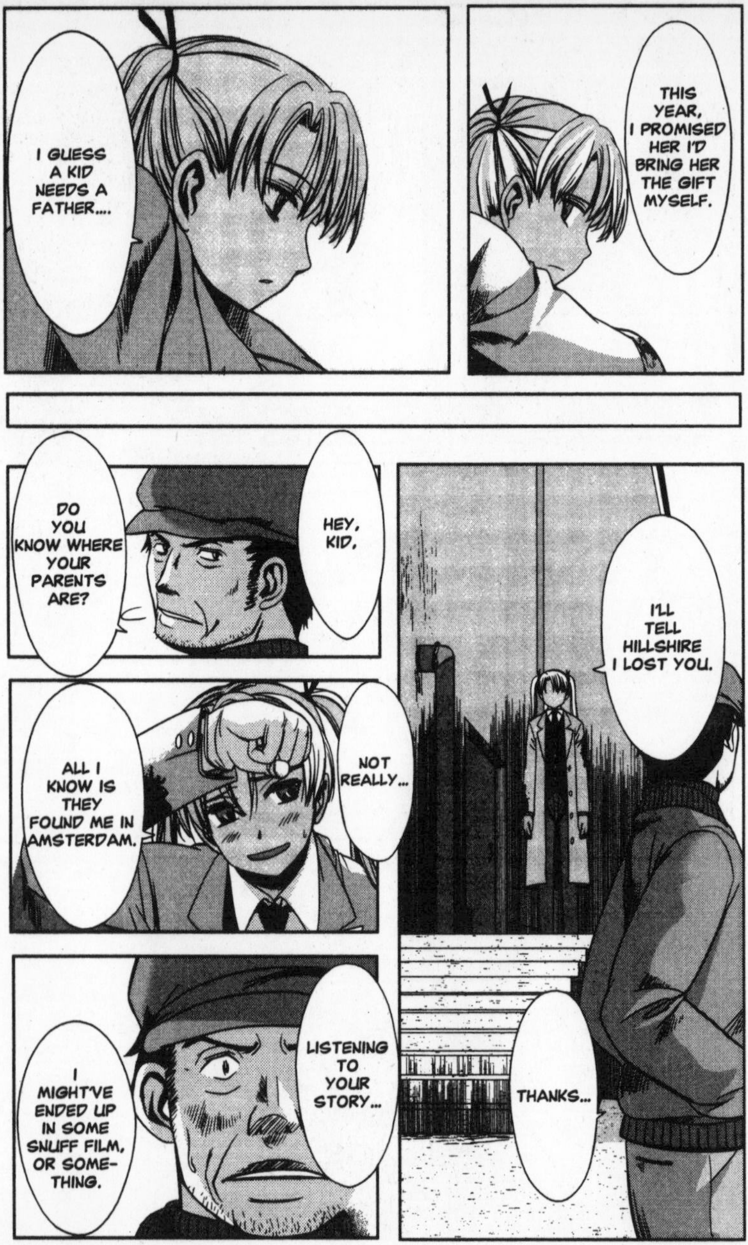
THIS YEAR, I PROMISED HER I'D BRING HER THE GIFT MYSELF.
I GUESS A KID NEEDS A FATHER....
HEY, KID,
DO YOU KNOW WHERE YOUR PARENTS ARE?
NOT REALLY...
ALL I KNOW IS THEY FOUND ME IN AMSTERDAM.
LISTENING TO YOUR STORY...
I MIGHT'VE ENDED UP IN SOME SNUFF FILM, OR SOME-THING.
I'LL TELL HILLSHIRE I LOST YOU.
THANKS...

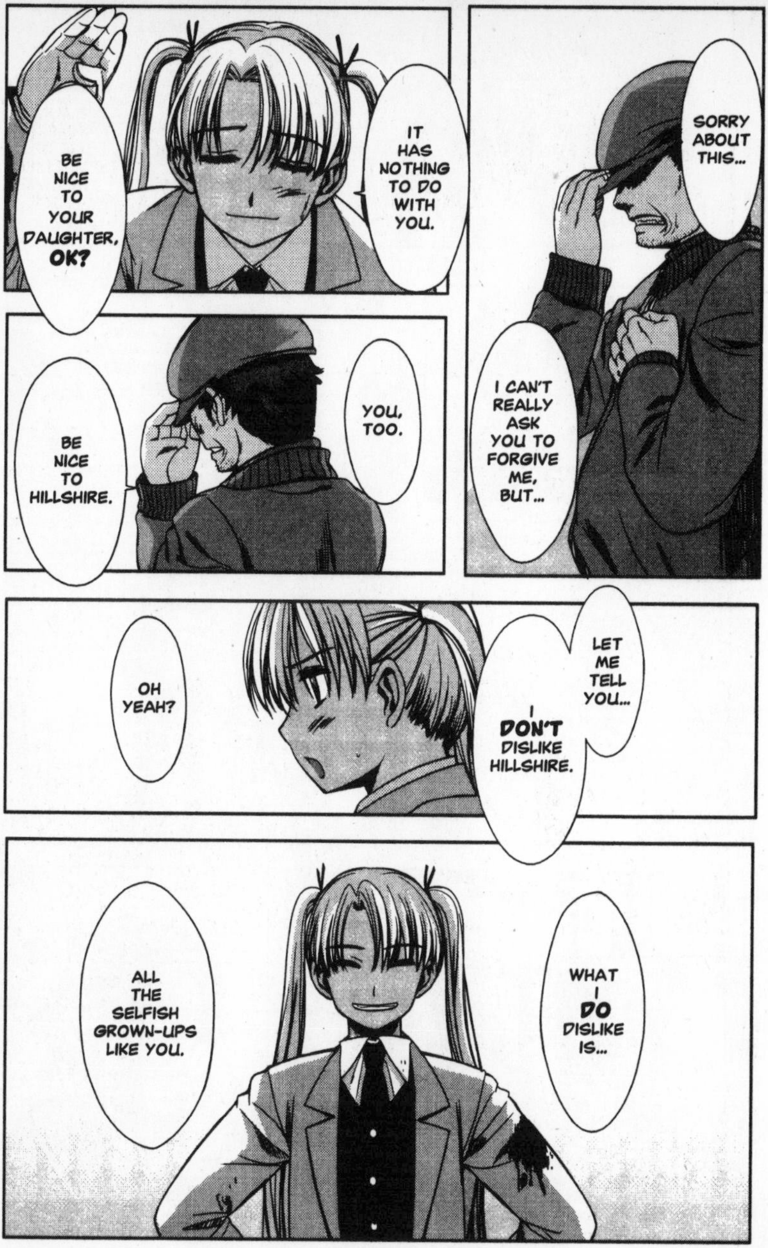
SORRY ABOUT THIS...
I CAN'T REALLY ASK YOU TO FORGIVE ME, BUT...
IT HAS NOTHING TO DO WITH YOU.
BE NICE TO YOUR DAUGHTER, OK?
YOU, TOO.
BE NICE TO HILLSHIRE.
LET ME TELL YOU...
I DON'T DISLIKE HILLSHIRE.
OH YEAH?
WHAT I DO DISLIKE IS...
ALL THE SELFISH GROWN-UPS LIKE YOU.

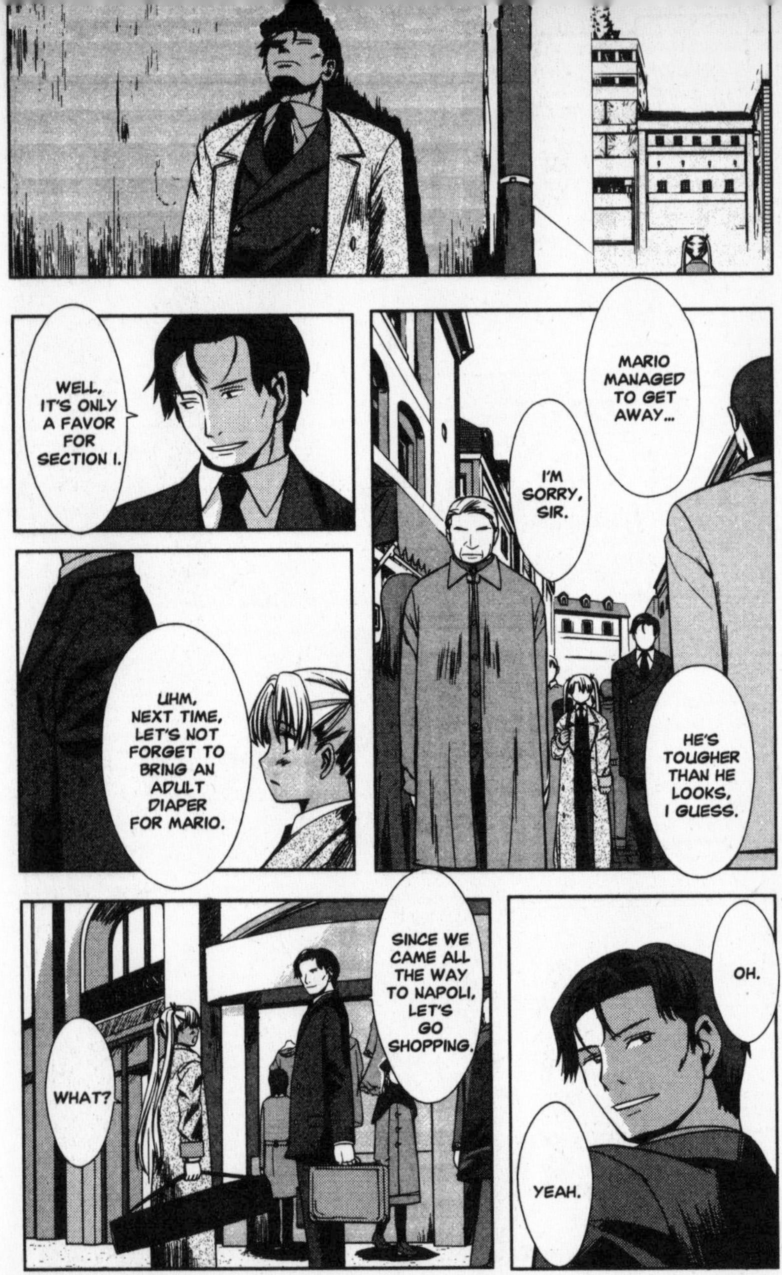
WELL, IT'S ONLY A FAVOR FOR SECTION I.
MARIO MANAGED TO GET AWAY...
I'M SORRY, SIR.
UHM, NEXT TIME, LET'S NOT FORGET TO BRING AN ADULT DIAPER FOR MARIO.
HE'S TOUGHER THAN HE LOOKS, I GUESS.
SINCE WE CAME ALL THE WAY TO NAPOLI, LET'S GO SHOPPING.
WHAT?
OH.
YEAH.

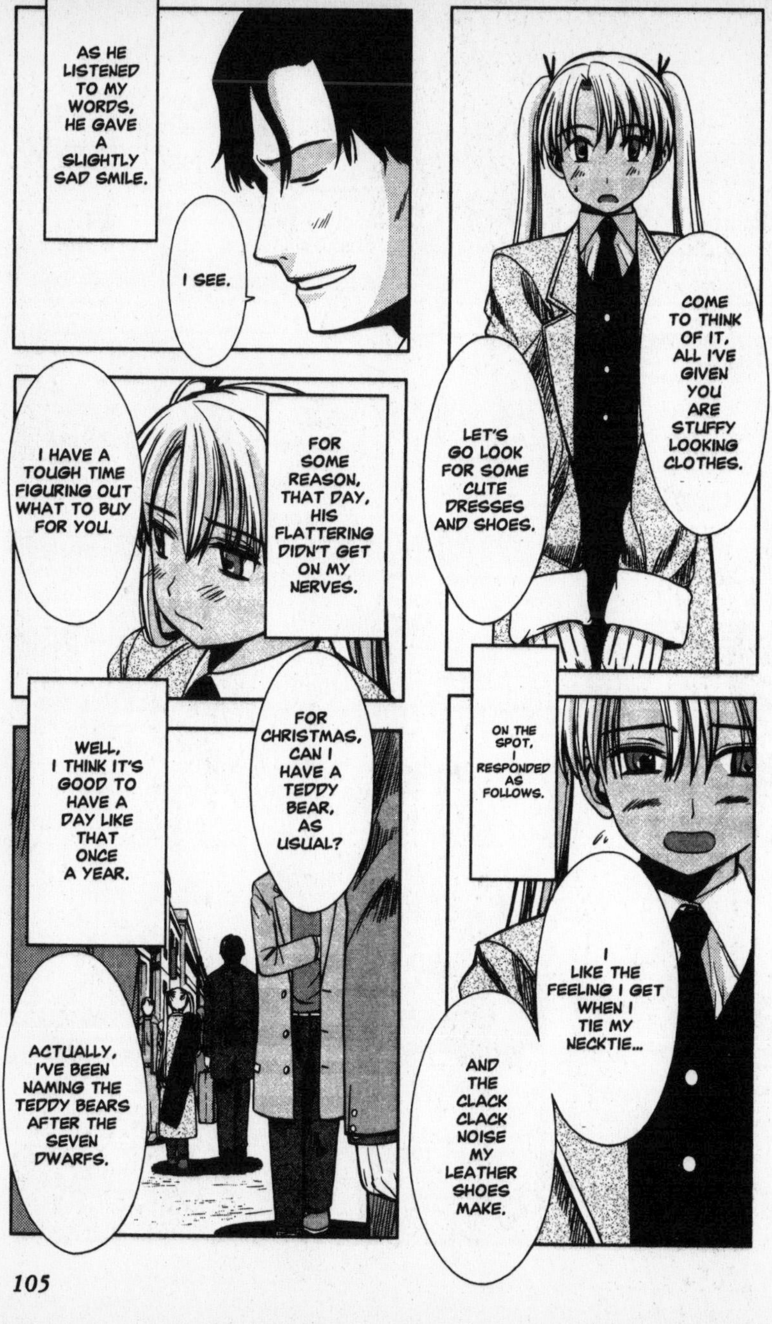
COME TO THINK OF IT, ALL I'VE GIVEN YOU ARE STUFFY LOOKING CLOTHES.
LET'S GO LOOK FOR SOME CUTE DRESSES AND SHOES.
AS HE LISTENED TO MY WORDS, HE GAVE A SLIGHTLY SAD SMILE.
I SEE.
FOR SOME REASON, THAT DAY, HIS FLATTERING DIDN'T GET ON MY NERVES.
I HAVE A TOUGH TIME FIGURING OUT WHAT TO BUY FOR YOU.
ON THE SPOT, I RESPONDED AS FOLLOWS.
I LIKE THE FEELING I GET WHEN I TIE MY NECKTIE...
AND THE CLACK CLACK NOISE MY LEATHER SHOES MAKE.
FOR CHRISTMAS, CAN I HAVE A TEDDY BEAR, AS USUAL?
WELL, I THINK IT'S GOOD TO HAVE A DAY LIKE THAT ONCE A YEAR.
ACTUALLY, I'VE BEEN NAMING THE TEDDY BEARS AFTER THE SEVEN DWARFS.

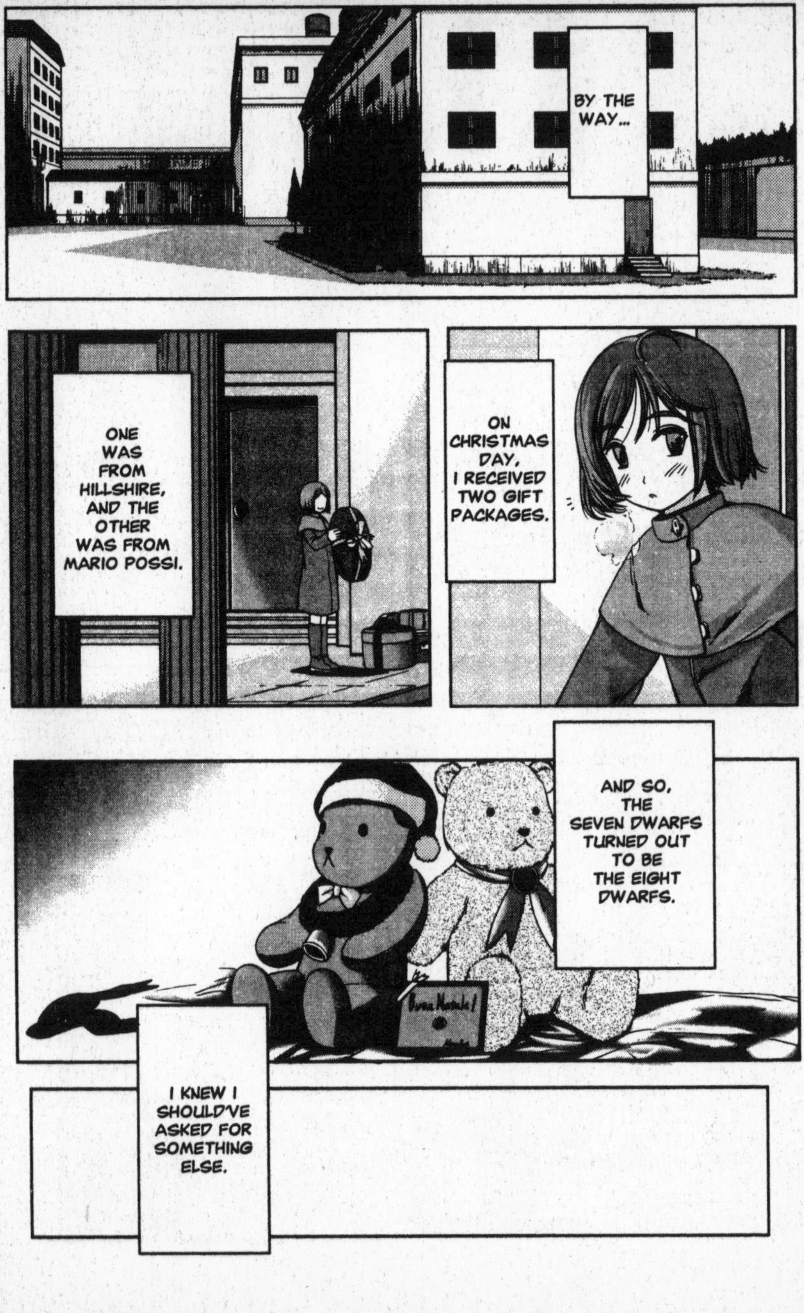
BY THE WAY...
ON CHRISTMAS DAY, I RECEIVED TWO GIFT PACKAGES.
ONE WAS FROM HILLSHIRE, AND THE OTHER WAS FROM MARIO POSSI.
AND SO, THE SEVEN DWARFS TURNED OUT TO BE THE EIGHT DWARFS.
I KNEW I SHOULD'VE ASKED FOR SOMETHING ELSE.

GUNSLINGERGIRL

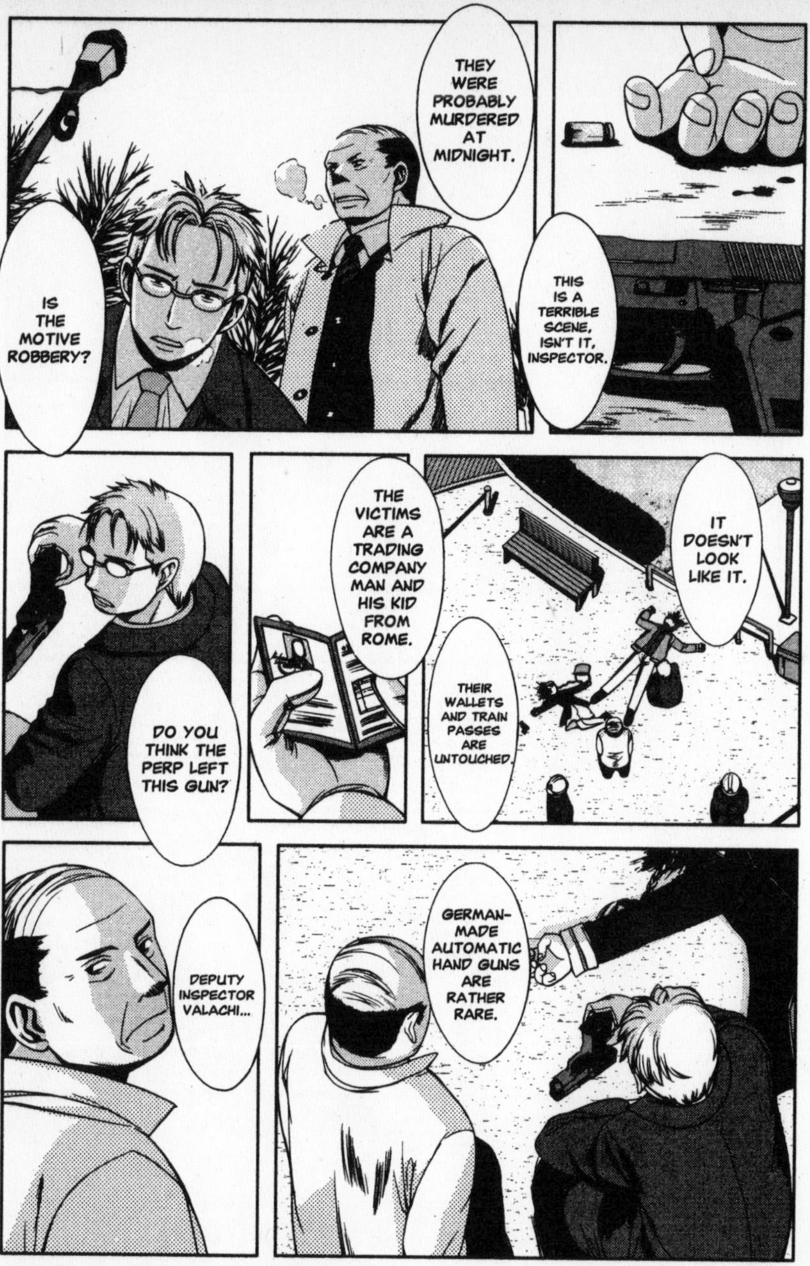
THIS IS A TERRIBLE SCENE, ISN'T IT, INSPECTOR.
THEY WERE PROBABLY MURDERED AT MIDNIGHT.
IS THE MOTIVE ROBBERY?
IT DOESN'T LOOK LIKE IT.
THEIR WALLETS AND TRAIN PASSES ARE UNTOUCHED.
THE VICTIMS ARE A TRADING COMPANY MAN AND HIS KID FROM ROME.
DO YOU THINK THE PERP LEFT THIS GUN?
GERMAN-MADE AUTOMATIC HAND GUNS ARE RATHER RARE.
DEPUTY INSPECTOR VALACHI...

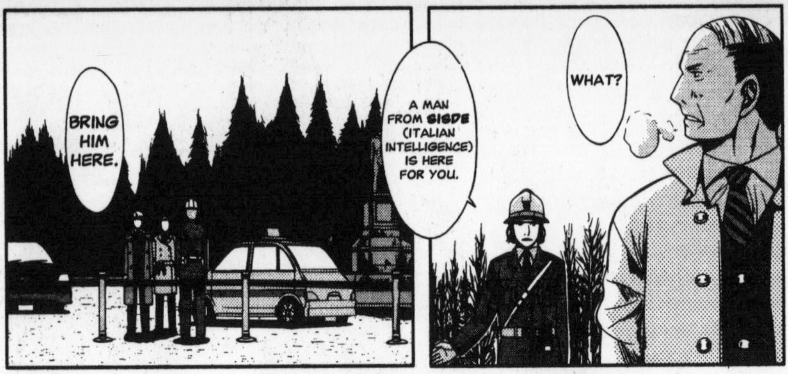

A MAN FROM SISDE (ITALIAN INTELLIGENCE) IS HERE FOR YOU.
WHAT?
BRING HIM HERE.

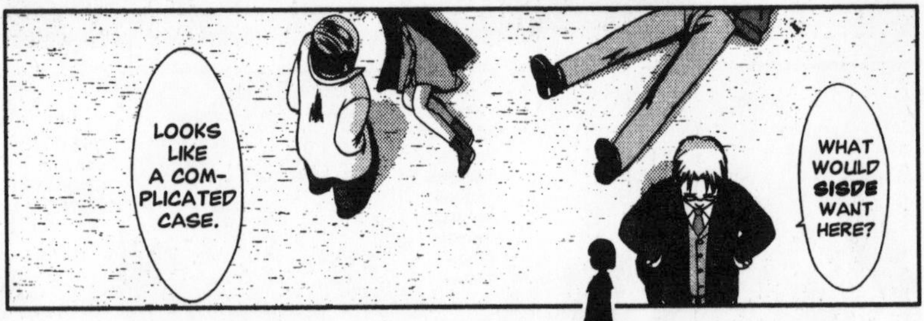

WHAT WOULD SISDE WANT HERE?
LOOKS LIKE A COMPLICATED CASE.

The girl has a mechanical body. However, she is still an adolescent child.

GUNSLINGER GIRL.

ガンスリンガー・ガール

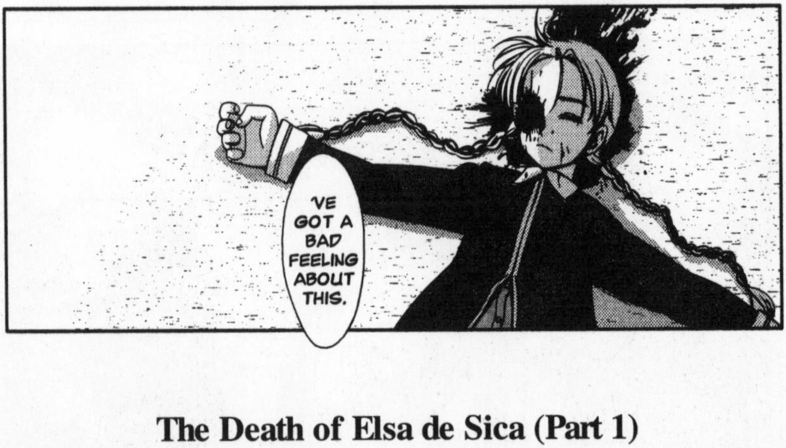

'VE GOT A BAD FEELING ABOUT THIS.

The Death of Elsa de Sica (Part 1)

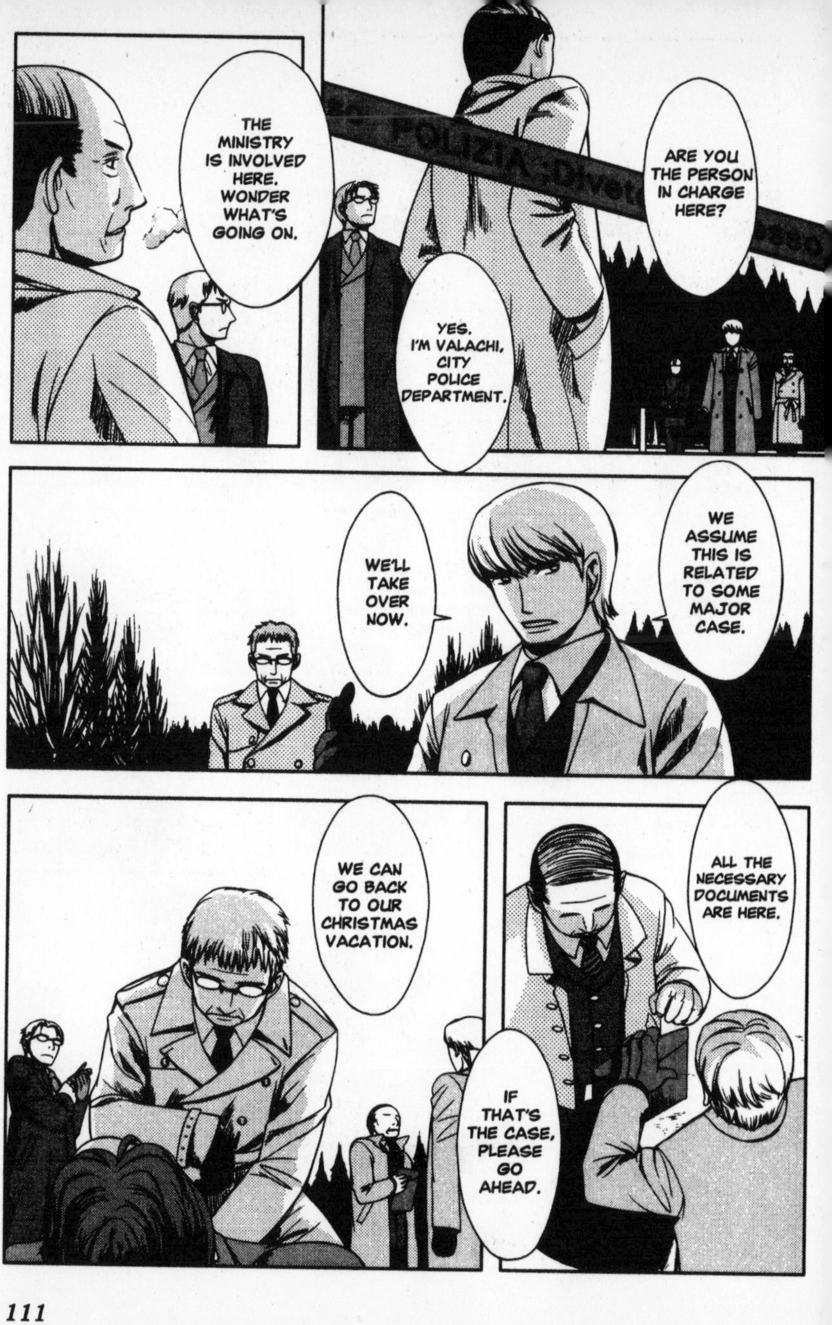
THE MINISTRY IS INVOLVED HERE. WONDER WHAT'S GOING ON.
POLIZIA
ARE YOU THE PERSON IN CHARGE HERE?
YES. I'M VALACHI, CITY POLICE DEPARTMENT.
WE ASSUME THIS IS RELATED TO SOME MAJOR CASE.
WE'LL TAKE OVER NOW.
ALL THE NECESSARY DOCUMENTS ARE HERE.
IF THAT'S THE CASE, PLEASE GO AHEAD.
WE CAN GO BACK TO OUR CHRISTMAS VACATION.

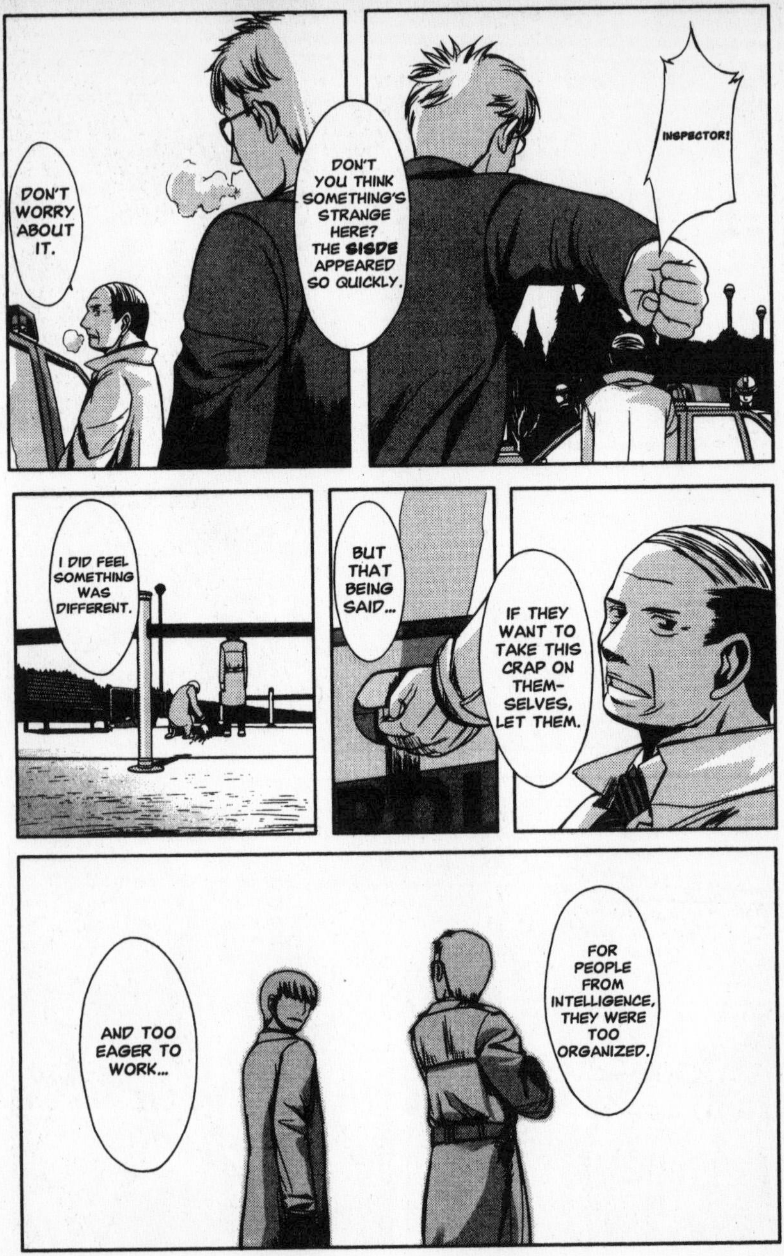
INSPECTOR!
DON'T YOU THINK SOMETHING'S STRANGE HERE? THE SISDE APPEARED SO QUICKLY.
DON'T WORRY ABOUT IT.
I DID FEEL SOMETHING WAS DIFFERENT.
BUT THAT BEING SAID...
IF THEY WANT TO TAKE THIS CRAP ON THEM-SELVES, LET THEM.
FOR PEOPLE FROM INTELLIGENCE, THEY WERE TOO ORGANIZED.
AND TOO EAGER TO WORK...

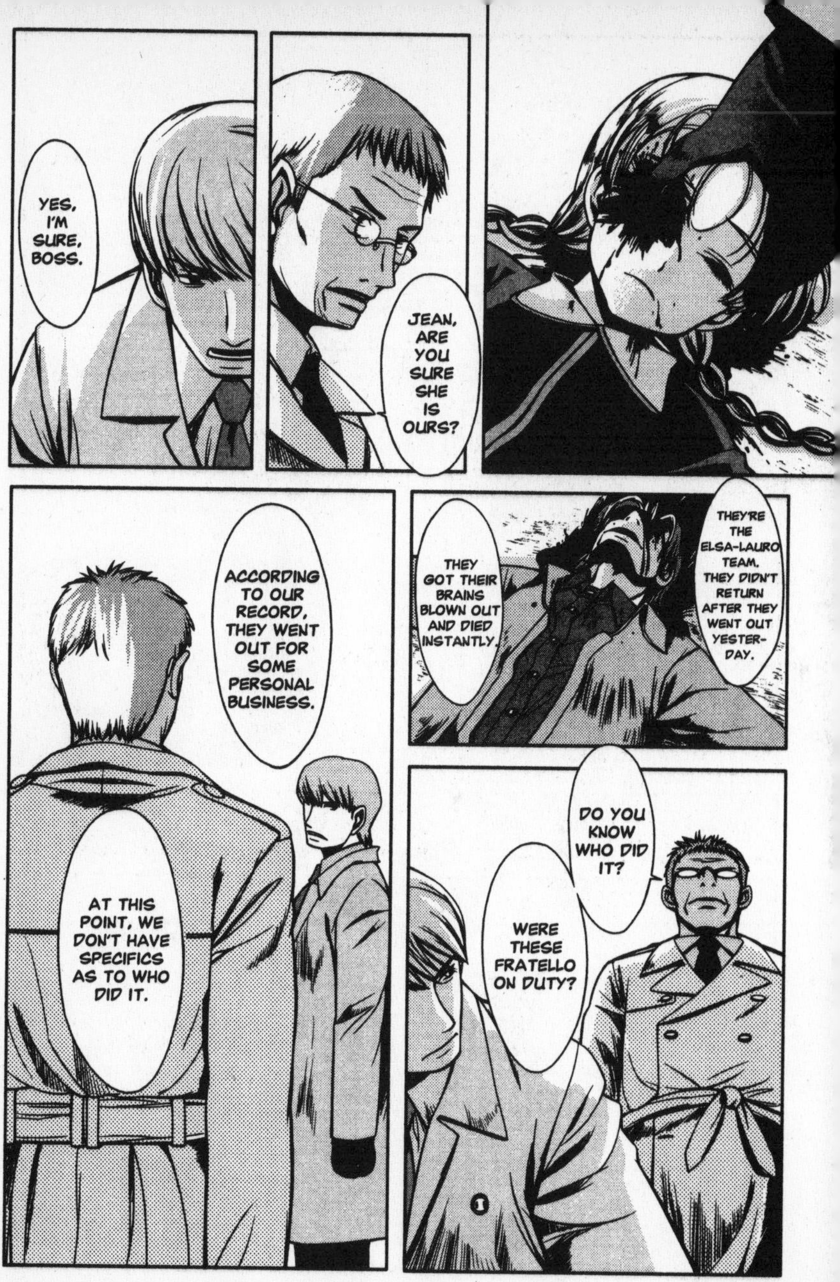
JEAN, ARE YOU SURE SHE IS OURS?
YES, I'M SURE, BOSS.
THEY'RE THE ELSA-LAURO TEAM. THEY DIDN'T RETURN AFTER THEY WENT OUT YESTER-DAY.
THEY GOT THEIR BRAINS BLOWN OUT AND DIED INSTANTLY.
DO YOU KNOW WHO DID IT?
WERE THESE FRATELLO ON DUTY?
ACCORDING TO OUR RECORD, THEY WENT OUT FOR SOME PERSONAL BUSINESS.
AT THIS POINT, WE DON'T HAVE SPECIFICS AS TO WHO DID IT.

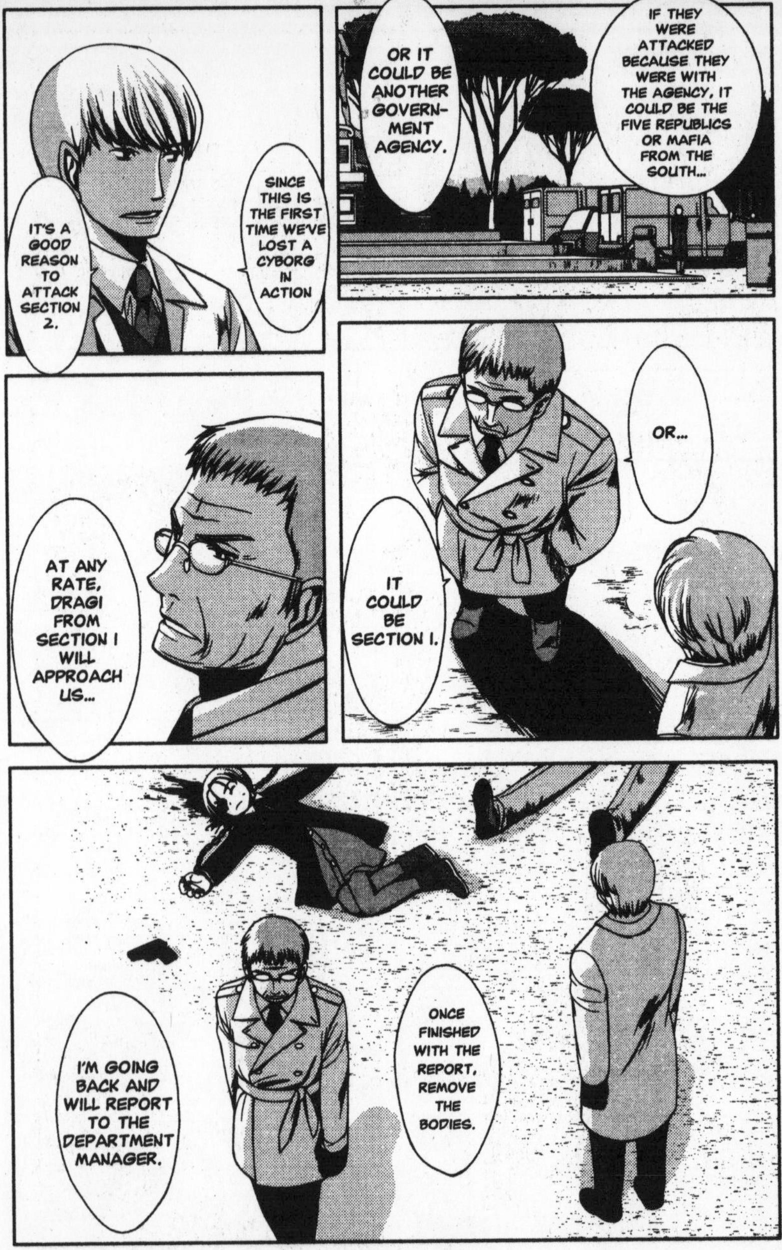
IF THEY WERE ATTACKED BECAUSE THEY WERE WITH THE AGENCY, IT COULD BE THE FIVE REPUBLICS OR MAFIA FROM THE SOUTH...
OR IT COULD BE ANOTHER GOVERN-MENT AGENCY.
SINCE THIS IS THE FIRST TIME WE'VE LOST A CYBORG IN ACTION
IT'S A GOOD REASON TO ATTACK SECTION 2.
OR...
IT COULD BE SECTION 1.
AT ANY RATE, DRAGI FROM SECTION 1 WILL APPROACH US...
ONCE FINISHED WITH THE REPORT, REMOVE THE BODIES.
I'M GOING BACK AND WILL REPORT TO THE DEPARTMENT MANAGER.

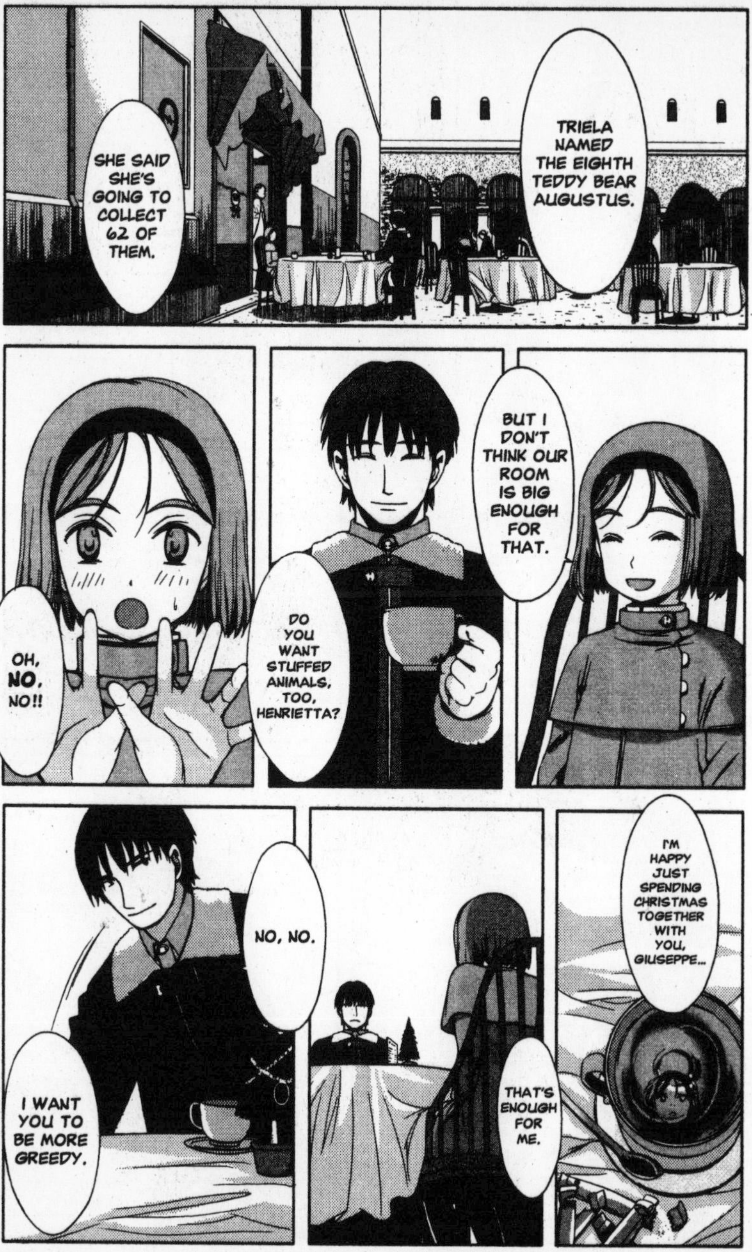
TRIELA NAMED THE EIGHTH TEDDY BEAR AUGUSTUS.
SHE SAID SHE'S GOING TO COLLECT 62 OF THEM.
BUT I DON'T THINK OUR ROOM IS BIG ENOUGH FOR THAT.
DO YOU WANT STUFFED ANIMALS, TOO, HENRIETTA?
OH, **NO**, NO!!
I'M HAPPY JUST SPENDING CHRISTMAS TOGETHER WITH YOU, GIUSEPPE...
THAT'S ENOUGH FOR ME.
NO, NO.
I WANT YOU TO BE MORE GREEDY.

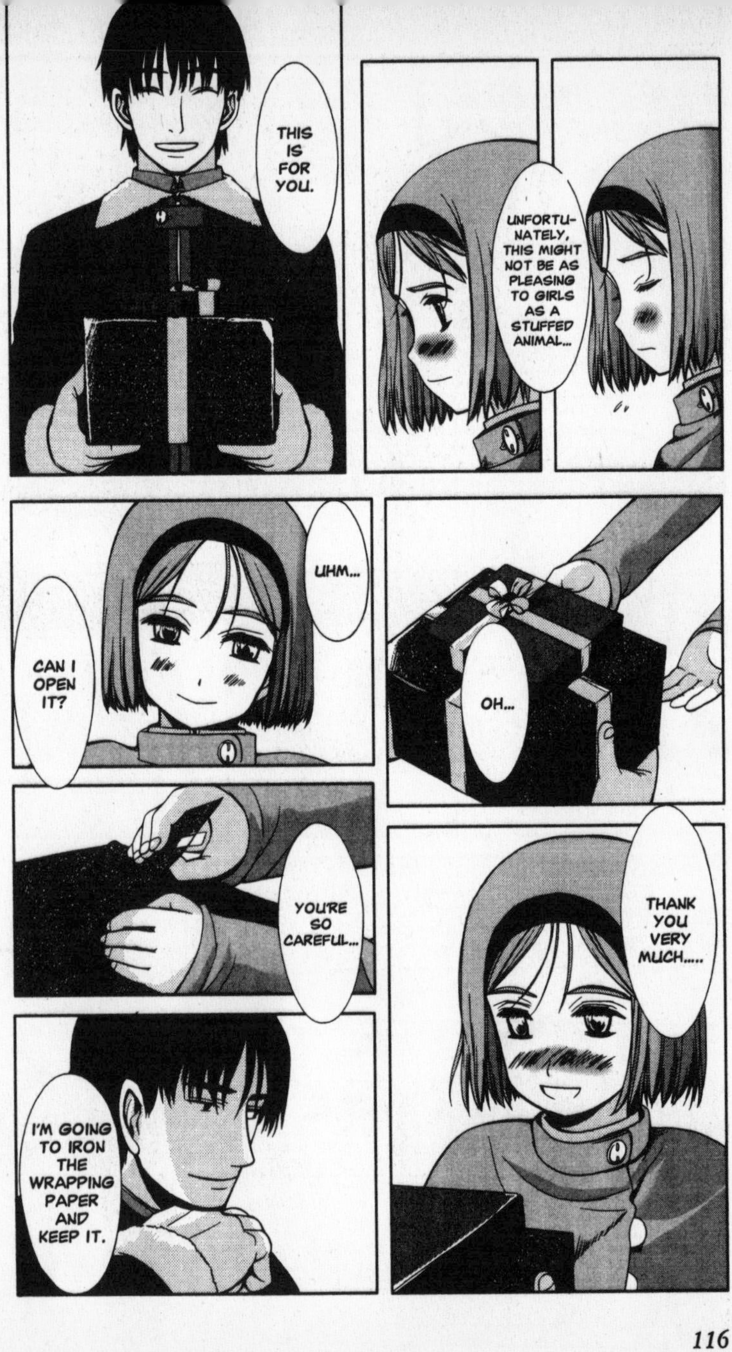
THIS IS FOR YOU.
UNFORTUNATELY, THIS MIGHT NOT BE AS PLEASING TO GIRLS AS A STUFFED ANIMAL...
UHM...
CAN I OPEN IT?
OH...
YOU'RE SO CAREFUL...
I'M GOING TO IRON THE WRAPPING PAPER AND KEEP IT.
THANK YOU VERY MUCH.....

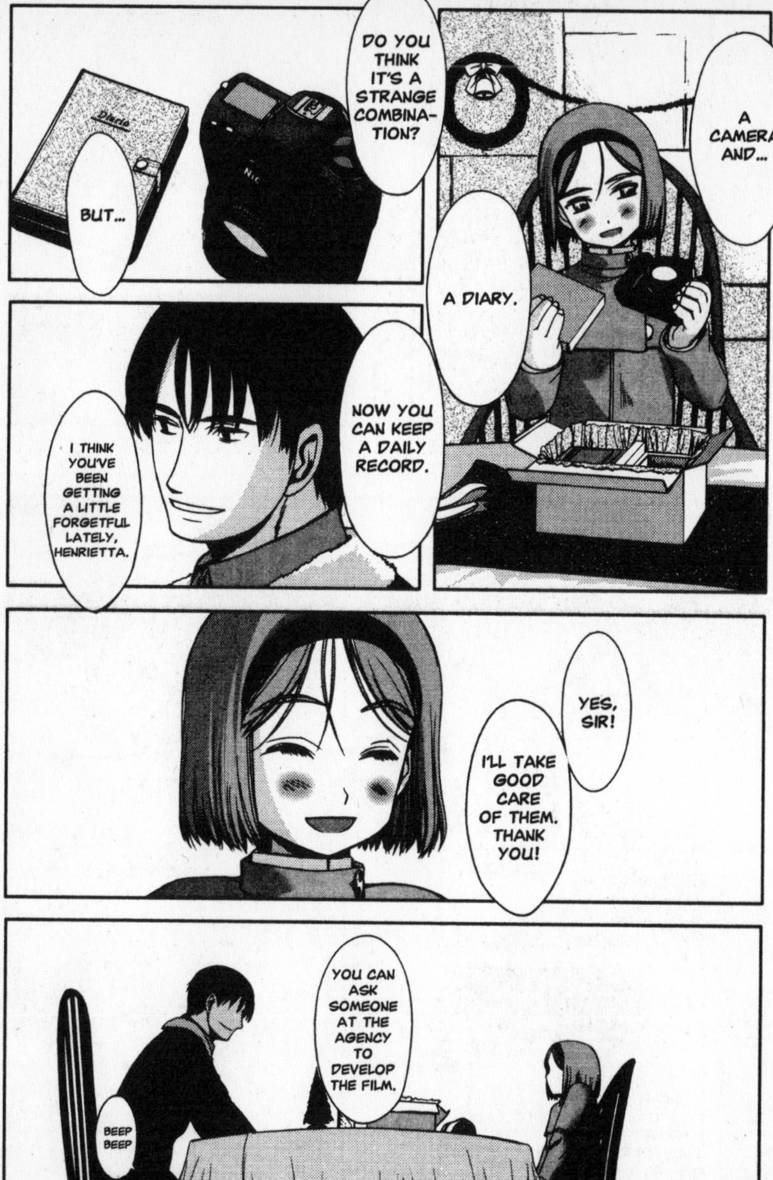
A CAMERA AND...
A DIARY.
DO YOU THINK IT'S A STRANGE COMBINATION?
BUT...
NOW YOU CAN KEEP A DAILY RECORD.
I THINK YOU'VE BEEN GETTING A LITTLE FORGETFUL LATELY, HENRIETTA.
YES, SIR!
I'LL TAKE GOOD CARE OF THEM. THANK YOU!
YOU CAN ASK SOMEONE AT THE AGENCY TO DEVELOP THE FILM.
BEEP BEEP

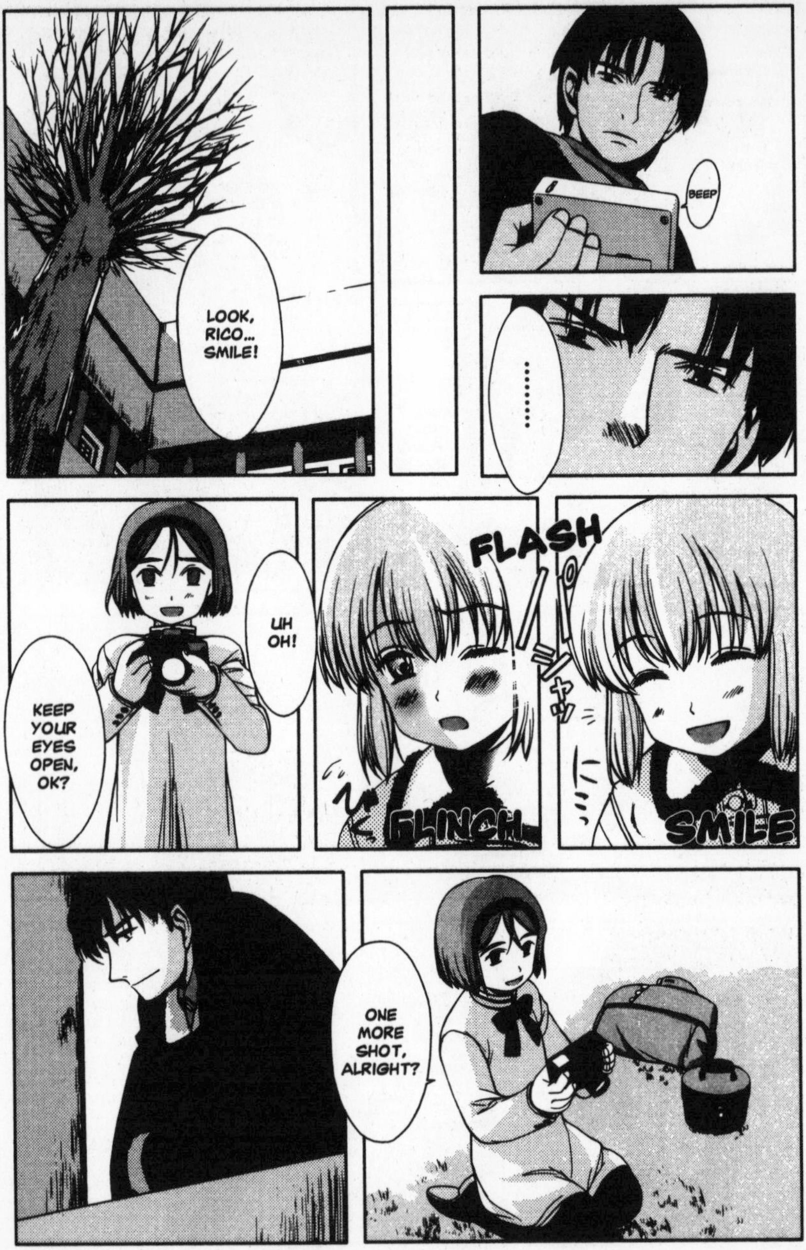
BEEP
....
LOOK, RICO... SMILE!
FLASH
SMILE
FLINCH
UH OH!
KEEP YOUR EYES OPEN, OK?
ONE MORE SHOT, ALRIGHT?

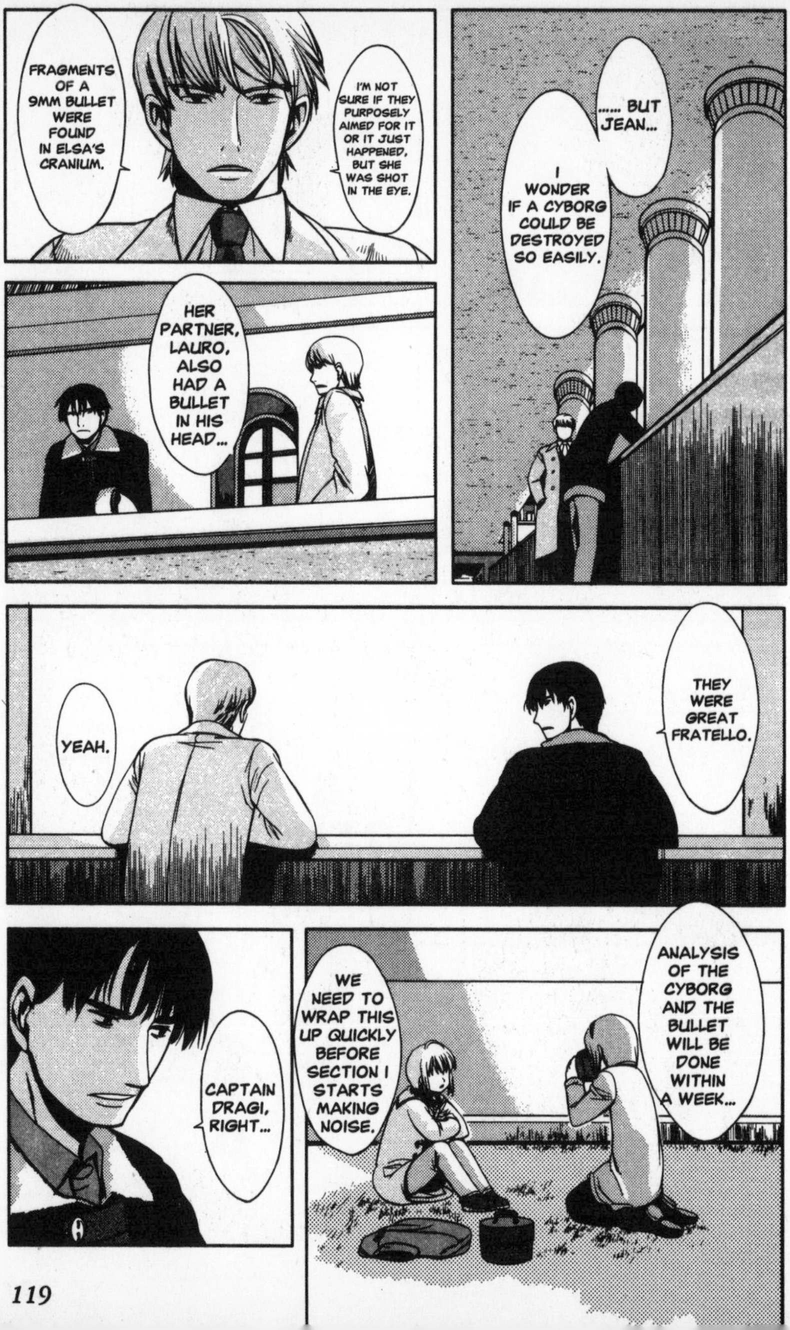
...... BUT JEAN...
I WONDER IF A CYBORG COULD BE DESTROYED SO EASILY.
FRAGMENTS OF A 9MM BULLET WERE FOUND IN ELSA'S CRANIUM.
I'M NOT SURE IF THEY PURPOSELY AIMED FOR IT OR IT JUST HAPPENED, BUT SHE WAS SHOT IN THE EYE.
HER PARTNER, LAURO, ALSO HAD A BULLET IN HIS HEAD...
THEY WERE GREAT FRATELLO.
YEAH.
ANALYSIS OF THE CYBORG AND THE BULLET WILL BE DONE WITHIN A WEEK...
WE NEED TO WRAP THIS UP QUICKLY BEFORE SECTION I STARTS MAKING NOISE.
CAPTAIN DRAGI, RIGHT...

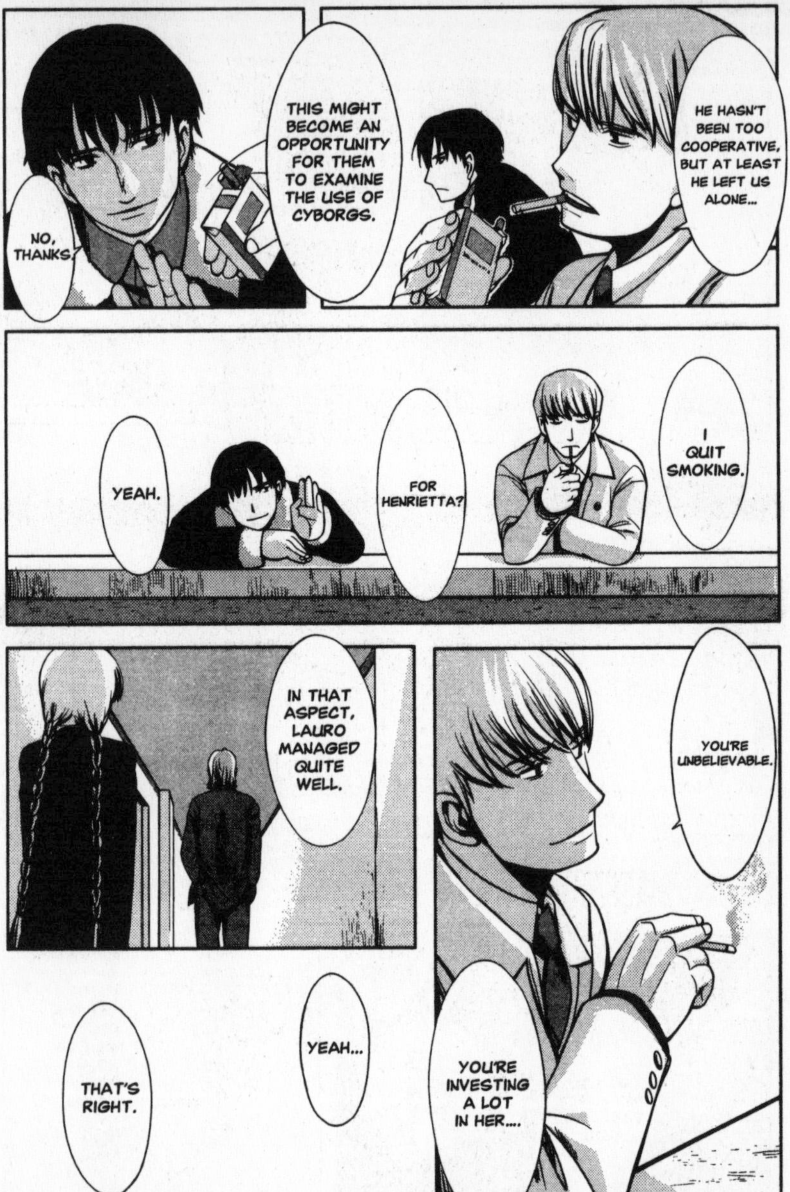
HE HASN'T BEEN TOO COOPERATIVE, BUT AT LEAST HE LEFT US ALONE...
THIS MIGHT BECOME AN OPPORTUNITY FOR THEM TO EXAMINE THE USE OF CYBORGS.
NO, THANKS.
I QUIT SMOKING.
FOR HENRIETTA?
YEAH.
YOU'RE UNBELIEVABLE.
YOU'RE INVESTING A LOT IN HER....
IN THAT ASPECT, LAURO MANAGED QUITE WELL.
YEAH...
THAT'S RIGHT.

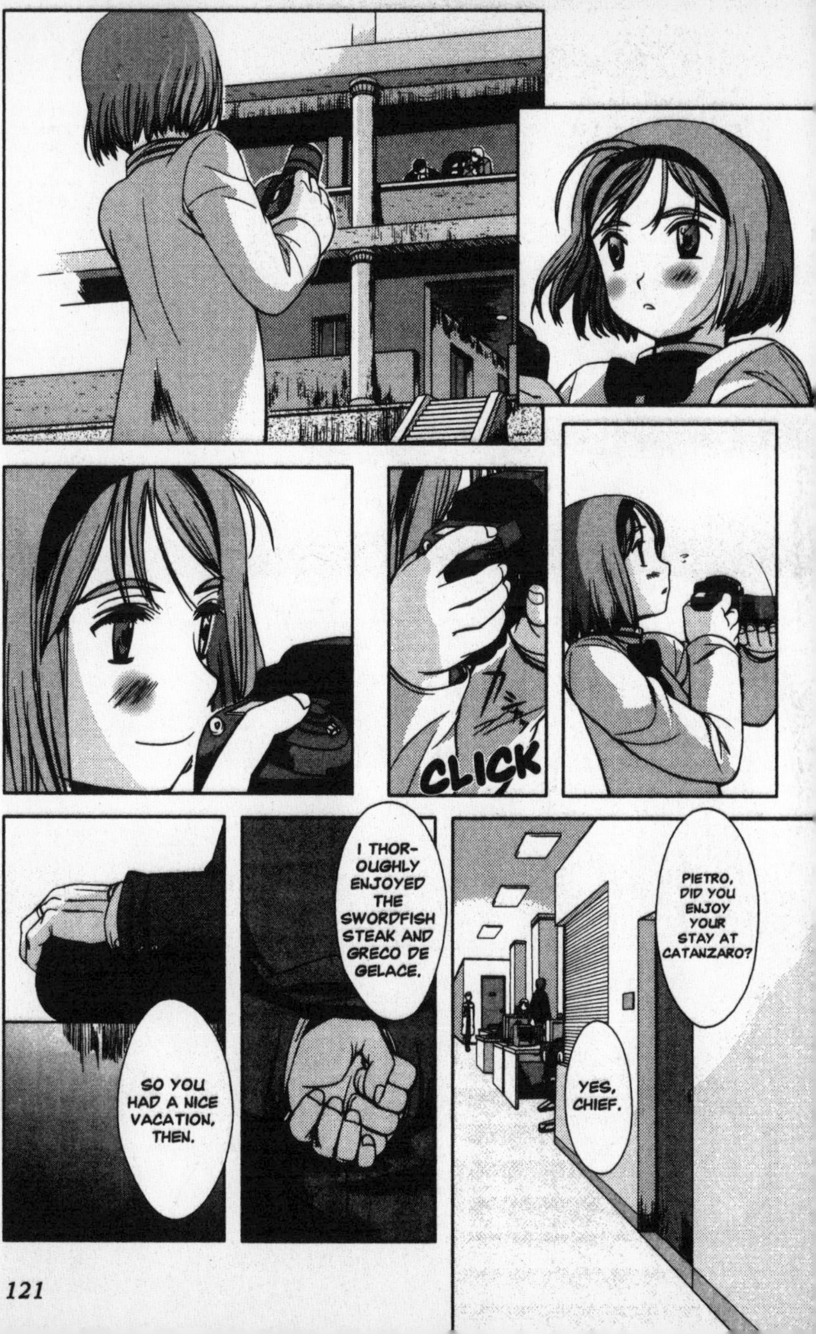
CLICK
PIETRO, DID YOU ENJOY YOUR STAY AT CATANZARO?
YES, CHIEF.
I THOROUGHLY ENJOYED THE SWORDFISH STEAK AND GRECO DE GELACE.
SO YOU HAD A NICE VACATION, THEN.

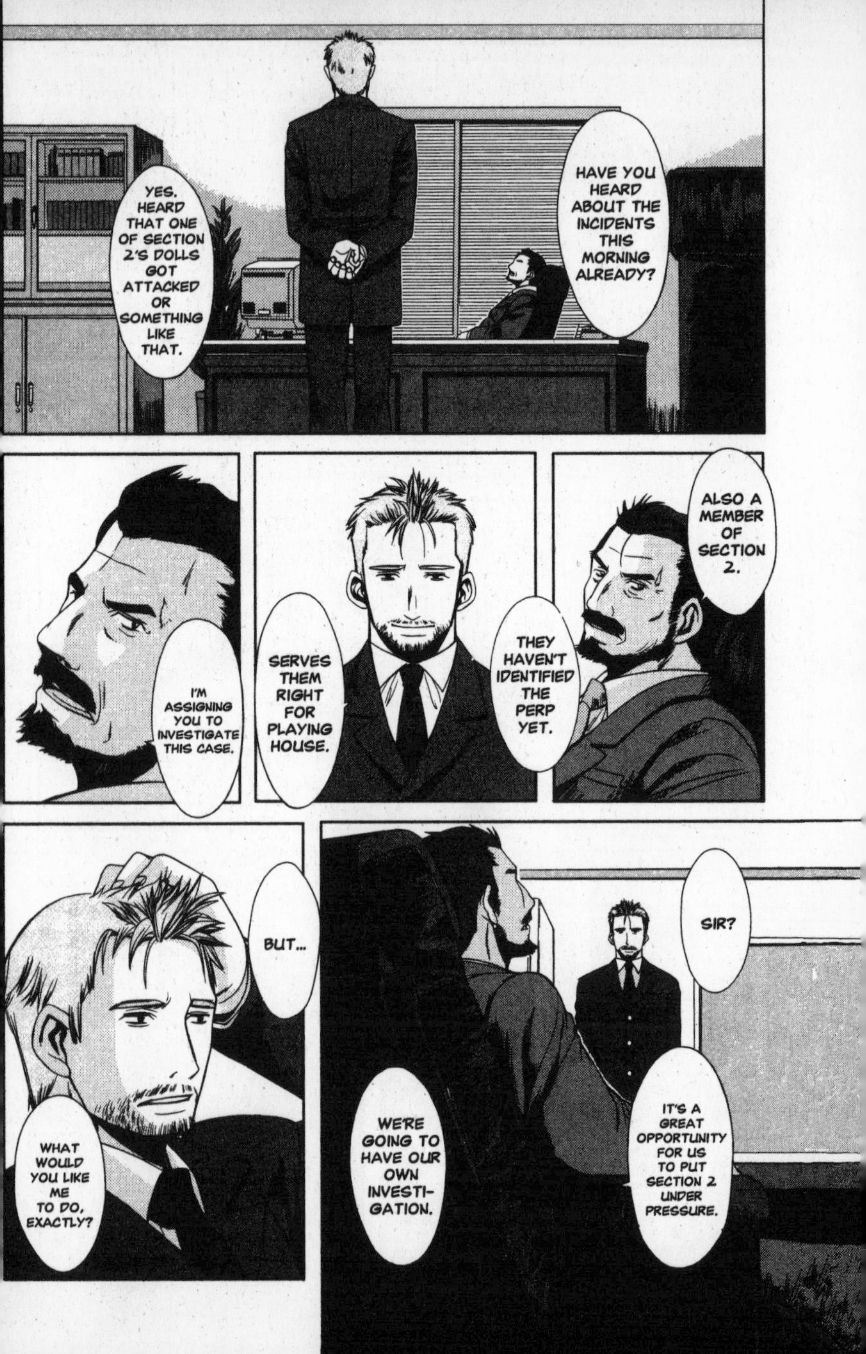
HAVE YOU HEARD ABOUT THE INCIDENTS THIS MORNING ALREADY?
YES. HEARD THAT ONE OF SECTION 2'S DOLLS GOT ATTACKED OR SOMETHING LIKE THAT.
ALSO A MEMBER OF SECTION 2.
THEY HAVEN'T IDENTIFIED THE PERP YET.
SERVES THEM RIGHT FOR PLAYING HOUSE.
I'M ASSIGNING YOU TO INVESTIGATE THIS CASE.
SIR?
IT'S A GREAT OPPORTUNITY FOR US TO PUT SECTION 2 UNDER PRESSURE.
WE'RE GOING TO HAVE OUR OWN INVESTI-GATION.
BUT...
WHAT WOULD YOU LIKE ME TO DO, EXACTLY?

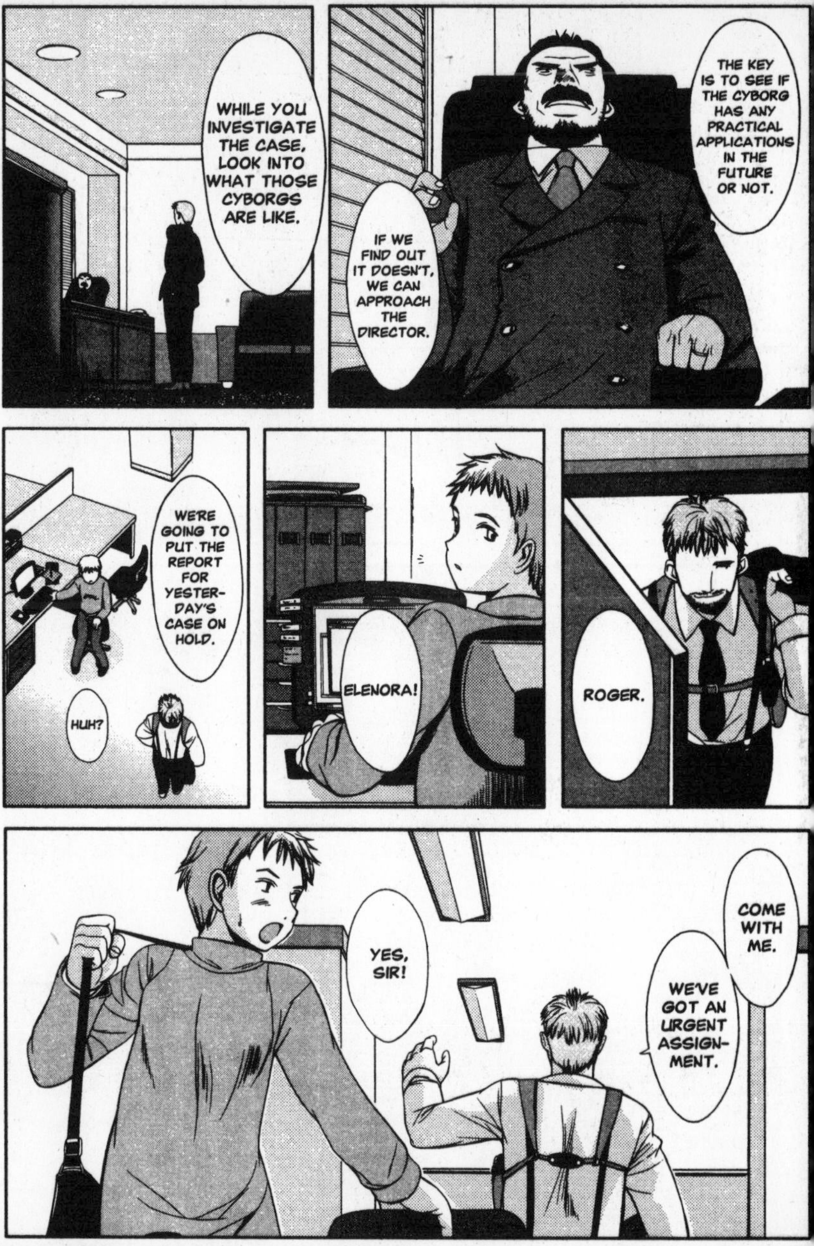
WHILE YOU INVESTIGATE THE CASE, LOOK INTO WHAT THOSE CYBORGS ARE LIKE.
THE KEY IS TO SEE IF THE CYBORG HAS ANY PRACTICAL APPLICATIONS IN THE FUTURE OR NOT.
IF WE FIND OUT IT DOESN'T, WE CAN APPROACH THE DIRECTOR.
WE'RE GOING TO PUT THE REPORT FOR YESTER-DAY'S CASE ON HOLD.
HUH?
ELENORA!
ROGER.
COME WITH ME.
WE'VE GOT AN URGENT ASSIGN-MENT.
YES, SIR!

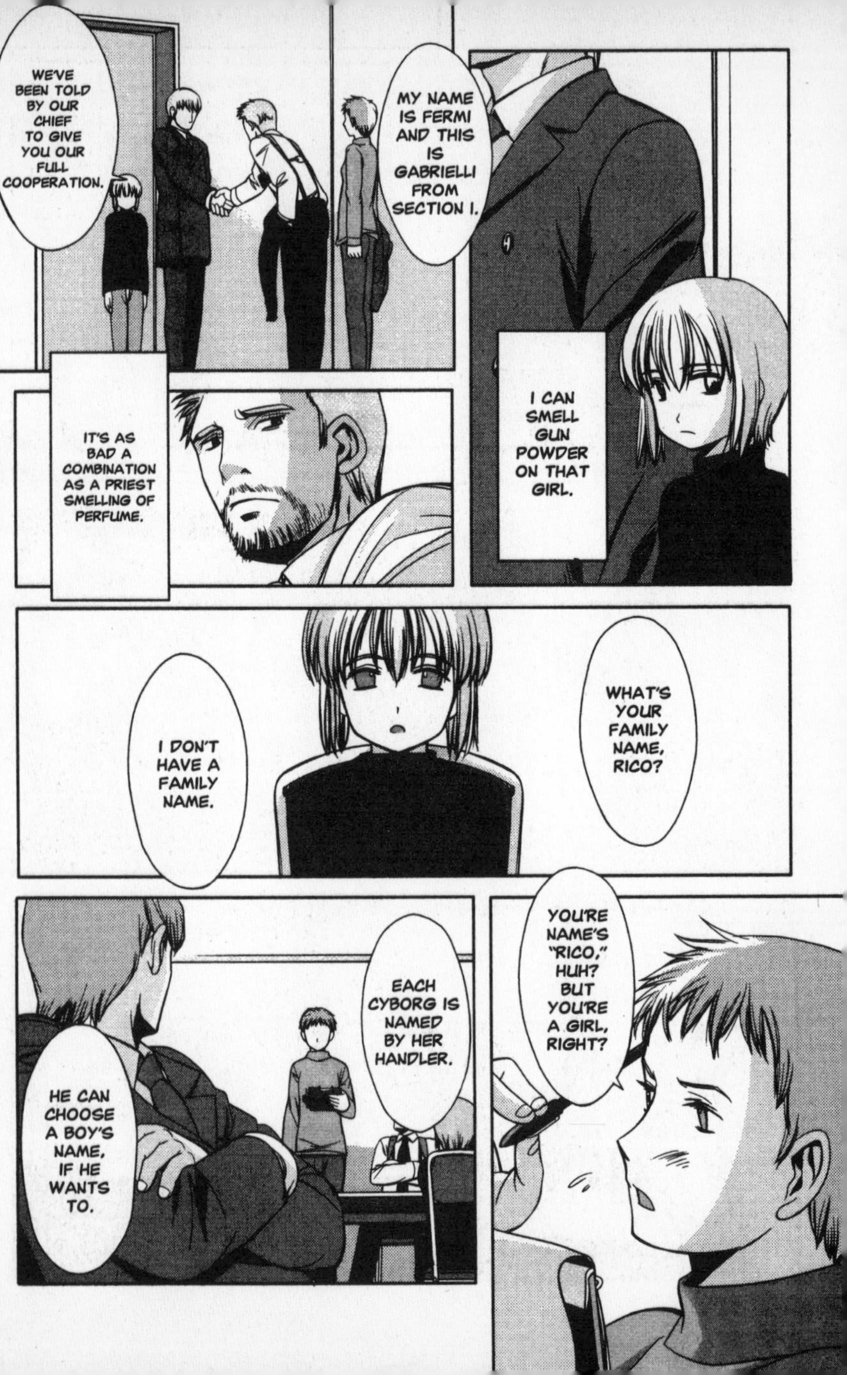
MY NAME IS FERMI AND THIS IS GABRIELLI FROM SECTION I.
WE'VE BEEN TOLD BY OUR CHIEF TO GIVE YOU OUR FULL COOPERATION.
I CAN SMELL GUN POWDER ON THAT GIRL.
IT'S AS BAD A COMBINATION AS A PRIEST SMELLING OF PERFUME.
WHAT'S YOUR FAMILY NAME, RICO?
I DON'T HAVE A FAMILY NAME.
YOU'RE NAME'S "RICO," HUH? BUT YOU'RE A GIRL, RIGHT?
EACH CYBORG IS NAMED BY HER HANDLER.
HE CAN CHOOSE A BOY'S NAME, IF HE WANTS TO.

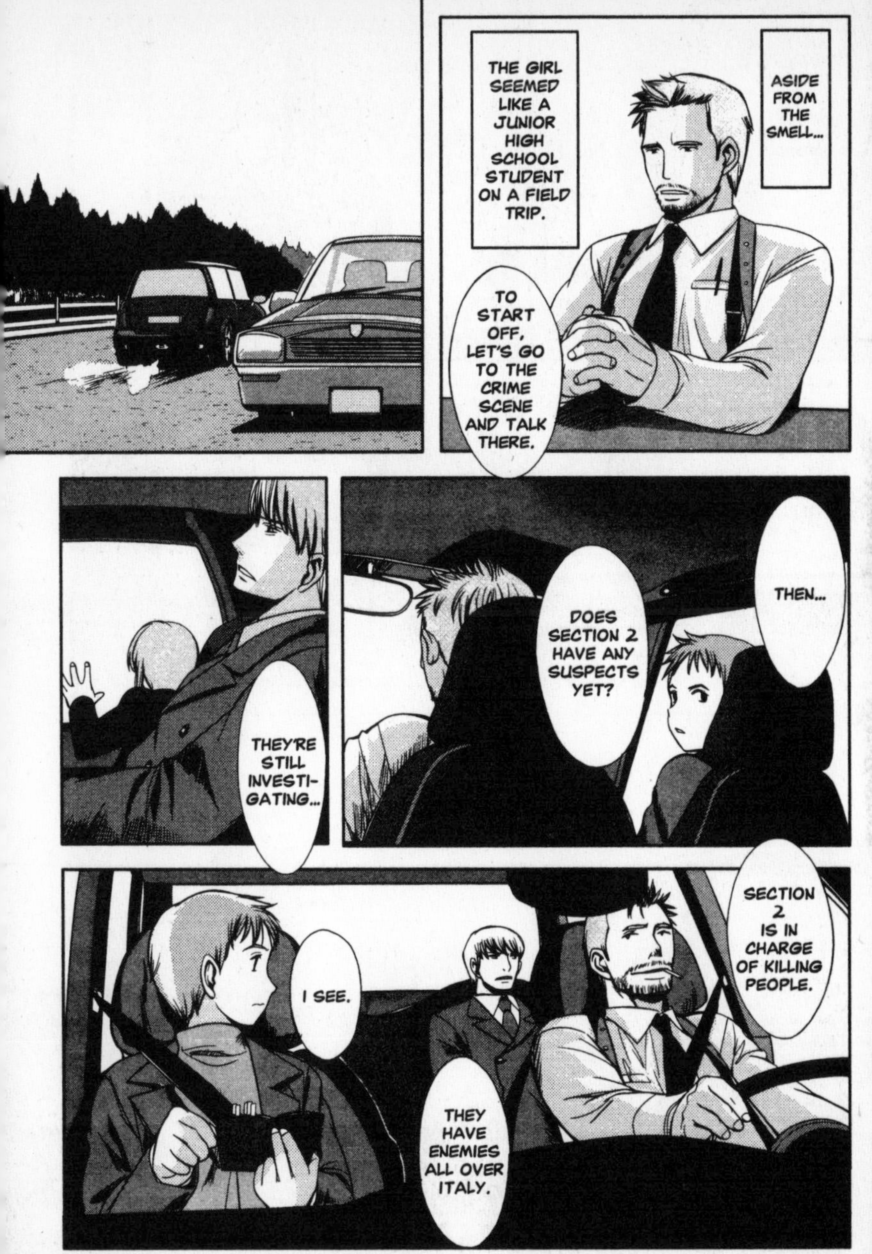
ASIDE FROM THE SMELL...
THE GIRL SEEMED LIKE A JUNIOR HIGH SCHOOL STUDENT ON A FIELD TRIP.
TO START OFF, LET'S GO TO THE CRIME SCENE AND TALK THERE.
THEN...
DOES SECTION 2 HAVE ANY SUSPECTS YET?
THEY'RE STILL INVESTI-GATING...
SECTION 2 IS IN CHARGE OF KILLING PEOPLE.
THEY HAVE ENEMIES ALL OVER ITALY.
I SEE.

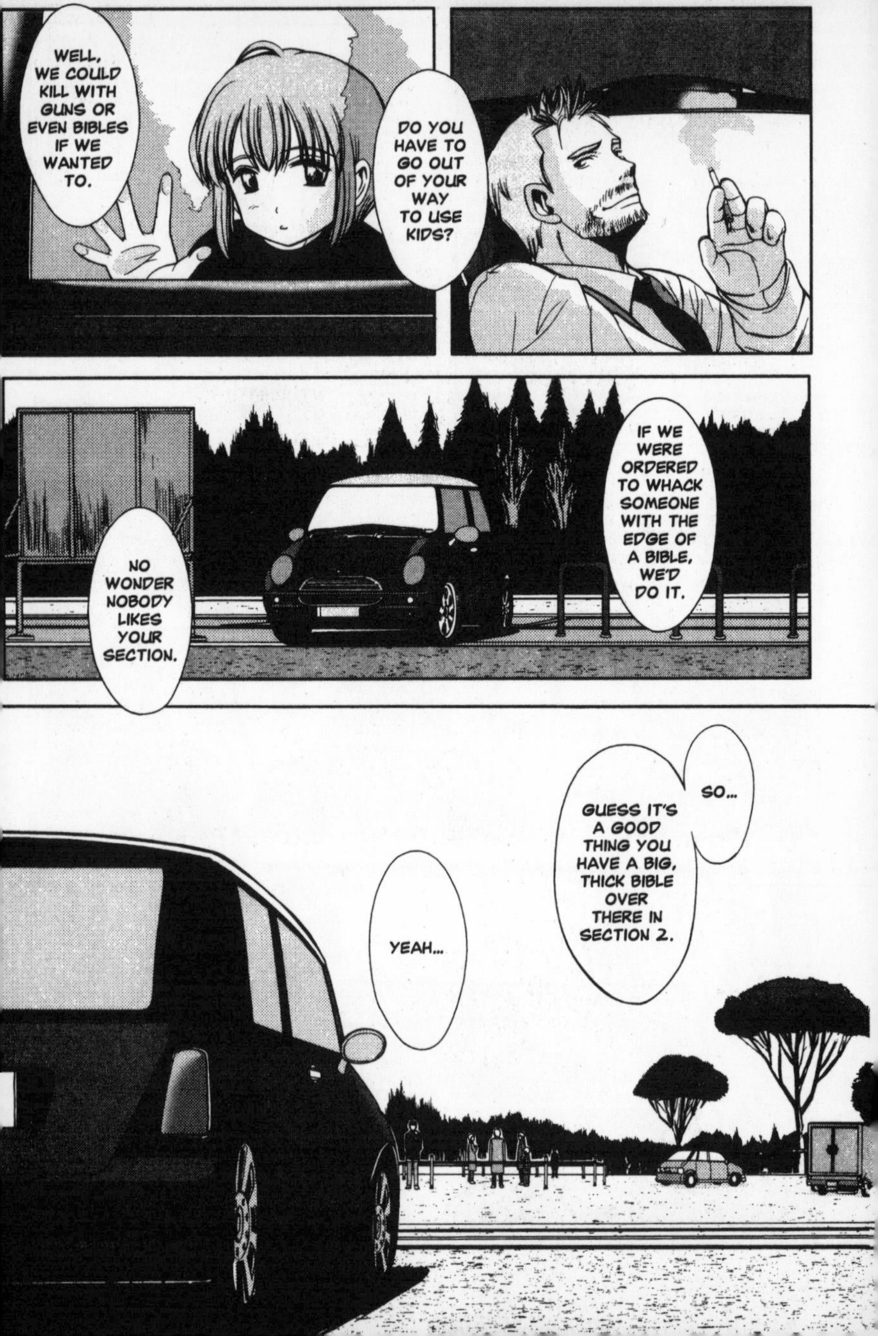
DO YOU HAVE TO GO OUT OF YOUR WAY TO USE KIDS?
WELL, WE COULD KILL WITH GUNS OR EVEN BIBLES IF WE WANTED TO.
IF WE WERE ORDERED TO WHACK SOMEONE WITH THE EDGE OF A BIBLE, WE'D DO IT.
NO WONDER NOBODY LIKES YOUR SECTION.
SO...
GUESS IT'S A GOOD THING YOU HAVE A BIG, THICK BIBLE OVER THERE IN SECTION 2.
YEAH...

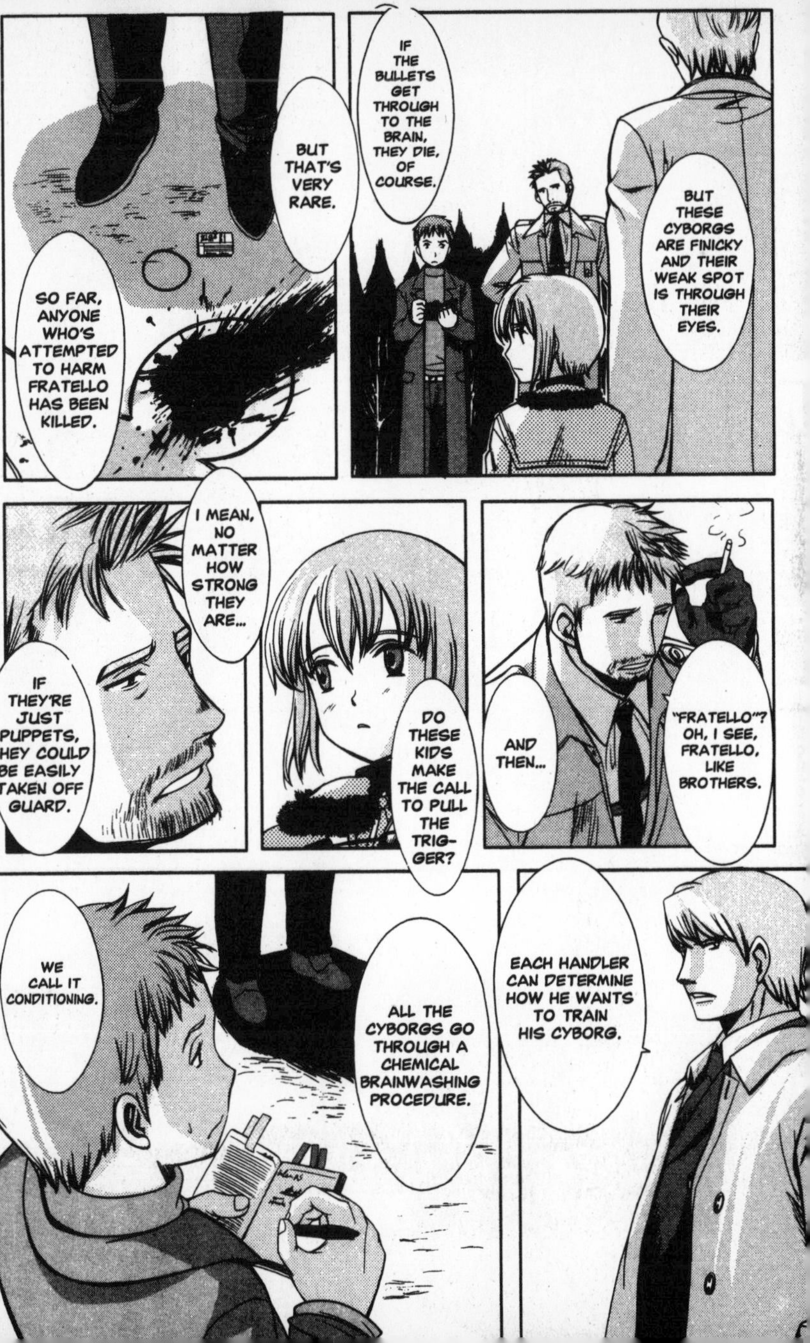
BUT THESE CYBORGS ARE FINICKY AND THEIR WEAK SPOT IS THROUGH THEIR EYES.
IF THE BULLETS GET THROUGH TO THE BRAIN, THEY DIE, OF COURSE.
BUT THAT'S VERY RARE.
SO FAR, ANYONE WHO'S ATTEMPTED TO HARM FRATELLO HAS BEEN KILLED.
"FRATELLO"? OH, I SEE, FRATELLO, LIKE BROTHERS.
AND THEN...
DO THESE KIDS MAKE THE CALL TO PULL THE TRIG-GER?
I MEAN, NO MATTER HOW STRONG THEY ARE...
IF THEY'RE JUST PUPPETS, THEY COULD BE EASILY TAKEN OFF GUARD.
EACH HANDLER CAN DETERMINE HOW HE WANTS TO TRAIN HIS CYBORG.
ALL THE CYBORGS GO THROUGH A CHEMICAL BRAINWASHING PROCEDURE.
WE CALL IT CONDITIONING.

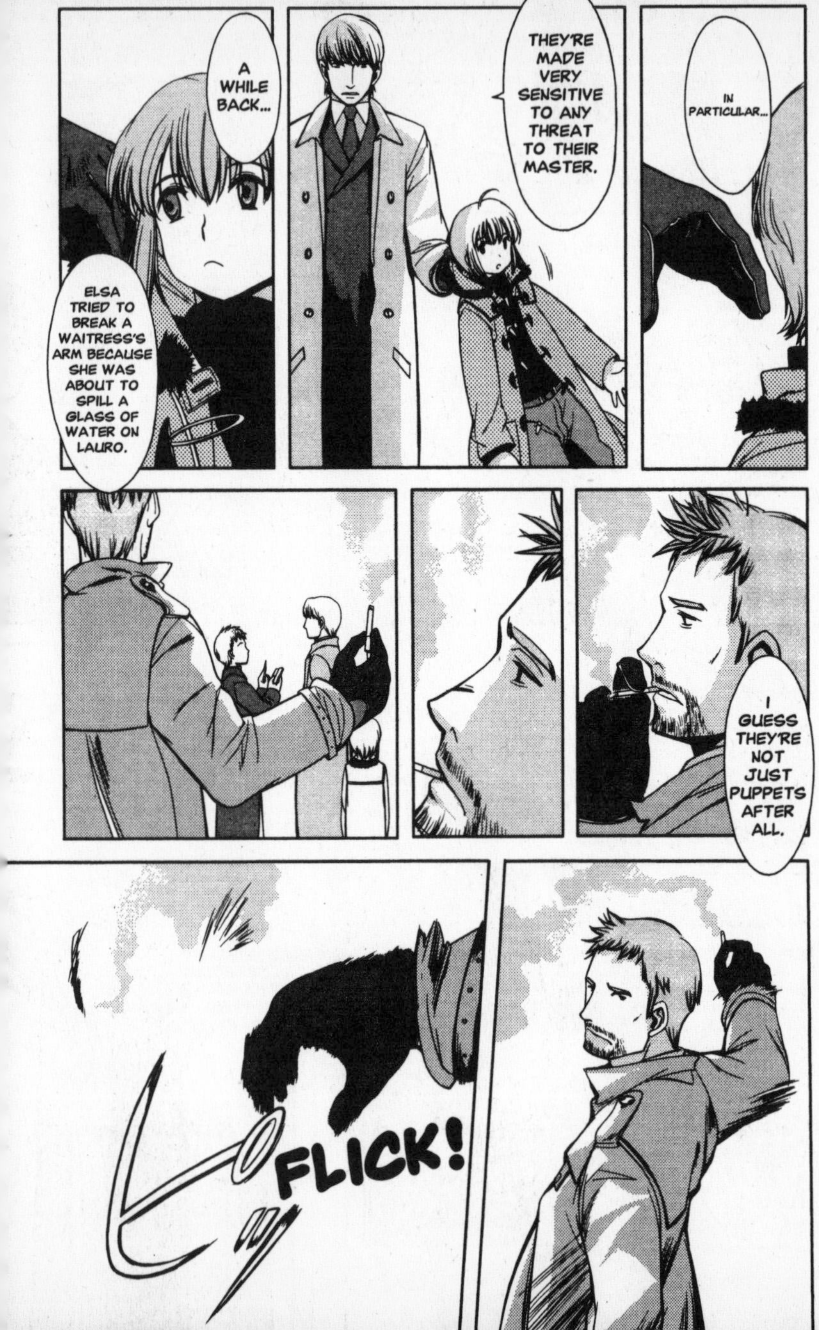
A WHILE BACK...
THEY'RE MADE VERY SENSITIVE TO ANY THREAT TO THEIR MASTER.
IN PARTICULAR...
ELSA TRIED TO BREAK A WAITRESS'S ARM BECAUSE SHE WAS ABOUT TO SPILL A GLASS OF WATER ON LAURO.
I GUESS THEY'RE NOT JUST PUPPETS AFTER ALL.
FLICK!

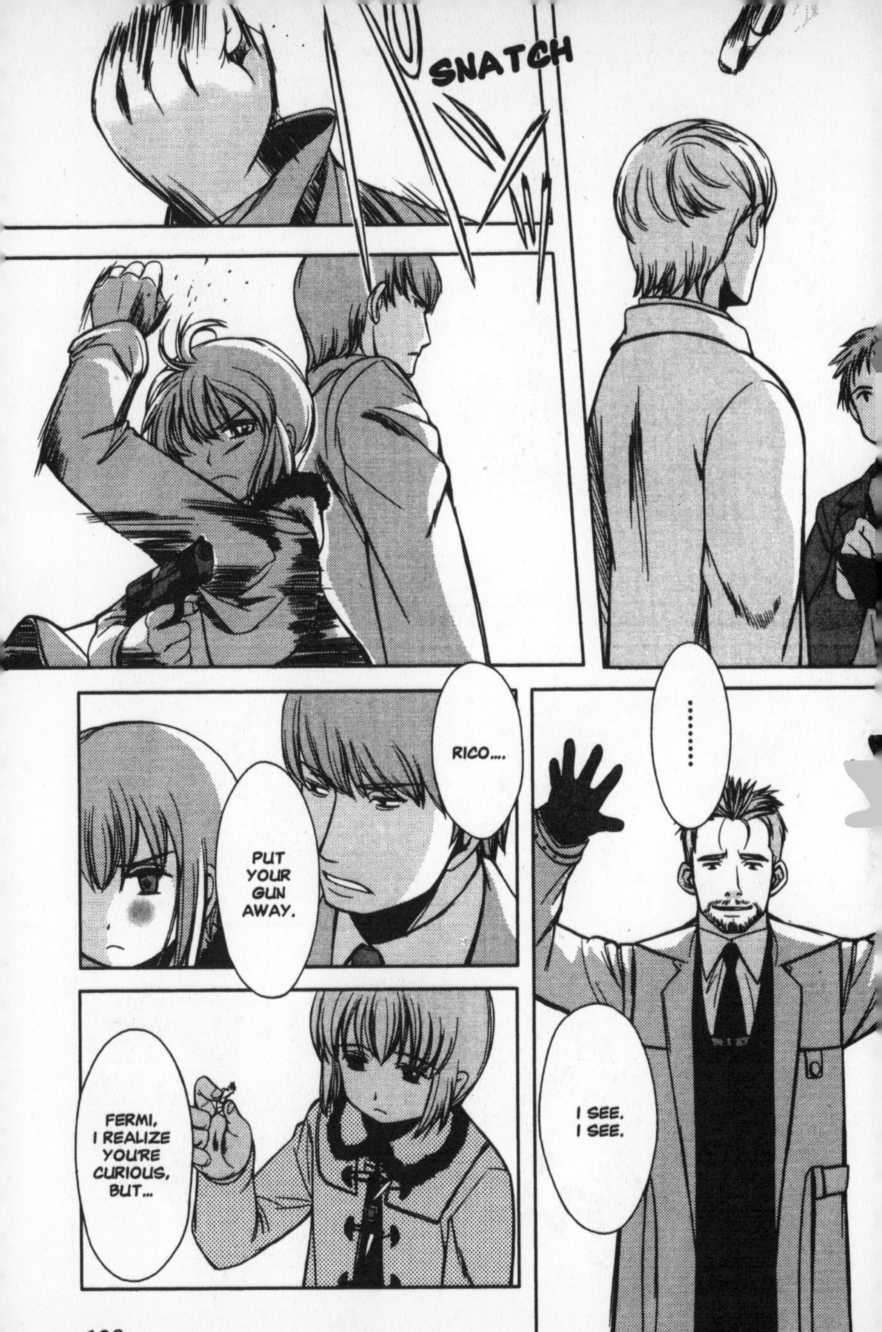
SNATCH
RICO....
PUT YOUR GUN AWAY.
....
I SEE. I SEE.
FERMI, I REALIZE YOU'RE CURIOUS, BUT...

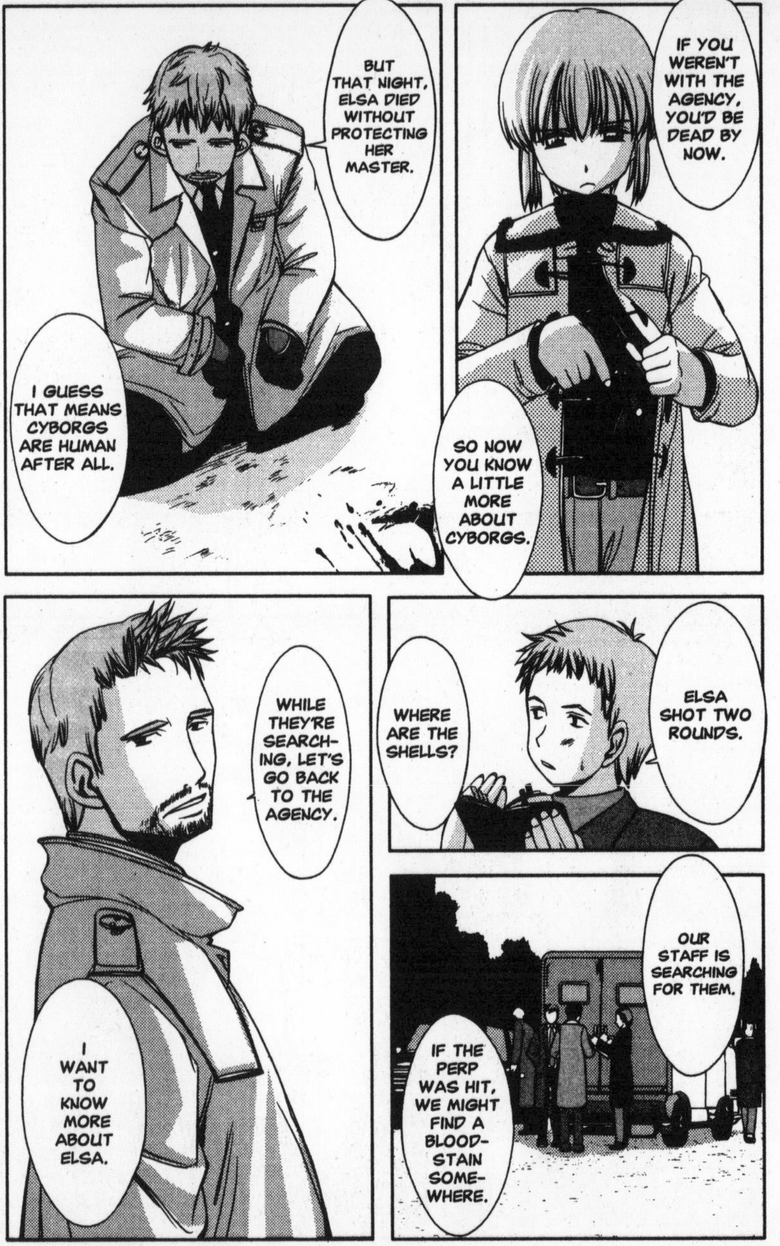
IF YOU WEREN'T WITH THE AGENCY, YOU'D BE DEAD BY NOW.
SO NOW YOU KNOW A LITTLE MORE ABOUT CYBORGS.
BUT THAT NIGHT, ELSA DIED WITHOUT PROTECTING HER MASTER.
I GUESS THAT MEANS CYBORGS ARE HUMAN AFTER ALL.
ELSA SHOT TWO ROUNDS.
WHERE ARE THE SHELLS?
OUR STAFF IS SEARCHING FOR THEM.
IF THE PERP WAS HIT, WE MIGHT FIND A BLOOD-STAIN SOME-WHERE.
WHILE THEY'RE SEARCH-ING, LET'S GO BACK TO THE AGENCY.
I WANT TO KNOW MORE ABOUT ELSA.

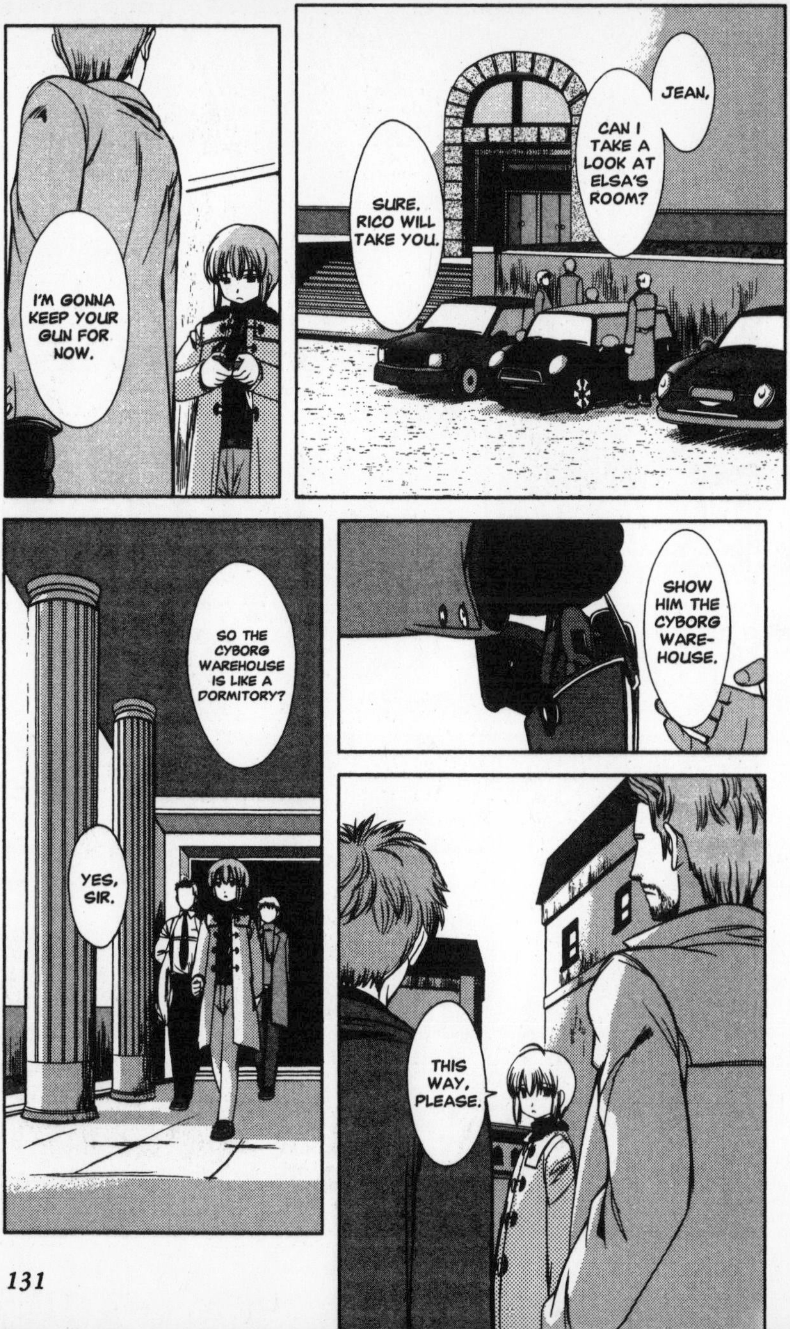
JEAN,
CAN I TAKE A LOOK AT ELSA'S ROOM?
SURE. RICO WILL TAKE YOU.
I'M GONNA KEEP YOUR GUN FOR NOW.
SHOW HIM THE CYBORG WARE-HOUSE.
THIS WAY, PLEASE.
SO THE CYBORG WAREHOUSE IS LIKE A DORMITORY?
YES, SIR.

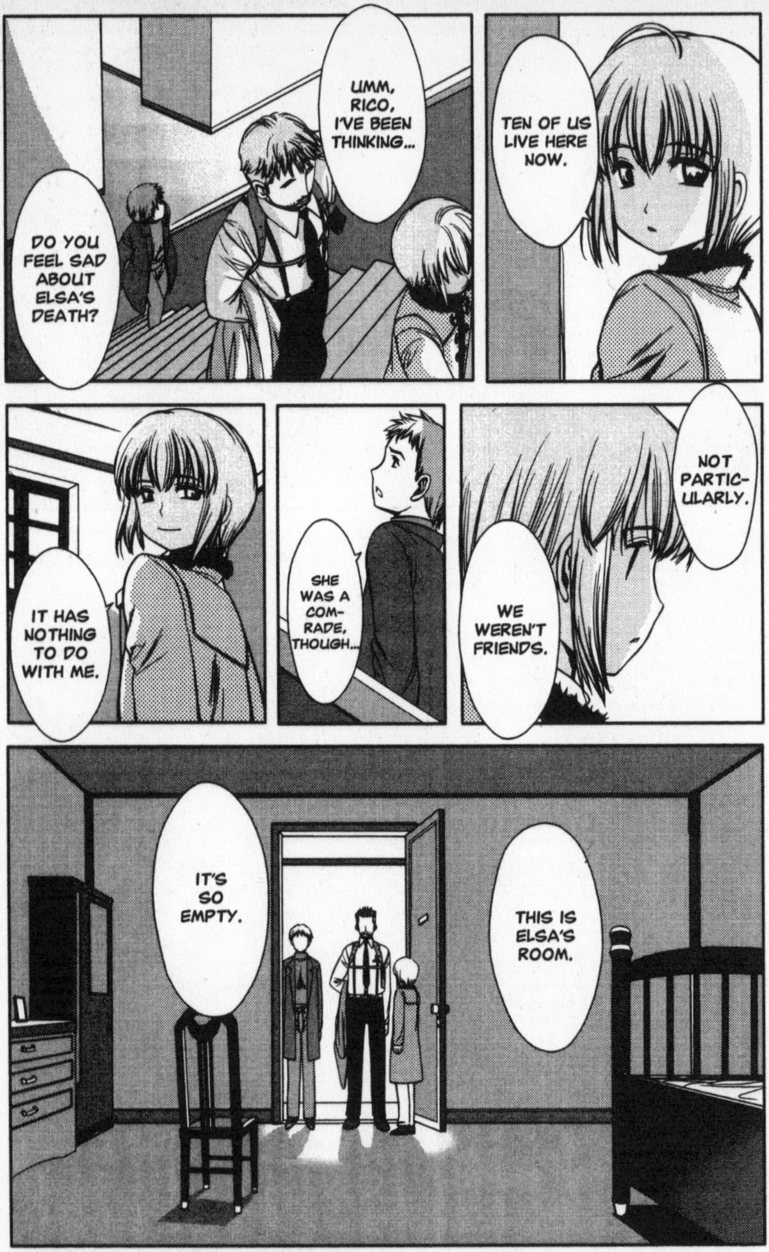
TEN OF US LIVE HERE NOW.
UMM, RICO, I'VE BEEN THINKING...
DO YOU FEEL SAD ABOUT ELSA'S DEATH?
NOT PARTIC-ULARLY.
WE WEREN'T FRIENDS.
SHE WAS A COM-RADE, THOUGH...
IT HAS NOTHING TO DO WITH ME.
THIS IS ELSA'S ROOM.
IT'S SO EMPTY.

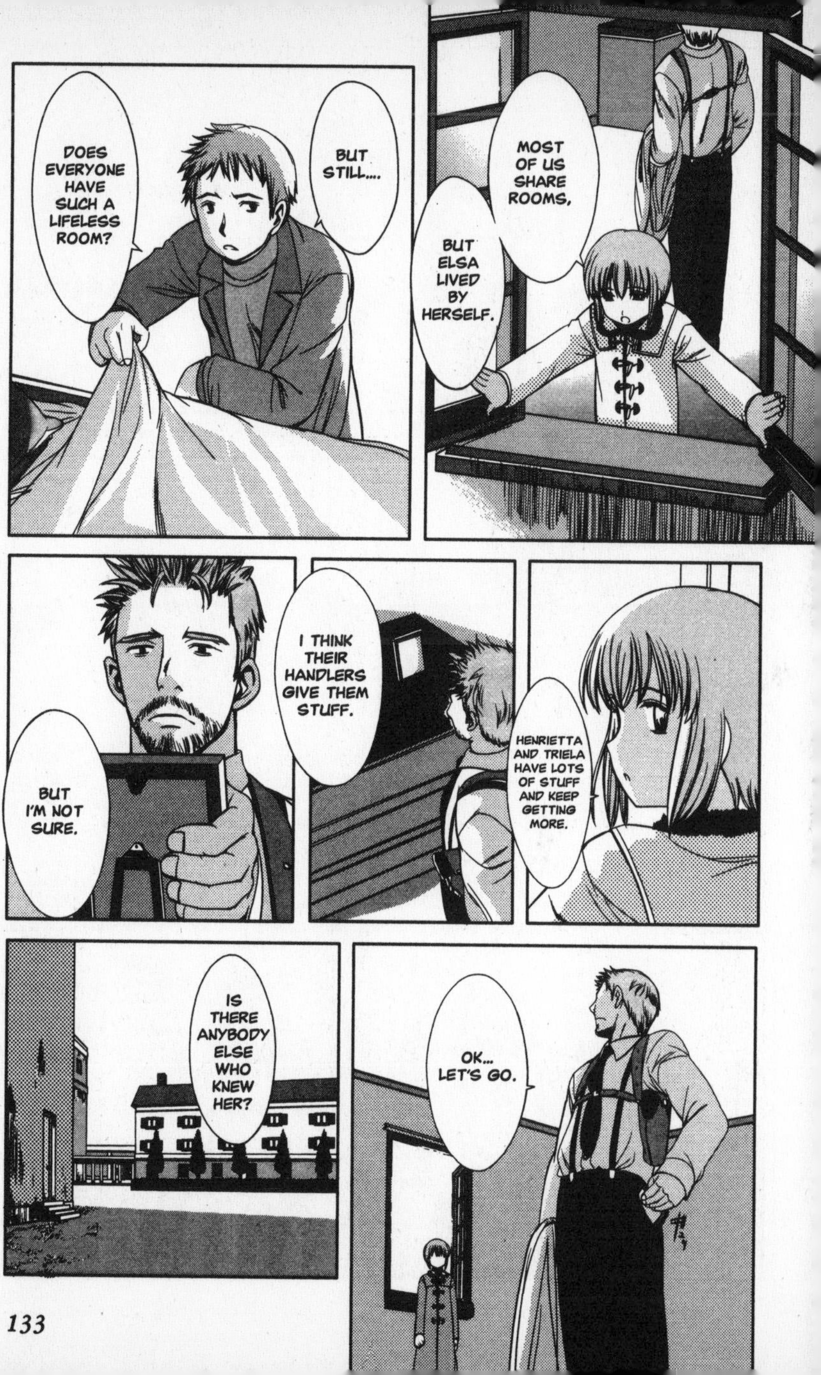
DOES EVERYONE HAVE SUCH A LIFELESS ROOM?
BUT STILL....
MOST OF US SHARE ROOMS,
BUT ELSA LIVED BY HERSELF.
I THINK THEIR HANDLERS GIVE THEM STUFF.
BUT I'M NOT SURE.
HENRIETTA AND TRIELA HAVE LOTS OF STUFF AND KEEP GETTING MORE.
IS THERE ANYBODY ELSE WHO KNEW HER?
OK... LET'S GO.

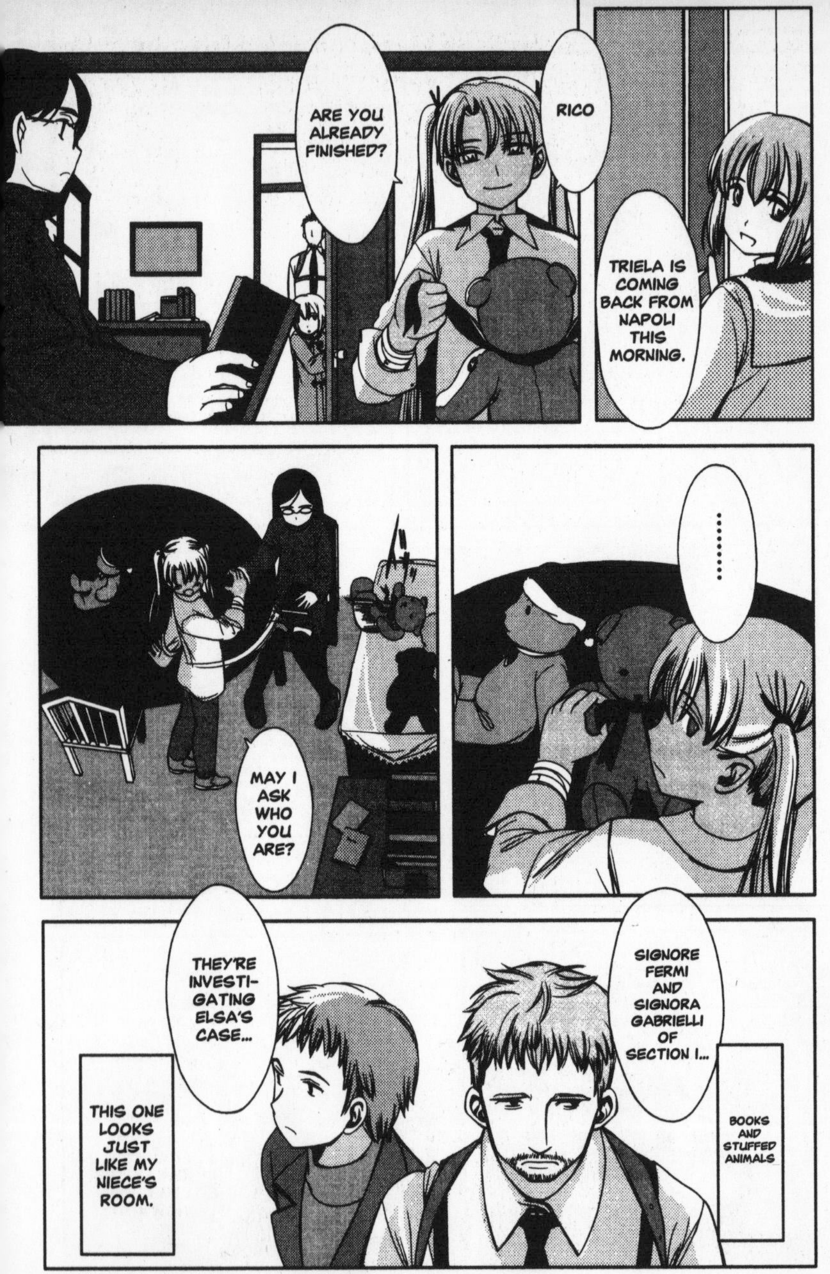
RICO
TRIELA IS COMING BACK FROM NAPOLI THIS MORNING.
ARE YOU ALREADY FINISHED?
......
MAY I ASK WHO YOU ARE?
SIGNORE FERMI AND SIGNORA GABRIELLI OF SECTION I...
THEY'RE INVESTI-GATING ELSA'S CASE...
BOOKS AND STUFFED ANIMALS
THIS ONE LOOKS JUST LIKE MY NIECE'S ROOM.

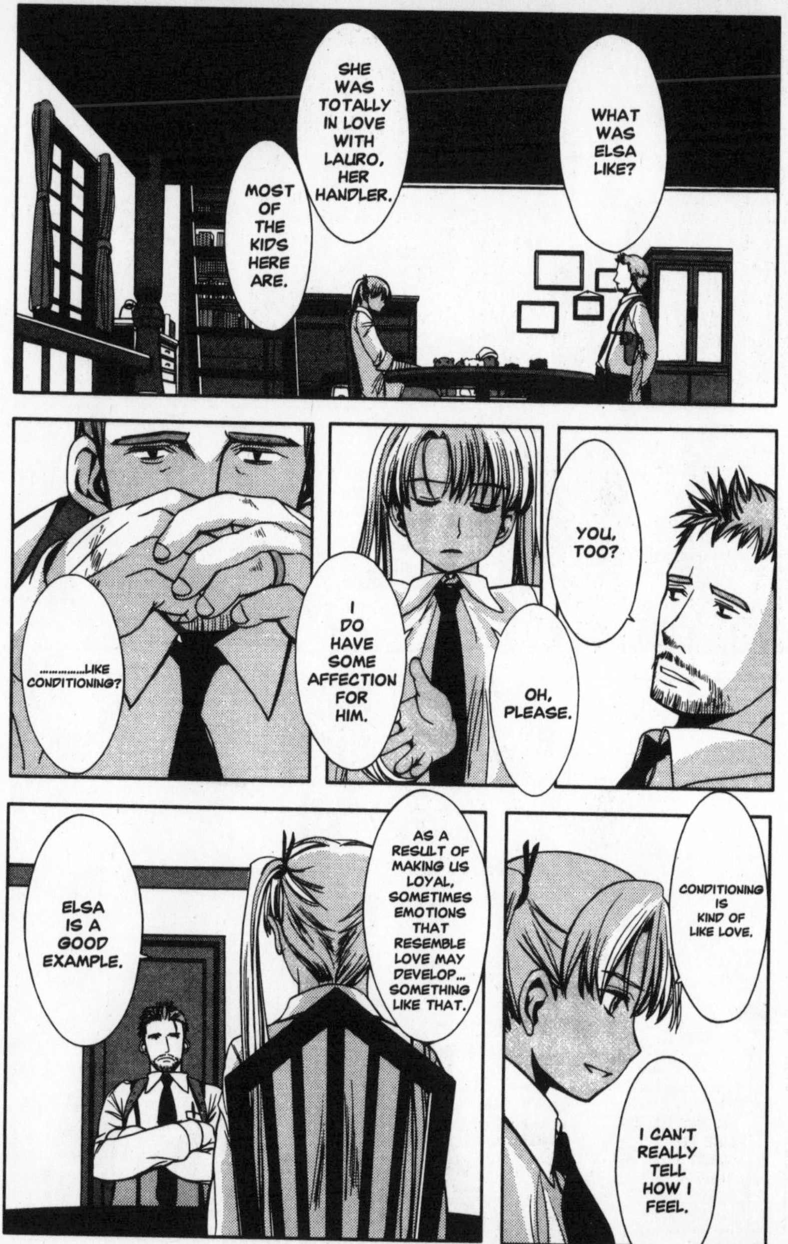
WHAT WAS ELSA LIKE?
SHE WAS TOTALLY IN LOVE WITH LAURO, HER HANDLER.
MOST OF THE KIDS HERE ARE.
YOU, TOO?
OH, PLEASE.
I DO HAVE SOME AFFECTION FOR HIM.
..............LIKE CONDITIONING?
CONDITIONING IS KIND OF LIKE LOVE.
I CAN'T REALLY TELL HOW I FEEL.
AS A RESULT OF MAKING US LOYAL, SOMETIMES EMOTIONS THAT RESEMBLE LOVE MAY DEVELOP... SOMETHING LIKE THAT.
ELSA IS A GOOD EXAMPLE.

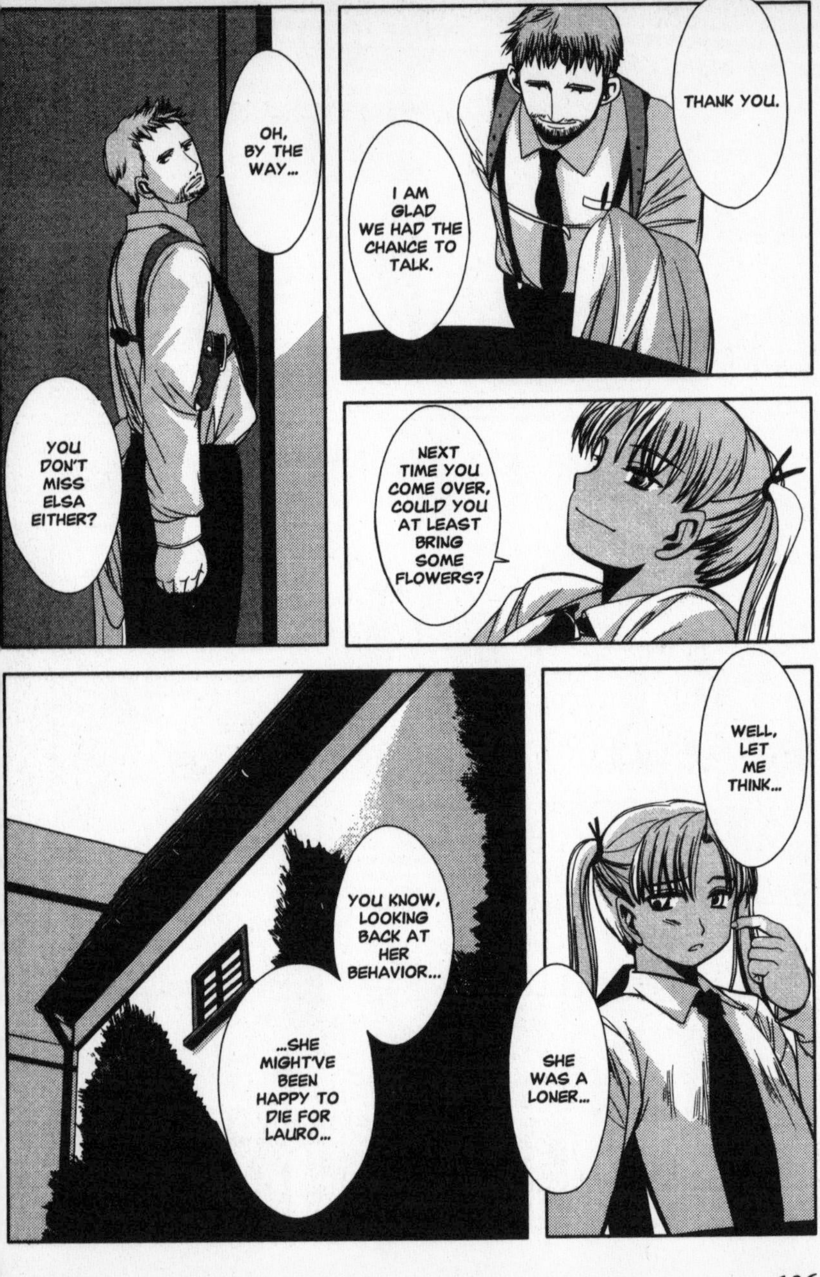
THANK YOU.
I AM GLAD WE HAD THE CHANCE TO TALK.
NEXT TIME YOU COME OVER, COULD YOU AT LEAST BRING SOME FLOWERS?
OH, BY THE WAY...
YOU DON'T MISS ELSA EITHER?
WELL, LET ME THINK...
SHE WAS A LONER...
YOU KNOW, LOOKING BACK AT HER BEHAVIOR...
...SHE MIGHT'VE BEEN HAPPY TO DIE FOR LAURO...

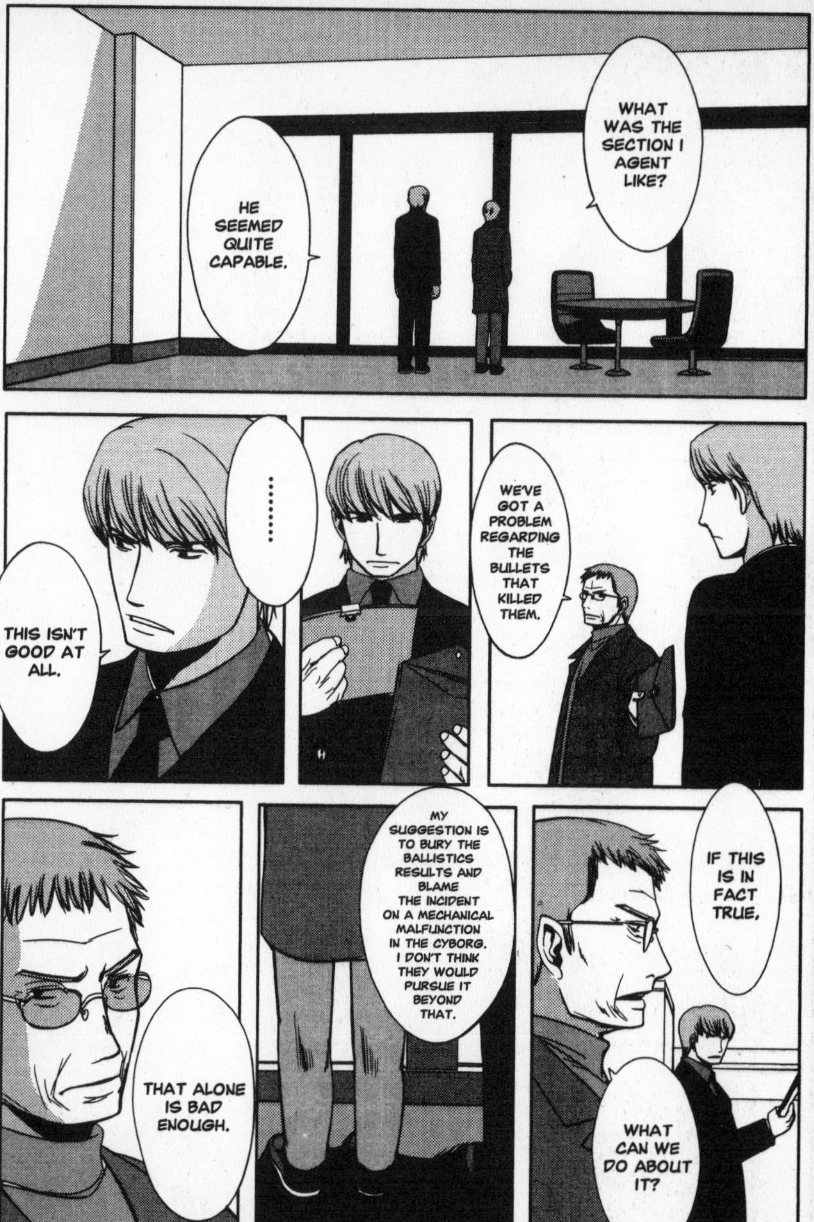
WHAT WAS THE SECTION I AGENT LIKE?
HE SEEMED QUITE CAPABLE.
......
THIS ISN'T GOOD AT ALL.
WE'VE GOT A PROBLEM REGARDING THE BULLETS THAT KILLED THEM.
THAT ALONE IS BAD ENOUGH.
MY SUGGESTION IS TO BURY THE BALLISTICS RESULTS AND BLAME THE INCIDENT ON A MECHANICAL MALFUNCTION IN THE CYBORG. I DON'T THINK THEY WOULD PURSUE IT BEYOND THAT.
IF THIS IS IN FACT TRUE,
WHAT CAN WE DO ABOUT IT?

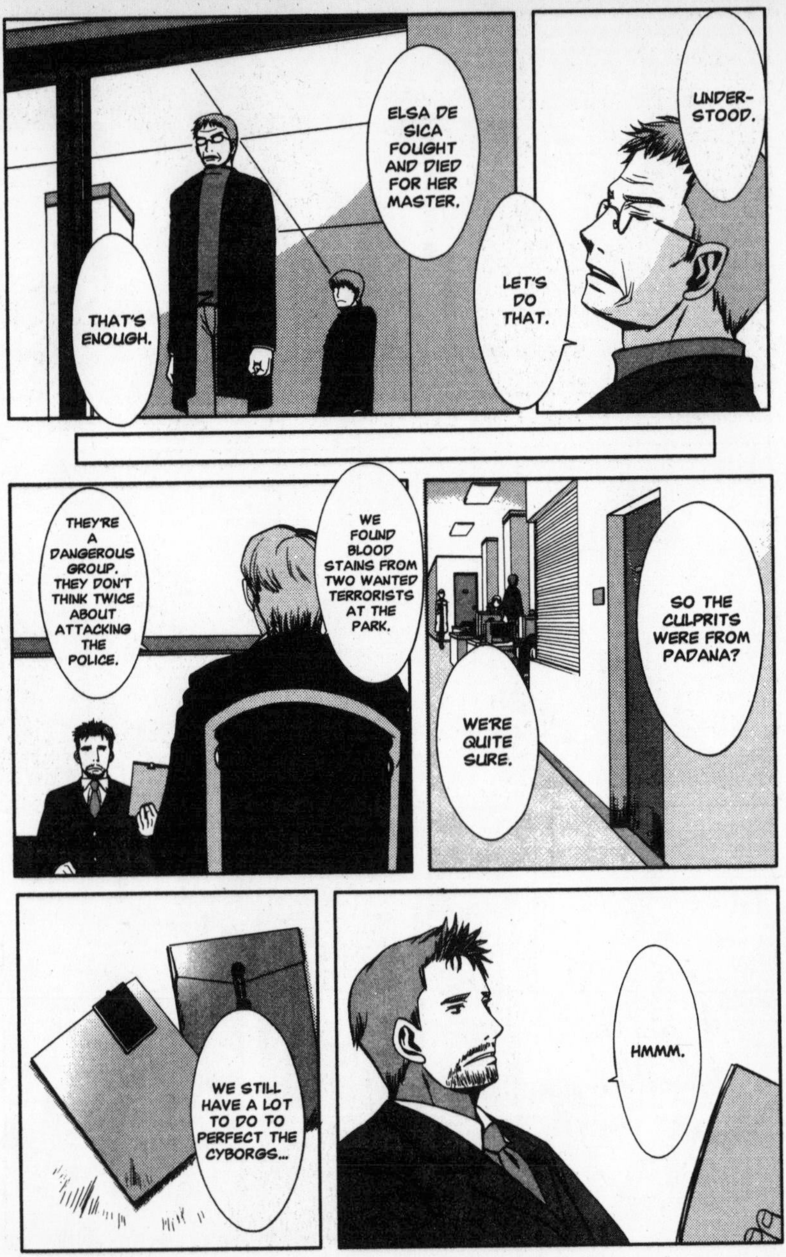
UNDER-STOOD.
LET'S DO THAT.
ELSA DE SICA FOUGHT AND DIED FOR HER MASTER.
THAT'S ENOUGH.
SO THE CULPRITS WERE FROM PADANA?
WE'RE QUITE SURE.
WE FOUND BLOOD STAINS FROM TWO WANTED TERRORISTS AT THE PARK.
THEY'RE A DANGEROUS GROUP. THEY DON'T THINK TWICE ABOUT ATTACKING THE POLICE.
HMMM.
WE STILL HAVE A LOT TO DO TO PERFECT THE CYBORGS...

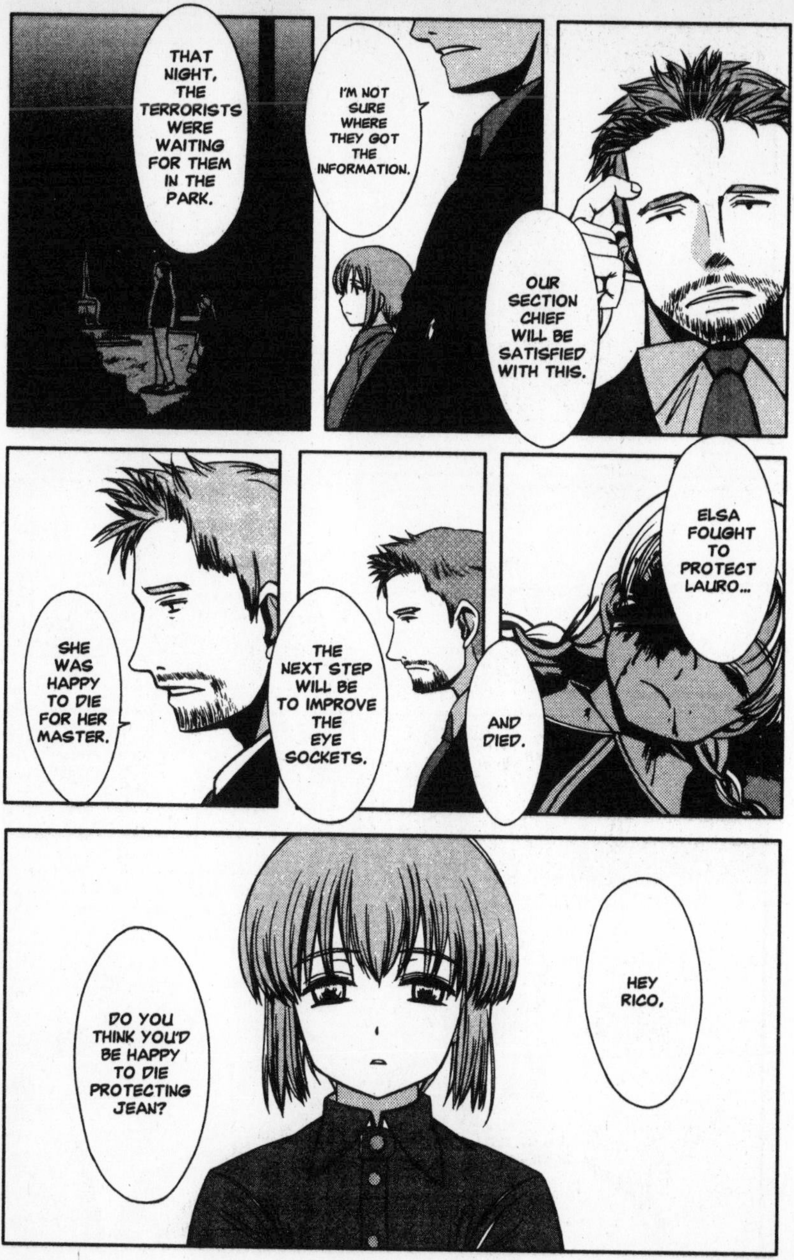
OUR SECTION CHIEF WILL BE SATISFIED WITH THIS.
I'M NOT SURE WHERE THEY GOT THE INFORMATION.
THAT NIGHT, THE TERRORISTS WERE WAITING FOR THEM IN THE PARK.
ELSA FOUGHT TO PROTECT LAURO...
AND DIED.
THE NEXT STEP WILL BE TO IMPROVE THE EYE SOCKETS.
SHE WAS HAPPY TO DIE FOR HER MASTER.
HEY RICO,
DO YOU THINK YOU'D BE HAPPY TO DIE PROTECTING JEAN?

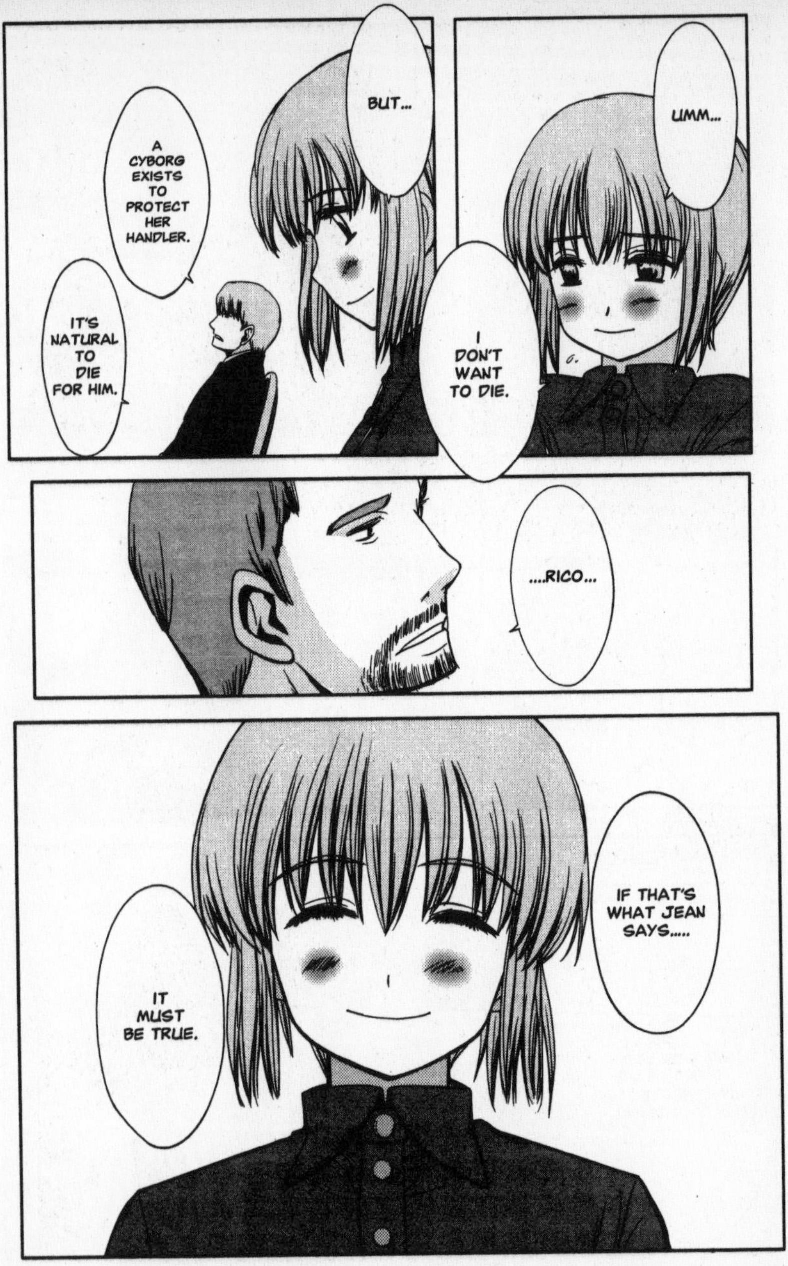
UMM...
I DON'T WANT TO DIE.
BUT...
A CYBORG EXISTS TO PROTECT HER HANDLER.
IT'S NATURAL TO DIE FOR HIM.
....RICO...
IF THAT'S WHAT JEAN SAYS.....
IT MUST BE TRUE.

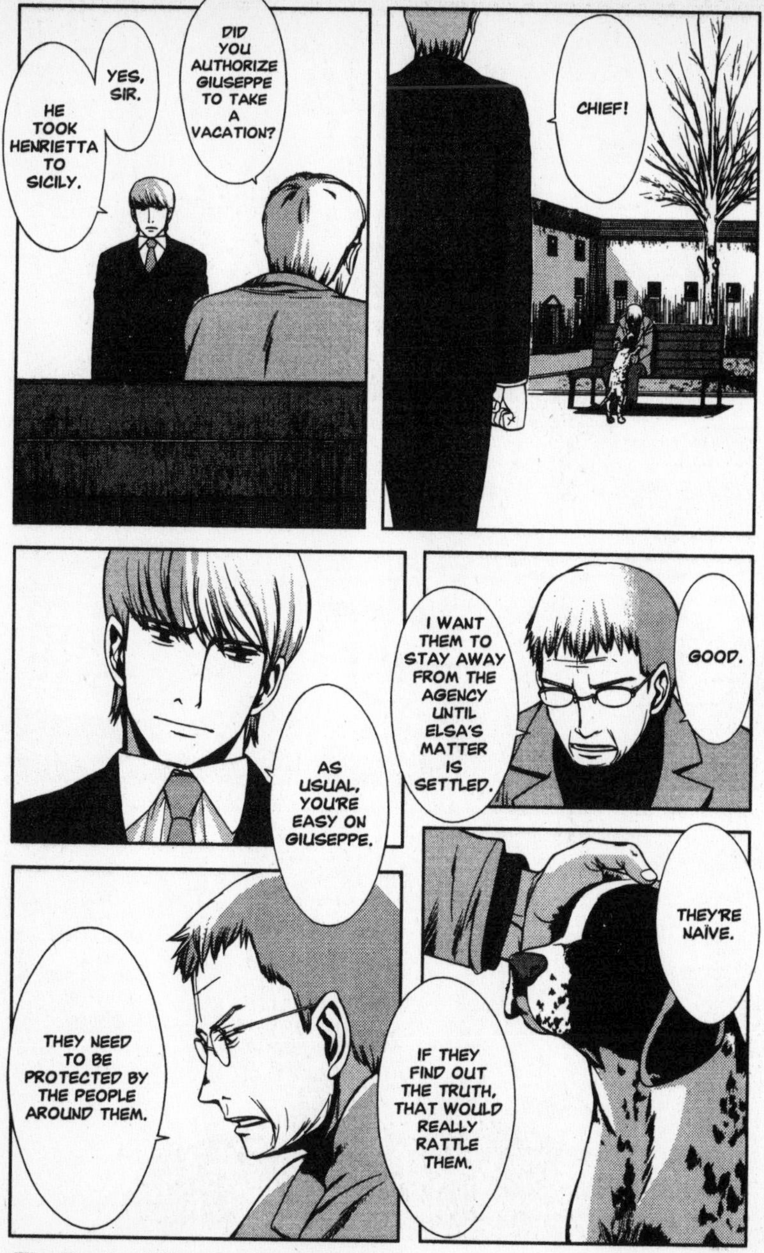

CHIEF!
DID YOU AUTHORIZE GIUSEPPE TO TAKE A VACATION?
YES, SIR.
HE TOOK HENRIETTA TO SICILY.
GOOD.
I WANT THEM TO STAY AWAY FROM THE AGENCY UNTIL ELSA'S MATTER IS SETTLED.
AS USUAL, YOU'RE EASY ON GIUSEPPE.
THEY'RE NAÏVE.
IF THEY FIND OUT THE TRUTH, THAT WOULD REALLY RATTLE THEM.
THEY NEED TO BE PROTECTED BY THE PEOPLE AROUND THEM.

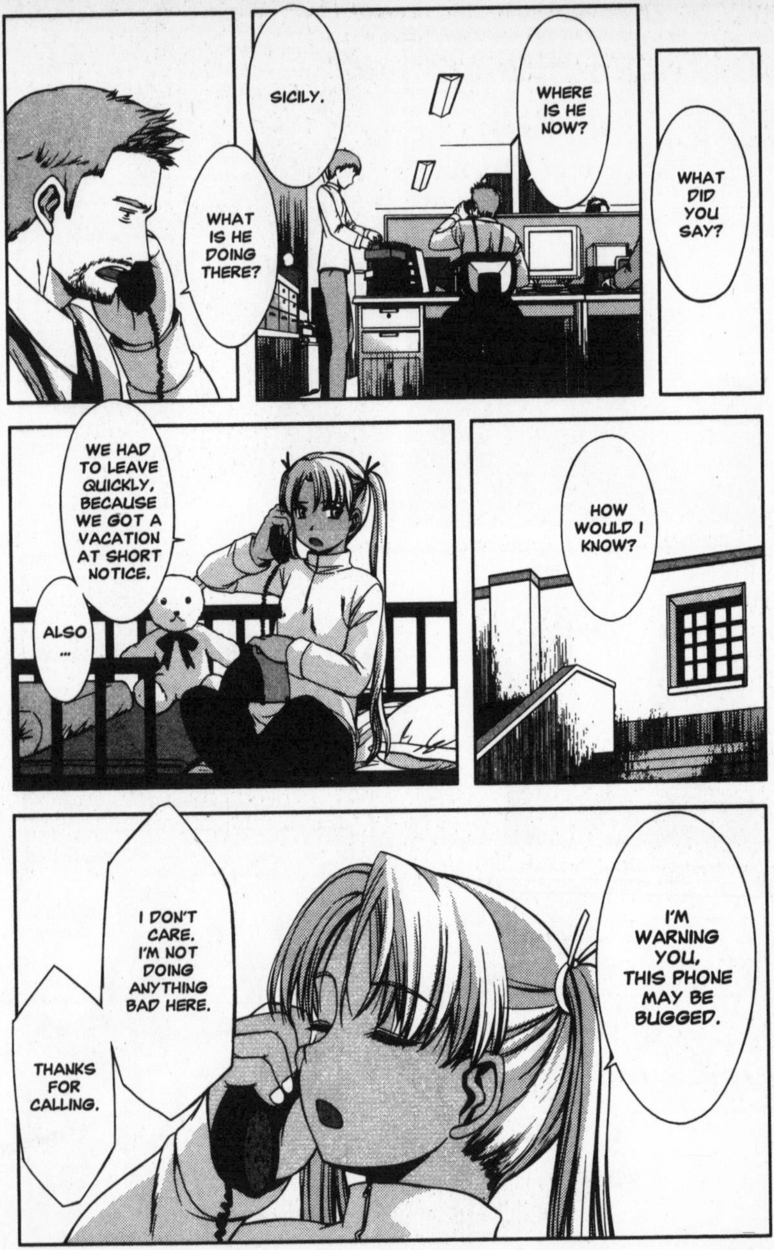
WHAT DID YOU SAY?
WHERE IS HE NOW?
SICILY.
WHAT IS HE DOING THERE?
HOW WOULD I KNOW?
WE HAD TO LEAVE QUICKLY, BECAUSE WE GOT A VACATION AT SHORT NOTICE.
ALSO ...
I'M WARNING YOU, THIS PHONE MAY BE BUGGED.
I DON'T CARE. I'M NOT DOING ANYTHING BAD HERE.
THANKS FOR CALLING.

第5話　エルザ・デ・シーカの死(後編)

The Death of Elsa de Sica (Part 2)

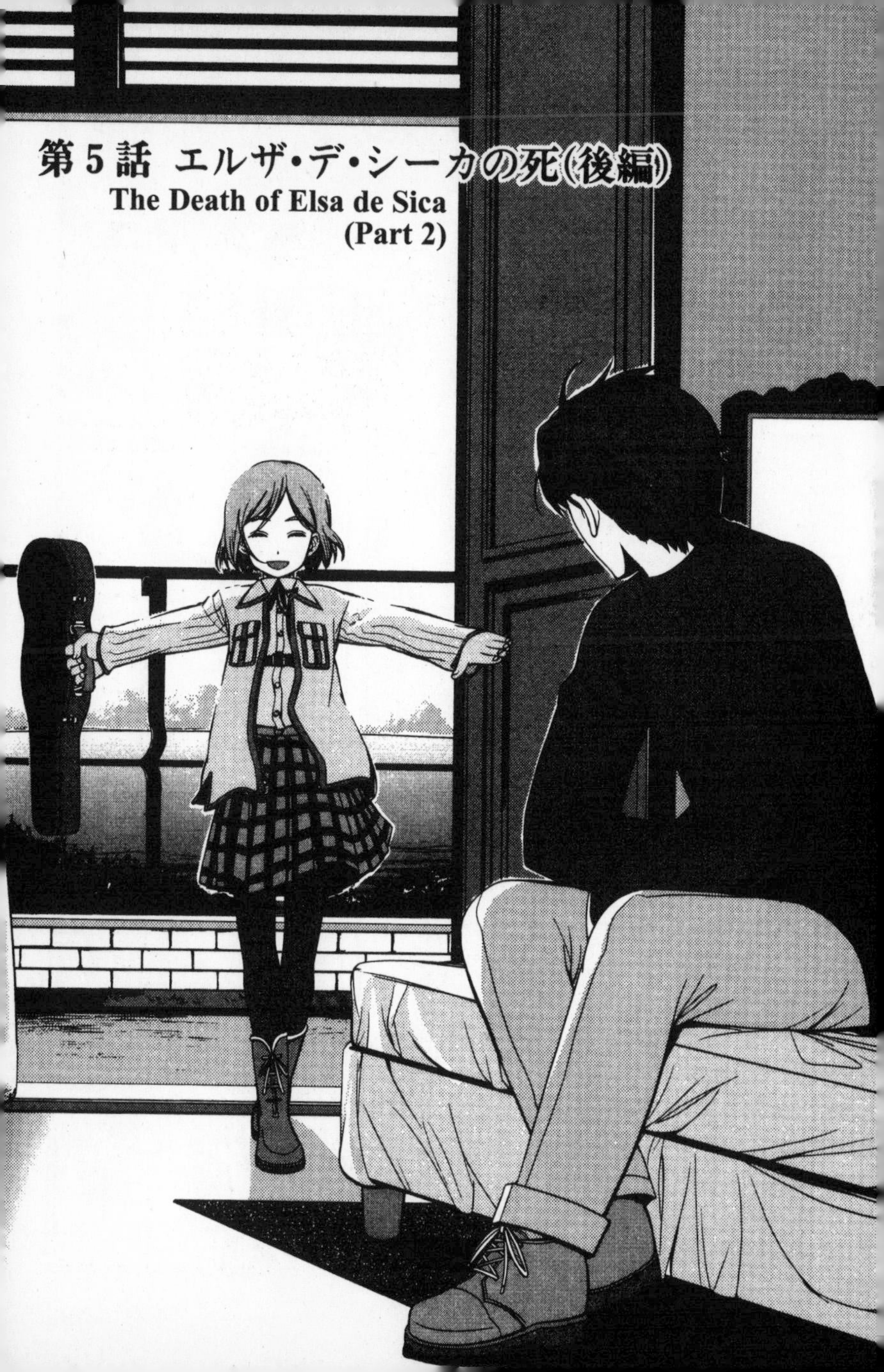

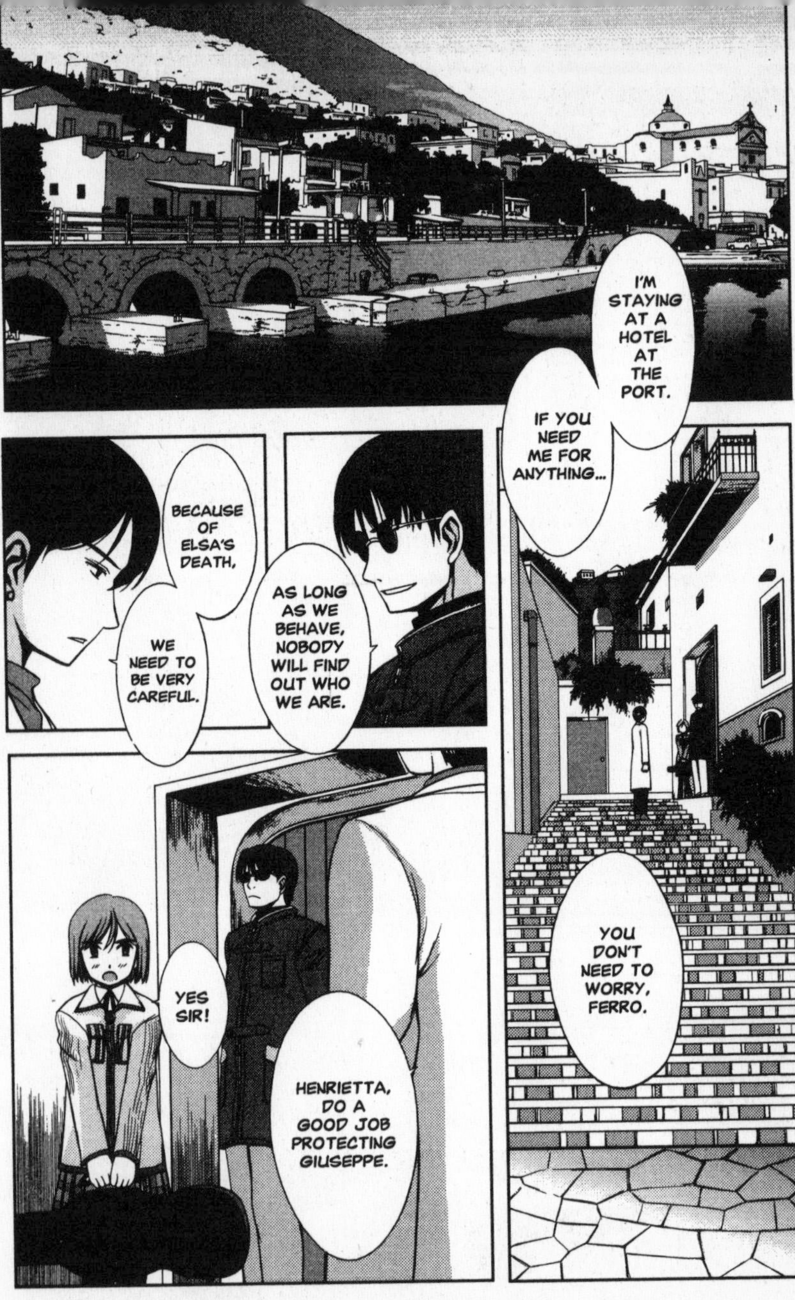
I'M STAYING AT A HOTEL AT THE PORT.
IF YOU NEED ME FOR ANYTHING...
YOU DON'T NEED TO WORRY, FERRO.
AS LONG AS WE BEHAVE, NOBODY WILL FIND OUT WHO WE ARE.
BECAUSE OF ELSA'S DEATH,
WE NEED TO BE VERY CAREFUL.
HENRIETTA, DO A GOOD JOB PROTECTING GIUSEPPE.
YES SIR!

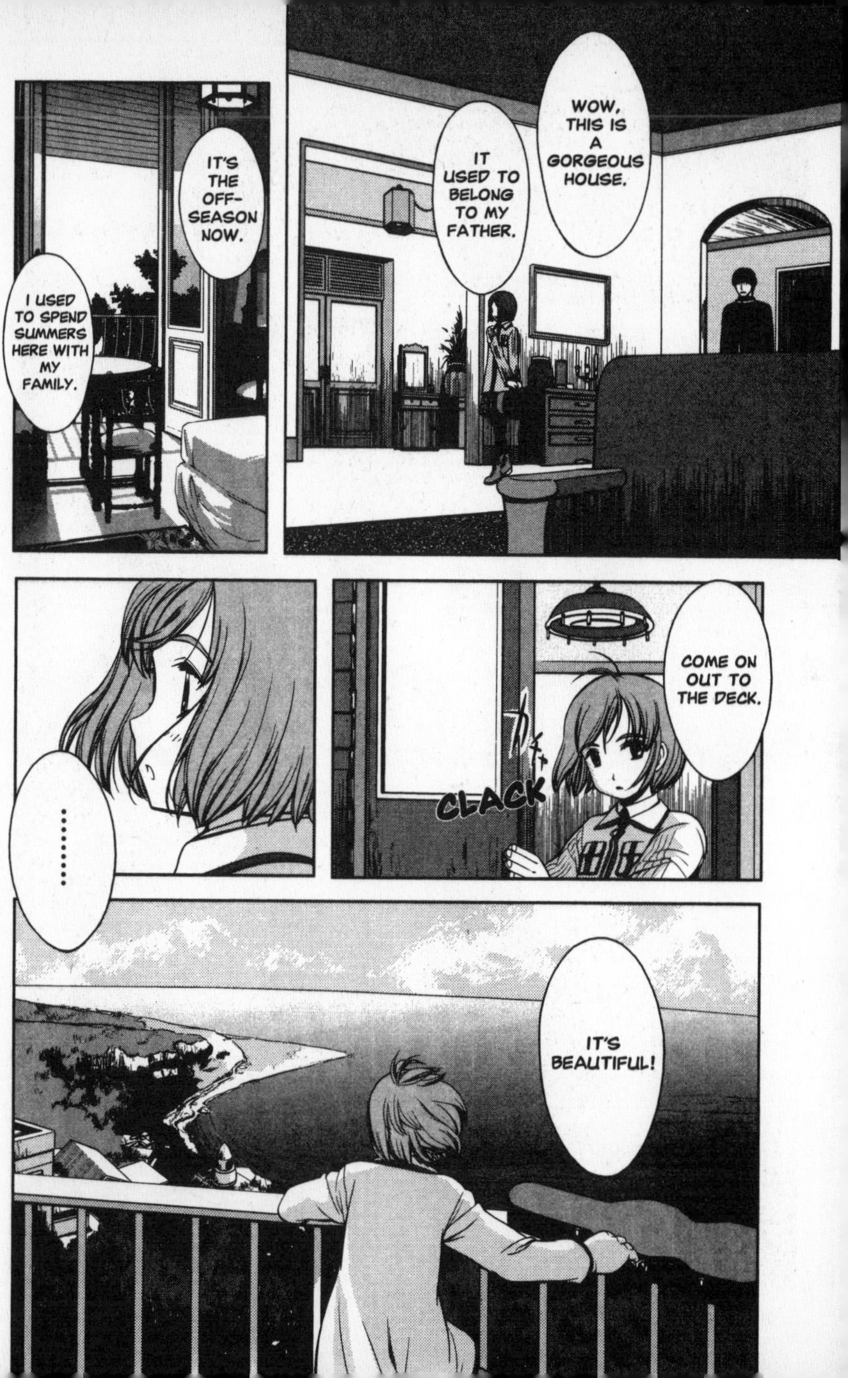
WOW, THIS IS A GORGEOUS HOUSE.
IT USED TO BELONG TO MY FATHER.
IT'S THE OFF-SEASON NOW.
I USED TO SPEND SUMMERS HERE WITH MY FAMILY.
COME ON OUT TO THE DECK.
CLACK
....
IT'S BEAUTIFUL!

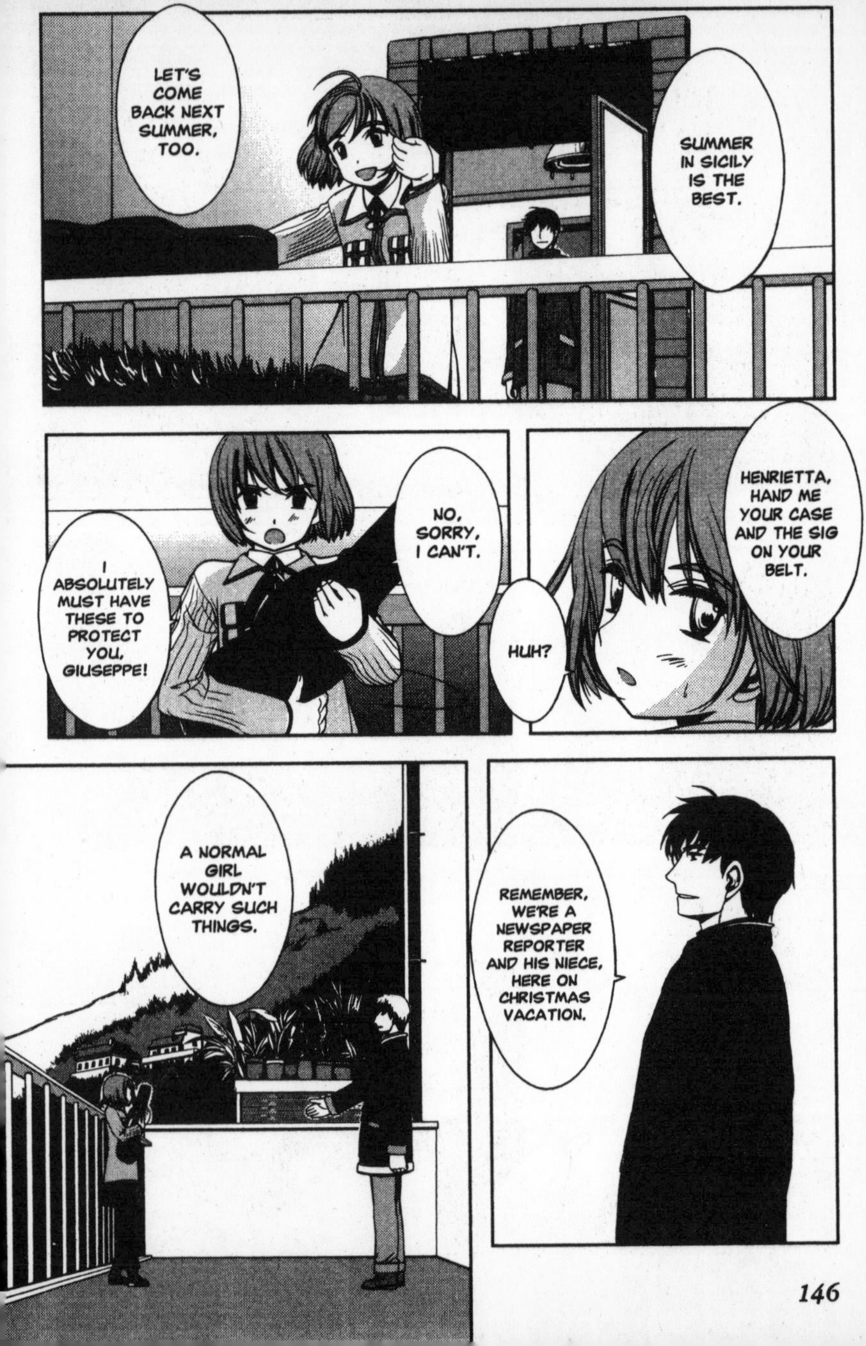
SUMMER IN SICILY IS THE BEST.
LET'S COME BACK NEXT SUMMER, TOO.
HENRIETTA, HAND ME YOUR CASE AND THE SIG ON YOUR BELT.
HUH?
NO, SORRY, I CAN'T.
I ABSOLUTELY MUST HAVE THESE TO PROTECT YOU, GIUSEPPE!
REMEMBER, WE'RE A NEWSPAPER REPORTER AND HIS NIECE, HERE ON CHRISTMAS VACATION.
A NORMAL GIRL WOULDN'T CARRY SUCH THINGS.

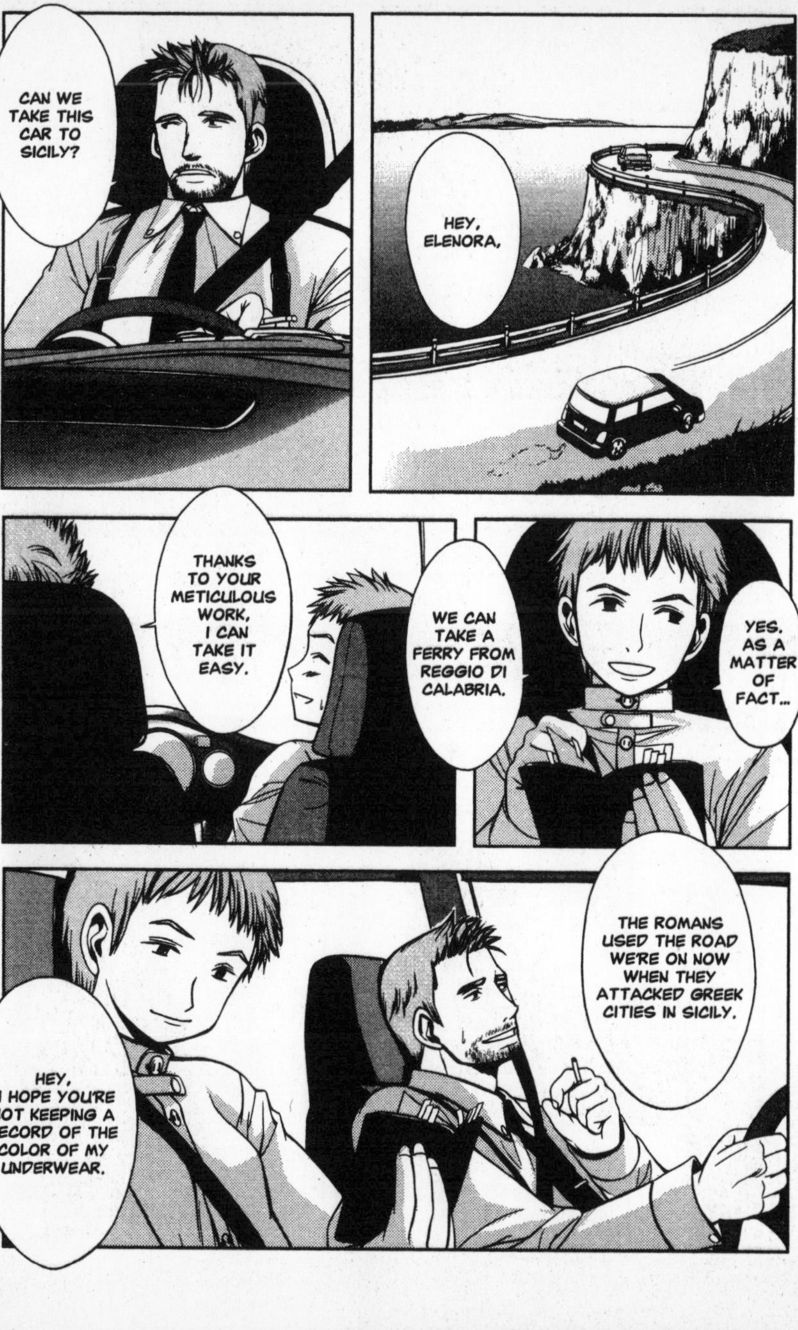
HEY, ELENORA,
CAN WE TAKE THIS CAR TO SICILY?
YES. AS A MATTER OF FACT...
WE CAN TAKE A FERRY FROM REGGIO DI CALABRIA.
THANKS TO YOUR METICULOUS WORK, I CAN TAKE IT EASY.
THE ROMANS USED THE ROAD WE'RE ON NOW WHEN THEY ATTACKED GREEK CITIES IN SICILY.
HEY, I HOPE YOU'RE NOT KEEPING A RECORD OF THE COLOR OF MY UNDERWEAR.

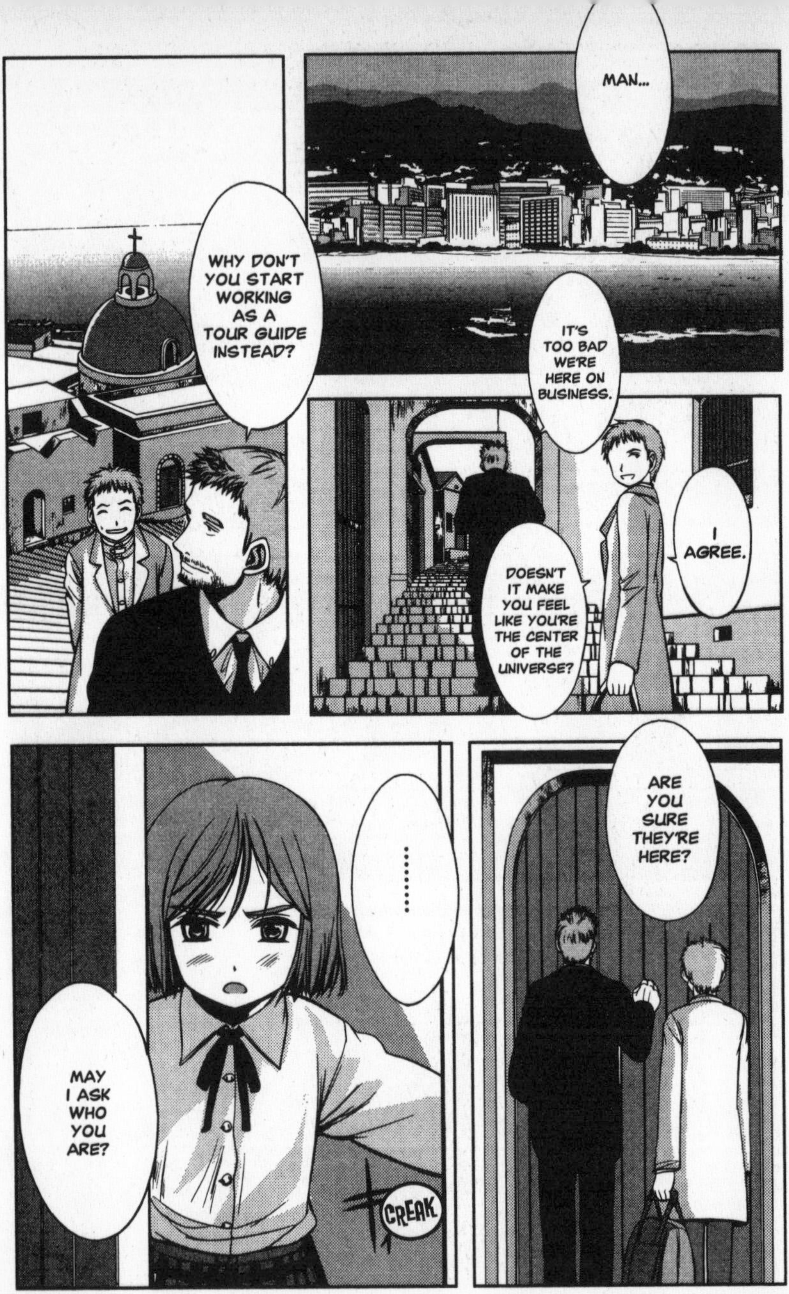
MAN...
WHY DON'T YOU START WORKING AS A TOUR GUIDE INSTEAD?
IT'S TOO BAD WE'RE HERE ON BUSINESS.
I AGREE.
DOESN'T IT MAKE YOU FEEL LIKE YOU'RE THE CENTER OF THE UNIVERSE?
ARE YOU SURE THEY'RE HERE?
CREAK
......
MAY I ASK WHO YOU ARE?

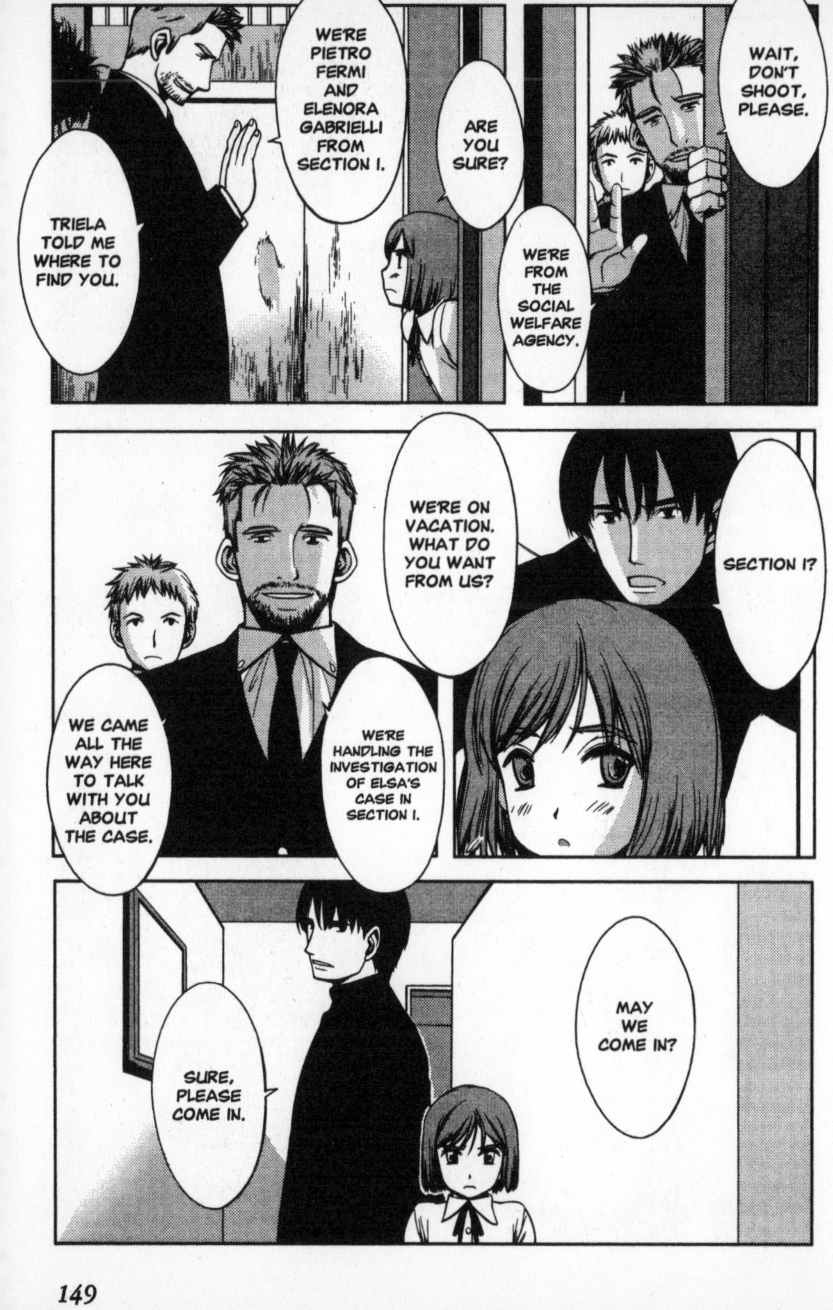
WAIT, DON'T SHOOT, PLEASE.
WE'RE FROM THE SOCIAL WELFARE AGENCY.
ARE YOU SURE?
WE'RE PIETRO FERMI AND ELENORA GABRIELLI FROM SECTION 1.
TRIELA TOLD ME WHERE TO FIND YOU.
SECTION 1?
WE'RE ON VACATION. WHAT DO YOU WANT FROM US?
WE'RE HANDLING THE INVESTIGATION OF ELSA'S CASE IN SECTION 1.
WE CAME ALL THE WAY HERE TO TALK WITH YOU ABOUT THE CASE.
MAY WE COME IN?
SURE, PLEASE COME IN.

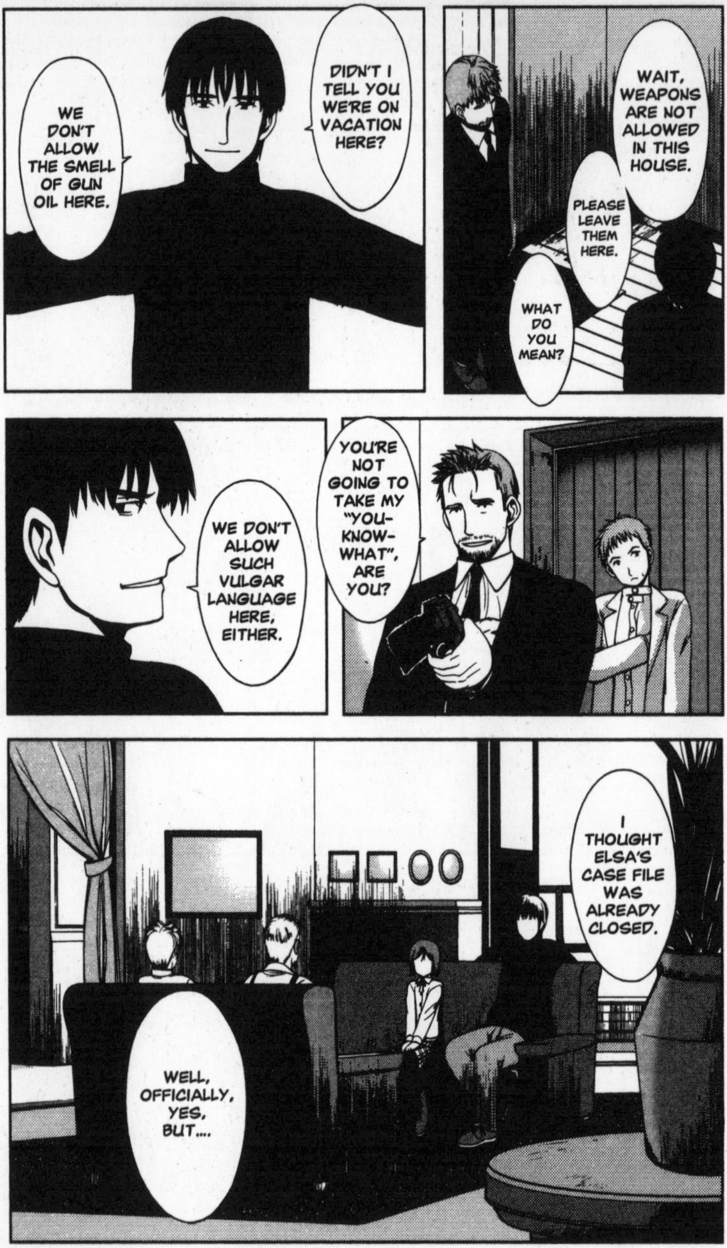
WAIT, WEAPONS ARE NOT ALLOWED IN THIS HOUSE.
PLEASE LEAVE THEM HERE.
WHAT DO YOU MEAN?
DIDN'T I TELL YOU WE'RE ON VACATION HERE?
WE DON'T ALLOW THE SMELL OF GUN OIL HERE.
YOU'RE NOT GOING TO TAKE MY "YOU-KNOW-WHAT", ARE YOU?
WE DON'T ALLOW SUCH VULGAR LANGUAGE HERE, EITHER.
I THOUGHT ELSA'S CASE FILE WAS ALREADY CLOSED.
WELL, OFFICIALLY, YES, BUT....

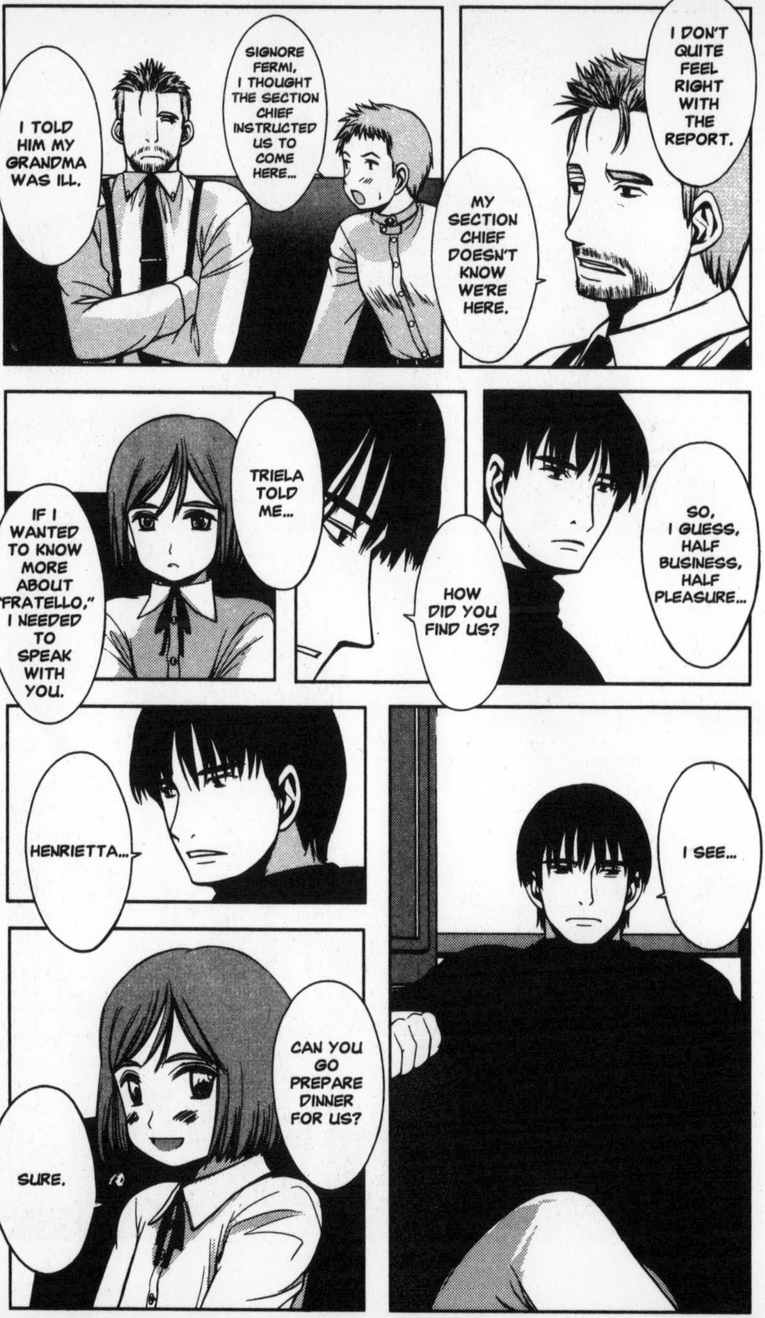
I DON'T QUITE FEEL RIGHT WITH THE REPORT.
MY SECTION CHIEF DOESN'T KNOW WE'RE HERE.
SIGNORE FERMI, I THOUGHT THE SECTION CHIEF INSTRUCTED US TO COME HERE...
I TOLD HIM MY GRANDMA WAS ILL.
SO, I GUESS, HALF BUSINESS, HALF PLEASURE...
HOW DID YOU FIND US?
TRIELA TOLD ME...
IF I WANTED TO KNOW MORE ABOUT "FRATELLO," I NEEDED TO SPEAK WITH YOU.
I SEE...
HENRIETTA...
CAN YOU GO PREPARE DINNER FOR US?
SURE.

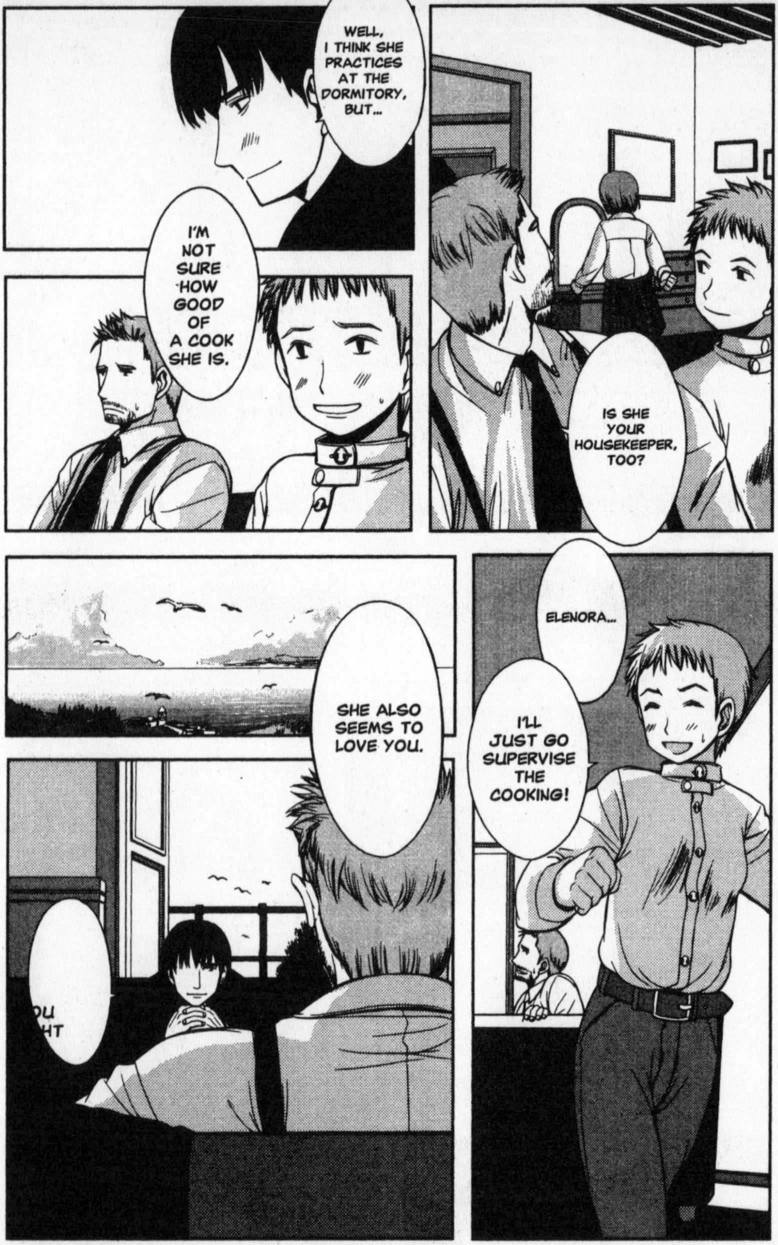
IS SHE YOUR HOUSEKEEPER, TOO?
WELL, I THINK SHE PRACTICES AT THE DORMITORY, BUT...
I'M NOT SURE HOW GOOD OF A COOK SHE IS.
ELENORA...
I'LL JUST GO SUPERVISE THE COOKING!
SHE ALSO SEEMS TO LOVE YOU.

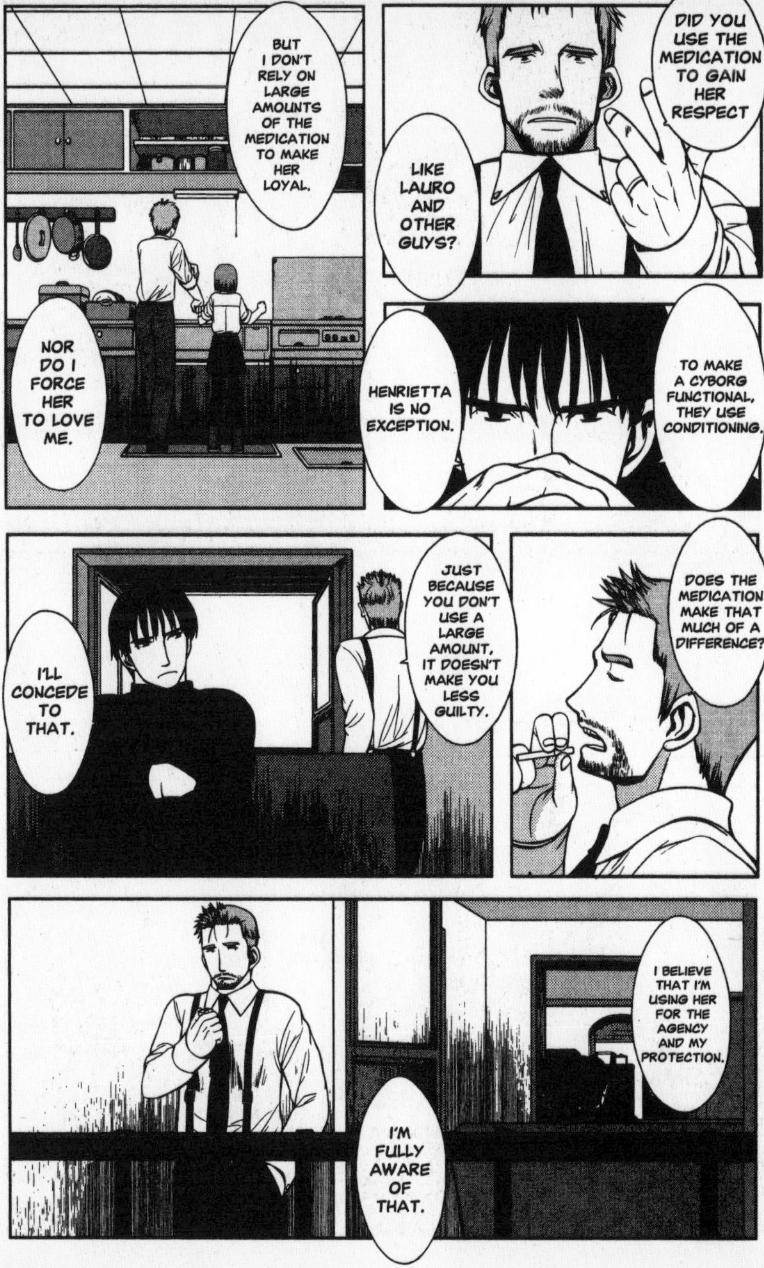
DID YOU USE THE MEDICATION TO GAIN HER RESPECT
LIKE LAURO AND OTHER GUYS?
BUT I DON'T RELY ON LARGE AMOUNTS OF THE MEDICATION TO MAKE HER LOYAL.
NOR DO I FORCE HER TO LOVE ME.
TO MAKE A CYBORG FUNCTIONAL, THEY USE CONDITIONING.
HENRIETTA IS NO EXCEPTION.
DOES THE MEDICATION MAKE THAT MUCH OF A DIFFERENCE?
JUST BECAUSE YOU DON'T USE A LARGE AMOUNT, IT DOESN'T MAKE YOU LESS GUILTY.
I'LL CONCEDE TO THAT.
I BELIEVE THAT I'M USING HER FOR THE AGENCY AND MY PROTECTION.
I'M FULLY AWARE OF THAT.

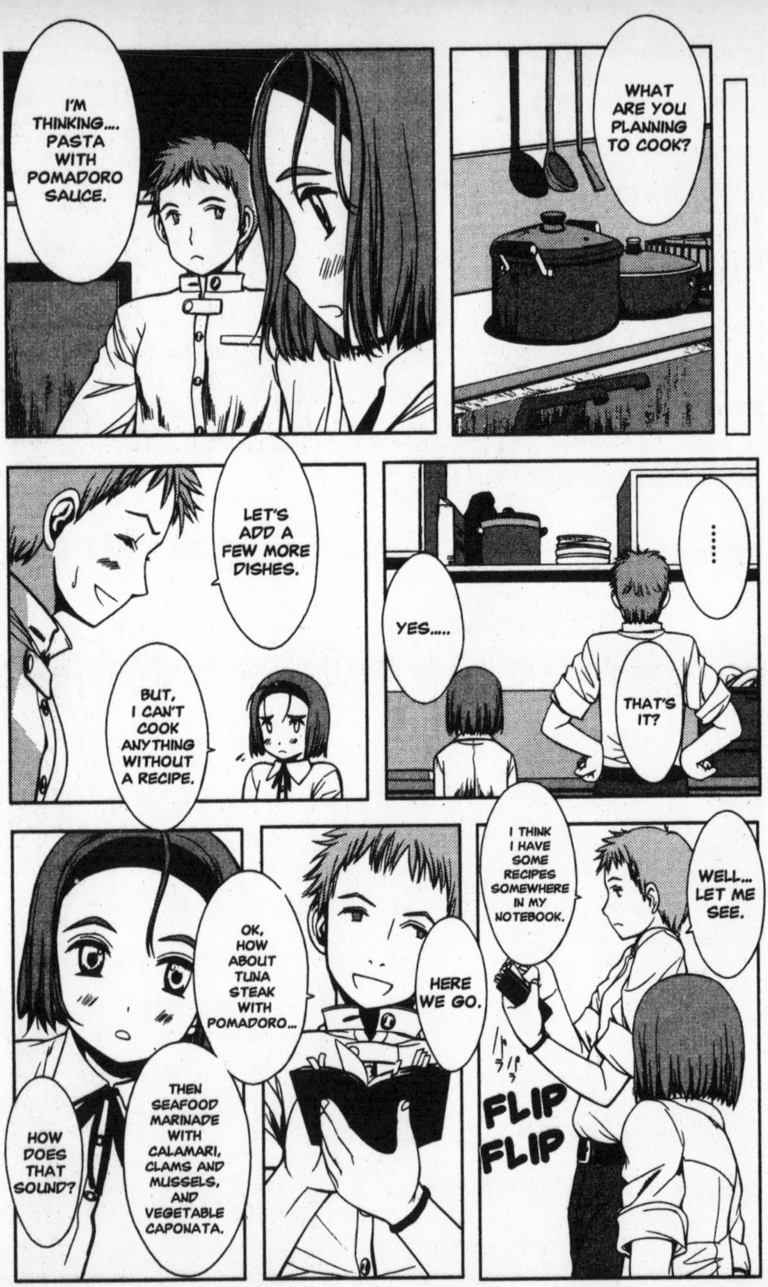
WHAT ARE YOU PLANNING TO COOK?
I'M THINKING.... PASTA WITH POMADORO SAUCE.
......
THAT'S IT?
YES.....
LET'S ADD A FEW MORE DISHES.
BUT, I CAN'T COOK ANYTHING WITHOUT A RECIPE.
WELL... LET ME SEE.
I THINK I HAVE SOME RECIPES SOMEWHERE IN MY NOTEBOOK.
FLIP FLIP
HERE WE GO.
OK, HOW ABOUT TUNA STEAK WITH POMADORO...
THEN SEAFOOD MARINADE WITH CALAMARI, CLAMS AND MUSSELS, AND VEGETABLE CAPONATA.
HOW DOES THAT SOUND?

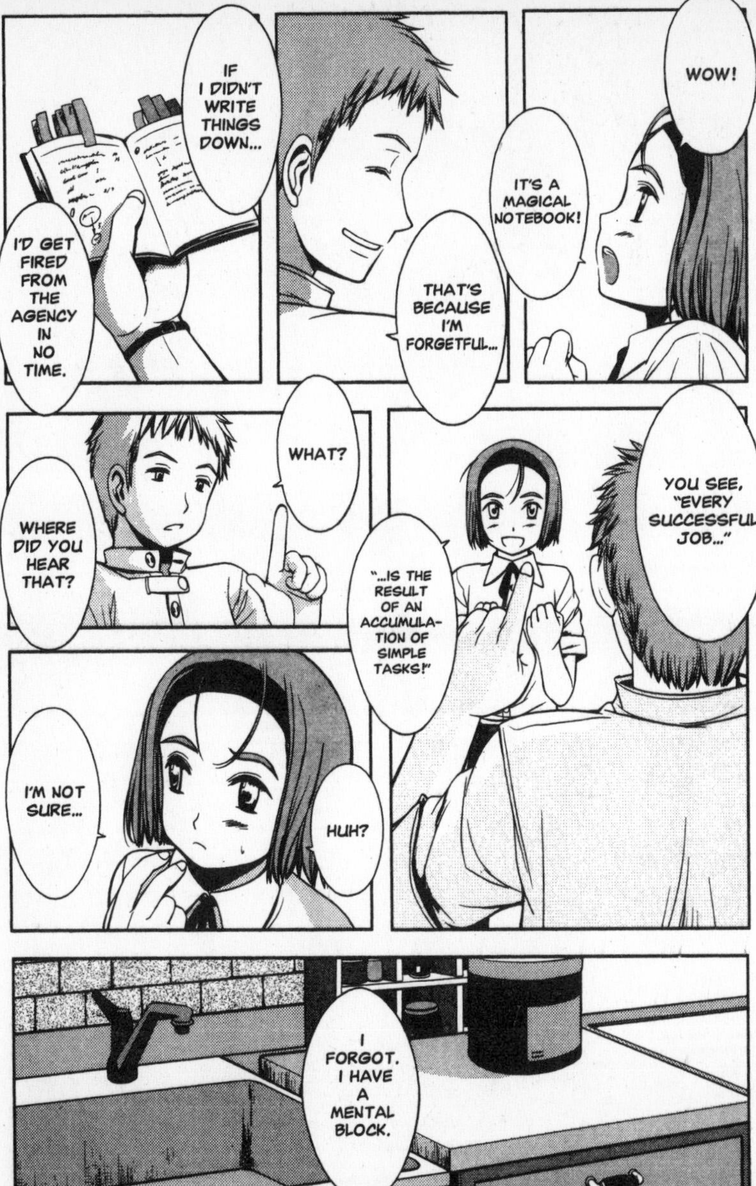
WOW!
IT'S A MAGICAL NOTEBOOK!
THAT'S BECAUSE I'M FORGETFUL...
IF I DIDN'T WRITE THINGS DOWN...
I'D GET FIRED FROM THE AGENCY IN NO TIME.
YOU SEE, "EVERY SUCCESSFUL JOB..."
"...IS THE RESULT OF AN ACCUMULATION OF SIMPLE TASKS!"
WHAT?
WHERE DID YOU HEAR THAT?
HUH?
I'M NOT SURE...
I FORGOT. I HAVE A MENTAL BLOCK.

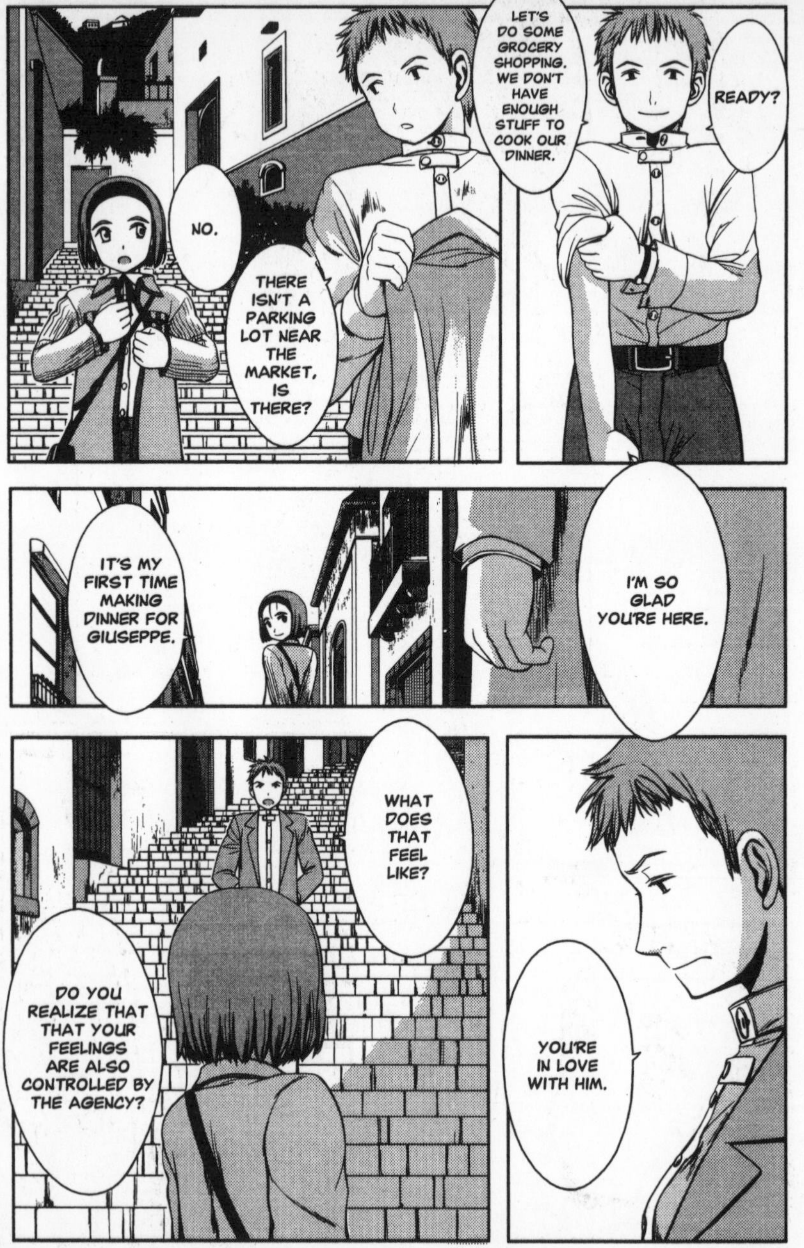
READY?
LET'S DO SOME GROCERY SHOPPING. WE DON'T HAVE ENOUGH STUFF TO COOK OUR DINNER.
THERE ISN'T A PARKING LOT NEAR THE MARKET, IS THERE?
NO.
I'M SO GLAD YOU'RE HERE.
IT'S MY FIRST TIME MAKING DINNER FOR GIUSEPPE.
YOU'RE IN LOVE WITH HIM.
WHAT DOES THAT FEEL LIKE?
DO YOU REALIZE THAT THAT YOUR FEELINGS ARE ALSO CONTROLLED BY THE AGENCY?

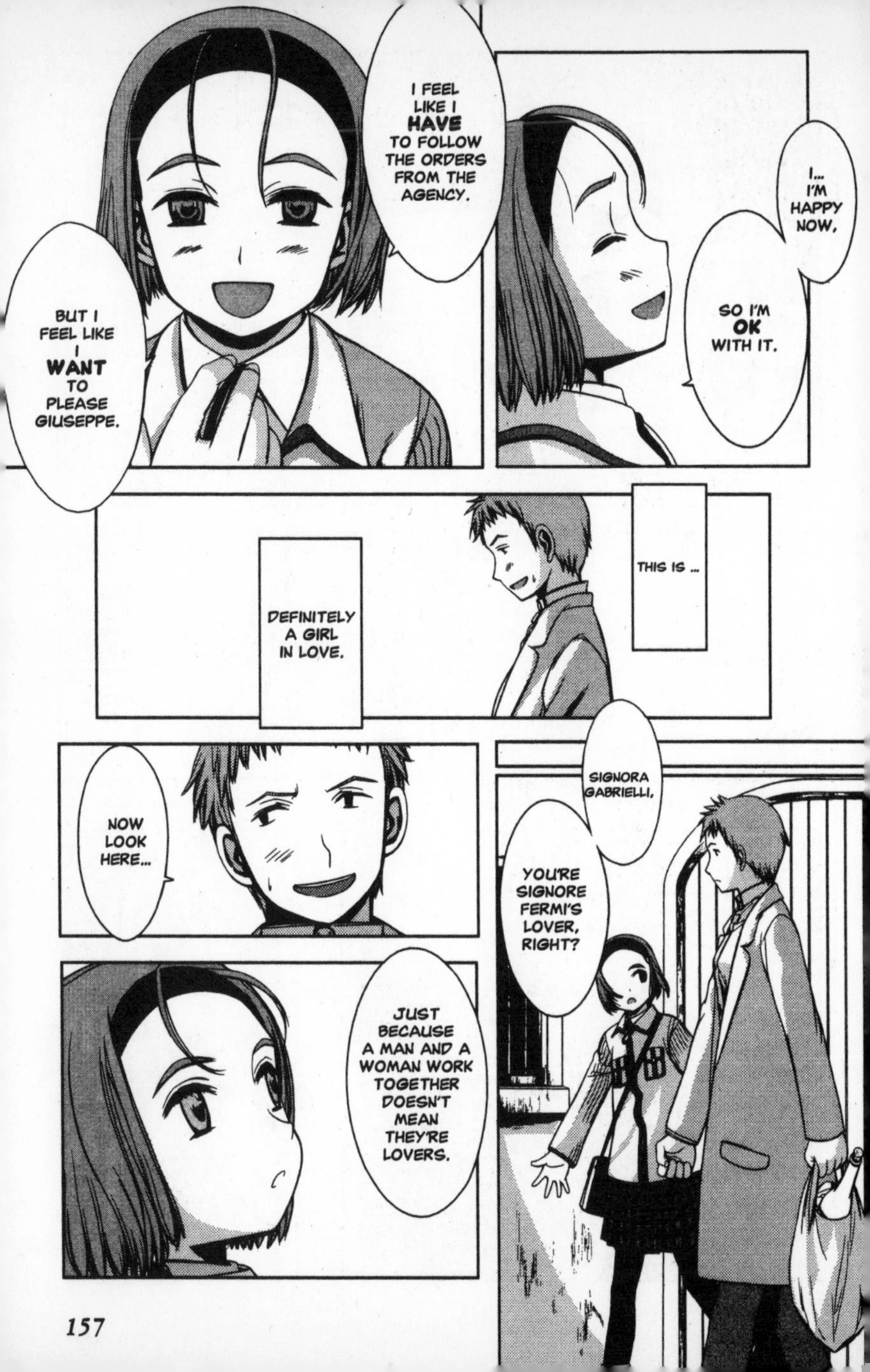
I... I'M HAPPY NOW.
SO I'M OK WITH IT.
I FEEL LIKE I HAVE TO FOLLOW THE ORDERS FROM THE AGENCY.
BUT I FEEL LIKE I WANT TO PLEASE GIUSEPPE.
THIS IS ...
DEFINITELY A GIRL IN LOVE.
SIGNORA GABRIELLI,
YOU'RE SIGNORE FERMI'S LOVER, RIGHT?
NOW LOOK HERE...
JUST BECAUSE A MAN AND A WOMAN WORK TOGETHER DOESN'T MEAN THEY'RE LOVERS.

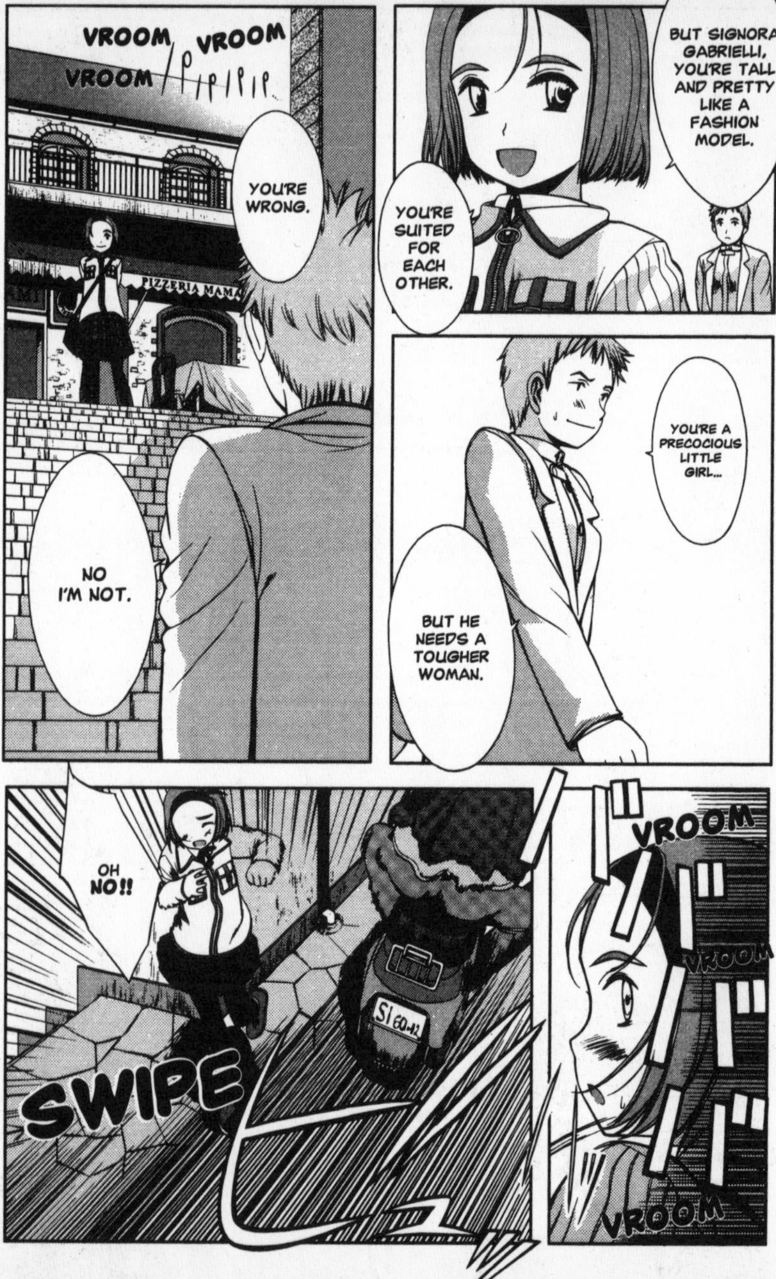

BUT SIGNORA GABRIELLI, YOU'RE TALL AND PRETTY LIKE A FASHION MODEL.
YOU'RE SUITED FOR EACH OTHER.
YOU'RE A PRECOCIOUS LITTLE GIRL...
BUT HE NEEDS A TOUGHER WOMAN.
VROOM
VROOM
VROOM
PIPIPIP
PIZZERIA MAMA
YOU'RE WRONG.
NO I'M NOT.
VROOM
VROOM
VROOM
OH NO!!
SWIPE

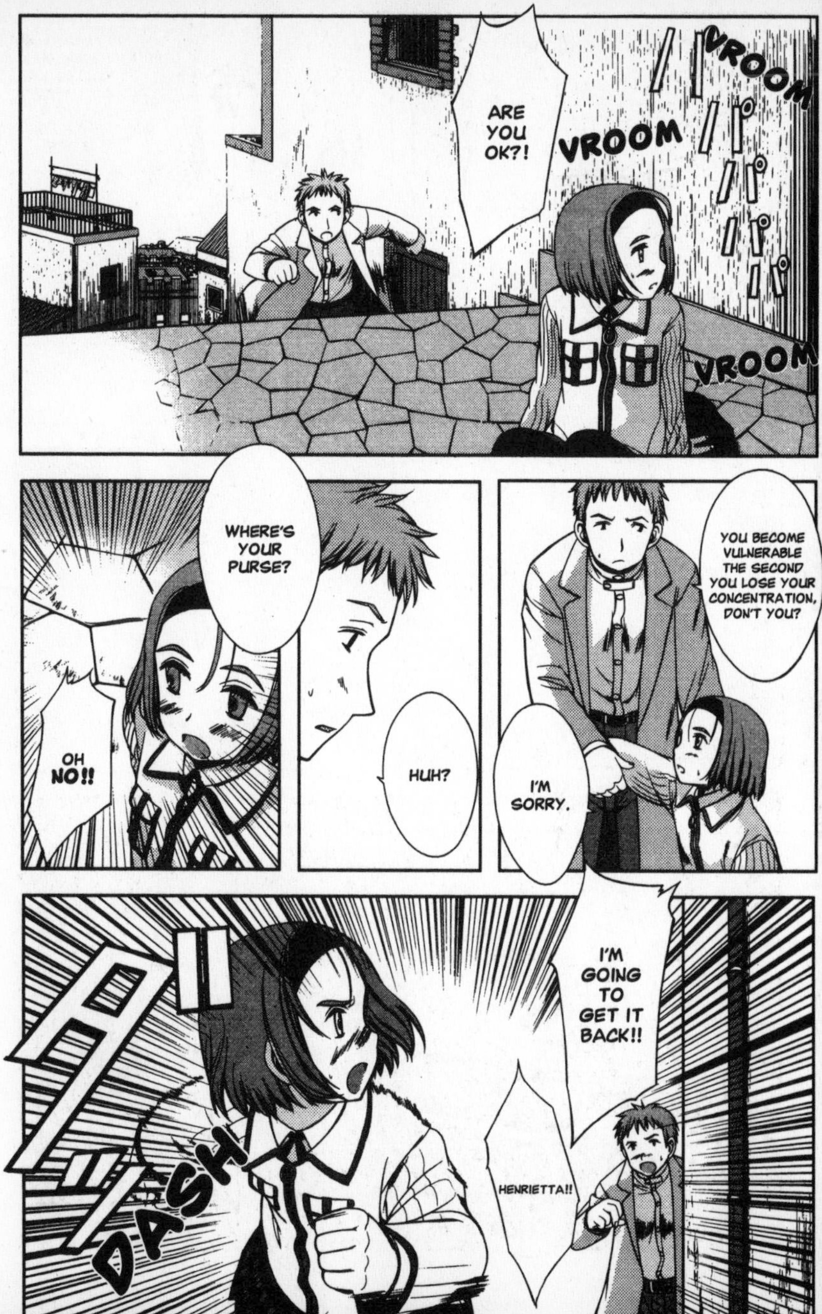
ARE YOU OK?!
VROOM
VROOM
VROOM
WHERE'S YOUR PURSE?
OH NO!!
HUH?
YOU BECOME VULNERABLE THE SECOND YOU LOSE YOUR CONCENTRATION, DON'T YOU?
I'M SORRY.
I'M GOING TO GET IT BACK!!
DASH
HENRIETTA!!

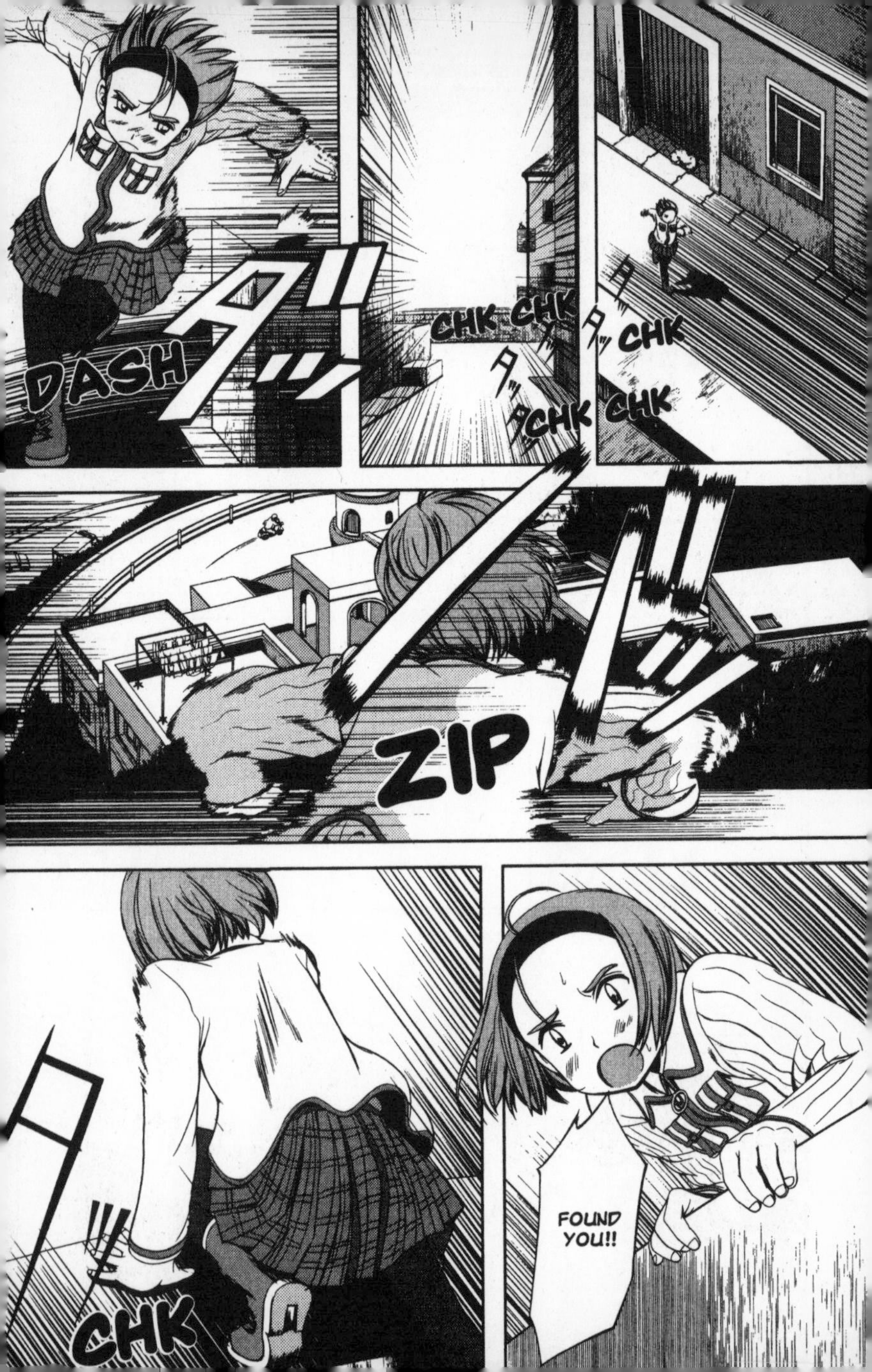
CHK
CHK CHK
CHK CHK
DASH
ZIP
FOUND YOU!!
CHK

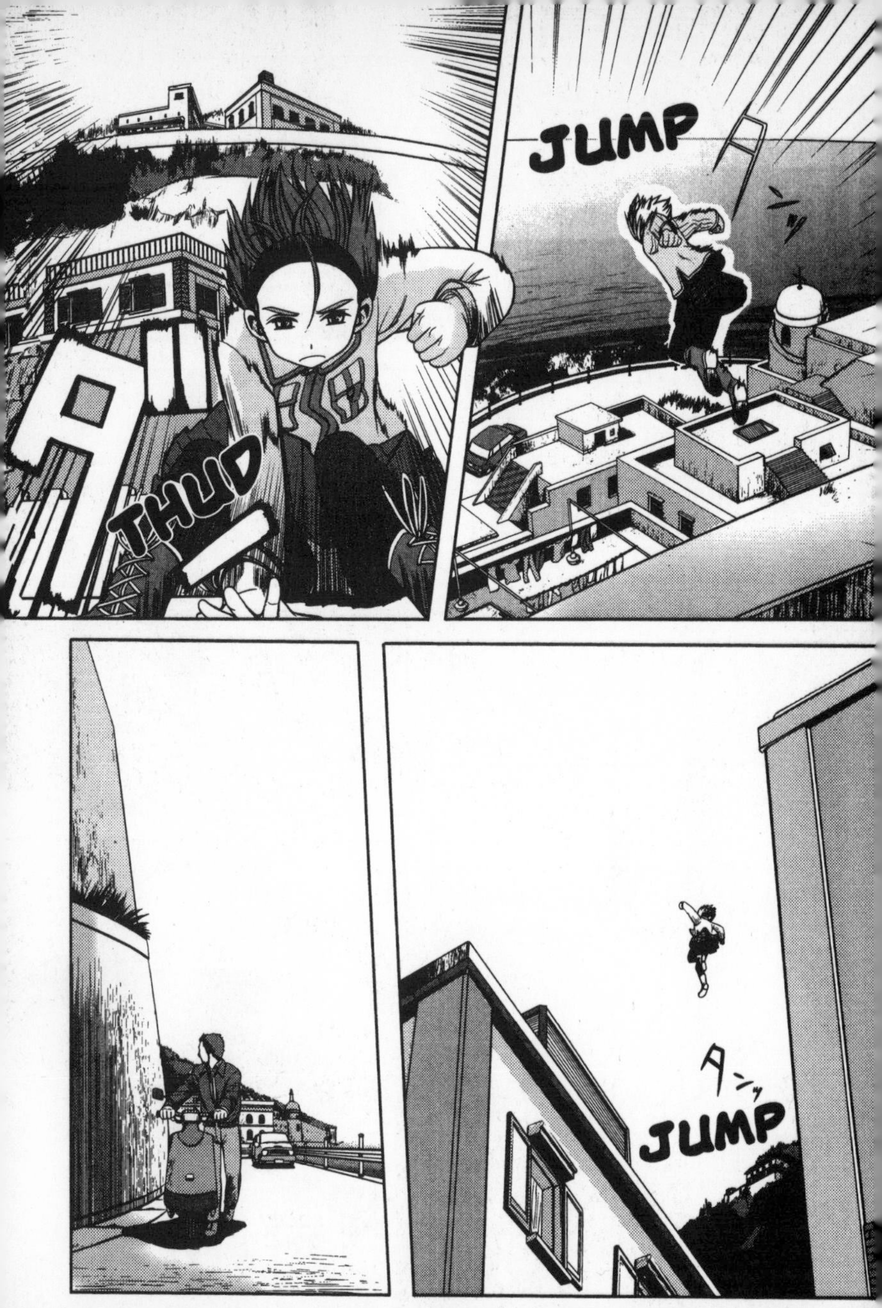
JUMP
THUD
JUMP

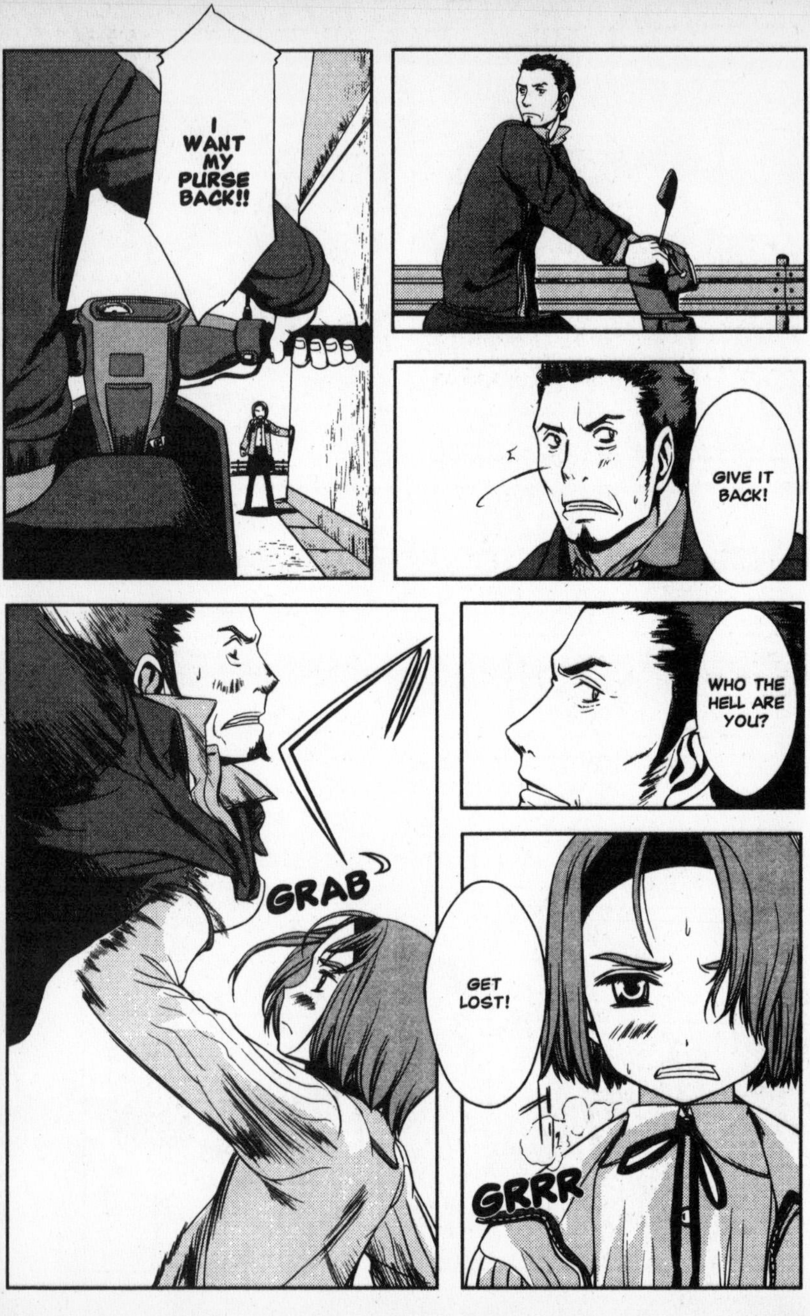
I WANT MY PURSE BACK!!
GIVE IT BACK!
WHO THE HELL ARE YOU?
GET LOST!
GRRR
GRAB

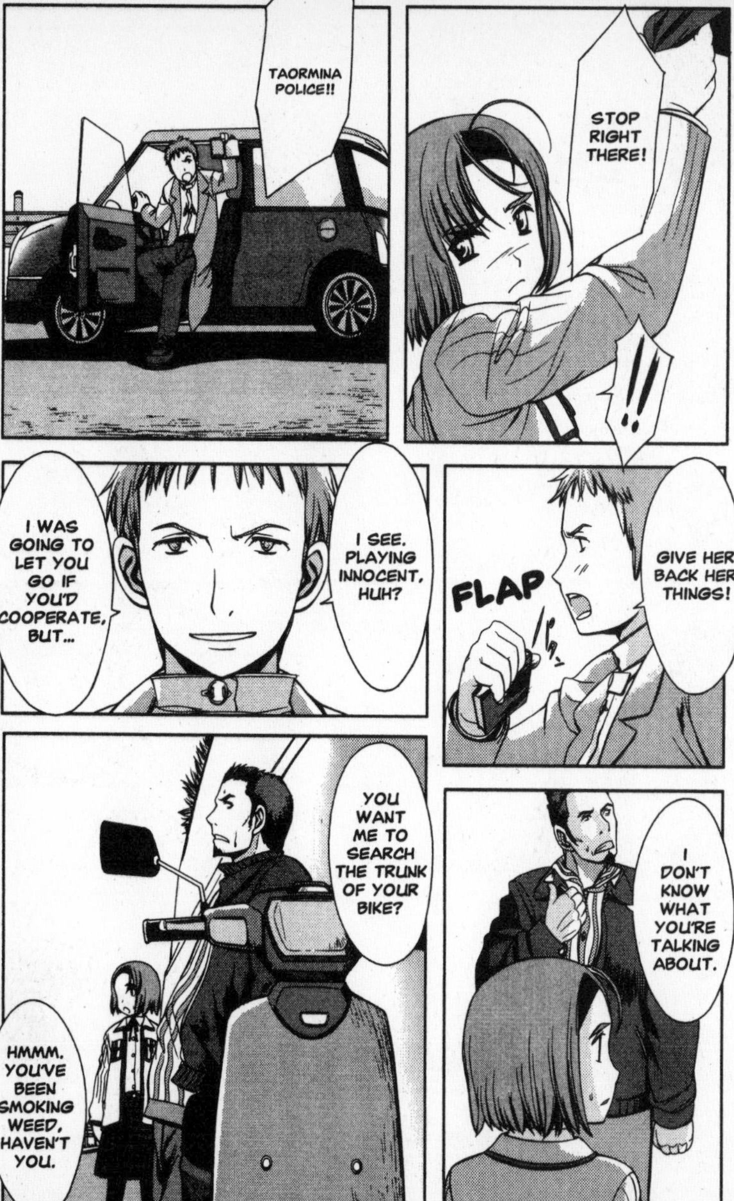
STOP RIGHT THERE!
TAORMINA POLICE!!
!!
GIVE HER BACK HER THINGS!
FLAP
I SEE. PLAYING INNOCENT, HUH?
I WAS GOING TO LET YOU GO IF YOU'D COOPERATE, BUT...
I DON'T KNOW WHAT YOU'RE TALKING ABOUT.
YOU WANT ME TO SEARCH THE TRUNK OF YOUR BIKE?
HMMM. YOU'VE BEEN SMOKING WEED, HAVEN'T YOU.

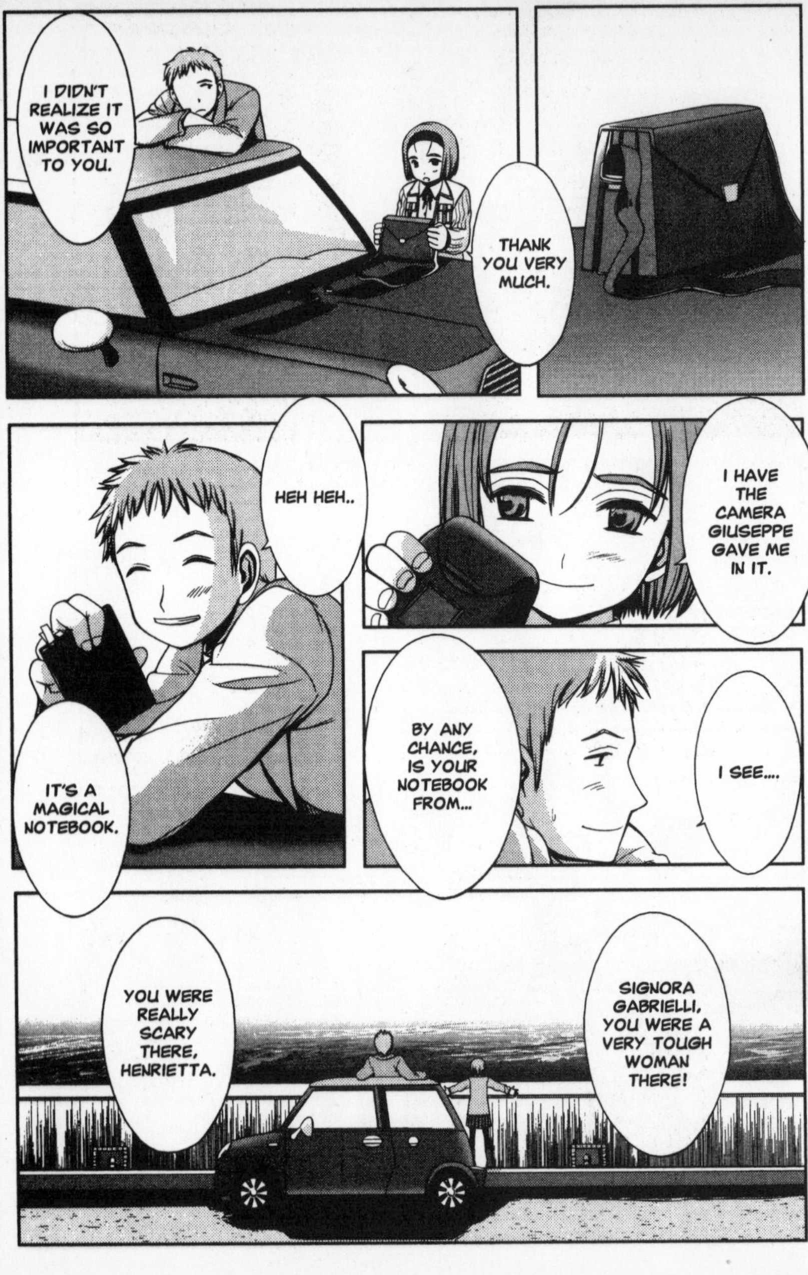
THANK YOU VERY MUCH.
I DIDN'T REALIZE IT WAS SO IMPORTANT TO YOU.
I HAVE THE CAMERA GIUSEPPE GAVE ME IN IT.
I SEE....
BY ANY CHANCE, IS YOUR NOTEBOOK FROM...
HEH HEH..
IT'S A MAGICAL NOTEBOOK.
SIGNORA GABRIELLI, YOU WERE A VERY TOUGH WOMAN THERE!
YOU WERE REALLY SCARY THERE, HENRIETTA.

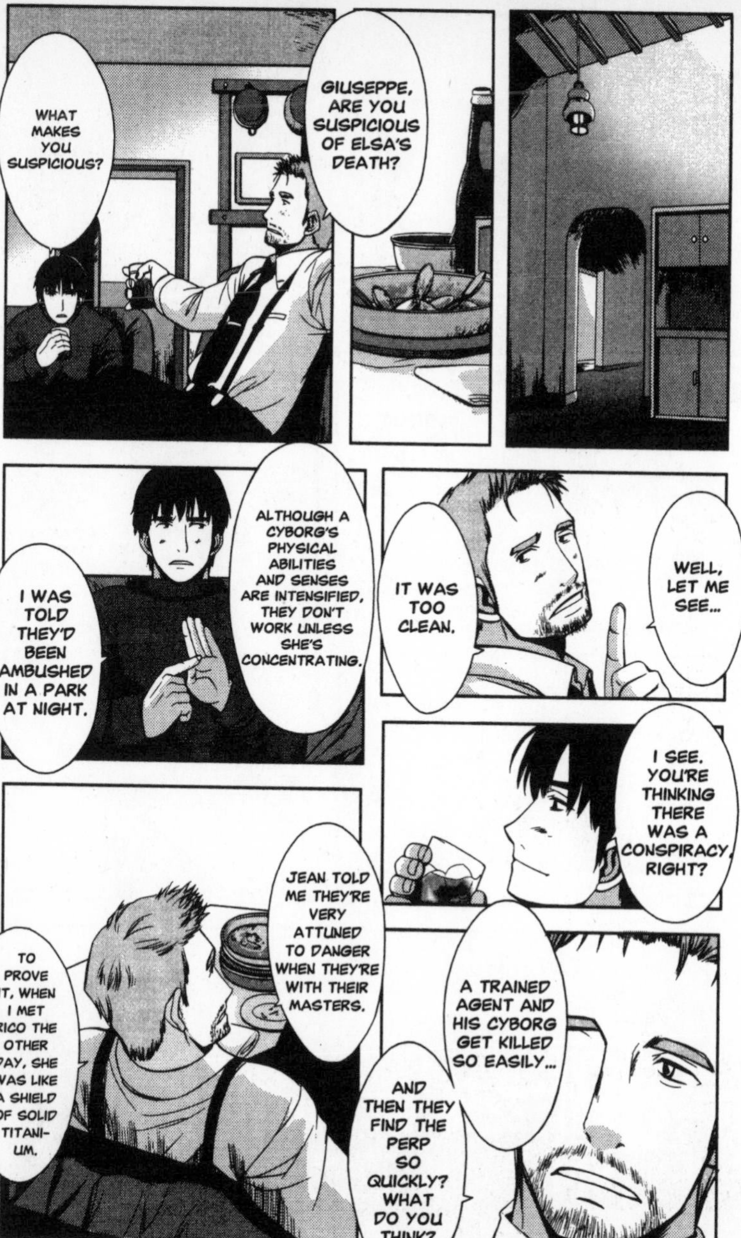
GIUSEPPE, ARE YOU SUSPICIOUS OF ELSA'S DEATH?
WHAT MAKES YOU SUSPICIOUS?
WELL, LET ME SEE...
IT WAS TOO CLEAN.
ALTHOUGH A CYBORG'S PHYSICAL ABILITIES AND SENSES ARE INTENSIFIED, THEY DON'T WORK UNLESS SHE'S CONCENTRATING.
I WAS TOLD THEY'D BEEN AMBUSHED IN A PARK AT NIGHT.
I SEE. YOU'RE THINKING THERE WAS A CONSPIRACY, RIGHT?
JEAN TOLD ME THEY'RE VERY ATTUNED TO DANGER WHEN THEY'RE WITH THEIR MASTERS.
TO PROVE IT, WHEN I MET RICO THE OTHER DAY, SHE WAS LIKE A SHIELD OF SOLID TITANI-UM.
A TRAINED AGENT AND HIS CYBORG GET KILLED SO EASILY...
AND THEN THEY FIND THE PERP SO QUICKLY? WHAT DO YOU THINK?

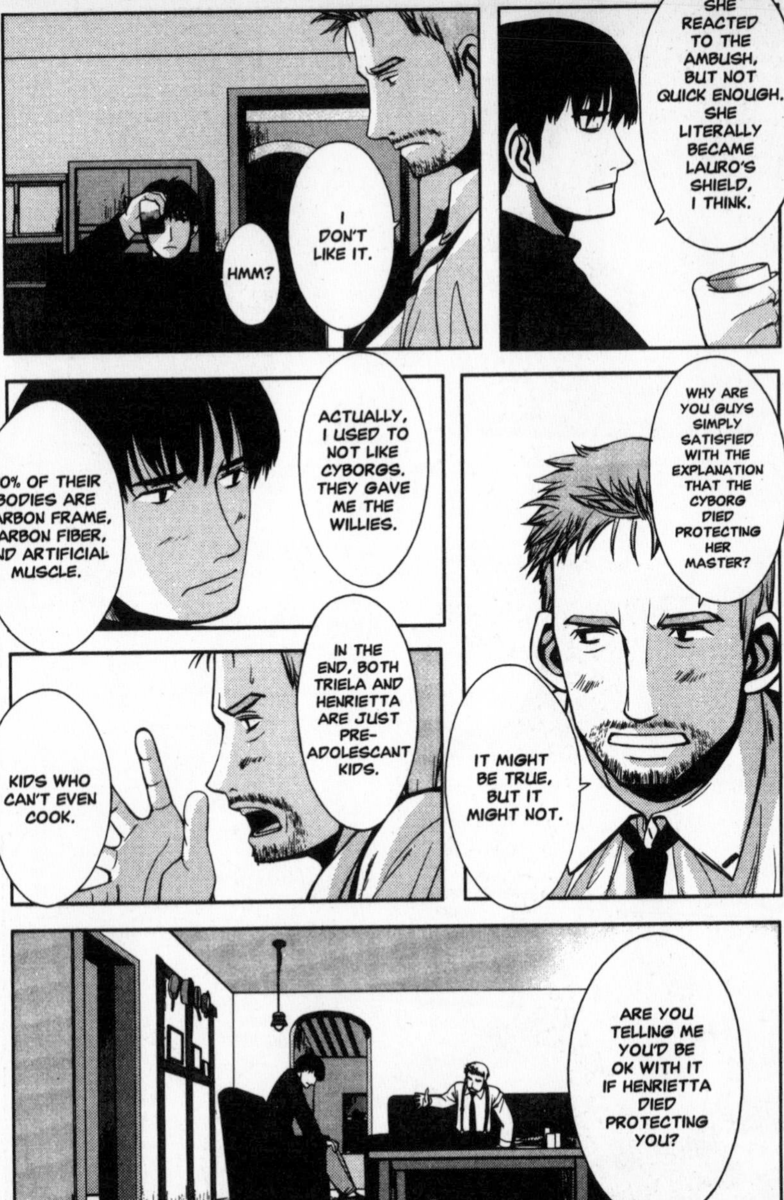

SHE REACTED TO THE AMBUSH, BUT NOT QUICK ENOUGH. SHE LITERALLY BECAME LAURO'S SHIELD, I THINK.
I DON'T LIKE IT.
HMM?
WHY ARE YOU GUYS SIMPLY SATISFIED WITH THE EXPLANATION THAT THE CYBORG DIED PROTECTING HER MASTER?
IT MIGHT BE TRUE, BUT IT MIGHT NOT.
ACTUALLY, I USED TO NOT LIKE CYBORGS. THEY GAVE ME THE WILLIES.
80% OF THEIR BODIES ARE CARBON FRAME, CARBON FIBER, AND ARTIFICIAL MUSCLE.
IN THE END, BOTH TRIELA AND HENRIETTA ARE JUST PRE-ADOLESCANT KIDS.
KIDS WHO CAN'T EVEN COOK.
ARE YOU TELLING ME YOU'D BE OK WITH IT IF HENRIETTA DIED PROTECTING YOU?

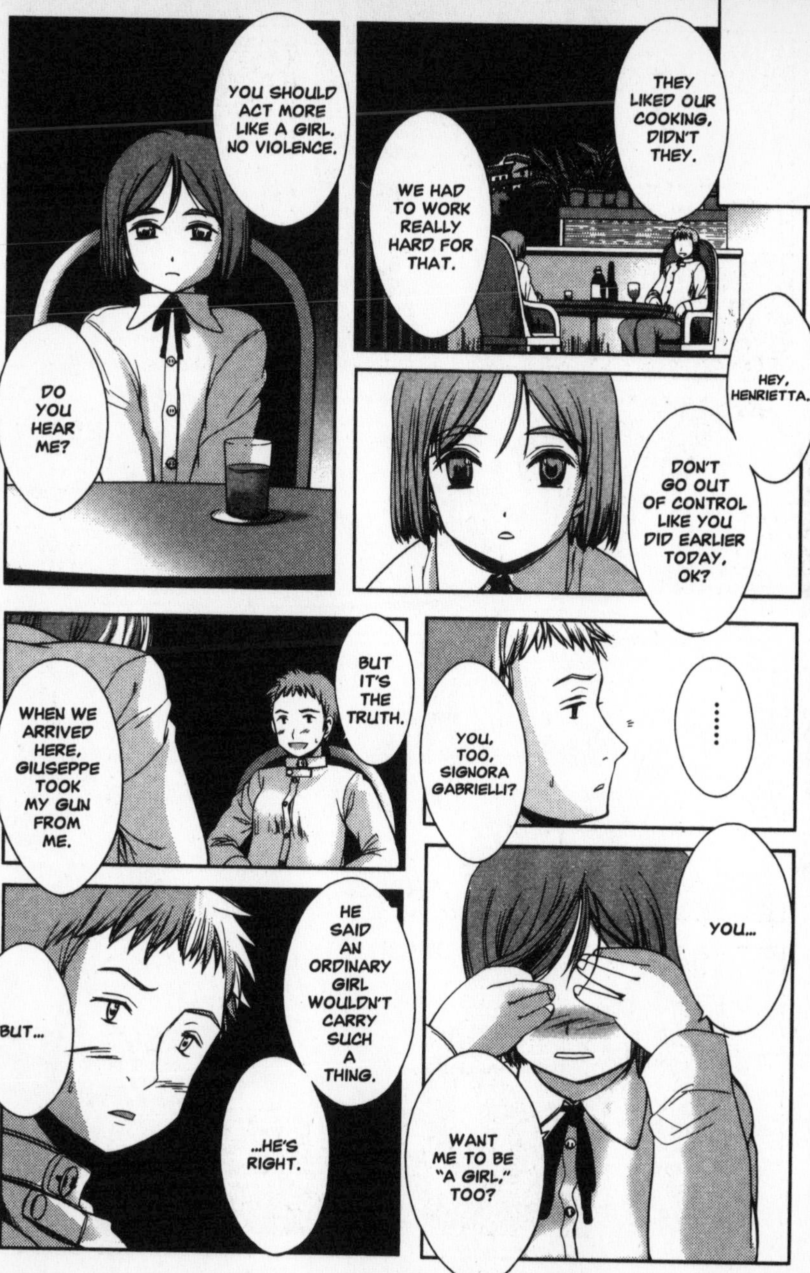
THEY LIKED OUR COOKING, DIDN'T THEY.
WE HAD TO WORK REALLY HARD FOR THAT.
HEY, HENRIETTA...
DON'T GO OUT OF CONTROL LIKE YOU DID EARLIER TODAY, OK?
YOU SHOULD ACT MORE LIKE A GIRL. NO VIOLENCE.
DO YOU HEAR ME?
......
YOU, TOO, SIGNORA GABRIELLI?
BUT IT'S THE TRUTH.
WHEN WE ARRIVED HERE, GIUSEPPE TOOK MY GUN FROM ME.
YOU...
WANT ME TO BE "A GIRL," TOO?
HE SAID AN ORDINARY GIRL WOULDN'T CARRY SUCH A THING.
...HE'S RIGHT.
BUT...

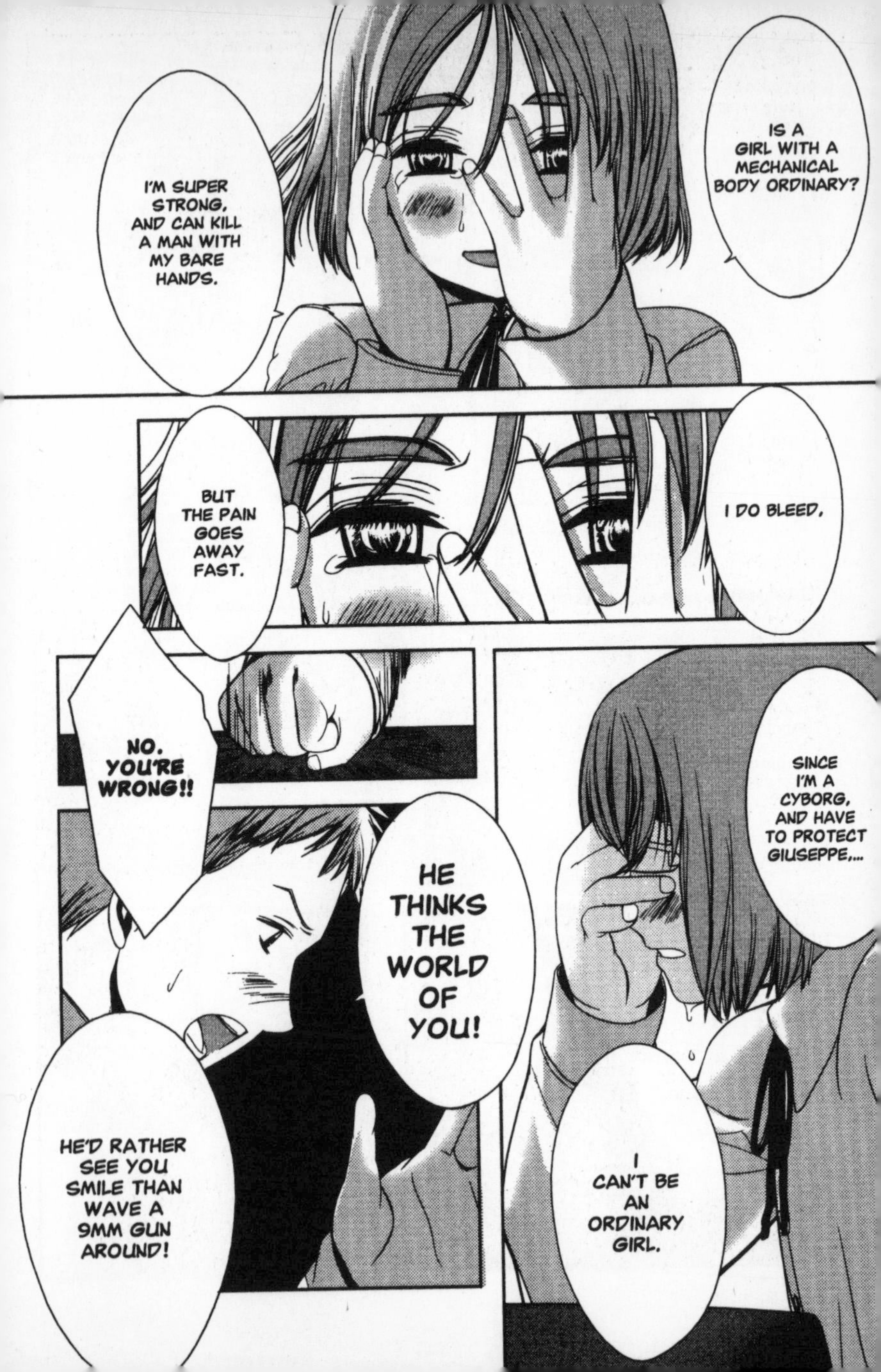
IS A GIRL WITH A MECHANICAL BODY ORDINARY?
I'M SUPER STRONG, AND CAN KILL A MAN WITH MY BARE HANDS.
I DO BLEED.
BUT THE PAIN GOES AWAY FAST.
SINCE I'M A CYBORG, AND HAVE TO PROTECT GIUSEPPE,...
I CAN'T BE AN ORDINARY GIRL.
NO. YOU'RE WRONG!!
HE THINKS THE WORLD OF YOU!
HE'D RATHER SEE YOU SMILE THAN WAVE A 9MM GUN AROUND!

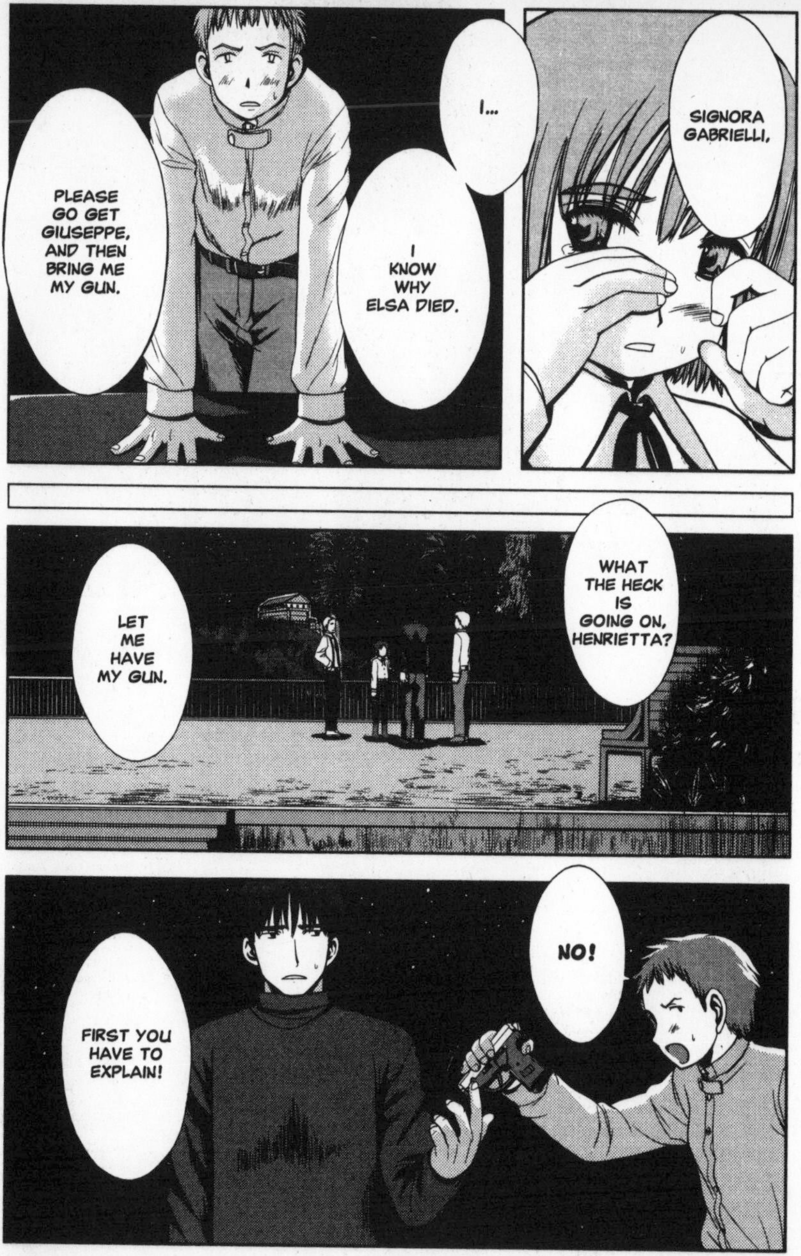
SIGNORA GABRIELLI,
I...
I KNOW WHY ELSA DIED.
PLEASE GO GET GIUSEPPE, AND THEN BRING ME MY GUN.
WHAT THE HECK IS GOING ON, HENRIETTA?
LET ME HAVE MY GUN.
NO!
FIRST YOU HAVE TO EXPLAIN!

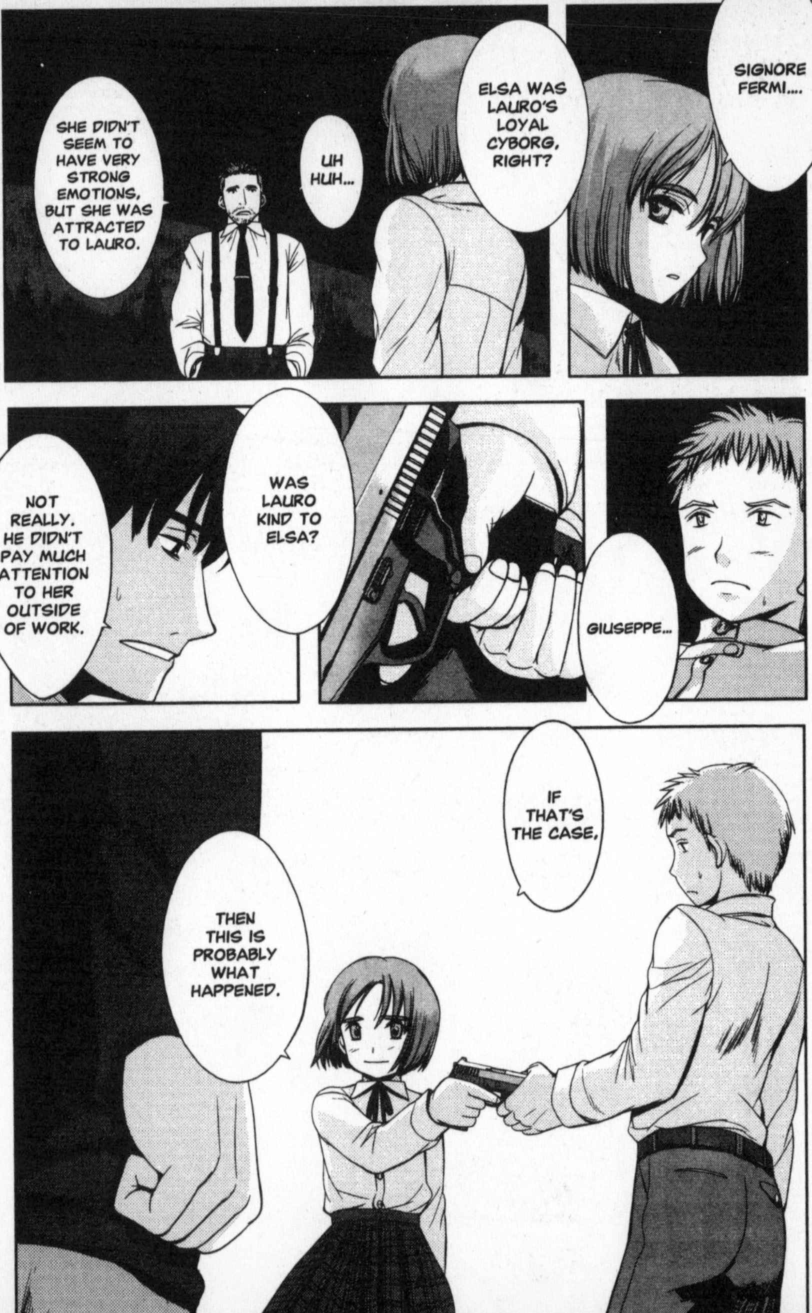
SIGNORE FERMI....
ELSA WAS LAURO'S LOYAL CYBORG, RIGHT?
UH HUH...
SHE DIDN'T SEEM TO HAVE VERY STRONG EMOTIONS, BUT SHE WAS ATTRACTED TO LAURO.
GIUSEPPE...
WAS LAURO KIND TO ELSA?
NOT REALLY. HE DIDN'T PAY MUCH ATTENTION TO HER OUTSIDE OF WORK.
IF THAT'S THE CASE,
THEN THIS IS PROBABLY WHAT HAPPENED.

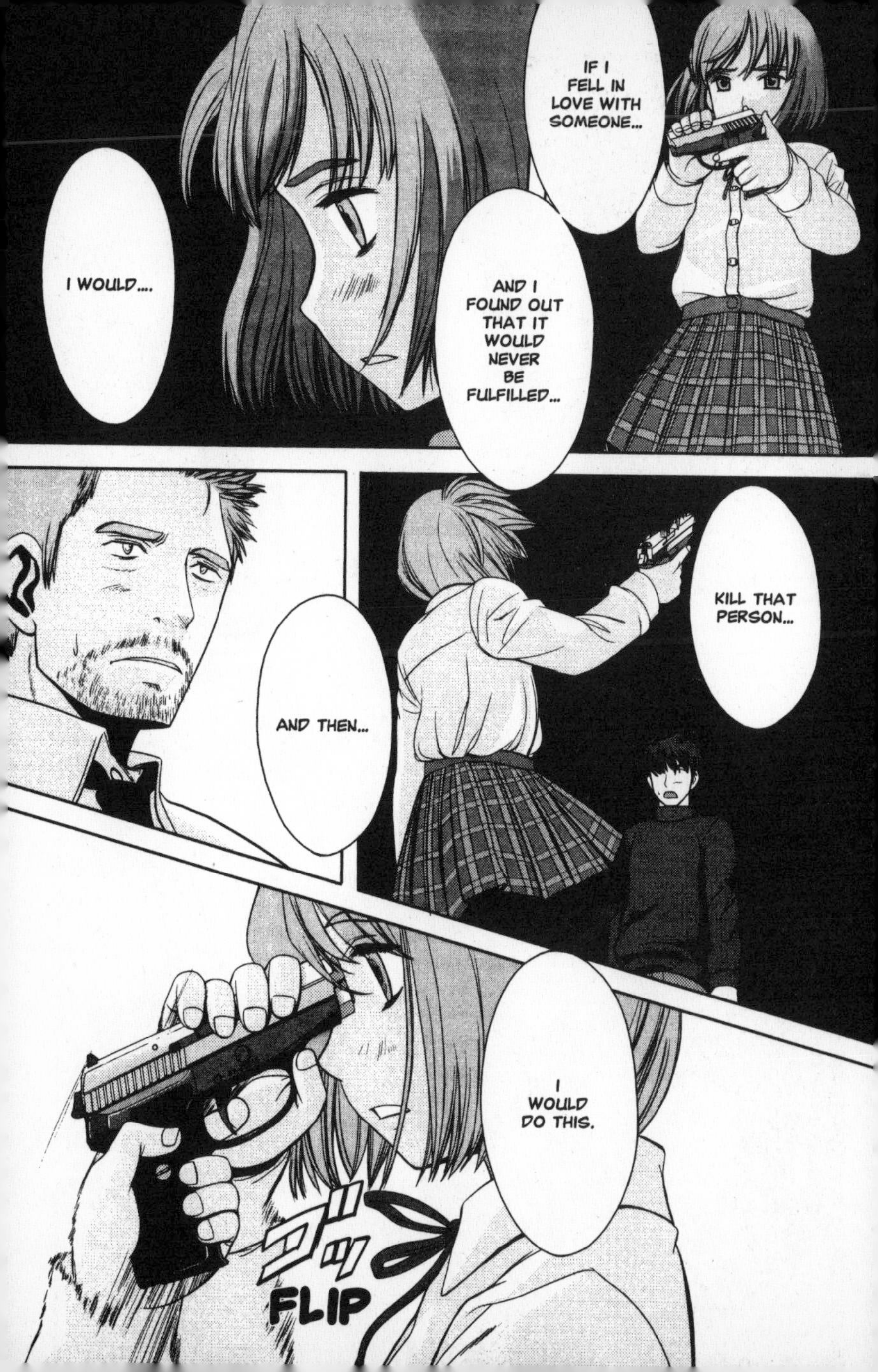
IF I FELL IN LOVE WITH SOMEONE...
AND I FOUND OUT THAT IT WOULD NEVER BE FULFILLED...
I WOULD....
KILL THAT PERSON...
AND THEN...
I WOULD DO THIS.
FLIP

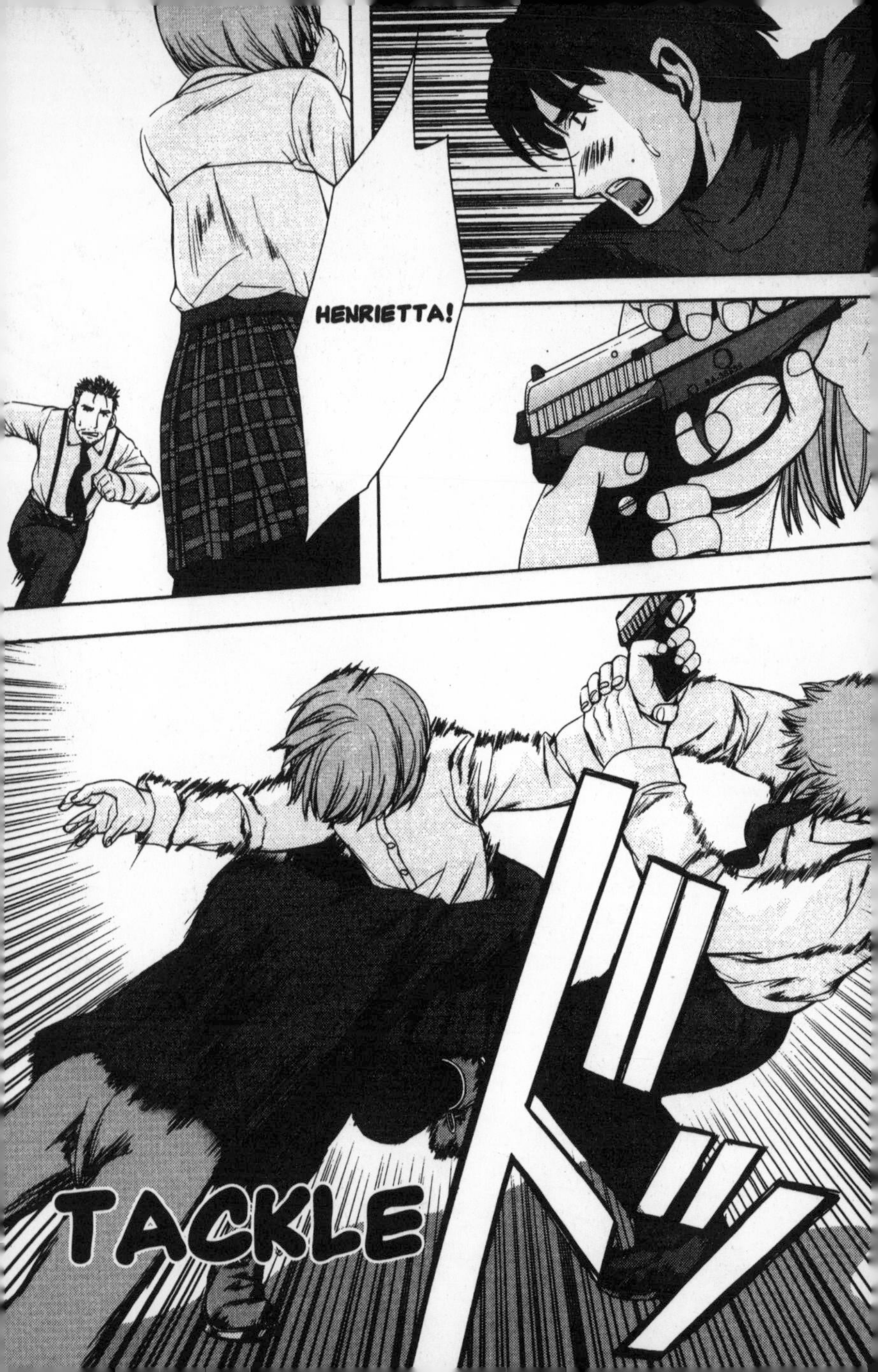
HENRIETTA!
TACKLE

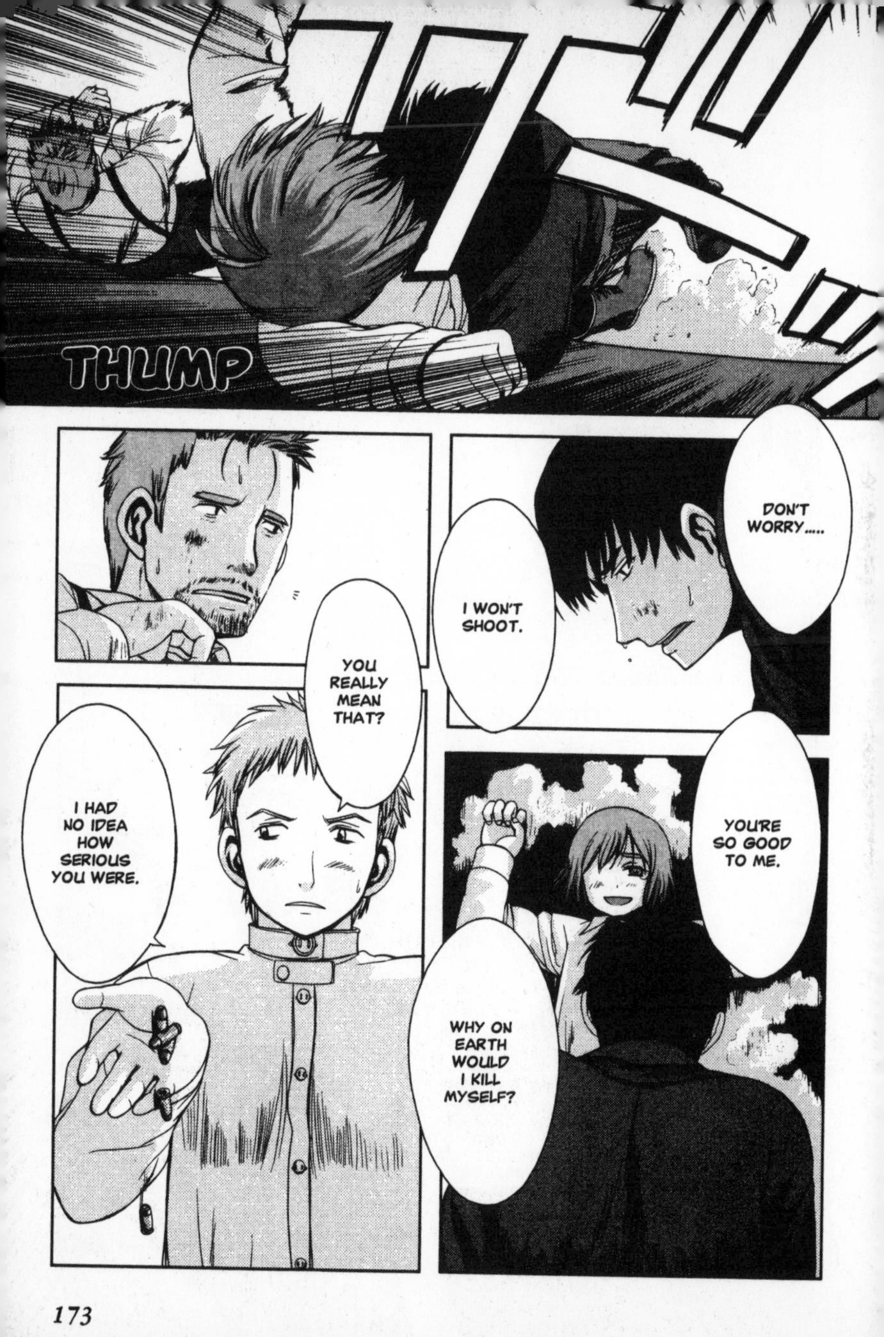
THUMP
DON'T WORRY.....
I WON'T SHOOT.
YOU REALLY MEAN THAT?
YOU'RE SO GOOD TO ME.
WHY ON EARTH WOULD I KILL MYSELF?
I HAD NO IDEA HOW SERIOUS YOU WERE.

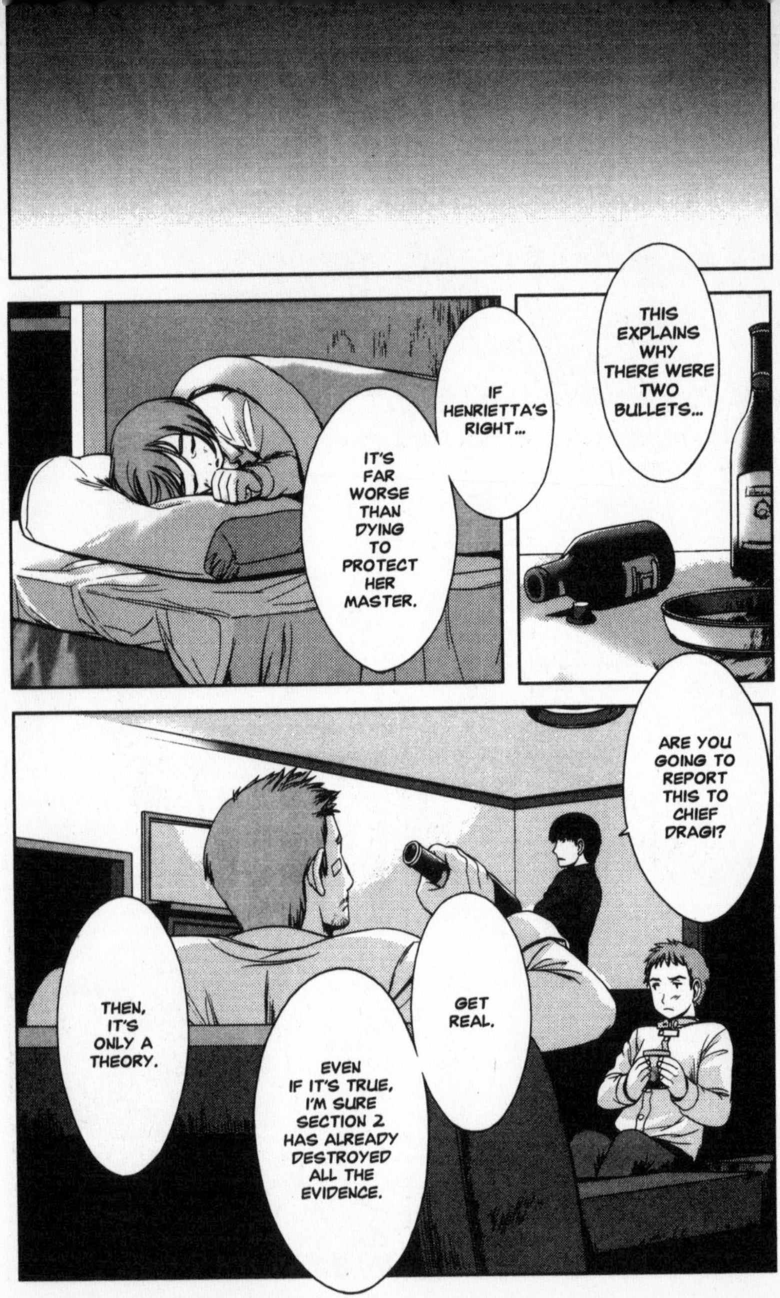
THIS EXPLAINS WHY THERE WERE TWO BULLETS...
IF HENRIETTA'S RIGHT...
IT'S FAR WORSE THAN DYING TO PROTECT HER MASTER.
ARE YOU GOING TO REPORT THIS TO CHIEF DRAGI?
GET REAL.
EVEN IF IT'S TRUE, I'M SURE SECTION 2 HAS ALREADY DESTROYED ALL THE EVIDENCE.
THEN, IT'S ONLY A THEORY.

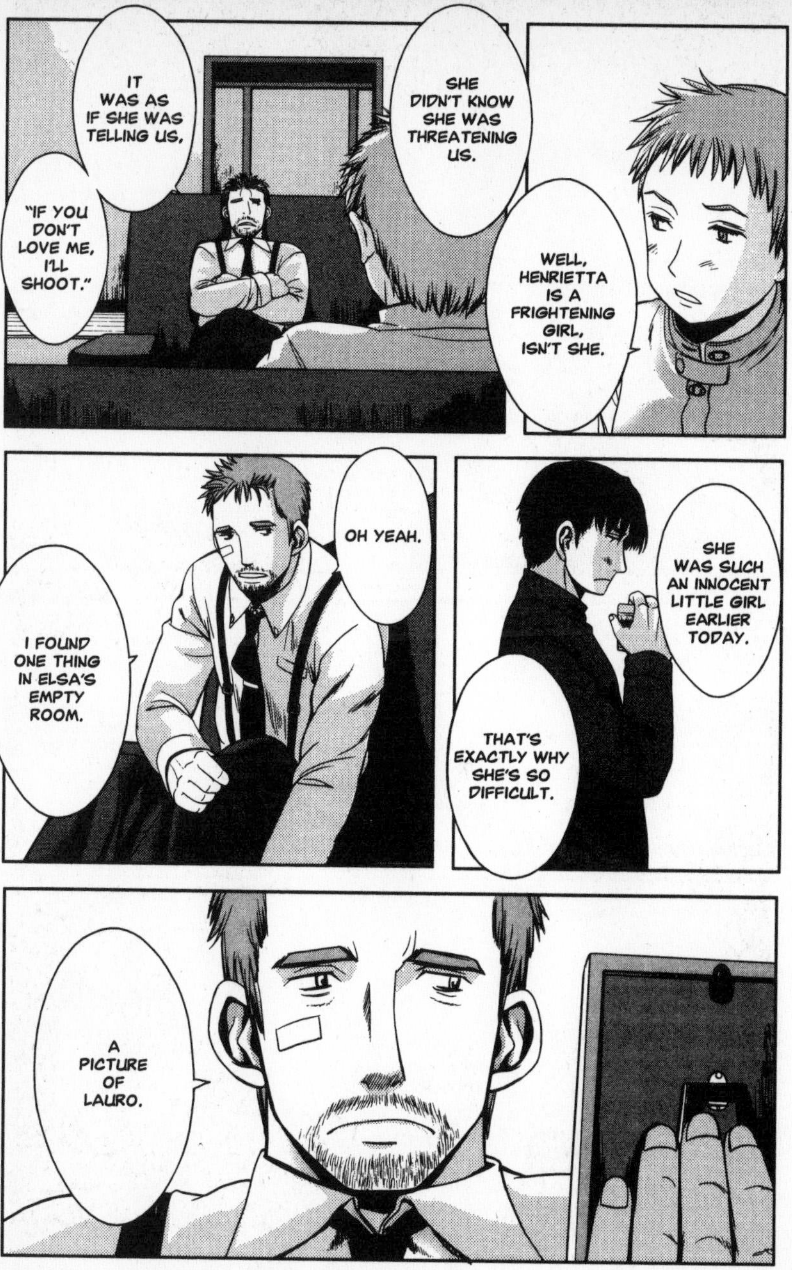
IT WAS AS IF SHE WAS TELLING US,
"IF YOU DON'T LOVE ME, I'LL SHOOT."
SHE DIDN'T KNOW SHE WAS THREATENING US.
WELL, HENRIETTA IS A FRIGHTENING GIRL, ISN'T SHE.
OH YEAH.
I FOUND ONE THING IN ELSA'S EMPTY ROOM.
SHE WAS SUCH AN INNOCENT LITTLE GIRL EARLIER TODAY.
THAT'S EXACTLY WHY SHE'S SO DIFFICULT.
A PICTURE OF LAURO.

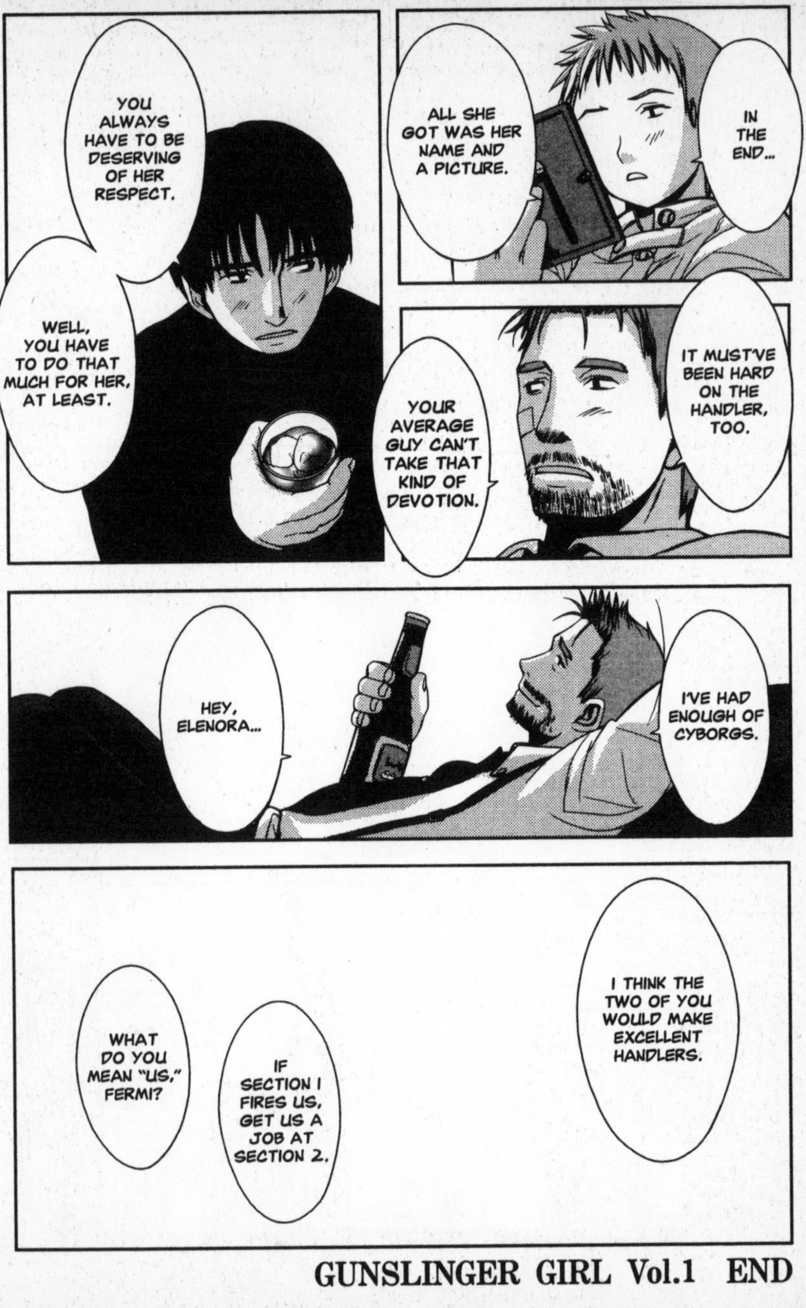
IN THE END...
ALL SHE GOT WAS HER NAME AND A PICTURE.
IT MUST'VE BEEN HARD ON THE HANDLER, TOO.
YOUR AVERAGE GUY CAN'T TAKE THAT KIND OF DEVOTION.
YOU ALWAYS HAVE TO BE DESERVING OF HER RESPECT.
WELL, YOU HAVE TO DO THAT MUCH FOR HER, AT LEAST.
I'VE HAD ENOUGH OF CYBORGS.
HEY, ELENORA...
I THINK THE TWO OF YOU WOULD MAKE EXCELLENT HANDLERS.
IF SECTION 1 FIRES US, GET US A JOB AT SECTION 2.
WHAT DO YOU MEAN "US," FERMI?

GUNSLINGER GIRL Vol.1 END

Gunslinger Girl Volume One

© YU AIDA 2002
First published in 2002 by MEDIA WORKS, Inc., Tokyo, Japan.

English translation rights arranged with MEDIA WORKS, Inc.

Translator EIKO McGREGOR
ADV Manga Translation Staff JAVIER LOPEZ, AMY FORSYTH, BRENDAN FRAYNE
Graphic Designer WINDI MARTIN
Graphic Artists JORGE ALVARADO, KRISTINA MILESKI, RYAN MASON, SHANNON RASBERRY
International Coordinators TORU IWAKAMI
                          ATSUSHI KANBAYASHI

Publishing Editor SUSAN ITIN
Editorial Assistant MARGARET SCHAROLD
President, C.E.O. & Publisher JOHN LEDFORD

Email: editor@adv-manga.com
www.adv-manga.com
www.advfilms.com

For sales and distribution inquiries please call 1.800.282.7202

 is a division of A.D. Vision, Inc.
10114 W. Sam Houston Parkway, Suite 200, Houston, Texas 77099

English Edition © 2003
Produced by A.D. Vision, Inc. under exclusive license.
ADV MANGA is a trademark of A.D. Vision, Inc.

ISBN: 1-4139-0020-8

First printing, October 2003
10 9 8 7 6 5 4 3 2 1
Printed in Canada

KYOYA'S NOT DONE YET... NOT BY A LONG SHOT!

THE SWORD ASHURA SLASHES THROUGH
TWO OTHER EXCITING SERIES FROM ADV MANGA!

[A PALACE APPEARS IN THE SKY OVER TOKYO, AND KYOYA'S INVITED ABOARD—FOR SINISTER REASONS!]

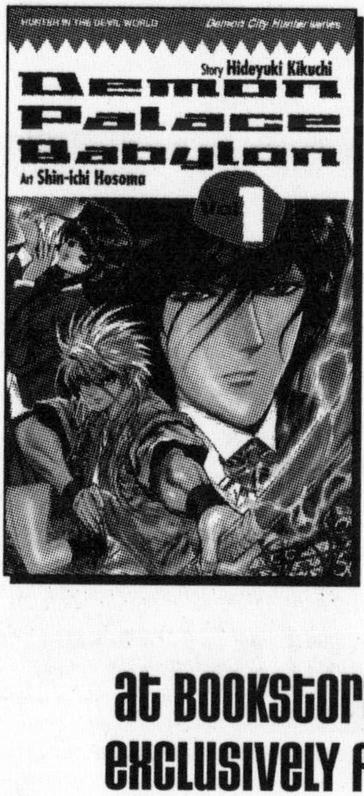
HUNTER IN THE DEVIL WORLD
Demon City Hunter series
Story Hideyuki Kikuchi
Demon Palace Babylon
Art Shin-ichi Hosoma
1

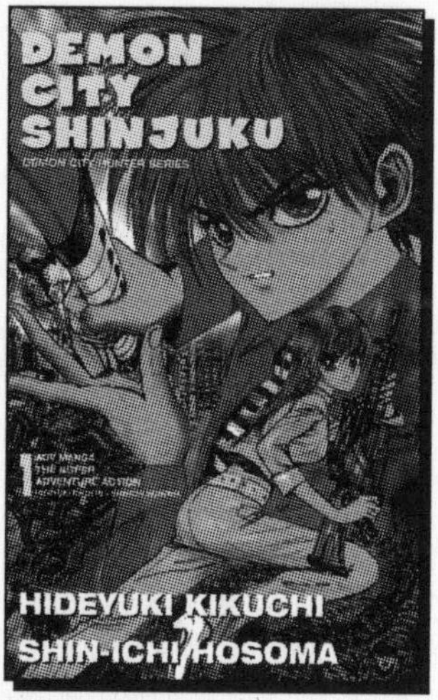
DEMON CITY SHINJUKU
HIDEYUKI KIKUCHI
SHIN-ICHI HOSOMA

[THE PRESIDENT OF EARTH'S RULING FEDERATION IS DYING FROM A DEMONIC CURSE, AND ONLY KYOYA CAN SAVE HIM!]

AT BOOKSTORES EVERYWHERE, EXCLUSIVELY FROM ADV MANGA!

ADV Manga

www.adv-manga.com

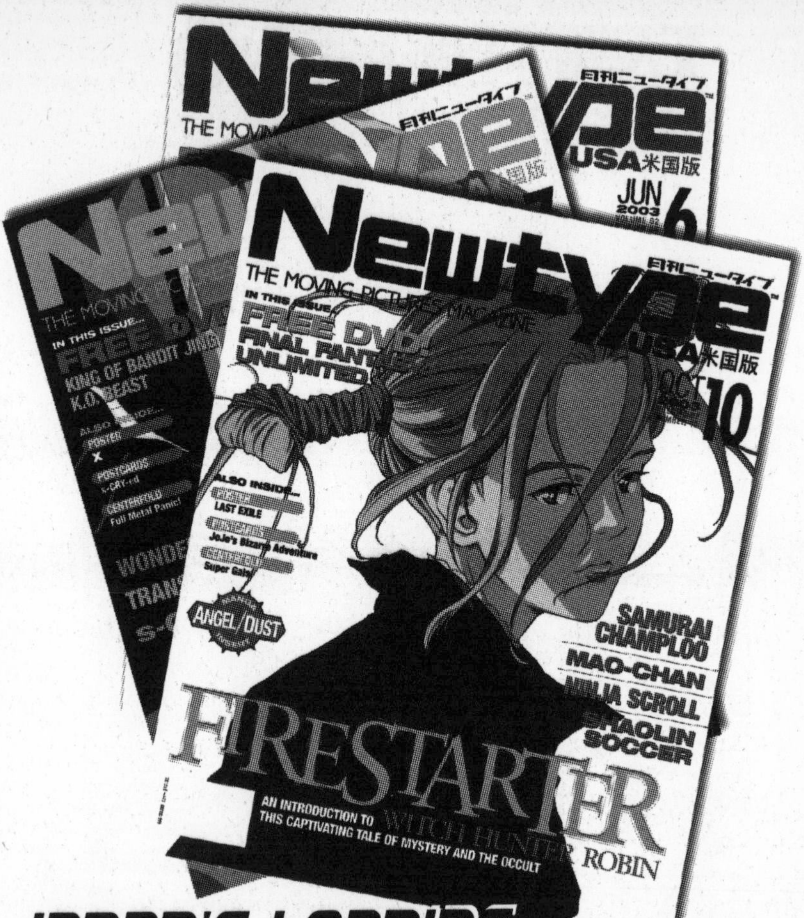
Newtype
THE MOVING PICTURES MAGAZINE
USA
JUN 2003 6
IN THIS ISSUE...
FREE DVD!
FINAL FANTASY UNLIMITED
KING OF BANDIT JING
K.O. BEAST
ALSO INSIDE...
POSTER
X
POSTCARDS
s-CRY-ed
CENTERFOLD
Full Metal Panic!
LAST EXILE
JoJo's Bizarre Adventure
Super Gals
ANGEL/DUST
OCT 10
SAMURAI CHAMPLOO
MAO-CHAN
NINJA SCROLL
SHAOLIN SOCCER
FIRESTARTER
AN INTRODUCTION TO THIS CAPTIVATING TALE OF MYSTERY AND THE OCCULT
WITCH HUNTER ROBIN

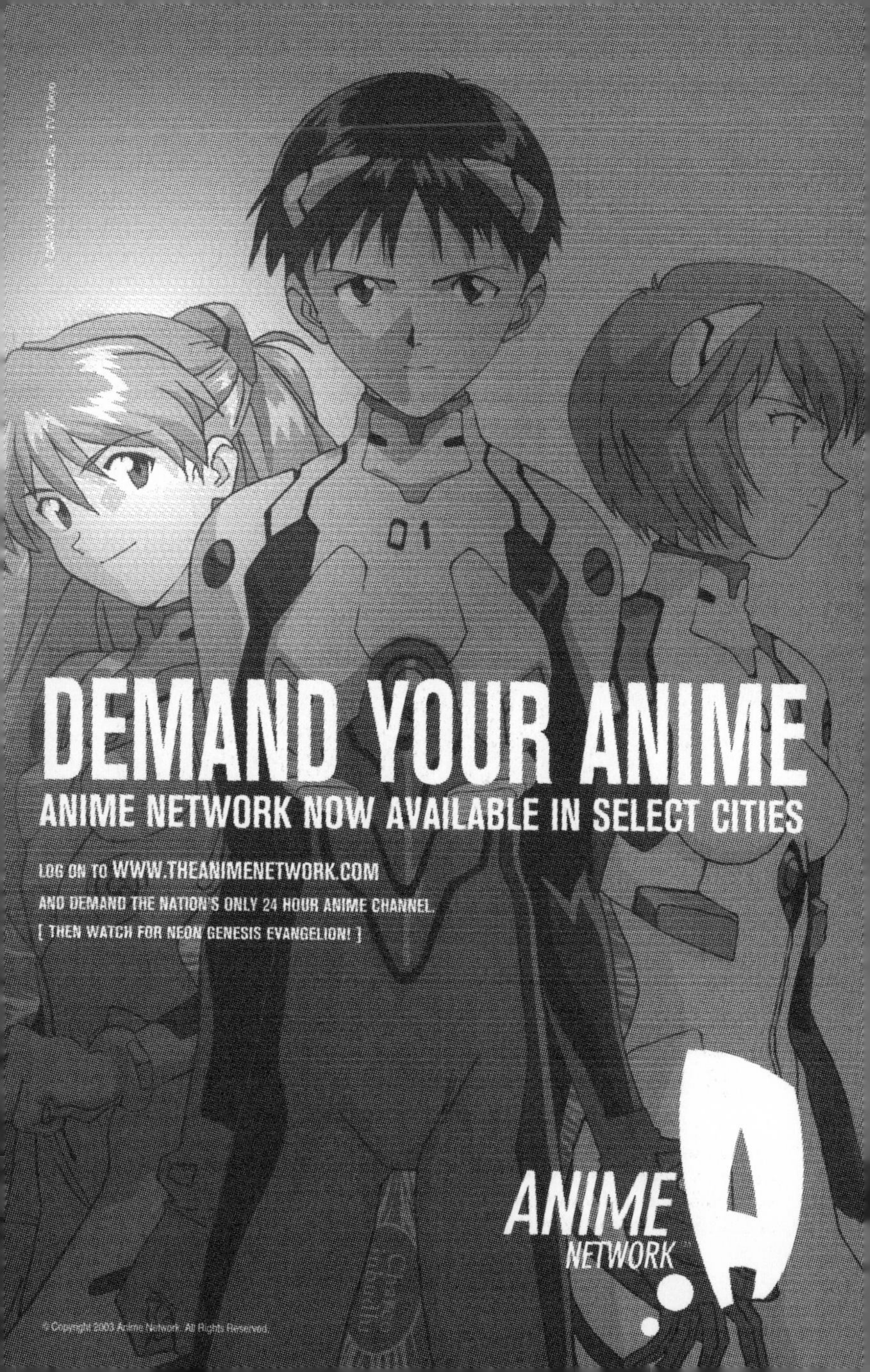

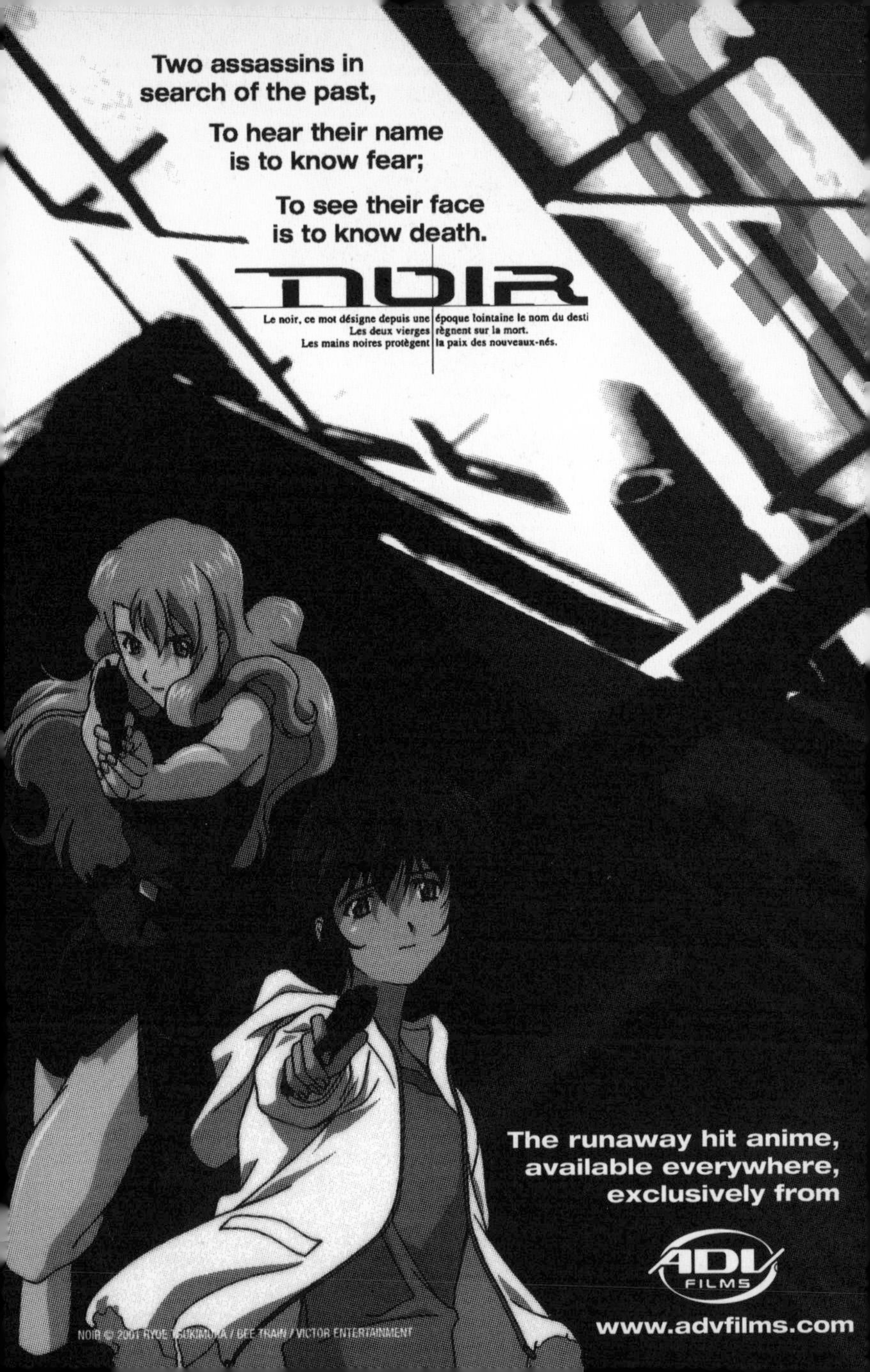

Two assassins in search of the past,
To hear their name is to know fear;
To see their face is to know death.
NOIR
Le noir, ce mot désigne depuis une époque lointaine le nom du desti
Les deux vierges règnent sur la mort.
Les mains noires protègent la paix des nouveaux-nés.
The runaway hit anime, available everywhere, exclusively from
ADV FILMS
www.advfilms.com
NOIR © 2001 RYOE TSUKIMURA / BEE TRAIN / VICTOR ENTERTAINMENT

ANIME SURVEY

FILL IT OUT AND YOU COULD WIN FABULOUS PRIZES!

PLEASE MAIL THE COMPLETED FORM TO: EDITOR – ADV MANGA
℅ A.D. Vision, Inc. 10114 W. Sam Houston Pkwy., Suite 200 Houston, TX 77099

Name: ______________________________
Address: ______________________________
City: State: Zip: ______________________________

E-Mail: ______________________________
Male ☐ Female ☐ Age: ______________________________
Cable Provider: ______________________________

☐ ***CHECK HERE IF YOU WOULD LIKE TO RECEIVE OTHER INFORMATION OR FUTURE OFFERS FROM ADV.***

1. Annual Household Income (*check only one*)

- Under $25,000
- ☐ $25,000 to $50,000
- ☐ $50,000 to $75,000
- ☐ Over $75,000

2. How do you hear about new Anime releases? (*Check all that apply*)

- ☐ Browsing in Store
- ☐ Internet Reviews
- ☐ Anime News Websites
- ☐ Direct Email Campaigns
- ☐ Online forums (message boards and chat rooms)
- ☐ Carrier pigeon
- ☐ Other:__________
- ☐ Magazine Ad
- ☐ Online Advertising
- ☐ Conventions
- ☐ TV Advertising

3. Which magazines do you read? (*Check all that apply*)

- ☐ Wizard
- ☐ SPIN
- ☐ Animerica
- ☐ Rolling Stone
- ☐ Maxim
- ☐ DC Comics
- ☐ URB
- ☐ Polygon
- ☐ Original Play Station Magazine
- ☐ Entertainment Weekly
- ☐ YRB
- ☐ EGM
- ☐ Newtype USA
- ☐ SciFi
- ☐ Starlog
- ☐ Wired
- ☐ Vice
- ☐ BPM
- ☐ I hate reading
- ☐ Other:

4. Would you subscribe to digital cable if you could get a 24 hour/7 day a week anime channel (like the Anime Network)?

- ☐ Yes
- ☐ No

5. Would you like to see the Anime Network in your area?

- ☐ Yes
- ☐ No

6. Would you pay $6.99/month for the Anime Network?

- ☐ Yes
- ☐ No

7. DEMAND YOUR ANIME! Yes, please sign me up for the Demand Your Anime Sweepstakes, with a chance to win a brand new Honda Civic Si and let my cable provider know that I'm interested in a 24/7 Anime channel!*

- ☐ Yes
- ☐ No

8. What genre of manga and anime would you like to see from ADV?
(*Check all that apply*)

- ☐ adventure
- ☐ romance
- ☐ detective
- ☐ fighting
- ☐ horror
- ☐ sci-fi/fantasy
- ☐ sports

9. How many manga titles have you purchased in the last year?

- ☐ none
- ☐ 1-4
- ☐ 5-10
- ☐ 11+

10. Where do you make your manga purchases? (*Check all that apply*)

- ☐ comic store
- ☐ bookstore
- ☐ newsstand
- ☐ online
- ☐ other: _____
- ☐ department store
- ☐ grocery store
- ☐ video store
- ☐ video game store

11. What's your favorite anime-related website?

- ☐ advfilms.com
- ☐ anipike.com
- ☐ rightstuf.com
- ☐ animenewsservice.com
- ☐ animenewsnetwork.com
- ☐ animeondvd.com
- ☐ animenation.com
- ☐ animeonline.net
- ☐ planetanime.com
- ☐ other:

***ENTRIES MUST BE RECEIVED BY DECEMBER 4, 2003**

All information provided will be used for internal purposes only. We promise not to sell or otherwise divulge your information.